Rethinking India's Past

Rethinking India's Past

By

R.S. SHARMA

OXFORD
UNIVERSITY PRESS

OXFORD
UNIVERSITY PRESS

Oxford University Press is a department of the University of Oxford. It furthers the University's objective of excellence in research, scholarship, and education by publishing worldwide. Oxford is a registered trademark of Oxford University Press in the UK and in certain other countries

Published in India by
Oxford University Press
22 Workspace, 2nd Floor, 1/22 Asaf Ali Road, New Delhi 110002

First Edition published in 2009
Oxford India Paperbacks 2010
Sixth impression 2015

ISBN-13: 978-0-19-806829-7
ISBN-10: 0-19-806829-8

Typeset in Naurang
by Guru Typograph Technology, New Delhi 110 075
Printed in India by Replika Press Pvt. Ltd

Dedicated to my parents

MATUK SINGH AND BARTO DEVI

Contents

Publisher's Note

The notes and references of the chapters have been kept in the form in which they appeared in the original. At few places the notes and references could not be reconstructed in their entirety as the publications were old and unapproachable. There are repetitions in some of the essays in this volume which result from their being written over a long and fruitful career.

Introduction

Looking at Ancient Social Formations*

Recent years have shown a happy awareness of 'no theory, no history' among historians. Seminars held to examine the assumptions underlying historical writings have given rise to a healthy, though still weak, reaction against colonialistic, pseudo-nationalistic, chauvinistic and obscurantist approaches to the study of Indian history. But the search for theories and models has led some writers into the sociological trap. In India, till the fifties the historical method and approach was applied to sociology, political science, economics, linguistics, etc. Although the concepts of growth in economics and of modernization and industrialization in sociology owe much to history, there is also a clamour for applying the models of the other social sciences to history. There are however models and models. We have to decide which ones are of the right type and can be used as tools of analysis. Insights from allied disciplines are always welcome, but history should not be allowed to dissolve into a welter of multidisciplinary clap-trap. Social history does not mean 'a backward projection of sociology', nor economic history an application of economic theory with 'retrospective' effect. Sociological generalizations which transcend time and place and deliberately attempt to prove the unchangeable character of Indian society pose a real danger to historians.

For comprehending and explaining the past in India we naturally look for models and typologies, but the intellectual market in social sciences, like any other market, is flooded with 'western' commodities, and we have very little choice in the matter. The obsession of some social anthropologists with kinship, caste, ritual, language, social customs,

*Previously published as, 'Problems of Social Formations in Early India' in R.S. Sharma, *Material Culture and Social Formations in Ancient India* (Delhi: Macmillan, 1983).

etc.—problems of superstructure—has given rise to several theories. A few of these can explain the structure, composition and functions of a society, but most of them founder on the fundamental problem of change from one social foundation to the other. Many of these models may enlighten static societies but do not help the study of social processes. The *jajmāni* system, for example, may explain the social and economic relations of the feudal phase but not of the pre-feudal phases. Whatever be the date of the *Arthaśāstra* of Kauṭilya, there is nothing of the *jajmāni* system in the whole of the text. Of the theories meant to explain social dynamics, those of Sanskritization and of the Great and Little Tradition touch only the outer cultural veneer and throw little light on socio-economic formations. Much is being made of the elite theory, and irrespective of their place in the system of production, the 'elite' (literally, the choice part, the best) are being seen as the prime motive force behind all social change. But the simple historical truth, that generally the literati and the intelligentsia are the subordinate allies of the ruling class in class societies cannot be overlooked. The theory of tradition and modernity is used to cover the whole history of society, which is also sought to be encompassed by 'simpler' and 'complex' societies. But as a matter of fact human society passed through four or more different modes/stages of production extending over centuries.

Advances in historical knowledge during the last hundred years have altered to some extent the model of social formations provided by historical materialism, and here we should gratefully record our debt to Gordon Childe, who has provided us with valuable insights into the social formations of the bronze age, but much more still remains to be done on the differences between bronze age societies and iron age societies, and particularly on the Asiatic mode of production, to the critique of which D.D. Kosambi and other Indian historians have made valuable contributions. A deep study of sources in the light of the fundamentals of historical materialism may open up exciting possibilities of discovering new and transitional types of societies. The sociological model of tribe/folk–peasant–industrial society is considered to be an alternative to the model provided by historical materialism, but it has a number of limitations. It is held that in primitive or folk/ tribal society kinship is the governing force, but it is doubtful whether it is far stronger than the tribal mode of production. The idea of the peasant stage envisages a tribute- and tithe-paying agricultural society ruled by priests and warriors, but the peasant phase does not necessarily correspond to the feudal phase.

If the problem is to articulate and characterize the mode and relations of production, 'feudal' and 'peasant' societies may not convey the same meaning. Peasants constitute the overwhelming majority of the population, but they do not from the ruling class. Therefore the dominant culture and ideology is not that of the peasant. Industrial society may cover both classless and class-based societies. The concept 'industrial' mainly means technological transformation and not social formation. This transformation may apply to capitalist, non-capitalist, and socialist societies.

We can dilate on some of these problems. Let us consider the idea of peasant society. Here the peasant is shown as meeting his hundred and one needs out of his produce and also paying tax and tithe. If the idea is to emphasize the crucial role of the peasant household production unit as the prime support of social structure in a pre-capitalist society, the term peasant society can prove to be useful. But if the idea is to get at the nature of the surplus provided for managers of production and consumption, the static connotation of this term cannot enlighten us much, for the amount and method of surplus collection and the mode of its distribution keep on changing. The concept of peasant society, therefore, may serve as an omnibus term for different types of formations in which peasants pay taxes, tithes, tributes, gifts, etc., but since these forms of payment and the mechanism for their assessment and collection keep on changing, the term would not be able to bear the weight of the theory which stresses the changing nature of class relations.

Again, peasants do not always constitute a homogeneous group. When tribal people take to full-fledged agriculture and adopt it as the main source of their livelihood, their bonds of kinship are initially strengthened and tribal traits continue in the management of land. They may have to pay taxes and tithes, but they can be better described as tribal peasantry. We also have to draw a distinction between free peasantry and servile peasantry which may coexist in a society, but a society with more of free peasantry will certainly be different from that having more of servile peasantry. Servile peasantry is characteristic of a feudal society. The peasantry controlled by market laws is found in a colonial/capitalist society. It may be added that a large-scale free peasantry is generally found in either a pre-feudal society or in a capitalist society.

Although in many pre-capitalist societies the peasantry may be the principal source of surplus meant for the maintenance of various non-producing segments of society, it would be wrong to think that a homogeneous peasantry guided and shaped the course of history. Peasants came to be divided into different strata, and substantial peasants certainly mattered more than their poor cousins. Even in the age of the Buddha we encounter the affluent landowning peasant called the *kassaka gahapati*. Some *gahapatis* employed a large number of slaves and agricultural labourers; others carried on agriculture mainly with the help of family labour supplemented by a few slaves and hired workers. The substantial peasants seem to have formed the backbone of the lay following of the Buddha. It was in their interest that Buddhism never thought of the abolition of slavery. Kauṭilya mentions sharecroppers who obviously were exploited by rich peasants. At a later stage rich peasants called *mahattara* eventually grew into local landlords living on the rents and services of the common peasantry. In other words the problem of stratification among the peasantry is linked up with changes in religion, social structures, etc. At the same time certain broad characteristics, such as sentimental attachment to land, worship of fertility divinities, local patriotism and some amount of conservatism may have been shared by all categories of peasants. Love for fairs, festivals, entertainment, etc., and also the need for protection could draw them towards the priests and princes by creating an illusion of cohesion. Feedback distribution on the occasion of sacrificial feasts by princes not only helps to maintain the sense of collectivity but also tempers the rigours of taxation.

Certain historians tend to attribute the formation of a slave society to conquest; examples are cited from Roman history.[1] But conquest itself is caused primarily by such internal dynamics as the compelling need for procuring labour power and obtaining land for colonization, particularly on the part of the ruling class. In the pre-capitalist phases of society such a use of force may be considered an extra-economic method adopted to maintain and perpetuate a class-based or slave-based society, as happened in Greece and Rome, and perhaps occasionally in India.

A large number of theoreticians frequently raise the problem of status, so popular with many sociologists, and in explaining the structure and dynamics of a society, the use of status is preferred by those who feel fed up with the 'worn-out', concept of class. It is argued that the brāhmaṇa, kṣatriya, vaiśya and śūdra form statuses and not classes. Varṇa is also translated as order, estate, etc., which obscures its identity as class, and it is said that in each case the economic status of a varṇa does not approximate to its social and ritualistic status. Apparently this view seems to be true to a degree. But the real question is not to investigate the nature of correspondence between the varṇa and its economic presence, although in the pre-colonial phase in most cases the economic functions and position of the two higher varṇas would roughly correspond to their social and ritualistic status. The same was broadly true of the two lower varṇas. However it will be more fruitful to find out the nature of the role of different 'statuses' in the overall management of production and in the sharing of its surplus. The problem is not to find out who is rich and who is poor but to assess the role members of a varṇa play in the mode of production which keeps society going.

Some scholars want to reconstruct the history of social formations on the basis of what the ancient people thought of their own roles in society. They argue that we should look at the conduct of ancient people as they perceived it themselves. But if we are convinced that the evolutionary view of history, which is now strongly corroborated by anthropological studies, is correct and if we think that a comparative yardstick in terms of time and places is necessary to have a more meaningful appreciation, of the past, it is essential to follow a consistent scientific method and objective approach in the study of the past. Whereas it is necessary to detect the various types of prejudices permeating our written records, it is all the more necessary to examine the nature of the material culture revealed by them and also the material remains of ancient cultures brought to light through excavation and exploration.

A few scholars who take an anthropological view of history hold that consideration of kinship played a vital part in ancient times.[2] Although in a great deal of their discussion the need for lineage and acquisition of manpower as a result of the advent of food production is not underlined, this approach has enabled scholars to explain some creation myths and to understand the nature of various types of marriage practices, inheritance, etc. Now the idea is being applied to some ancient and medieval dynastic kingdoms, which are called segmentary or kin-based states. Attempts are being made, though unsuccessfully, to apply the African model of tribal polity to some early medieval kingdoms of south India. Though kinship considerations might govern and condition a few areas of social conduct, as they do even now in Indian villages, it would be wrong to call those societies kin-based. There is no doubt that in the evolutionary scale the kin-based or tribal society was superseded by state-based and class-based society. But although it is possible to identify in this process certain landmarks defined by time and place, it is difficult to find clear cut-off or terminal points for one type of society giving place to another type of society. Strong survivals from earlier societies are always noticeable in later societies, and for this phenomenon various terms such as 'continuum', 'overlap', 'interlocking', etc., are used. But the study of change, divergence, disjuncture and discontinuity is possibly more important. It is difficult to think of unpunctuated development.

Wherever evidence points to more than one type of society in the same period and the same region, the student of history has to underline the dominant element which differentiates the emerging social formation from the decaying one.

If in a transitional phase two elements are equally balanced, that situation has also to be admitted. Some people would like to call it a dualistic phase; others might call it a counter-balancing situation containing contradictory elements. But all the same historians and anthropologists accept the existence of such a phase. While some anthropologists feel elated at their illusory achievement in demolishing the epochal findings of Morgan recorded in his *Ancient Society*, in recent years radical anthropologists have evinced a strong renewed interest in Morgan's ideas and methods. Adopting more sophisticated methods used by anthropologists currently, several of them have not only confirmed the basic findings of Morgan but have carried them further. In the process of the re-examination of the conclusions of Morgan and Engels, some Marxist anthropologists have now substantially modified the stages in the history of early evolution uncovered by the two 'thinker-scholars'. The new findings start with the advent of band which is a collection or group of people for hunting or other similar primitive foodgathering activities, but not necessarily bound by ties of kinship. In the second stage we come across tribe—whatever may be its meaning—although for us the element of kinship is most important in it. An important development of 'tribe' is the rise of tribal chiefdom, and then finally we find a state-based and class-based society.

Marxist anthropologists, however, are not in agreement on the relative importance of kinship and of the mode of production in a tribal society. Some consider kinship as a determining factor in regulating relations in a tribal community. In their opinion all economic activities including production, distribution and war are moulded by kinship relations.[3] But this view is not accepted by others. As already shown, in the pre-kinship stage a band of people belonging to unrelated kin may form a collective for gathering food by various methods. What is important to note is that a full-fledged tribal society is inextricably associated with certain basic conditions of material existence, and the moment those are disturbed, the tribal society begins to disintegrate, although it may rally, reform and reorganize itself, obtaining a fresh lease of tribal life. However the reorganized tribal community may lose some of the tribal elements, and this process would ultimately lead to its undermining and eventual break-up. The same analogy applies to the caste system, whose 'vigour' and 'persistence' have earned the unstinted admiration of some western sociologists and their Indian counterparts; they overlook the process of the older system under the impact of a new type of economy and derive satisfaction from demonstrating the continuity of caste.

The formation and the growth of the caste system are attributed to notions of purity and impurity. The theory is old hat which has been mended to serve those who find themselves fascinated by the outer manifestations of caste and untouchabiity. But only a historical approach based on considerations of time, place and social situations can unravel the causes and character of outer manifestations. It is clear that several crafts, especially those connected with leather, did not bear any stigma of impurity in early Vedic times when society had not completely transcended the tribal and pastoral stage and had not fully entered a class-based phase. The role of the socio-economic factor in contributing to the origin of caste and untouchability has been ably made out by several researchers.[4] Although we notice a few signs of untouchability even in pre-Gupta times it is only in early medieval times that untouchability attracts our attention as a significant social phenomenon.[5]

Notions of impurity connected with such events as death and menstruation in tribal societies were not sufficient to create conditions for the origin of untouchability. Only when manual work was completely divorced from religious/intellectual and administrative work, and a large number of men were separated from the land, the chief source of production, only then could members of the higher varṇas, particularly the first two, claim a number of exploitative privileges. The higher varṇas wanted to perpetuate their power and position by keeping themselves at a safe distance from a good section of primary producers, mainly artisans and agricultural labourers. How could this be done easily? By inventing and refining the rituals of purity and impurity and by creating a mechanism of barriers and hierarchy so that the buffer zones would be invested with varying degrees of purity/impurity. Some Indologists underscore the role of religion in shaping the course of Indian history and assert that it held back the economic progress of the country. This game has been going on for more than a century, and somehow because of ceaseless propaganda, religion has stuck to Indian studies so fast that it is difficult to extricate historical research from its yoke. The respectability conferred on the religious factor by orientalists and Sanskritists has been reinforced by recent publications of some sociologists. Whereas the former relied on texts, mostly written by priests, the latter swear by field work. A few Sanskritists are attracted by the findings of these sociologists and try to look similarly at ancient texts.

Scholars have suggested various types of approaches. They argue, for example, that the four goals of *dharma* (concern for social order or religion), *artha* (wealth), *kāma* (pleasure) and *mokṣa* (deliverance from the travails of life, or spiritualism), guided the activities of man in India. There is hardly any evidence to show that as a concept *trivarga* or *caturvarga* was known in the Vedic period which covered nearly a thousand years. Even in post-Vedic times, the *trivarga* appeared first, and *mokṣa*, which was used in the sense of divorce, or of manumission of a slave, was added to it later. The *caturvarga* ideal as a whole was popularized not before post-Maurya and Gupta times. Those who want to demonstrate that ancient Indian life was guided by these fourfold norms and values have to prove that the common man was aware of these objectives. Even now very few members of the intelligentsia, who boast of a knowledge of the Indian cultural heritage, are acquainted with the *caturvarga* ideal, not to speak of a far more limited number in ancient times. Incidentally the use of the term *artha* in this ideal as well as its relative importance in the list of the four objectives has to be appreciated. Several texts repeatedly state that *artha* constitutes the root (*mūla*) of *dharma* and other ingredients. In any case while the dominant class in ancient India was not without ideologies, it would be wrong to make *caturvarga* the common ideal of one and all and to consider it the motor force of all developments of ancient times. On the contrary it might prove rewarding to investigate the linkages between the four varṇas/*āśramas* on the one hand and the four goals on the other. On the face of it the hierarchy of the four goals starting with *dharma*, to which the law books or Dharmaśāstras were devoted, was a logical ideal for a varṇa-divided society.

No serious student of social formations in early India can overlook religious ideology and practices. But these cannot be studied in isolation from changes in material life. In fact Vedic and post-Vedic rituals serve as an indispensable guide to both social and economic developments. Unfortunately some scholars who consider the four-goal ideal as a key to the unfolding of the ancient Indian cultural treasure discard rituals as meaningless symbols. But myths and rituals have their origin and growth in reality. Even the wild growth of plants and vegetation is governed by certain laws. Myths and rituals therefore do not grow in a vacuum or in barren soil. They owe their origin to certain material and social environments which they subserve and perpetuate. With a change in environment, they might lose their relevance and become empty formalities, but they retain their significance as long as the original situation lasts. Even those who suspect their historical value consider many myths and rituals as symbols of fertility. But fertility represents production and reproduction without which human society cannot continue.

It would appear that the search for substitutes for the materialist explanation of history, developed through the concepts of class and mode of production, have thrown up a varied crop of alternatives such as concepts of status, kinship, peasant society, purity/impurity, religion, *caturvarga* ideals, etc. The exploration of each one of these the context of ancient Indian society has introduced a good measure of fresh air and also posed a few questions which need historical explanation. But none of these formulations appear to be effective substitutes. They may explain the growth of the outer dimensions of social institutions, but they do not provide convincing explanations for changes in the inner or basic social structure. Whatever may be its weaknesses regarding foolproof explanation, the Marxist theory, with its refinements in recent years, continues to be the most satisfying and effective tool for analysing and explaining historical events.

The mode of production occupies the pivotal position in the materialist explanation of history. In explaining its operation a distinction is rightly made between structure and superstructure; social units, religion, ideology, art and literature, polity, etc., are placed in the realm of superstructure. This distinction is sometimes questioned by those who include the ideological outfit in the mode of production. Emphasis on the hegemony of ideology may be considered as one of the ramifications of the 'elitist' theory, for it implies an emphasis on the role of intellectuals, who in most class societies have been an integral part of the establishment. It is likely that some Marxists want the intellectuals to play a very full and effective role in close cooperation with the working masses, but that purpose is not necessarily served by making ideology part and parcel of the mode of production. In the case of India if we accept this position we will have to accept the primacy of religion in shaping the course of history. But whatever little work has been done in this direction from the materialist point of view shows that religion subserved the interests of the ruling class because of the existing mode of production. The first essential therefore is to understand the nature of the mode of production and then of the resultant ideology. Those who investigate on these lines are dubbed mechanical materialists, but it is better to be called mechanical in the age of the machine than to give undue weight to the role of intellectuals. It is true that if the same material conditions persist for centuries, the religious paraphernalia assumes the character of a materialistic force and continues to keep its grip over the minds of the people even when the conditions which gave rise to it and sustained it have disappeared. But just as a rootless tree cannot retain its green leaves for ever, so also the religious facade without a materialistic framework cannot last for long.

The object of making ideology a part of the mode of production may be to strengthen the struggle against the hold of obscurantist and irrational ideas, but unless the basis of such ideas is assailed and shattered the system will continue. Though a study of interaction between the structure and superstructure cannot be ignored, a mixing-up of the two may hamper an analysis of the real nature of the inner structure of society and consequently may obscure our understanding of past societies. Such a mixing-up will particularly confuse the minds of those who have to deal with present societies and will affect the direction of their struggle against social injustice.

During the last twenty years or so the idea of the heartland and hinterland or of the core and periphery, advanced in the context of settlement geography, is being used by some scholars who want to utilize archaeological and other types of evidence for the study of ancient cultural patterns. There is no doubt that the idea originated in the context of a highly industrialized society with enormous transport facilities, and it emphasizes the dominance of the metropolitan cities in relation to smaller cities lying on the periphery. Only in such a society can we think of continuous commercial linkages on a substantial scale. It is difficult to imagine continued commercial traffic in the Vedic period or in the age of the Buddha. However the idea of diffusion of the elements of material culture associated with the PGW or NBPW from their epicentre to the peripheral zones through trade, conquest or missionary activities can be explored. There is also the possibility of feedback from less developed areas to more developed areas.

In the case of ancient India the concept of nuclear zones was first put forward forcefully by Subba Rao in his *Personality of India*. But it is not merely the geographical set-up or availability of resources which confers nuclear importance on any zone. Much depends on the technological knowledge available to people at various stages of the development of human society. It is obvious that despite the middle Gangetic basin being one of the most fertile areas and despite it lying adjacent to rich mineral resources including iron in south Bihar, it could only come into the historical limelight with the increased use and better knowledge of iron technology and of rice transplantation in the middle of the first millennium BC. It is therefore more meaningful to analyse the various elements that go into the making of the production system of a zone and help it to emerge as a unit. It helps further if we discover the processes of the spatial expansion of such units of production under the leadership of the dominant sections of society. The *janapadaniveśa* or *śunyaniveśa* of Kauṭilya presents a practical picture of these processes. When advanced zonal units of production come into contact with less developed units, they impart their advanced skill and knowledge, provided there is a congenial climate for receptivity. They also adopt from their neighbours new elements, refine them and assimilate them into their production system. It is a two-way traffic in which the advanced production zone may be a dominant giver, though its dominant classes consist of people who enjoy taxes and tributes made available through the spatial expansion of the production zone.

In the context of ancient India smaller towns were not the satellites of larger towns. Possibly the upper classes of towns were involved in transactions with one another in semiprecious beads, *de luxe* pottery, costly cloth and spices, some other luxury goods and prestige objects. Most townsmen however would have nothing to do with these objects. It may therefore be more fruitful to look for the rural base of towns whose inhabitants were mostly non-agriculturists. Here the archaeological method might pay. If the same types of pottery (NBPW and associated ware) are found in a town site in excavation and in the neighbouring area in excavation/exploration it may be possible to establish some kind of links between towns and the adjacent countryside. Unfortunately such an effort has not been made so far. In any case some insights from settlement geography may prove useful in the ancient Indian context, but the fact that some of these are far more relevant to highly industrialized communities should not be lost sight of.

Happily the prospects of applying the psycho-analytical approach to early Indian history do not seem to be bright because we do not possess authentic accounts of the childhood of great individuals. I have however a lurking suspicion that this will not deter enthusiasts, who might try their hands at interpreting the numerous legends we have. In any case what is needed is not only an awareness of the various models that are being peddled in the field but also their careful examination, otherwise we would just become middlemen and paraphrasers. I would prefer to be damned as old-fashioned than go in for the latest without assessing its analytical validity and social relevance. New terms are needed to express new ideas, but phrase-mongering should not be confused with advance in historical knowledge.

In this study we do not have any new approach to commend to the reader. We have based our methodology on an application of what is commonly known as historical materialism. Stated in the simplest terms it means 'no production, no history'. A study of ancient Indian history on this basis involves a study of (*i*) the labour process and the labouring masses; (*ii*) of the raw materials or the natural resources on which they worked; and (*iii*) of the artefacts which they used. It further means an inquiry into (*a*) the use, utilization and allocation of raw materials and other resources; (*b*) appropriation and distribution of surplus labour and surplus product; and (*c*) finally the nature of the relations that were established between different categories of primary producers themselves, and again between the primary producers on the one hand, and users, organizers, managers, and distributors of production on the other. Since clear and adequate information about the allocation and possession of resources cannot be gathered from the earliest written texts in India, it is far more important to consider the factors which govern the lack of availability of surplus and also its distribution. Although Gordon Childe's study of social evolution based on the application of the theory of surplus has been criticized, the critics do realize the need for an empirical study of increases in production and institutional arrangements for the identification and use of surplus.[6] Even the Polanyi school recognizes 'the relative importance of methods of production and efficiency in exploiting the environment and of procedures of allocation, in the study of economic anthropology'.[7]

Not much has been done to examine the potentialities of historical materialism in regard to the medieval and modern periods of Indian history, not to speak of ancient Indian history. What was the role of family and especially of women in the process of production? The problem of division of labour between the labouring masses and the leisured classes calls for investigation. Among the labouring masses we will have to consider the process of specialization. We need a thorough and detailed analytical history of the working population, free or servile, of vaiśyas/peasants, of śūdras/slaves, hired labourers, sharecroppers, serfs, of artisans touchable and untouchable, etc. We ought to know about their size, the calamities and diseases they suffered, and how they lived and died. Further we have to know how the primary producer managed to survive and multiply.

A study of the raw material and natural resources on which the people laboured would involve an areawise history of climatic conditions such as soil, rainfall, vegetation; of the change of river courses as in the case of the Indus, Gangetic and other systems which provide fiscal and administrative boundaries as well as cultural and linguistic limits; of the occurrence of floods, droughts and famines; and above all the history of mines and metals. A Sanskrit maxim asks us not to bother about the origins of great men. We may therefore ignore the great men of ancient India for the time being and look for the origin of the things which made them great. We need to examine the sources and availability of tin, copper and, more important, of iron. The progressive use of metal artefacts played a crucial role in man's perpetual struggle against nature, and in man's struggle against man. It is significant that a major part of India did not have a proper bronze age, although certain parts passed through the copper phase. In many parts of the country the intermediate stages between the neolithic stage and the iron age were skipped over.

The study of the history of artefacts and artifices, tools and weapons, has been vitiated by two extreme points of view. The Aryanists and chauvinists think that everything that is great and good in the history of world civilization including some of the latest inventions originated in ancient India. On the other hand the diffusionists think that the technique of making bronze, fire-baked bricks, painted grey ware, steel, metallic money, even stone implements, the art of writing and urban life came to India from outside. If eastern and southern India are looked upon as the borrowers of elements of material culture from South-East Asia, and northern and western India as the borrowers from Western Asia, then India as a cultural unit stands dissolved. It will have to be written off so far as indigenous developments are concerned. It reflects a colonial attitude projected back into our past history. Similarities do not always mean imitations. Even borrowing pre-supposes a congenial climate for acceptance and adoption, and the presence of optimum environmental conditions always opens up possibilities of the indigenous origin of tools, implements and technological knowledge.

We need more and more work on the history of mining and metallurgy, and particularly the history of iron technology. It is now widely recognized that there would have been no large-scale habitations in thick-vegetation areas such as the middle Gangetic or lower Gangetic basin without the use of iron for crafts, clearance, and cultivation. This makes us question the long-lived Purāṇic lists of dynasties in Kosala, Videha and Vaiśālī before 600 BC, notwithstanding the existence of a few chalcolithic settlements on the river banks or the confluence of rivers. An examination of place names found in early Pāli texts might throw light on the processes of clearance and cultivation. In the fourth century BC the classical accounts mention Indian steel and experts also ascribe the appearance of a minor kind of steel to the fifth century BC. But real steel appeared in the second century BC. The history of tools and agricultural implements, especially the iron plough share which provided an assured means of livelihood and led to the establishment of sedentary life, social formation and state formation merits attention. In addition to this we ought to know more about the means of water supply such as various types of wells, tanks, canals, waterlifts, *arahaṭṭas* (Persian water-wheels), etc. In ancient times animals, the constant companions of the labouring masses, 'provided not only dairy products and non-vegetarian food but also helped ploughing and cultivation, and hence served as an important means of production. The history of cattle economy and animal husbandry becomes important although the history of the buffalo, camel, horse and elephant cannot be ignored. A history of agricultural technology would also involve the study of the cultivation of such cereals as barley, wheat, rice, lentils, jowar, etc., of the various types of agriculture, of the size and location of fields, of the rotation of crops, and of seasons and rainfall.

In any study of the mode of production in early India, investigation into the use, occupation and ownership of land, pasture grounds, trees, forests, water reservoirs, mines, etc., constitutes the key to the understanding of all social developments. Since the British took over *diwani* rights in 1765 in Bengal, Bihar and Orissa, there has been an on-going debate, mainly from the legalistic point of view, on the nature of land rights in pre-British India. Not much consideration has been given to different schools or traditions derived from various communities at various times in various regions of the country. Changes in land rights are linked up with changes in the law of inheritance. The Dharmaśāstra laws regarding primogeniture, special share of the eldest son, equal share of all the legitimate sons, varying shares of adopted sons, shares of the sons born of *niyoga* and from wives of different castes, and enlargement of the scope of *strīdhana* (a woman's special movable property) indicate the nature of family and property relationships in a landed society. In Gupta and post-Gupta times the Smṛti laws, mostly meant for higher varṇas, recommend *sati* and child marriage for daughters, and condemn *niyoga* (levirate) and widow remarriage, which are reserved for lower orders. The dominant ideology not only increasingly places woman and śūdra in the same category but also brackets woman with property. Is there any linkage between these family laws on the one hand and the growth of private rights in land on the other in early medieval times? What could be the social implications of the Smṛti laws of partition of landed property which appear in the fifth-sixth centuries AD? A study of interaction between property distribution known from the land grants on the one hand and inheritance laws known from the Dharmaśāstras on the other should prove fruitful to the institutional historian.

Although we notice clear signs of change in the land system in Gupta and post-Gupta times, the technological base of the feudal phase has still to be explored. Without doubt agriculture expanded in peripheral areas, as indicated by land grants, and by the *Bṛhatsaṃhitā*, *Agni Purāṇa, Uktivyaktiprakaraṇa, Vṛkṣa-Āyurveda* and above all, by the *Kṛṣi-Parāśara*. All these texts contain advanced knowledge of crops, weather, rainfall, fertilizers, implements, etc. There is also clear evidence about the use of the Persian water-wheel (*arahaṭṭa*) in northern India during the early medieval period. Alongside all this the supply of iron artefacts had become so common that it was possible to put it to non-functional, non-utilitarian uses such as the Mehrauli pillar of the AD fourth century and the Dhara pillar of the twelfth century. Without increase in production it could not have been possible to support a large number of landed magnates and their retinue who appear in this period all over the country.

The study of technology is important for the study of the lack or availability of the social surplus. So is the study of the problem of appropriation and distribution of the surplus product in kind or cash and of surplus labour through the mechanism of kinship, religion, war, plunder, gifts (*dāna*), ritualistic ranks, taxes, tributes, tithes, trade, grants, rewards, salaries, etc. In the context of time and place each one of these can be a good subject for detailed investigation. Was the social surplus distributed in the earliest phase through the mechanism of war, kinship and community sacrifice? It is held that the producers contributed their mite to a central pool which distributed the collected stuff among all the members of the production unit. This is called 'redistribution', and credited with removing inequalities, but it also led to unequal allocation and social disparities. How did the voluntary gift system of the tribal phase assume the form of tax, tithes, tribute, trade, usury and bribery in the class-divided society? How did the brāhmaṇas come to monopolize the gifts unilaterally? Was the social surplus appropriated in the second stage through the mechanism of the varṇa system? Ancient India's juridico-legal device for the distribution of the social surplus lay in the ritual-based varṇa just as that of Greece and Rome lay in the device of citizenship. The varying ritual status conferred on the two upper varṇas several economic, political, social and ideological privileges which enabled them to claim taxes from the vaiśyas and services from the śūdras. A certain amount of agricultural commodity production existed because payment to many employees was made in cash, at least in Maurya times. It seems that in the third phase, that is, in the Gupta and more importantly in the post-Gupta phase, surplus in the form of rent in kind and labour was extracted from the peasants through land grants sanctified by religio-legal compulsions rather than through politico-legal compulsions, as was the case in Europe. The basic truth that the surplus produced by the peasant supports the state, landlords, traders, creditors, priests, prostitutes, pleaders, and people in towns is known to the peasants, as appears from the songs of the kisan movement of the thirties and forties of the present century, but it has to be grasped by historians and worked back with its implications in terms of time and place.

Trade and towns played an important part in the distribution of the social surplus. Whatever may have been the role of religion, political power and other similar non-economic factors in the origin of towns, the towns could not have existed without the availability of the social surplus. Similarly whatever be its other functions, the town never ceased to be a market. The question is from where did the social surplus and commodities come to the market? Did the town live on the taxes and tributes collected from the countryside? Did town–country relations indicate a form of class conflict? Was the ancient Indian town a centre of manufacture and export rather than of consumption and import? Do towns in post-Gupta times become primary centres of import and consumption? The remark of Marx that Asian history shows an undifferentiated unity of towns and country and that the town was mostly a princely camp superimposed upon the economic structure has to be examined. The earliest models of rural and urban settlements are provided by Kauṭilya, but in order to understand the nature of the relations between the two and their precise role in the overall mode of production written texts and material remains have to be studied together. Only if towns are seen as indicators of socio-economic change or as forms of concentration and consumption of the surplus, leading to social differentiation, their study becomes meaningful.

A few words can be said on the flourish and decline of towns. If we leave out the Harappa phase, archaeology makes it evident that Kuṣāṇa India saw the highest peak of urbanization. Excavations at Sonkh (Mathurā) have revealed seven layers of Kuṣāṇa structures, and only one or two layers of Gupta structures. The poverty of the Gupta layer structures in comparison with those of the Kuṣāṇa layer may be shocking to believers of the golden age, but it is an archaeological fact in northern

India. The Kuṣāṇa phase appears to be so thriving in coins, towns and structures that it has been called the golden age of Pakistan. The myth of the golden age is needed by all nations at one stage or another, but the glamour of the golden age under the Kuṣāṇas has to be shared by India, Pakistan, Afghanistan, Iran and Soviet Central Asia. Apparently this phase saw not only the peak of urbanization, but also of crafts, commerce and monetary economy.

The decline and disappearance of towns in Gupta and post-Gupta times is attested by excavations, though limited, and also by the Chinese accounts. This connected with falling trade, less use of metal money, and the almost total absence of gold coins in the seventh to tenth centuries. The lack of gold coins is similar to their paucity in Europe in the ninth to the thirteenth century. In early times we know little about various types of payments for different types of goods and services, and less about different classes of payers and recipients. If the decay of towns in the early medieval period is viewed in the context of slow-moving trade, fossilizing of craft-guilds into stagnant castes, sagging coinage, and growing payment in kind and land grants, all these processes fall into a pattern.

The problem of surplus appropriation led us into the question of trade and towns. But we may also examine the agrarian aspects of production and distribution. The nature of relations that were established between the primary producers and those who organized production and appropriated its surplus. Thus the relations between labourers and non-labourer have to be reviewed. In the ancient period priests, warriors, nobles and independent peasants used the services of hired labourers and slaves (both being śūdras), in craft and agricultural production. There were three components in production: free peasantry, slavery and wage labour. Their relative importance kept on changing. In the age of the Buddha peasantry was more important, but in state production under the Mauryas, slavery and wage labour also gained in importance. Nevertheless by and large the vaiśyas or peasants, who were the principal taxpayers, provided the surplus produce, and the śūdras, held in collective bondage, provided the labour. Political and legal institutions and instruments of coercion, as outlined in the Dharmaśāstras, were sanctified by religion and were geared to this supreme need. We have no single term to characterize this social formation, but on the whole the social structure from the sixth century BC to the AD fifth century in mid-India may be called vaiśya–śūdra based society in the sense that vaiśyas were peasants, and śūdras were artisans, slaves, and hired labourers. Irrespective of the change in relations between the two higher varṇas, the social and ritualistic distance between the two lower varṇas remained considerable. The social fabric probably underwent temporal and regional variations and also coexisted with other formations. In some areas tribute-paying peasants may have formed the backbone of society, in other areas sharecroppers and wage-labourers, in some other areas slaves and wage-labourers, and yet in still other areas primitive tribal villages with communal traits. Written texts may help in pursuing this line of inquiry, but archaeology of rural settlements and social anthropology might fill in the large gaps.

The ancient production relations embodied in the varṇa system encountered a serious social crisis in the early Christian centuries. In this period Manu stresses the need to discipline vaiśyas and śūdras and some of the earliest Purāṇas describe the evils of the Kali age. There is no doubt about the symptoms of the crisis, but its causes have to be explored. The crisis was overcome by modifying the varṇa order in which vaiśya peasants were relegated to the position of servile śūdras. What is more important, outside mid-India in the outer areas extensive land grants were made to religious beneficiaries, with the result that the inhabitants of these backward areas, who were hitherto almost complete masters of these lands, had now to make payments in kind and render agricultural and craft services to the beneficiaries. In mid-India, the śūdras were probably given pieces of land formerly cultivated by them as slaves, hired labourers, etc., for shares and rents which they had to pay to the landlords. In any case during this period land and other agrarian resources came to be privately controlled by a considerable class of beneficiaries, religious and 'secular'. On account of this, society was divided into two basic classes, one of landlords who came to have titles to lands and villages on the strength of state charters, and the other of peasant producers who were in effective possession of land which was the chief means of production. But, because of several fiscal and administrative rights, the beneficiaries could deprive the peasants of their means of production or at any rate curtail their rights to the unfettered use of land and pastures. Thus there developed the feudal type of society in which we notice the lordship of the landed magnates over the peasants and their indirect control over the instruments of production operated by the peasants.

The impact of land grants in various regions of the country was felt unevenly according to the existing substratum of agrarian rights—tribal, communal, familial, individual, royal, etc.—and also according to the existing extent of crafts and commerce. We may visualize several subtypes of social formations within the broad feudal framework such as servile peasantry verging on serfdom in northern Orissa and eastern Madhya Pradesh, insecure tenantry supplying forced labour in Maharashtra, Gujarat, Malwa and Rajasthan, feudalized urban pockets in the coastal areas of western India, intensely subinfeuded landed hierarchy in Rajasthan, taxpaying religious beneficiaries in south India, etc. A study of land grants in depth might reveal shades of variations in the social formation.

I have indicated some of the problems that arise out of the theory of 'no production, no history'. We may suggest a few methods that have to be used to study those problems. While I am rather wary of the models offered by sociology and social anthropology, I would unreservedly commend many techniques of research used by them. In particular I would like to stress the role of statistics in the interpretation of data. Generalizations acquire solidity and win acceptance only when they are backed by facts and figures. But some historians look upon facts in the same manner as a brāhmaṇa looks upon manual labour, with the result that these are entrusted to the sole charge of research assistants. Facts and figures lend credibility not only to written evidence but also to archaeological evidence. For determining the comparative prevalence of a ceramic it may be necessary to count the potsherds belonging to a particular fabric, colour and typology trench-wise, site-wise and period-wise. Possibly in northern India *c.* 1000-500 BC was mainly a period of the use of iron weapons and not of iron tools, which became equally important about *c.* 500 BC. But for this purpose the iron artefacts of the two phases will have to be counted, classified, and compared. Similarly coins, whose main functions are economic, have to be subjected to statistical analysis in order to determine their number and volume in circulation; the same technique has to be applied to the seals.

The relation between the material remains and the literary remains of ancient times deserves our special attention. We started with text-aided archaeology, which has now led to the search for the epic sites. But now we have reached a stage in which we need to practise archaeology-aided texts. Though some beginnings have been made in correlating archaeological data with documentary data, several complexities are involved in the method. Since very few ancient texts were composed by a single author at a single time and place, the first task is to differentiate the various strata of a text and establish its stratigraphic sequence. We can locate the narrative, descriptive and didactic portions of the *Mahābhārata*, but we have yet to identify satisfactorily the *Jaya*, the kernel of the text consisting of 8800 verses in the first phase, the *Bhārata* raised to 24,000 verses in the second phase, and the *Mahābhārata* elaborated to 100,000 verses in the final phase. For this internal criteria regarding style and contents and external comparisons will have to be evolved. It may be necessary to find the frequency rate of certain terms, through the computer, as has been done in the *Arthaśāstra* of Kauṭilya. Text vocabulary may be compared with inscriptional vocabulary. Curiously enough some fiscal and administrative terms used by Kauṭilya are in inscriptions of the eighth to tenth centuries from Orissa. Once literary stratigraphy has been established, it can be put to better use in conjunction and comparison with archaeological stratigraphy. In many cases literary evidence may have to be modified and sometimes even discarded in favour of archaeological data.

Whatever be the other functions of language, it has primarily been a medium for expressing social and economic needs, transactions, and relationships in day-to-day life. Therefore, the subject of the diffusion of elements of material culture, and interaction between various peoples, in and outside India, can be pursued through comparative linguistics. Location of loan words for cereals, fruits, animals, metals, tools, weapons, places, gods, kin relationships, social differentiation, etc., adopted by one language from another throws light on the nature of cultural contacts. Thus ancient Australian words for rice, coin (*paṇa*), silk-cotton and processing of cotton are found in Indo-Aryan languages in eastern India These Australian words may have been connected with the Mundari language, for the Mundas appeared in Australia much before they appeared in India around 50,000 BC. Similarly the Indo-Aryan terms for months, seasons, wheat, wood, brick, brass, ironrod, axe, axle, scissors, oil-press, sugarcane-press, tank-diggers, cowherd caste, forced labour (*viṣṭi*), etc., are found in several Dravidian dialects and languages of central and south India. It is our job to find out when, where and how this exchange of terms takes place and what it signifies. For this we need a comprehensive comparative-dictionary of Indian languages. *A Comparative Dictionary of Indo-Aryan Languages*, R.L. Turner, London, 1966 is very useful, but we require such dictionaries of Dravidian, Mundari and other Indian languages. There are still some enclaves in which old archaic dialects survive. Several Vedic, classical and inscriptional terms can be explained with reference to their cognates still surviving in the areas in which these were used. On the other hand the changing meaning of the terms over centuries cannot be ignored, so that the meaning assigned to a Vedic word in a commentary of the fourteenth century cannot be always taken at face value. For communicating the same ideas within the same broad linguistic and cultural group different terms and styles are used by members of opposing social classes such as priests, nobles, traders, artisans and peasants. It would be therefore worthwhile to look not only into class and trade vocabulary but also into the idiom used by different classes in their mutual relations. Finally our attention may be directed to the residues and survivals of ancient customs and rituals many of which have undergone variations. For the elucidation of ancient texts and the reconstruction of the past they may sometimes be as important as the material remnants. These along with unrecorded oral folk traditions, which reflect the peasant mind and ideology, can be a good source for the social historian. Some artisan groups in the Tanjavur area retain not only oral traditions about their migrations from Saurashtra but also use the same words for their tools as are common in Kathiawar

I have stated my views on the theories and models that have to be discarded, discouraged, and modified, the alternatives that may be tried, the problems that have to be tackled, and the methods that may be employed. In all this my chief concern has been the study of social formations in early India in the context of the mode of production. I know that I have touched only the fringe of complex problems which do not easily lend themselves to the simplification I have attempted. But I could not resist the temptation of stating some of my thoughts on them, in the hope that they receive some consideration. In the chapters that follow we will try to apply some of these ideas and methods to the study of Vedic and post-Vedic material life and social formations.

I am grateful to Sitaram Rai who has contributed much to the preparation of the present book. I also thank Shiv Shankar Kumar, Anjan Kumar, and K.K. Mandal who worked hard to arrange the matter in the present volume.

NOTES

1. Keith Hopkins, *Slaves and Conquerors*, Cambridge, 1978.
2. In the Greek context the kinship system did not have important functions; this can be inferred from Hesiod's *Works and Days*; S.C. Humphreys' *Anthropology and the Greeks*, London, 1978, p. 70.
3. According to 'neo-Marxist' anthropologists in France and elsewhere, even the religious or political system of a society may function as relations of production. Humphreys, op. cit., pp. 73–4.
4. Suvira Jaiswal, 'Caste in the Socio-Economic Framework of Early India, Presidential Address, Section I, Indian History Congress, 38th Session, Bhubaneswar, 1977; 'Some Recent Theories of the Origin of Untouchability;

A Historiographical Assessment', *Indian History Congress, Proceedings of the Thirty-Ninth Session*, Hyderabad, 1978. pp. 218–29; Vivekananda Jha, 'Untouchables in Early Indian History', unpublished Ph.D. Thesis, Patna University, 1972.

5. R.N. Nandi, 'Aspects of Untouchability in Early South India', *Indian History Congress, Proceedings of the Thirty-Fourth session*, i, Chandigarh, 1973, pp. 120–5.
6. S.C. Humphreys, op. cit., pp. 61–2; see also fns. 129 and 130 on p. 282, ibid.
7. Ibid., p. 62. Karl Polanyi became influential through *Trade and Market in the Early Empires*, eds, K. Polanyi, C. Aresberg and H.W. Pearson, Chicago, 1957, although his publications ranged between 1922 and 1974. A bibliographical list is given in S.C. Humphreys, op. cit., pp. 339–40.

1

Sources and Review of Early Socio-Economic History*

Political history has been the main concern of historians for long, and therefore the sources have been discussed chiefly in this context But the same sources can also be largely used for the reconstruction of social, economic and cultural history. On the other hand many sources including archaeology can be used primarily for non-political history. The relics of the settlements in which ancient Indians lived, the artefacts which they used to earn their subsistence and the places where they worshipped are found all over the country. In the south temples made of stone and in the east mathas and monasteries made of brick tell us not only about the religious beliefs and practices of the people but also about their social and economic life. Ancient remains are found in the country in the form of mounds which are called sites. Several successive material cultures may be found at the same site, and such sites are known as multi-culture sites. On the other hand some sites show only one type of culture and they are known as single-culture sites. Various stages of Harappan culture appear in many mounds which do not possess the remains of other cultures. The Harappan sites are found in very large numbers in the Indus valley. Territorially they are found in Pakistan, Punjab, Haryana and in the western part of U.P. Traces of this culture also appear in Rajasthan, Gujarat and Maharashtra. The Harappan culture is identified by its red pottery, form of writing and bronze tools. Granaries are also found at the sites of Harappa and Mohenjodaro.

If we study the remains of the Harappan culture we can learn about the way of life led by the urban people in the Bronze Age. Various antiquities

*Previously published as 'Sources of Economic and Social History', in R.S. Sharma, *Perspectives in Social and Economic History of Early India* (Delhi: Munshiram Manoharlal, 1983).

found in the neighbourhood of the Harappan settlements and even in distant places throw light on the nature of trade carried on at that time. They enable us to locate the resources that were available to the Harappans. The seals of Harappa have been discovered in Mesopotamia, and they show that the Indus valley people carried on trade with the land of the two rivers between *c.* 2500 BC and *c.* 1900 BC. Thus the excavation of the Harappan sites throws light on the economic life of the people in the Bronze Age. Numerous tools, metals and other antiquities help us to form an idea of the specialized artisans and traders who lived between *c.* 3000 BC and *c.* 2000 BC.

The small and large structures indicate social stratification. The rulers and members of the affluent section lived in bigger buildings in Harappan times whereas the ordinary people lived in modest two-roomed houses. Several images of mother goddesses found in course of excavations testify to the high position of women. Phallic emblems indicate that people believed in fertility cults. They seem to have thought that such emblems would help the families to multiply and have more earning members. Since *c.* 1000 BC onwards we find a new type of archaeological material in Punjab, Haryana, western U.P., and in the neighbouring areas of Rajasthan. They suggest a new type of material culture and a new type of settlement. This culture is identified by a new type of pottery called Painted Grey Ware. The PGW earthen pots abound in dishes (*thālīs*) arid bowls (*loṭās*). The excavation of the PGW sites in Atranjikhera and Hastināpur have exposed rice, wheat and other cereals which show the people to be basically agriculturists. They lived in thatched houses and their settlements were much smaller than those of the Harappans. Certain post-holes meant for erecting posts for thatched roofs have been found. Since burnt bricks were not used, no extant house has been recovered. But iron tools appear in Atranjikhera and other places. They are in the form of spearheads and arrowheads which suggests that the Painted Grey Ware people also practised hunting and war as sources of livelihood. The material associated with the Painted Grey Ware people indicates that their social structure was of a simpler type; it was not as complex as that of the Harappans. Tools and other material remains recovered from the Painted Grey Ware sites do not speak of much social differentiation. The PGW culture came to an end around 400 BC although social and economic life associated with it continued in later times.

When the Painted Grey Ware Culture thrived in western U.P., Haryana, Punjab and the neighbouring areas of Rajasthan, a new type of culture emerged in the plains of eastern U.P. and Bihar. This is marked by the appearance of a pottery called Northern Black Polished Ware that is, NBPW. Historical archaeology in northern India starts with the advent of this type of pottery around 600 BC. The NBPW sherds are found at numerous places in the middle Ganga plains in association with iron objects. The use of burnt bricks started in the middle Ganga plains in about 550 BC although it seems to have become common about a century later. The excavations at Kauśāmbī, Rajghat (Varanasi), Vaiśālī, Campā, etc. show that the Ganga plains were fairly settled and people lived here on farming supplemented by handicrafts. Although the earliest farming settlements in this area are generally associated with the people who used black-and-red ware since *c.* 1500 BC onwards and lived in the chalcolithic stage of culture, the artefacts left by them suggest extremely poor settlements. What distinguished the NBPW people was not only their expertise in manufacturing polished pottery but also their use of iron tools. The fabric of NBPW shows that this ware was used by affluent sections of society; the common people evidently used grey, red, and black-and-red ware. With the advent of the NBPW people urbanization starts in the middle Ganga plains. Several places mentioned in the Pāli texts ascribed to Buddha's time have been excavated, and show good signs of habitation in pre-Maurya times. The iron tools found there suggest that they were used not only in war and hunting but also in agriculture and crafts.

Since about 800 BC we find the commencement of an archaeological phase known as the megalithic in the Deccan and south India. The megalithic burials show blocks of stone and also iron. The excavations of these burials have exposed many iron implements, black-and-red pottery and cereals. This type of burial continued till 200 BC or even after it. The burials show the beginnings of settlements of farmers in the Deccan and south India.

Archaeology together with literary sources form the main source for the reconstruction of social and economic history until coins appear in *c.* 500 BC and inscriptions two centuries later. However because of the less certain chronology and mythical nature of literary texts we have to fall back on archaeology in many ways even when such texts are available. There is no doubt that the pottery, the terracottas, the structures, and the iron, copper tools or stone tools recovered in excavations from a region enable us to reconstruct its social and economic life. On their basis we can form an idea of the people who lived in any town or any rural region. They also show the type of crafts and agriculture that were practised. On their basis we can also suggest the nature of class inequality, of the size of family and also of the position of women.

In the construction of social and economic history numismatic evidence plays an important role. Although symbolic seals have been found in the Indus valley civilization no coined money has been found. Metal money started in India around 500 BC, and the earliest money consists of punch-marked coins mainly made of silver and of cast coins made of copper. Such coins are found in pre-Maurya times and continue till 100 BC. The provenance of these coins shows that trade and commerce had become considerable in ancient India and the exchange through barter had been largely replaced by exchange through coined money. Coins throw light on the distribution of commodities, collection of revenues, and payment to the state and various employees. They were issued by merchants and goldsmiths with the permission of the rulers. Their use promoted crafts and commerce which formed an integral part of economy in northern India since *c.* 500 BC.

The largest number of coins belong to post-Maurya times when they were issued by various dynasties as well as various guilds and towns. The names of Indo-Greek, Śaka, Sātavāhana and other kings are found on the coins. The Kuṣāṇa rulers issued gold coins on a large scale in this country. The Sātavāhanas issued coins of lead, potin, copper, etc. The boat is represented on some of their coins which suggests trade by sea. It appears that trade and commerce reached its peak under the Sātavāhanas and the Kuṣāṇas. Many Roman gold and silver coins are found, especially in peninsular India. Moreover between 200 BC and AD 300 many cities also issued their coins.

Coins were made of lead, potin, copper, bronze, gold and silver. The largest number of gold coins was issued by the Gupta kings. Coined money shows that trade was considerable in post-Maurya times and in the earlier phase of Gupta times. This is consistent with archaeological finds which show that the towns continued to flourish.

In post-Gupta times coins decreased in number at least for three centuries between AD 600 and AD 900. Between AD 650 and AD 1000 gold coins almost disappeared. A few imitations of Gupta gold coins are found in a part of eastern India, but by and large they are absent. It seems that during this period heavy transactions had suffered and long-distance trade declined. This situation obtained in both north and south India. Coins made of other metals had also decreased. Cowries appeared in good numbers, specially in Bengal, but they could not compensate for the lack of coins. The coins that are found in early medieval times cannot be identified dynastically except in the case of a few coins in Kashmir, Punjab, and Bangladesh. Coins of the Gurjara-Pratīhāras have been found, but they mostly belong to the 10th and 11th centuries. They are similar to *gadhaiyā paisās* which are found in large numbers in western U.P., Rajasthan and Gujarat. The form of writing found on inscribed *gadhaiyās* indicates that this type was mainly current between the 11th and 14th centuries. Therefore the relative paucity of coins until the 11th century suggests that trade suffered a set-back and ancient towns fell on evil days.

The study of coins throws light on the customs and religious beliefs of the rulers and the common people. Various types of symbols found on punch-marked coins need to be studied adequately. Many coins carry the images of kings and gods. The famous Samudragupta is represented playing flute on his coins. The importance of horse in transport is indicated by its representation on Kuṣāṇa and Gupta coins. Their coins show that the Kusāṇas adopted the worship of Śiva and Viṣṇu. Fire altar appears on the *gadhaiyā paisās* which shows that in early medieval times the worship of the Iranian type had become prevalent in northern India. Significantly enough the mother goddess is generally not represented on the coins which shows that the issuers of coins were a patriarchal lot.

From the point of view of social history inscriptions are far more important than coins. Lack of space in small metal pieces of which the coins are made does not accommodate much matter. But this constraint does not apply to the inscriptions incised on stone or copper. The importance of early medieval land grant inscriptions for the reconstruction of social and economic history has been pointed out by me in the last two chapters of my *Perspectives in Social and Economic History of Early India*. Here we may discuss the value of ancient inscriptions for this purpose.

Though the Harappan inscriptions are the earliest in the sub-continent, they have not been deciphered so far. The latest study shows that they seem to carry pictographic script. Symbols of this script have been found among both the Mundas and Dravidans. The first came to this country in *c.* 50,050 BC and the second came in *c.* 30,000 BC. Perhaps this may be the foundation of the Harappan culture. The Aśokan inscriptions are the earliest deciphered ones. These are written in Prākrit language and Brāhmī script and are found on highways in the major part of the country. Some Aśokan inscriptions also appear in Kharoṣṭsthī, Aramaic and Greek scripts. They are found in the form of royal orders and are particularly important for the study of social history. Through his edicts Aśoka tried to establish harmonious relations between different classes and communities. His edicts enjoined the people to respect parents and also the śramanas and brāhmaṇas, and pay attention to slaves and hired labourers. They also stress that followers of various religions should develop mutual respect for religious beliefs and practices. In his edicts Aśoka emphasizes the importance of the essentials of all religions and in this manner he tries to inculcate religious harmony (*samavāya*) and goodwill.

Though many subjects of administrative interest appear in Aśokan inscriptions they lack in economic content. However one inscription shows that Aśoka reduced the royal tax to 1/8th of the produce in Lumbini which was the birthplace of Gautama Buddha. It is obvious that the regular royal tax was much higher; it may have been 1/4th or 1/6th of the produce. The pillars on which Aśokan inscriptions are inscribed were made of sandstone and they were taken to different parts of the country from Chunar in Mirzapur district. All these polished pillars appear on important trade routes. Although inscriptions do not give any idea of the nature of transport, the fact that pillars were taken to long distances from Chunar shows that the transport system of Maurya times was not bad.

The inscriptions belonging to post-Maurya and Gupta times can be divided into two categories, private and official. Private inscriptions are mostly in the form of donation records, which give the identity of the donor, donee and also the articles that are donated. In post-Maurya times Gaya, Mathura, Sanchi, Bharhut, Nasik, Junnar, etc. abound in many epigraphs which bear the names of those artisans and merchants who donated for the Jain and Buddhist cause. The inscriptions mention the amounts in *kārṣāpaṇa.* The gift of coins is also mentioned in royal or official inscriptions. If we make a total of the various gifts recorded in the Nasik cave inscriptions of the Sātavāhana queen Nayanikā, the aggregate would come to 1,50,000 *kārṣāpaṇas*. In the Sātavāhana kingdom many merchants mention their own names and those of their towns. Thus the names of merchants and artisans of Kalyāṇa, Sopara, Dhenukākaṭaka occur in the context of their gifts. Guilds are also mentioned in inscriptions. Therefore inscriptions provide information not only about merchants, artisans and their guilds but also about towns and the currency system.

Post-Maurya inscriptions also refer to different occupations. It seems that artisans and merchants played an important role in the society of that time. Trade meant mobility which undermined the rigidity of the caste system. Many Buddhist nuns are mentioned in inscriptions which shows that they left families and joined the Buddhist order. Many other inscriptions refer to the gifts made by them in the cause of Buddhism. It is therefore clear that such nuns had sufficient money in their hands.

It is ordinarily thought that ancient Indian society was always dominated by patriarchy. But Sātavāhana inscriptions mention the name of the mother of the king as a part of the name of the king himself. Such names are for example Gautamīputra Śātakarṇi, Vāsiṣṭhīputra Puḷumāvi. In addition to this the Nasik cave inscription also mentions various sacrifices performed by queen Nayanikā. According to the Vedic texts women had no right to perform such sacrifices, but the case of Nayanikā goes against it. Thus the Sātavāhana inscriptions show that matriarchy carried weight with the Sātavāhana ruling class. Since the Sātavāhanas claimed to be brāhmaṇas who were champions of patriarchy, the presence of matriarchal element becomes all the more important. As the sole important brāhmaṇa Gautamīputra Śātakarṇi claims to have destroyed not only the pride of the kṣatriyas but also put an end to the mixture of the four varṇas. Therefore the Sātavāhana inscriptions tell us both about the varṇa system and the position of women.

Gupta and post-Gupta inscriptions contain some eulogies which are typical of semi-biographical literature. Inscriptional eulogy starts with the Hathigumpha inscription of Khāravela who ruled Kaliṅga in the first century BC. This inscription records the events of his reign year-wise. It tells us about his donation and also refers to his relation with the rural and urban people. Further, the inscription speaks of the construction of a canal in Kaliṅganagara. More information about irrigation is found in Rudradāman's Junagarh inscription (AD 150) which cannot be regarded as pure eulogy.

In Gupta times the most important eulogical epigraph is the Allahabad inscription of Samudragupta composed by Hariṣeṇa. This record was inscribed on the same pillar as contains the inscriptions of Aśoka. It throws light on the nature of relation between high and influential classes of society consisting of vassals and conquered kings on the one hand and *sāmantas* on the other. The inscription throws light on the social and administrative relations that were maintained with them by the Gupta king.

A new type of royal inscription starts with the Sātavāhana kings. These are called land grant inscriptions. Their number is small under the Sātavāhanas but by the end of the Gupta period they are found in a major part of the country. They specify the taxes which the king made over to the brāhmaṇas, temples and other parties. These inscriptions contain many technical terms of social and economic importance, for example, *praṇaya, viṣṭi, hiraṇya, udraṅga, uparikara, parihāra*, etc. Inscriptions mention many villages which were given as grants and also specify their boundaries. They further lay down the conditions on which the grantees were allowed to enjoy the villages. Therefore on the basis of land grant inscriptions we can have an idea of the land system and the agrarian history of Gupta and post-Gupta times.

Many inscriptions contain dates. Those which do not mention any era can be dated on the basis of palaeographical evolution. But it is very difficult to fix the date of ancient literary texts. Without dating changes in society and economy they cannot be placed in any perspective. For example the epics contain several strata, and hence it is wrong to ascribe the whole epic material to Vedic times. As will be shown later, certain Vedic traditions can be traced in the epics, but really speaking they were compiled in the early centuries of the Christian era. The history of social and economic processes in Vedic times can be written only on the basis of Vedic literature. Of course the archaeological material from western U.P. and the neighbouring areas belonging to the later Vedic period can be used for the social and economic history of *c.* 1000–500 BC.

The *Ṛg Veda* is the oldest Vedic text. It may have been compiled around 1500 BC or earlier. Though its first and tenth books account for a large number of hymns, they belong to a much later period and may possibly represent the state of affairs in later Vedic times. In the Puruṣa-sūkta in the tenth book it is stated that the brāhmaṇa was born out of the head of the primeval man, the rājanya from his arms, the vaiśya from his thighs and the śūdra from his feet. This statement is considered to be an interpolation and cannot be made the basis of the generalization that the varṇa system is as old as the *Ṛg Veda.* Similarly more information about farming is found in the tenth book. We may note that it was a common practice to interpolate material in ancient texts and thus make it acceptable to the common people. Interpolation could be made easily either in the beginning or at the end of the book. Therefore unless we take account of the different strata found in Vedic and other texts it will not be possible to construct solid history.

Later Vedic literature contains numerous rituals in addition to hymns. The *Atharva Veda* contains magic charms and spells which are used to drive away diseases. It is dated around 1000 BC although it may have been completed later. It is held that it contains non-Vedic cultural elements.

The date of *Yajur Veda* falls more or less in the time-bracket of the *Atharva Veda*, and its different collections may have been completed by 800 BC. In addition to hymns the *Yajur Veda* collections contain numerous rituals, which are explained in detail in the Brāhmaṇas. Some of the Brāhmaṇas such as the *Aitareya, Pañcaviṃśa Śatapatha* are useful from the point of view of social history. The rituals found in them show how the raja or the rājanya tries to bring under his control the *viś*. In explaining the rituals, it is emphasized that the place of the rājanya/kṣatriya and brāhmaṇa is high and that of the vaiśya is low. Rituals show that on account of internal conflict within the same kinship group certain people emerged as chiefs and priests whereas the majority of their kinsmen were thrown into the ranks of ordinary peasants. Rituals prescribed by the later Vedic texts gradually deprived the śūdras of the right to participate in sacrifices. These texts mention *takṣan, karmāra, rathakāra* and various other artisans. They also refer to various metals including iron, and cereals including rice and wheat. Later Vedic literature gives us an idea of the economy of the Kuru-Pañcāla country. Its study becomes all the more fruitful if it is undertaken in combination with the archaeology of the PGW settlements.

From the point of view of social history the Dharmaśāstras are extremely important. Dharmaśāstra is the general name given to different categories of early legal writings which include (1) Dharmasūtra, (2) Smṛti, (3) Ṭīkā, and (4) Nibandha. The Dharmasūtras are ascribed roughly to 500–200 BC. Of them *Āpastamba* and *Baudhāyana* are considered to be most ancient. It is held that *Baudhāyana* contains some southern traditions. Although *Gautama* is also regarded to be 'ancient, it has many interpolations which seem to belong to the early century of the Christian era. The Dharmasūtras are generally written in prose although some of them also contain verses. These earliest law-books give the first systematic description of the varṇa system, and they specify the duties and obligations of the four varṇas clearly. They enjoin the king to uphold the varṇa-based social order and to see that members of every varṇa carry out their duties.

The Dharmasūtras prescribe eight forms of marriage. Some of these forms are called approved and others are called unapproved. The lawgivers prescribe the duties of women and deal with *niyoga* and widow remarriage. The untouchables and members of mixed varṇas come under the category of the śūdras. The lawgivers also specify the rights of son and lay down the law of inheritance. Therefore a study of the Dharmasūtras becomes essential for the history of marriage, family, property, varṇa system and untouchability.

The Dharmasūtras codify laws relating to the guilds of merchants and artisans. The internal administration of the guilds was carried on according to their own customs. The earliest law-books also mention the use of coins in trade and in the context of the judicial fines. Moneylending starts with the Dharmasūtras. Thus these texts throw considerable light on ancient Indian economy.

By the beginning of the Christian era the place of the Dharmasūtras was taken by the Smṛtis. The period of the composition of the Smṛtis can be placed between 200 BC and AD 900, but most Smṛtis were compiled by the end of sixth century AD. Whereas the Dharmasūtras are written in prose the Smṛtis are written in verse. The subjects treated in the Dharmasūtras are dealt with in detail in the Smṛtis which also include new topics not found in the earliest law-books.

The law-book of Manu is the oldest Smṛti. The German scholar Būhler placed it between 200 BC and AD 200. But it contains chapters which can be placed around the fifth century AD. Its 10th chapter enumerates 61 mixed castes which originate mainly as a result of marriage between men of lower castes and women of higher castes. If a śūdra has a brāhmaṇa wife the issue is called caṇḍāla and is known as a *pratiloma*. Numerous castes of *pratiloma* origin appear in the law-book of Manu, and are placed in the category of untouchables. According to the provisions of Manu śūdras and women occupy a very low status and they are looked at with great contempt. On the other hand brāhmaṇas occupy a special position and are given many privileges. However this kind of attitude is also found in the other Smṛtis. The law-book of Manu is therefore important not only for the study of the proliferation of castes but also for the study of the history of the family.

In Gupta times the law-books of Yājñavalkya, Nārada, Bṛhaspati and Kātyāyana are considered to be important. Yājñavalkya contains considerable material which is found in the *Arthaśāstra* of Kauṭilya and this raises some problems about the dating of the *Arthaśāstra*. All these Smṛtis, especially that of Nārada, prescribe many privileges for the brāhmaṇa varṇa. Nārada also has detailed provisions regarding the slaves and their manumission. The Smṛtis usually contain a chapter on the law of inheritance which prescribes the shares of the different types of sons in the family. The large Smṛtis contain chapters dealing with *vyavahāra, ācāra, prāyaścitta* and *rājanīti*. The section on *vyavahāra* contains laws regarding partnership which show how the traders formed corporate bodies and distributed profit according to the amount of the capital they invested. The sections dealing with *ācāra* and *prāyaścitta* throw light on the rituals and social status of different castes. The problem of purity and pollution occupies an important place in the section on *ācāra*. How members belonging to the higher castes get polluted by partaking food and cultivating bodily contact is stated in some detail. What a person should eat and avoid is prescribed not on grounds of health or nutrition but on the basis of caste.

The section on *prāyaścitta* shows that social regulations were to be enforced not only by the state but also by society. Under the influence of brāhmaṇical ideology the Smṛtis provide various types of penances. Those who deviate from their varṇa duties have to undergo these difficult rites. It is evident that people were compelled to perform penances because of the social pressure exerted on them through the brāhmaṇical ideology: the king had no hand in it. Several commentaries and digests were written on the Dharmasūtras and Smṛtis between the seventh and the eighteenth centuries AD. The commentators explained the provisions of ancient times. Specially several commentaries were written on the law of inheritance or *dāyabhāga* because the question of the partition of property was an ever present problem with the landed communities. Thus all the commentaries on the *Yājñavalkya Smṛti* give great attention to the *dāyabhāga*. Seven commentaries were written on Manu. Of these that of Medhātithi written in the ninth century is famous. The commentaries enable us to understand the meaning of obscure provisions. But .the commentators also explained the old provisions according to their times and prejudices. Thus although several law-books allow a woman to take a second husband (*pati*) if her husband is lost, dead, becomes an ascetic, is impotent or is excommunicated, Medhātithi takes the *pati* to mean protector in this context and thus prevents the affected woman from remarrying. Therefore if we only rely on the commentators we may not be always able to get the real intentions of the lawgivers. Further, the same material is repeated in the Dharmaśāstras and their commentaries *ad nauseum*, which suggests long changelessness in the social institutions of ancient India. There is also the problem of tackling the different views of lawgivers and commentators on the same subject. These views have to be placed in the perspective of time, place and circumstances; different views also show that changes took place in social institutions.

Many Gṛhyasūtras, which belonged to 500–200 BC, are important for the study of social and economic life. Khadira, Gobhila, Baudhāyana and Parāśara are some of the authors of these texts which describe the domestic rituals from birth to death. They deal with the ceremonies connected with the first eating of the child, tonsure, sacred thread, marriage, funeral rites, etc. These rites or *saṃskāras* are meant only for the twice-born. The śūdras could perform their rites without the use of the Vedic *mantras*. In the beginning the number of *saṃskāras* was 16 but gradually they rose to three dozen and in Gupta and post-Gupta times even the śūdras could perform many *saṃskāras*.

In domestic ceremonies numerous rituals have to be performed. The use of plants, cereals, metals, etc., is prescribed in their performance. A study of all the various articles that were needed for the performance of domestic rituals throws light on the economic life of ancient times.

Like the Dharmasūtras and the Gṛhyasūtras the *Arthaśāstra* of Kauṭilya was compiled in prose. It contains verses at some places, but they should be considered interpolations. Although Kauṭilya is used for a study of the economic and social condition of Maurya times the date of this text has not been established on a firm footing. The second, third and fifth books of this text include ancient material which can be used for Maurya times. Its remaining books reflect the state of affairs in post-Mauryan times. It is natural that the matter relating to economy receives the greatest attention in the *Arthaśāstra*. Book 2 of this text throws light on agriculture, trade, handicrafts, irrigation, minting of coins and several other economic activities. Kauṭilya enjoins the king to regulate economic life, and he provides for the appointment of a superintendent for each type of economic activity. He speaks of the superintendents of agriculture, commerce, weights and measures, mint, spinning, custom-house and several other economic sectors, and in each case the functions of the superintendent are laid down. Book 5 of the *Arthaśāstra* has a section dealing with the payment of employees. It mentions the amount of salary to be given to all the employees, great and small, appointed by the king. The maximum salary is 48,000 *paṇas* and the minimum is 60 *paṇas*. The *Arthaśāstra* also mentions employees who were given only 10 and 20 *paṇas*. Thus it shows a wide disparity in salaries. But it is clear that according to Kauṭilya salary was paid not in kind but in cash.

The *Arthaśāstra* of Kauṭilya contains considerable material on the social history of ancient India. A section deals with slaves and hired labourers and enumerates different types of slaves. Kauṭilya also speaks of eight types of marriage of which four are considered approved and the remaining four unapproved. Approved marriages take place with the consent of the father. Unapproved ones involve the consent of both the father and mother.

Apparently, the *Arthaśāstra* shows the dominance of the brāhmaṇical tradition. But its close examination reveals some differences between it and the Dharmaśāstras. Although brāhmaṇas are given several privileges in the Dharmaśāstras, all these are not mentioned by Kauṭilya who provides for the heavy punishment of a brāhmaṇa offender. The kṣatriyas seem to be quite important in the *Arthaśāstra* of Kauṭilya.

Several scholars think that the Purāṇas embody the kṣatriya tradition. These texts record genealogies of kṣatriya kings. However, many genealogies appear to be fabrications and cannot be relied upon. Post-Gupta inscriptions show that new dynasties traced their descent from the solar or the lunar line. These family trees were apparently not prepared by the kṣatriyas themselves but really by the brāhmaṇas who were granted land and other articles in return. In any case it is important to study the Purāṇas from the point of view of social history. The Purāṇas number 18. Out of these, *Viṣṇu, Brahmāṇḍa, Bhāgavata, Vāyu, Matsya*, and *Bhaviṣyat* are considered fairly old. Most Purāṇas were compiled by the end of Gupta times. But many of them continued to be compiled till the sixteenth century and interpolations continued to be made in them even in the nineteenth century and even later. The *Agni Purāṇa*, a text of about ninth-eleventh centuries, is important for the study of cultures and society. This text is in the form of an encyclopaedia. Like many other Purāṇas it deals with grammar, geography, genealogy, astrology and also polity. From the economic point of view the *Agni Purāṇa* contains the same type of knowledge about agriculture as appears in the *Bṛhat Saṃhitā* of Varāhamihira and in the *Parāśara Smṛti*. The *Agni Purāṇa* also contains considerable material on tantra which is wanting in the earliest Purāṇas.

Like the Purāṇas, the Smṛtis also number 18. Sometimes even the *jātis* and *prakṛtis* also number 18. Thus 18 is a conventional term which is used in different contexts. Therefore the number of the Purāṇa may not even be limited to 18. From the point of content the Purāṇa is a miscellany. The compilers arranged in the Purāṇas all the information that was available to them about the society, religion, *tīrthas,* geography, genealogy, astrology and many other subjects. Most Purāṇas contain a certain quantum of Dharmaśāstra material which was needed for the regulation of social institutions. The compilers of the Purāṇas were not unaware of the concept of change. They described four epochs consisting of *kṛta, tretā, dvāpara* and *kali*. Each succeeding epoch is described worse than the preceding one, and in every succeeding epoch moral values and social standards are supposed to suffer degeneration. In this manner the Kali is described as an age of social and religious crisis in which members of different varṇas discard the functions prescribed by the Dharmaśāstra and adopt those of others.

The two epics *Rāmāyaṇa* and the *Mahābhārata* resemble the Purāṇas in many ways. The *Mahābhārata* is attributed to Vyāsa who seems to be a mythical figure. In the beginning this epic consisted of 8,800 verses and it was called *Jaya,* which indicated that it was a story of victory. Subsequently the text was inflated to 24,000 verses and came to be known as *Bharata*, which suggests that it contained the story of the descendants of the earliest Vedic tribe known as Bhārata. By the Gupta period the number of verses rose to 100,000, and the text came to be known as *Mahābhārata.* The kernel of the story deals with the fight between the Kauravas and Pāṇḍavas. This event is dated around 950 BC which falls in later Vedic times. The *Mahābhārata* deals with social practices which may possibly be attributed to later Vedic times. The epic consists of narrative, descriptive and didactic portions. The narrative portion is so full of mythical stories that it is difficult to reconstruct history on its basis. However, the descriptive and the didactic portions of the epic can be used for identifying trends in social and economic history in post-Maurya and Gupta times. The Śānti Parva of the epic contains a good deal of material on polity. The principles of taxation propounded in it are important from the point of view of economic history. This Parva also deals with the functions of the castes. Many verses found in the Śānti Parva appear literally in the *Manu Smṛti* which suggests that the two texts were close to each other chronologically. The *Rāmāyaṇa* was authored by Vālmīki whose antecedents are as indefinite as that of Vyāsa. This epic originally consisted of 6,000 verses which were first inflated to 12,000 and finally to 24,000. The subject matter of the *Rāmāyaṇa* is comparatively homogeneous, and it does not abound in mythical stories like the *Mahābhārata.* But the didactic portions have been added to this epic also at a later stage. The compilation of this epic started around 500 BC. Since then it passed through five stages and the fifth stage is assigned to the twelfth century AD. On the whole the major portion of the *Rāmāyaṇa* seems to have been compiled after the writing of the *Mahābhārata.* We can learn about the nature of the family organization from this text, which also throws light on the position of women and śūdras.

Since the beginning of early medieval times around the sixth century AD we find a few semi-biographical texts, which throw light on the nature of the feudal hierarchy and the court life. The *Harṣacarita* of Bāṇabhaṭṭa written in the seventh century is a text of this type. Written in prose it is full of metaphors. It gives an account of the early life of Harṣa. The feudal character of Harṣa's court and aspects of social and religious life of the period can be studied on its basis. Several other texts were written afterwards. Sandhyākara Nandī wrote *Rāmacarita* in the twelfth century. The text gives an account of the revolt of the Kaivarta tribe against the Pāla ruler in the eleventh century and provides some glimpses of tribal life. The *Vikramāṅkadevacarita* written by Bilhaṇa in the eleventh century recounts the achievements of the Cālukya king of Kalyāna called Vikramāditya V. Because of increasing trade and commerce in the twelfth and thirteenth centuries several biographies of the *seṭhas* came to be written. A biography called *Jagaḍucarita* completed in the fourteenth century throws light on the social and economic conditions of western India in the thirteenth century. Jagadu traded with Persia and transported goods in his own ship. An eleventh century text called *Muṣikavaṃśa* found in north Kerala shows how the tribal chiefs succeeded in establishing ruling dynasties and obtained legitimation from the support of the brāhmaṇas. The best illustration of early history writing is furnished by Kalhaṇa's *Rājataraṅgiṇī* which literally means the stream of kings. This text recounts the exploits of Kashmir kings. Although it was written in the twelfth century, its account of Kashmir from the seventh century onwards can be used for social and political history. This work enables us to notice the changes that took place in the social structure and land system of Kashmir in early medieval times.

Besides biographical literature a good number of literary texts including dramas, *kāvyas*, etc., can be used for the reconstruction of social and economic life. The dramas of Bhāsa are attributed to post-Maurya times. They reflect contemporary social conditions. The great author Kālidāsa is attributed to Gupta times, and his works include *Meghadūta, Abhijñānaśākuntala, Raghuvaṃśa*, etc. On the basis of these texts attempts have been made to describe the economic, social and cultural conditions in the age of Kālidāsa. Similarly the *Mṛcchakaṭika* written by Śudraka and the *Mudrārākṣasa* written by Viśākhadatta tells us about the social conditions of Gupta and post-Gupta times. The *Daśakumāracarita* written by Daṇḍin in the seventh century provides us with glimpses of the social life of the Deccan and south India. The works of Māgha, Bhāravi and Rājaśekhara are similarly useful. The *Tilakamañjarī* of the Jain author Dhanapāla belongs to the eleventh century and furnishes information about the state of trade in that period.

Many technical works dealing with grammar, astronomy and astrology, lexicon, architecture, etc., are also useful for a study of social and economic life. The examples given to illustrate the grammatical rules in the *Aṣṭādhyāyī* of Pāṇini throw light on social and economic conditions. Pāṇini is placed around 400 BC and his grammar reflects the geography of north India. On the basis of the *Aṣṭādhyāyī* and its commentaries V.S. Agrawala has written a book called *India as Known to Pāṇini*. Around 150 BC Patañjali produced a commentary on the grammar of Pāṇini. The commentary contains valuable information about the social and economic conditions of India in post-Maurya times.

Texts on astronomy and astrology carry their own importance. In the sixth century AD, Varāhamihira wrote in Ujjain a text called *Bṛhat Saṃhitā*, which is used for the construction of the economic history of northern India in the Gupta period. This text deals with agriculture in some detail. It also lays down rules for the construction of the houses of different varṇas and different grades of dignitaries. These rules show clear discrimination between different social groups and functionaries.

From the point of view of agriculture the *Kṛṣiparāsara* and *Kāśyapa Kṛṣisūkti* are two important published texts. The first belongs to a period around the eleventh century and the second to a date after it in medieval times. It is, however, held that the second text on agriculture contains much material which can be attributed to the eighth and ninth centuries. The descriptions found in the *Kṛṣiparāśara* apply to northern India. On the other hand the *Kaśyapa Krsisūkti* seems to have been written in some paddy producing area. Although its manuscript has been found in south India it may belong to either the north or the south. These two texts on agriculture deal with various kinds of crops, cereals and seeds. The *Kṛṣiparāśara* also speaks of certain conditions on the basis of which rainfall can be predicted. Therefore such texts are useful for the study of agrarian history.

The *Amarakośa* written by Amarasiṃha throws light on social and economic conditions. It was compiled around AD 400 and it contains synonyms for many important terms. A study of these synonyms tell us not only about cultural, social and economic conditions but also about various types of provisions and resources.

The *Kāmasūtra* of Vātsyāyana, which was written in Gupta times, is useful for a study of urban life and position of women. It deals in considerable detail with the type of the life led by a typical citizen called *nāgaraka*. It shows that rich people living in towns did not do much work to earn their living. They possessed enough resources to live a comfortable life without doing any physical work. The *Kāmasūtra* also tells us that the village headman used to compel women to work in the field.

Numerous texts were written on art and architecture, particularly in early medieval times. Mention may be made of the *Mānasāra*, and the *Aparājitapṛcchā*. Both belong to the twelfth century, though the *Mānasāra* is sometimes assigned to the eighth century or even to an earlier period. These texts provide not only technological information but also throw light on the type of the houses that were meant for various grades of rajas and *sāmantas.* The rules laid down by them throw light on the hierarchy that obtained in the ruling class.

The Jain texts are important for the study of social and economic processes. Jainism made great efforts to eliminate the evils of the varṇa system and the performance of the Vedic rituals. In the initial stage the Jains discarded Sanskrit which was patronized by the brāhmaṇas and gave their religious sermons in the Prākrit language. Their religious texts, written in Ardhamāgadhī, were finally compiled in the sixth century in Valabhi which was a great centre of learning in Gujarat. The teachings of Jainism are found in the Āgamas. They include important texts as *Kalpasūtra, Bhagavatisūtra,* etc. and are placed around the sixth century BC. Whatever may be their exact date the Jain Prakrit texts throw light on the ancient varṇa system, towns and economic activities. They tell us about different types of urban and rural settlements in ancient India. Maritime trade receives considerable attention in these texts. After the sixth century several commentaries were written on the Jain texts, but except a few they have not been adequately studied. The Jain literature comprises Mahākāvyas, Purāṇas, dramas, etc. Special mention may be made of the two Jain Prākrit texts *Kuvalayamālā* and *Samarāic-cakahā*, both belonging to the eighth century AD. These two provide us with valuable information about the nature of trade in western India and also throw light on the type of feudal organization that developed in Rajasthan. It should be noted that a good number of later Jain texts were written in Sanskrit. Unlike the Buddhist texts many Jain texts have not been published so far. They lie deposited in the form of manuscripts in the Jain maṭhas of Gujarat and Rajasthan, and need to be critically edited and published. But even the published Jain texts are of great value for the social and economic history of western India between the seventh and the thirteenth century.

The Jains first wrote in Prākrit and then in Sanskrit and regional languages. But the Buddhists wrote in Pāli. Pāli is also considered a form of Prākrit which spread widely. The Pāli texts were taken to Sri Lanka, Myanmar (Burma), China and other countries. The Buddhist texts written in Pāli are divided into three categories, *Sutta Piṭaka, Vinaya Pitaka,* and *Abhidhamma Pitaka.* The *Sutta Piṭaka* contains the teachings of Gautama Buddha. The doctrines of Buddhism appear in the context of stories. The *Sutta Piṭaka* or the *Suttas* contain five bodies of collections called the Nikāyas. Mention may be made of the *Dīgha Nikāya* and the *Khuddaka Nikāya*. The *Dīgha Nikāya* contains many references to farming and trade. It shows that Gautama Buddha did not accord the highest place to the brāhmaṇas in society only on the basis of birth, he considered function far more important than birth. However, from the point of view of social and economic history the *Khuddaka Nikāya* is more important. It comprises the *Sutta Nipāta,* the oldest collection of Buddhist teachings, and the *Dhammapada* which was a popular text. More importantly it contains the Jātakas. The Buddhists believe that before the Buddha was born in the form of Gautama Buddha he had already passed through nearly 550 births. Every Jātaka tells the story of a previous birth of the Buddha and gives glimpses of the social and economic life of ancient times.

The Jātakas show that the traders, who traded by land and sea, occupied an important position in society. According to many scholars, the Jātakas belong to the sixth and fifth centuries BC, but really speaking matters of economic interest found in the Jātakas mainly belong to a period around 200 BC or a little earlier than that. The Jātaka stories are depicted in relief work at Sanchi and Bharhut whose date is fixed around 200 BC.

The *Vinaya Piṭaka* lays down rules and regulations meant for observance by monks and nuns, who were not allowed to touch gold and silver, and to practise trade and agriculture like lay devotees. They were required to lead a plain life through begging. The rules made for nuns throw light on the position of women. The *Vinaya* rules indicate the nature of relations of monks and nuns with people engaged in different vocations and also amongst themselves. The *Abhidhamma Piṭaka* deals with the *Suttas* or Buddhist doctrines in detail, and the illustrations given in it to propagate them throw light on the social outlook of the Buddhists.

Several commentaries were written on ancient Pāli texts in Sri Lanka in the fifth century. The two commentators were Buddhaghoṣa and Dharmapāla. Their commentaries show an attempt to explain ancient teachings and events in the light of changing social and economic conditions in the fifth century AD.

In addition to Sanskrit, Pāli and Prakrit sources we have some ancient Tamil texts which indicate the social and economic conditions of south India in the early centuries of the Christian era. The earliest Tamil texts are known as Sangama literature. The Sangama was an assembly of Tamil poets probably sponsored by kings or chiefs. We do not know how many assemblies were held and when. The Tamil commentaries written in the eighth century tell us that three Sangamas cover 99,990 years; they include 8,898 poets and they had 197 Pāṇḍya kings as their patrons. But all this seems to be extremely exaggerated. We can only say that the Sangamas were held under the auspices of the Pāṇḍya kings in Madurai. The major portion of Sangama literature was compiled between AD 300 and AD 600. But some of its portions may be as old as the second century BC. The *kāvya* portion of the Sangama literature comprises 30,000 lines, and they arc classified into different collections. There is no doubt that the Sangama literature contains several strata which were written or compiled one after the other. On the basis of style, contents and comparison with archaeological material attempts have been made to identify strata in the Sangama literature, but the results of the effort have not been accepted universally. Broadly speaking the Sangama literature can be divided into two groups—the narrative and the didactic. The narrative texts known as *Melkanakku* are called eighteen major texts, and the didactic texts known as *Kilkanakku* are known as eighteen minor texts.

The Sangama texts of both types enable us to identify the main stages in the development of society in south India. In the beginning the southerners lived under their chiefs and the narrative texts speak of the exploits of heroes and heroines. They repeatedly refer to continuous wars and cattle raids. It is therefore clear that the Tamils and their neighbours were mainly cattle rearers in the beginning. The Sangama literature shows that many people lived on the spoils of war. It is stated that when a hero dies he is reduced to a piece of stone. This is supported by the practice of megalithic burials in which graves were surrounded by huge blocks of stone.

The narrative Sangama texts tell us that the system of collecting tax and administering justice was rudimentary. They also speak of traders, artisans and agriculturists. Further, they refer to several towns of which Kanchi, Madurai, Puhar or Kaveripattanam are famous. Some of the Sangama sites have been excavated, and the material remains found in them testify to the prevalence of trade and commerce.

The didactic portions of the Sangama texts were composed by brāhmaṇa scholars who knew Sanskrit and Prākrit. These texts lay down the code of conduct not only for the king and his court but also for various social and professional groups. Probably this code was formulated after the fourth century AD when a good number of brāhmaṇas appeared in south India under the patronage of the Pallavas. The Sangama texts speak of the grant of villages and also mention lunar and solar ruling lines which suggest the influence of the Purāṇas on them.

In addition to the Sangama texts we have also some other ancient Tamil texts of which the *Tirukkuṛal* is a didactic text. The philosophical ideas and the maxims which it contains suggest that it was compiled in society influenced by brāhmaṇical ideas. The *Tolkkappiam* comprises elements of grammar and rhetoric but also refers to social practices.

Tamil is noted for its two epics, *Silppadikaram* and *Maṇimekhalai*, both of which were compiled around the sixth century AD. The first deals with a love story which reflects the position of women and the life of well-to-do people in Kaveripattanam. The second epic was written by a trader from Madurai who dealt in cereals. Both the epics provide gleanings of the society and economy of the Tamils around the sixth century AD.

Foreign accounts supplement the information obtained from literature, archaeology, coins, inscriptions, etc. Several Greek, Roman and Chinese travellers came to India arid many of them wanted to have a better understanding of Indian religion which they had adopted. Some foreign travellers came along with Alexander the Great and some followed him afterwards as ambassadors. Megasthenes came as an ambassador to the court of Candragupta Maurya and wrote *Indica.* A complete copy of his book has not been recovered, but later writers quote him in their writings. All these fragments have been put together and published as *Indica.* They provide valuable information about seven castes including brāhmaṇas, economic activities and the urban organization under the Mauryas. The *Indica* is full of exaggerations. According to it seven-year old mothers lived in the country of the Pāṇḍyas. Despite distortions the fragments can be used for comprehending the real nature of society. The social structure described by them does not exactly correspond to the varṇa system which is considered to be the norm in the Dharmasūtras. The *Indica* also describes the urban and the administrative organization of Pāṭaliputra or Palibothra which was the capital of the Mauryan empire.

In the first and the second centuries AD several Greek and Roman authors give detailed accounts of the Indian coast and the export and import of goods between India and the Roman empire. Ptolemy wrote *Geography* in the first century AD. Divided into eight chapters (books), this text lays down the principles of map making, and devotes considerable space to the geography of India and its neighbourhood. It mentions the important places on the western and eastern coasts of India from the mouth of the Indus to that of the Ganga. The author of this text speaks of six types of urban settlements in the Indus valley and the neighbouring areas. Altogether these settlements numbered forty-one, and were situated on highways of commerce. The second book written in Greek is called *The Periplus of the Erythraean Sea* written in about AD 150. The author was a Greek merchant who lived in Egypt. His account contains a long list of the commodities that were in demand in the Indian ports and also of those which were sent out by these ports. *Naturalis Historica* written by Pliny in Latin in the first century AD contains information about Indo-Roman trade. Pliny was an assiduous collector of information, but he was not so careful in verifying it. In his account he laments that Rome lost heavily in gold on account of trade with India. Pliny's account contains exaggerations, and he is called a liar by several writers, but what he says about Roman loss on account of trade with India is attested by some papyrus records found in Egypt.

Fa-hsien and Hsüan Tsang are considered to be important Chinese travellers. Both of them were Buddhists who came to India to visit Buddhist shrines and study Buddhism. Fa-hsien stayed in India during AD 399–414 and Hsüan Tsang in the first half of the seventh century. Fa-hsien has given an account of the social and economic conditions of India in Gupta times, and because of his Buddhist beliefs he throws special light on religious and cultural conditions. Hsüan Tsang presents a similar account of India in the age of Harṣa. Both of them tell us that the caṇḍālas were considered to be untouchable. Hsüan Tsang toured the major part of the country. He gives us an account of Buddhist monasteries and the monks living in them, and compares their numbers with those of the brāhmaṇical establishments. His account shows that the Buddhist monasteries were fading away and similar was the fate of the towns which were associated with Buddhism in ancient India. The account of I-tsing also enlightens us about the social and religious conditions of India in the second half of the seventh century.

In addition to these travellers several other important Chinese monks came to India in quest of the knowledge of Buddhism when the Tang dynasty ruled in China in AD 608–907. Biographies of these monks were translated into English in 1986 by Lotika Lahiri. These biographies provide valuable information about the social and economic conditions of India in early medieval tunes. A Chinese book written in 1225 by Chau Ju-kua is of great value for a study of the trade between India and China during the eleventh and twelfth centuries.

The writers of foreign accounts provide useful information about India, but at many places they project the conditions of their respective countries into the Indian situation. Sometimes they create the impression that they found in India the same kind of social, economic and administrative situation as prevailed in their respective countries. These accounts contain an element of exaggeration. Since the Chinese were deeply attached to

Buddhism their accounts also suffer from religious prejudices. Despite these limitations the foreign accounts are of great help in the construction of social, economic and religious history of India.

It is convenient to treat social and economic history separately, as has been done largely in the present book. But in order to comprehend the dynamics of history the social and economic processes need to be explained in their interconnections. This is a difficult exercise because social history is based primarily on literary sources which have to be aided by archaeology, numismatics, inscriptions, etc. for the reconstruction of economic history. The socio-economic history needs to be based on a comparative and correlated study of all the sources. But while the date, place and authenticity of a good many literary sources are yet to be settled, the reports of important excavations remain to be published. Though archaeology has made great strides in India after 1947, the results of excavations and explorations have not been placed in the mainstream of social and economic history. The stages through which Indian society has passed can be understood only if we begin with the prehistory of India and follow it up with a study of historical archaeology. Although more than 150 historical sites have been excavated in the country, in most cases their reports are not available. Even the meagre material that appears in print has not been adequately used for the study of social and economic processes. Reports dealing with historical archaeology are valuable for writing the history of rural and urban settlements. They are equally important for the study of commerce, handicrafts and technology.

To make social and economic history meaningful various types of literary sources need to be examined in relation to archaeological sources. As shown earlier, such an exercise can be fruitful for the study of society and economy in later Vedic and post-Vedic times. A study of coins has its own usefulness. So far coins have been used mainly for the study of political history and to some extent for that of religious history. But basically they were meant for the exchange of goods and services. How exchange through the medium of coined money took the place of barter system and mutual gift system and to what extent the coined money was used areawise and periodwise can be found out if the available coins are studied in relation to the remains of crafts and commerce recovered from the excavated sites. So far inscriptions have been used mainly for political history and occasionally for religions history. But numerous inscriptions speak of donation in cash and land. Cash donations indicate an economy which was different from a land grant economy.

Land grants enable us to discuss the process of state formations in new areas, the expansion of agriculture in them, and particularly the nature of changes that occurred in the land system in Gupta and post-Gupta times. Coins, inscriptions and archaeology are generally considered more reliable than the myths and traditions found in the *Rāmāyaṇa*, *Mahābhārata* and the Purāṇas. The myths were used to confirm and strengthen social practices, to make codes of conduct acceptable, and to legitimize the privileges or the disabilities of various social strata, but the events to which they refer cannot be regarded as true. To make the best of the sources discussed above it may be necessary to have a clear idea of tribal societies, to consider the remains of ancient social systems, and finally to compare social and economic developments in early India with those of contemporary societies outside India.

2

Exploiting History through Archaeology*

Until 1920 or so British archaeologists and their Indian associates showed more concern for the discovery of exotic objects which appealed to their romantic sense. They looked for something rare and unique. They also laid stress on exposing places and religious structures. The sequence of cultures or their interrelationship did not bother them. Although Mortimer Wheeler emphasized the need for establishing cultural sequences he was obsessed with the idea that important elements of culture came to India from outside. During the last fifty years South Asian and some other archaeologists have done considerable vertical digging and have established a workable sequence of cultures from paleolithic to historical times. They have also removed some distortions caused by the emphasis on outside influence on the cultures of the subcontinent.

The history of the material culture of India raises several problems. The archaeological identification of the Aryans appears to be almost intractable. The literature-based stand about India being the original home of the Aryans is supported by some archaeologists who assert that the material culture of the Aryans is to be originally found in India. Not all theories about the archaeological identity of the Aryans are inspired by chauvinistic feelings. There have been genuine differences in opinion. Those who hold the theory that the Aryans came from outside the subcontinent associate various types of culture including the Cemetry H culture, the copper-hoard culture, black-and-red ware culture of central and western India, the black-slipped ware culture and particularly the painted grey ware with the Aryan groups.

*Previously published as 'Exploiting History through Archaeology' in *The Statesman Festival*, 1995.

But the real problem is the formation of the 'Aryan' culture. This culture can be identified by the use of Indo-European languages, the use of the horse and the spoked wheel, the practice of horse sacrifice, the prevalence of cremation, the rituals of the Soma drink and fire altar, and by male domination. Some of these traits are as old as the sixth-fifth millennia BC and are found in both eastern and western Europe, South Russia, Central Asia and Western Asia. How they were combined to form the Aryan culture needs to be investigated.

We may also consider the question of the continuity of culture. In more than half a dozen sites in western India and the adjoining parts of central India the chalcolithic culture starts around 1700 BC or even 2000 BC and ends around 1000 BC or 900 BC. These sites are occupied in early historic times around 300 BC thus they remain deserted for more than 500 years. Such a break in the history of our culture comes as a rude shock to the fundamentalists who believe in the uninterrupted flow of the Indian cultural stream. However in Bihar such sites show continuous occupation right from chalcolithic to early historical times, though they undergo a fundamental change in material culture, in post-chalcolithic times.

Despite recent studies in the location of late Harappan sites over a large part of the country the disappearance of urban life marked by planning, use of bricks, seals and inscriptions is well known in Harappan sites from 1700 BC onwards. We notice a similar gap in the history of urbanism in historical times after the third century AD and at some sites after the sixth century AD. Such gaps are explained by archaeologists through hydrological changes on which there has been some work in the Harappan context. Sometimes ecological changes are also considered the cause of the decay of urbanism in post-Gupta times.

Whereas the introduction of the ecological and environmental perspectives provides new ways of looking at changes in human society, we cannot ignore the possible consequences of the measures adopted by the organized human agencies such as the state, social groups or classes or by ethnic solidarities. It is a moot point whether the records of disturbances caused by state agencies or by other organized groups can be detected in the archaeological record. Are disturbed layers caused only by extra-human factors or also by human factors, internal and external? Is there any archaeological evidence for the advent of the Kali yuga in the third and fourth centuries?

There is a tendency to push back the dates of the cultures discovered by the excavators. The feeling that antiquity confers respectability on the culture is too strong to resist. Several dates suggested by the excavators have been blown up by the radiocarbon dating. Such excavators are therefore shy of collecting samples for dates and getting them examined in the laboratories. The chauvinistic approach has filtered down to regional history. Under the influence of extreme regionalism local archaeologists try to glorify the achievements of their locality. Though elements of neolithic cultures have been discovered in the Gangetic plains, in dating them radiocarbon dates are ignored. The fact that wheel-made-with-hand-made pottery appears from the very beginning of the neolithic phase at several sites in the middle Gangetic zone is glossed over. The wheel evidence clearly points to the late neolithic phase. Similarly on the basis of a single radiocarbon date it is claimed that Hatikira in Birbhum district of West Bengal manufactured low-carbon steel as early as 1000 BC. This is based on a sample from French A Layer 6 at a depth of 192 centimetres attributed to the chalcolithic phase. But another sample from the same trench at a depth of 120 cm gives a date of AD 610. Five other samples from the Iron Age Phase of the same site give dates ranging from AD 370 to AD 1200.

Historical events inferred from epic and Puranic traditions can be broadly dated with the aid of archaeology. Formerly we had text-aided archaeology. Now it is better to date the texts with the aid of archaeology. Gautama Buddha is placed on this basis in the fourth century BC, for 400 BC is the archaeological base of several Gangetic towns he visited. Puranic genealogical tables suggest the beginning of Kosala and Magadha around 2000 BC or a few centuries earlier. But the archaeological material available from those regions betray no signs of any considerable settlement until the fourth century BC.

The use of iron was crucial to the clearance of the jungle cover of these areas as well as the large-scale cultivation of their alluvial soils. Since iron was not used in these areas on any scale for cultivation and for crafts until 500 BC settlements appear in the Ganga zone after 500 BC. It is significant that the calibrated date for the earliest settlement at Rama's Ayodhya is 400 BC.

Though the origin and diffusion of iron technology has been debated, it had a long period of gestation. It has been first reported from Mesopotamia in the fifth millennium BC, again from Egypt during third millennium BC. Black copper from nearer Anatolia during third millennium BC, used as gifts in West Asia till twelfth century BC. Emphasis by some western archaeologists on the role of ideas, beliefs and symbols, all typical of cognitive archaeology, has come as a boon to the Indian fundamentalists who deliberately underplay the importance of technology.

That there is a two-way traffic between the mind and the material culture is not realized by them. How the use of low-carbon steel from about 500 BC transformed agricultural operations and brought about a sea change in the production of craft goods has still to be investigated. It seems that in the Gangetic plains Ironization led to urbanization. The British archaeologist Andrew Sherratt notices a secondary products revolution in the neolithic age. A similar revolution in the production of craft goods in the middle Gangetic plains to place from about 500 BC onwards. This can be shown by a comparison of the quantity and quality of antiquities from the pre-iron or chalcolithic phase with those from the NBPW-iron phase. The latter phase registers a sudden and enormous increase in the number of semiprecious stones, bone tools, shell articles, wooden objects, glass goods, and copper artefacts, and, above all shows the appearance of metal coins. All this could not have been possible without the use of anvils, hammers, chisels, areo, drill, saws, and such other instruments, all made of iron.

The burgeoning of agriculture and handicrafts of account of the use of iron tools had much to do with the rise of the state, cities and varṇa-divided society and also with the expansion of the settled areas, particularly, the middle Gangetic plains from about 500 BC onwards.

Recently the study of settlement archaeology has been initiated in India. Settlements which indicate a complex or class divided society are attributed mainly to riverine areas. It is generally held that the earliest settlements appear only on river banks. But in the middle Gangetic plain they appear in good numbers in close proximity to water collections or reservoirs called *jhils* or *chaurs* formed by the abandonment of river beds or accumulation of water in lowlands. Narhan in Gorakhpur and Jaimanglagarh in Begusarai are good examples. While the people always faced the perennial problem of water supply, thickly forested riverine plains could not be settled on any scale because of the difficulty of removing the forest cover. The study of settlements in Haryana shows that these did not appear in riverine niches but mainly in semi-arid areas which could be cleared of vegetation even with stone tools.

In the study of settlements great importance is attached to the role of the state. In view of provisions about the founding of rural and urban settlements in the *Arthaśāstra* of Kauṭilya, it is logical to look at the initiative of the state in founding settlements. Amalanand Ghosh (the former director general of the Archaeological Survey of India), therefore has rightly underlined the role of the state in promoting urban settlements. But the state stands for an entity which collects taxes and maintains a regular army and therefore needs to be sustained by considerable agricultural surplus. In historical times this agricultural surplus was made available by the knowledge of growing two crops and of the art of paddy transplantation in the middle Gangetic plains, but more important by the use of iron. We find many of ploughshares, spades, sickles, and so on in the middle Gangetic plains, further the find of other iron implements and references to iron in literary texts leave little doubt that the black metal in the form of low-carbon steel was used substantially in these plains after 500 BC.

Swayed by chauvinistic feelings some excavators want to attribute every bit of their antiquities to indigenous efforts. Some of them seem to take advantage of processual archaeology which gives great importance to local processes. What is worse they are also guided by narrow prejudices derived from the sect to which they belong and the food habits developed on the basis of family practices. For instance in the report on Bhagwanpura (1933) A.K. Sharma, in his study of animal remains, calls the PGW people predominantly vegetarian. He argues that cattle bones do not bear cut marks and the bones of sheep and goat are 'superficially charred'. What 'superficially charred' means is unclear. For if the bone is charred obviously it was used for roasting. However according to J.P. Joshi, the excavator of Bhagwanpura, majority of cattle bones were charred, which in our view shows that cattle were used for food.

The problem of terms suitable terminologies in archaeological writings needs consideration. Fortunately social science jargons have not invaded archaeology so far. In describing the sequence of cultures Indian archaeologists use the terms that are widely accepted. Each phase of the development of material culture is indicated by a term which signifies the material of which the tools of that phase are made. Some of these terms now create difficulties when cultures using tools of two different materials overlap each other. Thus the term neolithic is used to describe the phase in which tools of polished stone were used. But some neolithic sites in Europe show the use of copper though this metal occupies only a marginal place in the tool equipment of the people. Further, the development of the neolithic culture as a whole shows that about 4500 BC cattle rearing, agriculture and dairy products all reach an advanced stage compared to what we find around 900 BC. (Thus the neolithic stage marked by the use of copper is called Eneolithic.) One could also think of early and late neolithic, but such terminologies are not preferred.

In India the term chalcolithic is used to describe the phase of culture in which copper and stone are used. Many tools of chalcolithic sites show a great, deal of microliths, but surprisingly enough some of these sites (which are distinguished by the use of microliths and black-and-red ware) do not show any copper at all in Bihar. Since such phases of culture generally belong to the pre-iron age they are called chalcolithic. But some suitable term needs to be coined for describing them. How can we apply the term chalcolithic to a phase of culture in which the use of copper is either nominal or none at all? However, copper generally appears in western India.

Another peculiarity of the chalcolithic sites in Bihar, West Bengal and eastern Madhya Pradesh is the appearance of iron in their later habitation, though the other items in the cultural equipment remain the same. Therefore the cultural complex as a whole is not placed in the Iron Age. A new term ferro-chalcolithic has been coined to connote the chalcolithic culture of this phase, but it lacks acceptability.

How does one designate the discoveries from a site which show mutual interrelationship and also a kind of uniformity in style followed in the manufacture of objects? Do they constitute a culture? The general term culture for a collective archaeological entity has been popularized. In earlier times 'culture' had a restricted meaning and signified art, architecture, literature and religion. Now culture is almost universally used by archaeologists in the sense of material culture. The Harappa culture is understood as a unified and integrated combination of artefacts that have been discovered at Harappa and other major Harappan sites. But now some archaeologists prefer to use the term tradition with a capital T. Tradition is an unsuitable term to describe an archaeological assemblage. According to *The Concise Oxford Dictionary* it means 'opinion or belief or custom handed down . . . from ancestors to posterity, especially orally or by practice'. It is also used in theological sense such as doctrine or theory supposed to have divine authority but not committed to writing as in the case of God's teachings communicated to Moses, and the teachings of Christ and Mohammed.

Thirdly, tradition means artistic or literary principles based on accumulated experience or continuous use. Fourthly, it is used in the sense of law or formal delivery. These meanings given to the term tradition hardly cover any element of archaeology except art. By and large tradition is primarily concerned with written or oral articulation; it does not signify artifactual articulation. Therefore the use of the term tradition in place of culture in the archaeological context creates confusion. Unless a better substitute for culture is coined it will be advisable to carry on with this term. The utmost we can do is to add an adjective and call it material culture. Whatever is discovered through digging or exploration constitutes concrete artefacts though they may indicate the ideas and religions of the users.

Sometimes the correct interpretation of the archaeological record becomes a casualty in the quarrel between the diffusionists and anti-diffusionists. The Harappan culture is internationalized in the sense that its origin and growth are traced to external factors, and it is localized in the sense that all its ingredients are traced to local sources. Those who stand by the indigenous origins of the Harappan culture boastfully highlight its influence in Shortugai in Afghanistan. Thus the anti-diffusionists who attribute local origins and growth to many cultures feel enthused when they find that these cultures have also spread in distant places. In this sense the anti-diffusionists become diffusionists.

Though there is a strong wave against the diffusionist and migrationist school in archaeology, even the leading lights of the anti-diffusionist and anti-migrationist school take to diffusion in interpreting the history of material culture in India. Thus the British archaeologist Professor Lord Colin Renfrew holds that agriculture came to the Indus valley when it spread with the advance of the Aryans from Anatolia in *c.* 6500 BC. Though this hypothesis cannot be accepted because of the beginnings of agriculture about that time in Iraq, Iran and above all in Mehrgarh in Baluchistan, it does show the nature of the unconscious ideological influence on a leading British archaeologist. He does not deliberately spread the colonialist idea, but such ideas are engrained in quite a few of the archaeologists who may not be conscious of them.

The theory of diffusion was the child of the Industrial Revolution. Inventions made in Britain in the eighteenth and early nineteenth centuries spread in Europe, the U.S.A. and the colonies of western powers. The theory had much to commend and leading archaeologists including Gordon Childe used it. But its strong colonialist overtones should not be ignored. Wheeler took the application of this theory to absurd limits. Some other archaeologists and many foreign historians gave the theory a completely colonialist colour. They argued that whatever was good and great in ancient India was borrowed by the Indians from outside. This was meant to convince the Indians and the world public opinion that the Indians were incapable of any achievement in the field of art and culture. This naturally gave rise to a strong reaction. Indian scholars ably demonstrated, for example, that Hellenic influence in India was not as strong as was made out by foreign waters. Unfortunately at present a few Indian scholars have adopted a chauvinistic approach and assert that whatever is good and great in the history of civilization originated in India from where it spread to the other parts of the world.

When diffusionism is overloaded with colonialist prejudices, and anti-diffusionism with local or national chauvinism, objective study of the archaeological material becomes very difficult. Diffusionism and anti-diffusionism also affect the study of literally texts. Some Indian writers trace all developments in science, technology, society, economy and culture to the *Rg Veda*. They speak of the uninterrupted tradition from Rg Vedic times to modern times and clamour for return to the past which is credited with all the achievements that mark the present age. Similarly some archaeologists trace all later developments in the Harappan culture, and even identify it with the Rg Vedic culture. The sharp contrast between the basically pastoral and horse-centred society of the early Vedic people and the urban and almost horse free character of the Harappans does not bother them. They find it difficult to think of any discontinuity in the Harappan stereotype although after 2000 BC or so even the use of the burnt bricks, characteristic of the mature Harappan culture, is rarely seen in post-Harappan cultures until we come to the third century BC. In Dholavira, which ranks in importance next to Harappa and Mohanjodaro, according to its excavator, R.S. Bisht, bricks disappear after 2000 BC. No horses exist at other Harappan sites they disappear around 2000 BC. The attribution of bricks to the PGW phase in Bhagwanpura in Haryana is doubted by several scholars. It was suggested earlier that a brick wall at Kausambi belonged to the tenth century BC, but now archaelogists ascribe it to the third century BC.

Distortions cannot be avoided unless archaeologists are free from national, regional or communal chauvinism. Indian archaeologists are noted for their digging skill and technical perfection. But what mars their efforts is a kind of fundamentalist prejudice with which their minds are saturated. The reports published fully in the form of monographs or partly in the form of summaries in *Indian Archaeology: A Review* do not dilate on cultures that belong to medieval times. Many sites in the Gangetic plains show medieval antiquities in the top layers. But since these belong to the Islamic period of the rule of the sultans or the Mughals, they are passed over in a few lines. Sometimes they are entirely discarded on the ground that the top layers contain flimsy materials. Real archaeology in northern India does not begin unless diggers reach the Gupta or the Kushan levels. Because of the negligence of the layers belonging to medieval times it is not possible to utilize archaeological material in the reconstruction of medieval life.

It is also interesting that some historians or archaeologists repeatedly speak of destruction of monuments by the Muslims, but they do not talk of such destruction in other contexts except occasionally in the case of the Hunas. In the archaeological record one could also think of possibilities of destruction caused by internal convulsions which are never taken into account. Kali convulsions, Kalabhra revolt in south and Kaivartta rebellion in Bengal are generally ignored.

Talking of digging methods, it is very difficult to salvage mud structures in the alluvial soil and rain-fed areas in the Gangetic and similar plains it is easy to brick structures but the distinction between mud sections and mud walls is so blurred in such areas that in all likelihood some of these structures may have been destroyed in course of digging the pre-brick levels. It is interesting to note that the mud stupa at Vaishali, which is now being publicized to attract Japanese and other Buddhist tourists, was in the process of being destroyed when Amalanand Ghosh detected a brick encasing and suggested that it might contain a mud stupa. It was in this way that the great Indologist A.S. Altekar was able to salvage the mud stupa at Vaishali in which a relic casket containing ashes was discovered; these ashes were supposed to be the earthly remains of Gautama Buddha.

Apart from improving the digging methods, in interpreting the literary or archaeological material for historical reconstruction we have to discard the type of diffusionism coloured by colonialism and also the type of anti-diffusionism inspired by local chauvinism and communalism. We have to lay stress on objectivity. We must realize that neither history nor archaeology can solve the political problems with which we are beset today. These disciplines can only throw light on the dimensions of those problems and can enable social and political actors to appreciate the complexities.

3

Writings on Early Indian Polity*

The first edition of *Aspects of Political Ideas and Institutions in Ancient India* was based on some pieces I had written in 1950–4. My study was particularly influenced by the ideas generated by historical materialism. In collecting, analysing and interpreting the evidence I relied on *Ancient Society by* Henry Morgan and *The Origin of the Family, Private Property and the State* by Frederick Engels. My approach enabled me to understand better the origin, growth and nature of the state in ancient India and also the history of its organs. Drekmeier, a political scientist, who adopted a sociological framework in his *Early Kingship and Community* (1962), found many of such findings acceptable. He underlined the primitive and tribal character of ancient rituals and institutions connected with polity. On the other hand although the importance given by me to the treatment of the *vidatha* was recognized by J.P. Sharma in his *Republics in Ancient India* (1965), he considered it to be a religious body and ignored the undifferentiated character of functions performed by the kin-ordered institutions of a pre-class Vedic society. However, the *nidatha* came to be regarded as an important Vedic assembly along with the *sabhā*, and *samiti* by many scholars including A.S. Altekar.

A.S. Altekar's *State and Government in Ancient India* has been a popular textbook. Published in 1949, it has undergone three editions, and the third edition (1958) was reprinted in 1972 and 1977. Although he generally admired ancient institutions, in the third edition he did take note of some unorthodox researches which were stimulated by anthropological and other ideas. He referred to the role of the family and property in explaining the origin of the state. In his view the 'institution of

*Previously published as 'Introduction' in R.S. Sharma, *Aspects of Political Ideas and Institutions in Ancient India* (New Delhi: Motilal Banarsidass Publishers, 1991).

the family with the notion of family and property thus played its own part in the origin of the State.'[1] He also states that 'the state in the early Vedic period was still tribal'[2] and that the Vedic tribes had for a long time no permanent territorial basis for their states.[3] These views are sound though Altekar and scholars of his generation were neither interested in the definitions of kin-ordered collectivities such as clan, tribes, etc., nor in the stages and processes of state formation and polity evolution. Altekar also gave some attention to the discussion of the character of the *vidatha*.[4] His concern with problems of social injustice is evident.[5] A revivalist and Hindu nationalist, he blames both the state and society for perpetuating an iniquitous social system.[6] However he singles out society for investigation and does not examine the linkage between the state and the dominant social classes. He defends the disabilities of the śūdras and untouchables on the ground that they 'believed that they were born in their particular caste as a natural result of certain sins committed by them in past lives'.[7] Altekar also discovered 'a welfare state'[8] which was the case with K.A. Nilakanta Sastri[9] and even A.L. Basham.[10] He not only tried to demonstrate the state's effort to establish harmonious relationship between castes and social classes,[11] but also put up the ideal of the Vedic kings and of the ancient republics[12] before modern citizens. He did not investigate whether these 'ideals' were the products of certain social situations. Altekar was deeply religious, but he did not adopt a consistent position on the role of religion in ancient Indian polity. He finds 'considerable force in the view that the ancient Indian state was theocratic to a great extent.'[13] However, he does not accept Willoughby's view that in all early Asiatic monarchies the rulers claimed a divine right to control the affairs of the state.[14] He asserts that religion and philosophical dogmas and concepts did not deeply influence Hindu political thought, practice and institutions.[15]

As in the earlier phase, Ghoshal's contribution in the post-independence period is marked by impeccable scholarship. In his, *A History of Hindu Public Life* (1957) and *A History of Political Ideas Ancient and Medieval* (1959) he elaborates the points made in his earlier publications and documents them so carefully that it is difficult to detect any error. His analysis is more or less on the lines of Western liberal writings on the history of political thought which he taught for long in Calcutta. Though associated for many years with a journal called *Greater India*, Ghoshal is not swayed by Hindu chauvinism. He substantially adds to our information on political ideas and institutions but does not *try* to link them to social and economic developments; he considered such an exercise to be 'speculative'.[16] Apart from his repetitive and involved style of writing, Ghoshal creates some problem because of the methods he adopts in using the sources. For example, he ascribes the major part of the Kauṭilyan material to pre-Maurya times on the ground that Kauṭilya frequently quotes from masters of political thought who preceded him. Unfortunately the writings of these teachers have not been discovered so far, and many of them may have been Kauṭilya's senior contemporaries. The more one examines the *Arthaśāstra* the more-difficult it becomes to use its major part even for Maurya times.[17]

The *Mahābhārata* continues to attract a good many researchers. In recent years at least four dissertations on political ideas and institutions in the *Mahābhārata* have appeared.[18] They certainly systematize much information bearing on ancient Indian polity.[19] Formerly more emphasis was placed on the *rājadharma* section of the *Śānti Parva*, but now references found in the *Sabhā, Anuśāsana* and other parvas are also used for research in polity which is seen in the perspective of political science.[20] These studies, however, ignore stratification in the text and do not situate references in the context of time, place and social evolution. Rituals surviving till today contain vestiges of various stages of evolution; and legends as well as descriptive and didactic portions in the *Mahābhārata* reflect ideas and practices prevalent in different regions and periods. A tentative explanatory framework for handling the epic material has been provided by us elsewhere.[21] But further progress in the field will depend on a more critical reconstruction of the Critical Edition text.[22]

Western Indologists of the nineteenth and the early twentieth centuries popularized the stereotypes of oriental despotism and the hold of religion and spiritualism.[23] These came under heavy attack, largely justified, from Indian scholars. After India attained independence, the West developed a kind of neo-orientalism based on sociology. As a concession to the independent republican status of India, Western historians and Indologists modified the idea of perpetual despotism, but they placed undue emphasis on the role of religion, particularly rituals, and on the divinity of kingship.[24]

J. Gonda overemphasizes the role of religion in the formation of kingship in ancient India.[25] The sources he uses to argue his case are unrelated, distant in time and place though they show some superficial continuity in tradition. Gonda frequently states that the honour shown to a sovereign is similar to the marks of veneration conferred on the images of the gods.[26] The fact that gods are conceived after the pattern of chiefs and kings and are given the latter's attributes and qualities does not strike him. Similarly he repeatedly asserts that in India divinity of king has always been accepted by the masses.[27] But the *Arthaśāstra* of Kauṭilya clearly shows that superstitious ideas about the miraculous powers of the king are deliberately propagated by the ruling class. Bāṇabhaṭṭa exposes the hollowness of the mass belief in royal divinity.[28]

Though Gonda's etymological and philological study of ancient Sanskrit terms from the angle of comparative religion is valuable, his decontexualized approach obscures the changing meanings of terms. For instance, the translation of *dharma* as religion or even moral order would not suit all the Sanskrit passages. In fact most allusions in which the king is called the upholder of the *dharma* or in which he is called *dharmaparavartaka*[29] (promoter or advancer of *dharma* according to Gonda) refer to the varṇa-based social order in which the brāhmaṇa and kṣatriyas either lived respectively on the gifts and taxes collected from the peasants (mainly the vaiśyas) or on śūdra labour. But Gonda completely misses this significance of *dharma*. He sees decay of *dharma* causing fatal losses in welfare and happiness though really it means mixing of the varṇas and upsetting of the society structured in favour of the two higher orders.

Gonda's pupil J.C. Heesterman overstresses the part played by ritual and tradition in the formation of polity. Some of his interpretations of the Vedic rituals are acceptable.[30] However it is not sufficiently realized that political power was made acceptable to people through rituals, legends, genealogies, marriage alliances, hierarchical ideology and various other means. Further, the fact that the Brāhmaṇas, Śrautasūtras, Gṛhyasūtras and some other texts deal with rituals should not create the impression that all Indian history is rituals. The inference of social and economic processes from archaeological and anthropological sources is equally important. Rituals and traditions may have their roots in reality but are usually manipulated by dominant social groups to serve their interests. Heesterman, who rules out any broad-based struggle of the Indian against the colonial rule and thinks that they fought between themselves and not with the Raj,[31] emphasizes fragmentation and atomization in Indian history. But we have instances of both local and pan-Indian supralocal political formations. The ancient Indian king in his view was primarily interested in mastering his senses *(indriya-jaya)* though real history shows more interest in territorial conquest and administration. He thinks that the king derives his ultimate authority from the brāhmaṇa who is a renouncer. The theory that the eternal and transcendent values of renunciation were meant for the guidance of the state[32] hardly worked in practice. The brāhmaṇa opposed the renunciatory religions of the Buddha and Mahāvīra, and prescribed renunciation only for the fourth stage (*āśrama*) of life which rarely materialized. The brāhmaṇas were an integral part of the varṇa divided society which they regulated with the help of the kṣatriyas. They occasionally quarrelled, but they together lived on the gifts, taxes, tributes and presents provided by artisans, peasants and other sections of society. Towards the end of the ancient period the brāhmaṇas were given substantial land grants and rituals were reoriented.

The French scholar Robert Lingat, who has produced 'a work of outstanding merit' on *dharma* or law,[33] takes a balanced view of the divinity of kingship as well as the relation between the temporal and spiritual power (*brahma* and *kṣatra*). He considers *dharma* 'essentially, a rule of interdependence founded on a hierarchy corresponding to the nature of things and necessary for the maintenance of social order'.[34] The king is considered indispensable to the social order,[35] in which 'religious aspirations do not monopolize all human activity'.[36] We may add that this social order is varṇa-divided and male-dominated, and its laws regarding person and property help the higher varṇas.

That the *puruṣārthas*, namely, *artha, dharma, kāma* and *mokṣa* shaped ancient political ideas and institutions is also held by some Indian writers. Ideas do shape the course of history, but there is nothing to show that the fourfold aims of life or the *puruṣārthas* determined the development of society. Such ideas hardly appear in Vedic times; nor do they figure in early Buddhist texts. They assume importance only in Gupta and post-Gupta times, especially in the Purāṇas. Initially only *artha, dharma* and *kāma* appear, and can be connected with the institutions of the family, property and varṇa. The idea of *mokṣa* or salvation linked to renunciation is tagged on to the original three ideals. What is really needed is an explanation of the origin and development of these ideals in the context of time, place and social milieu. How far ancient rulers, priests and others were influenced by the relative importance of such ideals in their policies and actions also requires investigation.

The establishment of the Republic of India in 1950 made some impact on researchers. It was no longer necessary to make a case for the existence of republics in ancient India, as was forcefully done by K.P. Jayaswal under the colonial rule, but to think of steps for the preservation of the Indian Republic. In this context A.S. Altekar finds it necessary to understand the causes of the disappearance of the republics in ancient India.[37] He adumberates the seven conditions laid down for the success of the Vajji republic and recommends that 'Modern India may carve on the gate of the Parliament the Buddha's prophesy'[38] about the decline or survival of that republic. The subject of the republics therefore assumed greater importance in the post-independence period than the study of limited monarchy. Republics in the popular notion came to be confounded with democratic governments, and this idea also influenced researchers. Thus in his book *Republics in Ancient India* (1963) J.P. Sharma discusses at length the various popular assemblies including the *vidatha* in Vedic times. Another book on the subject[39] makes a descriptive study of the republics and adds very little to what K.P. Jayaswal has written. The conclusion that the republics of today do not differ from those of ancient times in their essentials is naive.[40] S.N. Mishra has collected exhaustive data on the *gaṇa-rājya* and its different interpretations.[41] But except Ghoshal writers on polity hardly emphasize the clan or the oligarchical character of the republics that were set up in post-Vedic times.

Thus the questions which exercise the minds of scholars are not entirely new. Neither the influence of colonialism nor that of nationalism has been completely eliminated from writings on ancient Indian polity. The stress on spiritualism, which first appeared in the nineteenth century and the early twentieth century, is given a new form. Some writers, both Western and Indian, still consider religion to be an autonomous factor that influences the formation of the state and kingship and makes for permanent divisiveness.

Influenced by historical materialism D.D. Kosambi made a penetrating study of ancient Indian society,[42] but he did not give attention to polity. Karl Marx formulated primitive communist, ancient, slave, Germanic, Asiatic, feudal and capitalist modes of production.[43] Now the Asiatic mode is also applied to Latin American countries, and certain Marxist anthropologists advance the concepts of the 'African', 'lineage', 'domestic', 'foraging' and some other modes of production, but none of these has won any general acceptance.[44] Taking the cue from the lineage mode of production Romila Thapar[45] underlines the point that members of senior lineages claim special shares from those of junior lineages in Vedic times. But how patrilineages and genealogies are formed and manipulated and whether achievements determine seniority and ascriptive claims to spoils and shares in produce has to be investigated.[46]

In the light of historical materialism we propose to look at ancient political ideas and institutions in relation to socioeconomic processes. We will consider various modes of production including the tribal and the post-tribal. Insights derived from recent studies of tribal societies and archaeological discoveries will be used to explain the significance of rituals and institutions in ancient India. But in exploring the linkage between economy and polity historically we would not ignore comparisons with the ancient institutions of Asia and Europe.[47]

NOTES

1. A.S. Altekar, *State and Government in Ancient India*, 1958 edn, p. 36.
2. Ibid., p. 43.
3. Ibid.
4. Ibid., p. 141.
5. Ibid., pp. 49–51, 385.
6. Ibid., p. 385
7. Ibid.
8. Ibid., p. 60.
9. *Proceedings of the 16th Session of the All-India Oriental Conference*, Lucknow, 1951, pp. 67–8.
10. A.L. Basham, foreword to John W. Spellman, *Political Theory of Ancient India*, Oxford, 1964, p. vi. After the attainment of independence by India in 1947 Altekar saw the possibility of trying limited monarchy by the princely states on Vedic lines and implicitly regretted that it could not be done (ibid., p. 38). Also see K.N. Mishra, *State Sponsored Public Welfare Plans in the Mahābhārata*, Varanasi, 1972.
11. Altekar, op. cit., pp. 350, 325–6.
12. Ibid., pp. 379–21.
13. Op. cit., p. 53.
14. Ibid., pp. 94–5.
15. Ibid., p. 57.
16. This is what he told me in a discussion in Patna when he stayed with me in 1957.
17. R. Trautman identifies several strata in the *Arthaśāstra* on the basis of computerized mannerism in style. S.C. Mishra's inscriptional analysis of the text reveals four strata, the latest of which tallies with the inscriptional use of the terms in the 11th–12th centuries. See S.C. Mishra, 'An Inscriptional Approach to the *Arthaśāstra* of Kauṭilya', Ph.D. Thesis, University of Delhi, 1984.
18. S.L. Pande, *Bhisma Kā Rājadharma*, Lucknow, 1955; Premkumari Dikshit, *Mahābhārata mein Rājavyavasthā*, Lucknow, 1970; B.P. Roy, *Political Ideas and Institutions in the Mahābhārata*, Calcutta, 1975; N.K.P. Sinha, *Political Ideas and Ideals in the Mahābhārata (A Study of first two Parvans)*, New Delhi, 1976.
19. B.P. Roy, op. cit.
20. N.K.P. Sinha, op. cit.
21. R.S. Sharma, *Material Culture and Social Formations in Ancient India*, Delhi, 1983, ch. VIII.

22. An attempt has been made in this direction by Kcshavram K. Shashtree (*The Jaya-Samhitā*, that is, *the Ur-Mahābhārata*, vols I and II, Gujarat Research Society, Ahmedabad, 1977), but it is difficult to agree with the criteria he has adopted for selecting original 8800 verses constituting the *Jaya*.
23. Infra, ch.1.
24. J.W. Spellman, *Political Theory in Ancient India*, 1964; J. Gonda, *Ancient Indian Kingship from the Religious Point of View*, Leiden, 1969; J.C. Heesterman, *Inner Conflict of Indian Tradition*, Delhi, 1985.
25. *Ancient Indian Kingship from the Religious Point of View*, Leiden, 1969.
26. Ibid., p. 56.
27. Ibid., pp. 1–2, 15, 24, 67, 86, 127, 132, 138–9.
28. See *Śakanāsopadeśa* in *Kādambari.*
29. Ibid., p. 70.
30. J.C. Heesterman, *The Ancient Indian Royal Consecration*, The Hague, 1957.
31. Ibid., *Inner Conflict of Tradition in India*, Delhi, 1985, p. 176.
32. Ibid., pp. 43, 155, 160, 177.
33. *The Classical Law of India*, translated from French with additions by J. Duncan M. Derrett, University of California, 1973, p. xi.
34. Ibid., p. 211.
35. Ibid., p. 207.
36. Ibid., p. 5.
37. Altekar, op. cit., p. 378.
38. Ibid., p. 379.
39. Shobha Mukherji, *The Republican Trends in Ancient India*, Delhi, 1969.
40. Ibid., p. 205.
41. *Ancient Indian Republics from the Earliest Times to the Sixth Century A.D.*, Luknow, 1976.
42. D.D. Kosambi, *An Introduction to the Study of Indian History*, Bombay, 1956.
43. Karl Mara, *Pre-Capitalist Economic Formations*, ed. and introduction. E. Hobsbawm, London, 1964; *The Grundecisee*, ed. M. Nicolaus, Penguin, Harmondsworth, 1973, p. 472 ff.
44. Mathew Sprigg in *Marxist Perspectives in Archaeocology*, Cambridge, 1984, pp. 4–5.
45. *From Lineage to State*, Delhi, 1984.
46. During the last 30 years lineage studies have hardly gone beyond the Goros of Africa, and are confined to a few French anthropologists.
47. Pre-industrial India is considered similar to pre-industrial Europe and not to pre-colonial Africa in respect of family and systems of marriage in Jack Goody, *The Oriental, the Ancient and the Primitive*, Cambridge University Press, 1990. This also applies to ancient political institutions in several cases.

4

Studies in Ancient Polity*

The first serious attempt at the study of India's past, by both the Western as well as Indian scholars, began after the revolt of 1857–9.[1] A perusal of some introductions to the *Sacred Books of the East* reveals the motive underlying this great venture extending over years. It was felt by the British rulers that the revolt was due to lack of their knowledge of Indian religion, manners, customs and history. Further, the people could not be won over to Christianity and consequently to the empire unless the missionaries acquired an idea of the vulnerable points in their social structure. According to Max Müller, to the missionary an accurate knowledge of the sacred books was as indispensable as the knowledge of the enemy's country to a general.[2] In their study of the ancient history of India, Western scholars reached two important conclusions, which can be summed up in the words of Max Müller. In 1859 he wrote that the Indians are a nation of philosophers and Indian intellect is lacking in political or material speculation, and that the Indians never knew the feeling of nationality.[3] We do not know whether Max Müller drew upon the famous dictum of Aristotle that oriental rule is autocratic in character. But his idea was the stock-in-trade of the great European historians who wrote in the 18th and 19th centuries. Thus Gibbon pointed out that all oriental history is 'one unceasing record of valour, greatness, degeneracy and decay'. Green stated that 'the empires of the East are, in the main, tax-collecting institutions. They exercise coercive power on their subjects of the most violent kind . . . (and) do not impose laws as distinct from particular and occasional commands'.[4] Similar ideas continued to find expression in the work of eminent orientalists. Writing in 1898 Sénart stated that India never attained to the idea either of the

*Previously published as 'Historiography of Ancient Indian Polity up to 1930' in R.S. Sharma, *Aspects of Political Ideas and Institutions in Ancient India* (New Delhi: Motilal Banarsidass Publishers, 1991).

state or of the fatherland,[5] and that could not evolve any political constitution, even in conception.[6]

Such a view about India's past history and polity was obviously dominated by imperialist ideology. Its practical implications in the existing set-up were dangerous to the demand for self-government in India. If Indians were essentially philosophers, absorbed in the problems of the spiritual world, it followed that their material world should be managed for them by their imperialist masters. If Indians were accustomed to autocratic rule and never had any idea of nationhood, state or self-government, it was in keeping with their tradition that they should be ruled autocratically by the British Governor-General and Viceroy.

This colonialist ideology regarding ancient history and particularly the nature of the early Indian polity came as a challenge to Indian scholarship and to the few foreign scholars who were yet unaffected by imperialist ideology. In 1889, controverting Max Müller who had said that 'to the Greek, existence is full of life and reality, to the Hindu it is a dream and delusion',[7] the great American savant Hopkins pointed out that the religious element did not penetrate deeply into the vast mass of unpriestly classes.[8] But the biggest response to this challenge came from the Indian scholars themselves. During the last three decades of the nineteenth century Bhagwan Lal Indraji, R.G. Bhandarkar, R.L. Mitra and B.G. Tilak, most of whom actively associated themselves with the political and social movements of their time, tried to prove the falsity of the imperialist ideology. By their researches into the manifold aspects of the past history of their country they tried to build a powerful case for the political and social progress of the country in their own times. Since then the study of India's past was mainly guided by the nationalist ideology. This point can be especially illustrated by presenting a rapid survey of research on ancient Indian polity.

Just as there were two phases, moderate and radical, in the growth of the nationalist movement, so also there were two such phases in the progress of research on ancient Indian polity. It is well-known that the chief demand of the Indian nationalist movement in its earlier stages was to curtail the powers of the autocratic Viceroy by introducing a popular element at the Centre and in the Provincial Governments. Hence in 1887 R.C. Dutt wrote an article on the 'Civilisation in the Brāhmaṇa Period', in which he tried to show that in ancient times the king did justice to all.[9] He was followed by Purnendu Narayan Singh, who, in an article in 1894, strongly countered the statement of Sir Auckland Colvin that 'the British have taught for the first time that the end and aim of rule is the welfare of the people, and not the personal aggrandizement of the sovereign'. He argued that such an idea is due to the ignorance of the system of government in ancient India which, in his opinion, was limited monarchy.[10]

The strong nationalist movement that followed the partition of Bengal in 1905 gave further impetus to research in ancient Indian polity. Curzon's homily on the oriental character, his autocratic measures for the partition of Bengal, and his attack on the elected element in the Calcutta Corporation could not but influence the course of research on ancient polity. In an article written in 1907 A.C. Das repeated with greater emphasis the view of the previous scholars that 'it is a mistake to suppose that the Hindus have been accustomed to an autocratic form of government, and that the popular element never existed as a distinct force in the country'. He further said that 'it was not Absolute but Limited Monarchy that flourished in Ancient India'.[11] Perhaps by way of indirect suggestion that Curzon's attack on the elected element in the Calcutta Corporation was unwarranted, in another essay of the same year Das pointed out that 'Local Self-Government existed in Ancient India even in a better form than that in which it exists at present under British rule'.[12] Four years later, S.K. Aiyangar in his thesis on Cola Administration brought to light the working of elected village panchayats, exercising all functions in early mediaeval times under the Colas.[13]

The nationalist movement stimulated the search for ancient manuscripts, resulting in the discovery of the *Arthaśāstra* of Kauṭliya in 1905 and its publication by Shamasastry in 1909. The discovery was an epochmaking event in the history of the study of ancient Indian polity, for it provided valuable raw material which could be utilized in yielding 'political precedents for modern controversies'.[14] This was an important factor which contributed to many critical and descriptive studies of' the ancient Indian polity.[15]

The period from 1905 was a period of extremist politics. Extremists, who did not believe in constitutional methods for the attainment of slow reforms, set up a net work of revolutionary societies in Bengal and Maharashtra. The movement was coloured by the spirit of Hindu revivalism. The very names of' these societies betray their love for past culture. For instance the Anushilan Samiti, which was set up in 1905 and had about 550 branches by 1907, means the society for the promotion of culture and learning. It is legitimate to suspect that, although wedded to the cult of violence, it must have published certain research tracts of which we are unaware. These societies created a revolutionary temper in the country and prepared the minds of many intellectuals for the complete independence of their motherland. It was through them that the word Swaraj got the widest currency. As interpreted by a left-wing paper it means 'self-taxation, self-legislation and self-administration'.[16] It is not known whether K.P. Jayaswal was in any way connected with these societies, but the fact that he was made to resign his post in the postgraduate teaching department of Calcutta University by the Bengal Government in 1912–13 might suggest that he was considered a potential contributor to the 'seminaries of sedition'.[17] It is to the late K.P. Jayaswal that Indology owes its greatest work on ancient Indian polity. His articles contributed to *Modern Review* between 1912 and 1915—which appeared later in the form of his famous book *Hindu Polity* in 1924—were really pioneer works, as later admitted by D.R. Bhandarkar, R.C. Majumdar, B.K. Sarkar and other scholars who followed him. For the first time he showed the importance of republics in ancient Indian history. He tried to prove that the ancient Hindu political system was partly of republics of the Athenian type, and of constitutional monarchies such as that of Great Britain. There were popular assemblies such as the *paura* and *jānapada*, acting as checks on the powers of the king. According to him these organizations were more advanced than any thing which modern Switzerland or the United States can boast of. At the end of his study Jayaswal concluded: 'The constitutional progress made by the Hindus has probably not been equalled much less surpassed by any polity of antiquity'. And finally, he expressed the undying hope of a patriot that the 'Golden Age of his polity lies not only in the past but in the Future'.[18] The implications of his research are clear. His conclusions present the first solid ideological case for complete independence and a republican form of Government in India. It is because of this that no thesis on ancient Indian history has been so frequently quoted as *Hindu Polity.* It became the Bible of the Indian nationalists. Meet any educated old man and he knows about *Hindu Polity.*

Jayaswal was followed by a host of scholars, who flooded *Modern Review, Hindustan Review* and *Indian Antiquary* with a spate of articles and wrote a number of theses. In many ways the period between 1916 and 1925, coinciding with post-war nationalist and revolutionary movements sweeping over Europe and Asia, marked the peak of our nationalist movement. No other period of the present century has produced so many research works on ancient Indian polity as this period of nine years. Leaving aside the articles, the number of monographs on Hindu political theories and institutions would come to more than a dozen. It is not possible to notice the ideological basis of all works, but we can examine the important ones to find out the main trends.

To begin with works of a general nature on polity, P.N. Banerjea in his *Public Administration in Ancient India*, published in 1916, points out that the 'ancient system of government may thus be called constitutional monarchy'. It was 'Sachivatantra'.[19] He further says that not only in monarchies but also in republican states the popular assemblies were important in ancient times.[20] In the same year K.V. Rangaswami Aiyangar brought out *Some Aspects of Ancient Indian Polity*, which was based on his lectures delivered in 1914. In his work the author deprecates the tendency to look into the armoury of 'our' ancient polity for weapons to be used in the arena of modern political controversies.[21] But at the same time he points out that the undermining of the 'current' belief that ancient Indian institutions and political theory were unprogressive will long form a vital condition of a successful, historical study of ancient Indian polity.[22] In his book *Corporate Life in Ancient India* (1918) even a trained historian such as R.C. Majumdar admits that he was led to this line of inquiry through the importance of 'the spirit of co-operation' in the present highly developed stage of civilization.[23] In his opening lines in the introduction he says that 'India at present is very backward in this particular aspect of culture, but the following pages are intended to show that things were quite different in the past'. It pains him to find that it required great effort to believe that political institutions 'which we are accustomed to look upon as of western growth had also flourished in India long ago'.[24] He also assails the commonly held view that India was only absorbed in religion. His researches are intended to show that 'religion did not engross the whole or even an undue proportion of the public attention'. A similar view is expressed by Shamasastry in his book *Evolution of Indian Polity* (1920). He asserts that neither during the Vedic period nor in the time of Kauṭilya divine birth or right of kings seems to have been thought of.[25] Coming to the next publication, *Aspects of Ancient Indian Polity* by N.N. Law (1921). Keith says in his foreword that the development of a keen interest in the history of Indian theories of polity is one of the gratifying consequences of the awakening of political aspirations in India.[26] The longest chapter (IX) in the book is 'The Religious Aspects of Ancient Hindu Polity'. While concluding it, Law states that 'there were wide and various fields of political actions in which the Hindu showed considerable judgment and acumen undelegated by the force of beliefs'.[27] By 1922 B.K. Sarkar was ready with his *Political Institutions and Theories of the Hindus*. In its preface he claims that on fundamental points the volume delivers 'a frontal attack on the traditional Western prejudices regarding Asia, such as are concentrated in Hegel, Cousion, Max Müller, Maine, Janet, Smith, Willoughby and

Hutington'.[28] He deplores that the 'servile and degenerate Asia of to-day' should be compared with Asia which was the leader of humanity's progress.[29] Repudiating the suggestion of the influence of religion on politics he says that 'Hindu states were thoroughly secular'.[30] In *Development of Hindu Polity and Political Theories* (1927) N.C. Bandyopadhay asserts that the ancient Indian king could neither claim divinity nor possessed any prerogatives.[31] In his opinion the views of thinkers who justify the expulsion or destruction of a tyrant disprove the theory of divinity.[32]

In 1923 there appeared *A History of Hindu Political Theories* by U.N. Ghoshal.[33] He ably refutes the view of Max Müller and Bloomfield that Hindus, because of certain inherent tendencies in their character, could not conceive of the idea of the state and that there is no provision for the interest of the state in their scheme. His main targets of attack are Western writers of history of political thought such as Janet, Dunning and Willoughby. He questions Janet's estimate that the sole city for the Indian sages is the city divine. This, says Ghoshal, when tested in the light of sober fact, will appear no more than a half truth.[34] Dunning states that the Āryans in India could never develop Political Science as an independent branch of knowledge and free it from its theological and metaphysical environment as the European Āryans did, whereas Willoughby thinks that because of their supreme faith in the divine creation they were never impelled to enquire into the *rationale* of their institutions.[35] Rejecting this view Ghoshal says that the chief characteristic of the Buddhist political thought is 'bold and avowed appeal to human reason'.[36] Moreover, he asserts that the Indian states, contrary to the usual view, were not modelled after a uniform pattern, that of despotic monarchy.[37]

In his lectures *Some Aspects of Ancient Hindu Polity* delivered in 1925, D.R. Bhandarkar again quotes the same views of Dunning, Max Müller and Bloomfield in order to refute them. In case of Dunning he makes allowance for the fact that he had no direct knowledge of orientalia. But he sees no justification for the statement of oriental scholars such as Max Müller and Bloomfield, who hold that the Indian never knew the feeling of nationality and that his heart never trembled in the expectation of national applause.[38] He points out that particularly after the discovery of the *Arthaśāstra* 'it is no longer correct to assert that the Hindu mind did not conduce to the development of political theories, and that the Indians never set up politics as an independent branch of knowledge'.[39] While discussing the rules of business in the republican assembly he is apprehensive lest his conclusions are regarded 'as prompted by patriotic bias'.[40]

The high watermark of the nationalist ideology reflected in research on polity can be traced in V.R.R. Dikshitar. His work *Hindu Administrative Institutions*, which he took up as his thesis in 1923 and completed in 1927, goes rather too far in singing the glories of our past institutions. He regards Hindu polity as almost modern. Strongly rebutting the view that patriotism was not a phenomenon realized in ancient India, he argues that 'the oneness of the country and the ideal of every monarch to make a *digvijaya* and achieve sole rule over the world extending from the Cape Comorin to the Himalayas indicate beyond doubt the existence of a strong nationalist feeling in the country'. And then he quotes the famous verse *jananī janmabhūmiśca svargādapi garīyasti*.[41] His concluding lines carry exactly the same sense as those of Jayaswal. He says that, though every nation evolved its own polity, no polity had the inherent vitality that the Hindu polity possessed. At the end of his work he repeats the robust optimism of Jayaswal that 'the Golden Age of his (Hindu) Polity lies not in the past but in the future'.[42]

Thus a review of general works on polity during 1916–25 reveals a marked tendency to place an ideological weapon in the hands of Indian nationalists. The same is the case with certain special works such as those on Local Self-Government and International Law in Ancient India. R.K. Mookerji's *Local Government in Ancient India* seeks to modify the opinion of such critics as declare that 'In ancient India there was nothing of the nature of a political institution between the village and central government'.[43] Like other scholars, Mookerji also feels that to see endless repetitions of autocratic and theocratic institutions in Indian history is a great source of historical misinterpretation.[44] He claims that the study of ancient Indian local institutions will point the way to the lines of development on which reconstruction should proceed. On the other hand, 'to the people it will bring a new inspiration, a fresh stimulus to national self-respect that will look back with pride on the record of institutions which gave them at once the blessings of self-rule and a means of self-preservation amidst adverse political conditions'.[45]

Similar sentiments are expressed in P.N. Banerjea's work *International Law and Custom in Ancient India* (1920). Banerjea says that imbued with imperialistic ideas Hall considers International Law as a 'favoured monopoly' of the European family of nations.[46] He complains that even a considerate publicist such as Lawrence regards the Indian troops as 'semi-civilized or imperfectly civilized troops' and that he recommends their use against border tribes and in warfare with people of the same degree of education as themselves.[47] The object of Banerjea's thesis is 'to establish the apparently incredible fact that *the ancient Indians had a definite knowledge of the rules of International Law according to which they regard their international conduct*'.[48] S.V. Viswanath's *International Law in Ancient India* institutes a comparison between the First World War, which was waged in contravention of the accepted laws of nations and in defiance of all notions of international morality laying its hand on combatants and non-combatants alike,[49] and the wars in ancient India, which were fought according to the rules of *Dharmayuddha* and in which wholesale destruction and devastation were forbidden.[50]

Between 1925 and 1930 the number of works on ancient polity was comparatively fewer than what it was between 1916 and 1925. In 1927 N.C. Bandyopadhay brought out two books *Development of Hindu Polity and Political Theories* and *Kauṭilya*. Whereas in the former he tried to demolish the belief that India was the birthplace and the peculiar habitation of despotic power, in the latter he concluded that Kauṭilya 'dreams the prospect of a truly 'national king' who was to merge even his identity with customs and language'.[51] But Beni Prasad, who published his two books *State in Ancient India* and *Government in Ancient India* about the same time, sounded a word of warning against reading too much of modern ideas into ancient institutions. Nevertheless, to prove the superiority of early Indian institutions over the Greek and Roman systems he said that in ancient India there was no aristocracy in the Greek or Roman sense. Caste forbade a combination of office, wealth and prestige of birth as in other countries.[52] In 1931 S.K. Aiyangar published his *Evolution of Hindu Administrative Institutions in South India* 'for an understanding of the native Indian theory of government so that there may be a correct apprehension of the constitutional needs of the country'.[53] He flatters himself with the idea that the ancient 'administration seems to have made a clear, but close approach to these ideals which modern democracy is making an effort at realising.'[54] An important work of specific nature published in 1929 was *Contributions to the History of the Hindu Revenue System* of U.N. Ghoshal. Therein he states that the principles of taxation formulated in early times 'surpass the achievements of classical antiquity and tend to approach the ideas of European thinkers in the 18th and early 19th centuries'.[55] In his opinion the view that taxes are the king's dues for the service of protection is identical with the similar doctrine of the seventeenth and eighteenth century Europe.[56]

Thus a reviewer of Dikshitar's *Hindu Administrative Institutions* in 1929 rightly pointed out that 'the general trend of the works during the last fifteen years has been to show that the government of the country in ancient days was not irresponsible, that there was public opinion with recognized channels for the expression thereof, that public opinion was respected in almost all cases by the powers, that it could grow at times so powerful as to lead to the abdication or dethronement of the ruler, and so on'.[57] There is no doubt that this whole series of research works on the history of political theories and institutions was written with a purpose it was meant to bring grist to the nationalist mill and to sustain the nationalist movement. After 1930 there set in a stagnation in research, and few works on polity were produced in the following twenty years or so. The books that appeared during this period mostly covered the old ground.

Here let us pause and consider the merits and limitations of the nationalist and revivalist line of approach to the study of India's past polity. Its one great result was that by presenting an encouraging picture of the past it filled the people with great self-confidence. As a scholar of Hindu polity says in 1922, 'the nationalist movement of Young India which has won recognition as a world force in international politics since 7 August 1905, is receiving a conscious guidance and direction from the solid results of unquestionable antiquarian investigation'.[58] This knowledge of ancient polity gave tongue to those who advocated self-government and independence of India. If they had self-government in the past, there was no reason why they should not have it in the present. Secondly, this ideology produced splendid research works, and certain inferences regarding the prevalence of limited monarchy, republics, local self-government and international law in ancient India came to be accepted by nearly all scholars, despite the dissenting note of V. Smith that it was not safe to rely on the admonitions of the early sages about the ideal king.

But this nationalist ideology had also its limitations. First, though it did serve to rouse the educated middle class against alien rule, it hardly appealed to conscious intellectuals interested in the masses of peasants and workers who were being drawn into the national struggle from 1920 onward. By a fulsome adoration of ancient Hindu institutions it tended to antagonize the Muslims, though this was not done deliberately. Second, it gave us a false sense of past values. It glossed over the fact that, whether it was monarchy or republic, the two upper varṇas dominated the two lower varṇas, who were generally excluded from political offices. It also ignored the fact that fundamentally ancient legislation worked in the interests of the upper varṇas. It did not pay attention to the fact that the ruling class consciously exploited religion for the promotion of its political interests. It never took into consideration the fact that wealth and political offices went hand in hand.

Third, many Indian scholars fought shy of the religious aspects of ancient Indian polity and, as if to cover a sense of guilt, took too much pains to prove the secular character of the ancient Indian state. They realized that even in the Western world the first completely secular state did not come into existence until 1783 and that India was not the only country where religion influenced political ideas and actions.[59]

Fourth, in its craze for proving the superiority of our ancient institutions over those of the ancient West it hardly tried to examine them - in the light of the evolution of primitive tribes as known from anthropology or in the light of the early institutions of other Indo-European peoples. Because of these limitations it appears that the possibilities of research in ancient Indian polity on purely nationalistic lines have been almost exhausted. We are in need of an objective approach free from cheap nationalist generalisations.

NOTES

1. Although the establishment of the Asiatic Society of Bengal in 1784 marks the starting point of Western interest in ancient Indian studies the number of books that were published till 1859 was small. Max Müller, *A History of Ancient Sanskrit Literature*, p. 1.
2. *SBE*, i, pt. I, Preface, p. xi.
3. Max Müller, op. cit. p. 16.
4. Quoted in Beni Prasad, *The State in Ancient India.*
5. *Caste in India,* p. 198.
6. Ibid., p. 212.
7. *A History of Ancient Sanskrit Literature*, p. 18.
8. 'Position of the Ruling Caste etc.', *JAOS,* xiii, 182.
9. *Calcutta Review*, xxxv (1887), 266.
10. Ibid., xcviii (1894), 301.
11. 'Limited Monarchy in Ancient India', *Modern Review,* ii (1907), 346ff.
12. Ibid.
13. *Ancient India*, pp. 158–91.
14. K.V. Rangaswami Aiyangar, *Some Aspects of Ancient Indian Polity*, p. 87.
15. An up-to-date bibliography is found in R.P. Kangle, *The Kauṭiliya Arthaśāstra*, Part III, University of Bombay, 1965.
16. Quoted in Hiren Mukerjee, *India Struggles for Freedom*, p. 88.
17. *Hindu Polity*, p. xxv.

18. Ibid., p. 366.
19. Ibid., p. 51.
20. Ibid., p. 97.
21. K.V. Rangaswami Aiyangar, *Some Aspects of Ancient Indian Polity*, pp. 3–4. Although the 1935 edition of this book has been consulted, it does not mean any difference in matter except for footnotes and appendices.
22. K.V. Rangaswami Aiyangar, op. cit., p. 65.
23. Introduction, p. i.
24. *Corporate Life in Ancient India*, p. 122.
25. Ibid., p. 145.
26. *Aspects of Ancient Indian Polity*, p. iv.
27. Ibid., p. 218
28. B.K. Sarkar, *Political Institutions and Theories of the Hindus*, p. viii.
29. Ibid., p. 9.
30. Ibid., p. 13.
31. N.C. Bandyopadhyay, *Development of Hindu Polity and Political Theories*, p. 94.
32. Ibid., p. 294.
33. This book has been more than doubled in size and has been re-issued in 1959 under the title *A History of Indian Political Ideas* which is a good reference book for details but does not add substantially to the original work.
34. *A History of Indian Political Ideas*, p. 5.
35. Ibid., p. 8.
36. Ibid., p. 9.
37. Introduction, p. 2.
38. D.R. Bhandarkar, *Some Aspects of Ancient Hindu Polity*, p. 2.
39. Ibid., p. 3.
40. Ibid., p. 77.
41. Ibid., p. 78.
42. V.R.R. Dikshitar, *Hindu Administrative Institutions*, p. 384, bracketted portion ours.
43. Ibid., p. 316.
44. Mookerji, 'Introduction', *Local Government*, p. xiii.
45. Mookerji, *Local Government*, pp. 21–2.
46. *JDL*, i (1920). p. 202.
47. Ibid., p. 203.
48. Ibid.
49. S.V. Viswanath, *International Law in Ancient India*, pp. 3–4.
50. Ibid., p. 126.
51. Ibid., p. 298.
52. *The State in Ancient India*, pp. 7–8.
53. Ibid., p. v.

54. Ibid., p. 379.
55. U.N. Ghoshal, *Contributions to the History of the Hindu Revenue System*, p. 14.
56. Ibid., p. 17.
57. *JIH*, viii (1929), p. 405.
58. B.K. Sarkar, *The Political Institutions and Theories of the Hindus,* p. 4. 1
59. The religious aspect has been emphasised recently in several publications, as has been shown by us in our Introduction.

5

Early Story of Oriental Despotism: A Critique*

The pedigree of the idea of oriental despotism in Europe can be traced back to Plato and Aristotle. But it was only when the mercantilist and first-generation industrial powers had acquired colonies in India and other parts of Asia that the idea was popularized. Amongst others it is found in the writings of Adam Smith, Montesquieu, Richard Jones and Hegel, and was propagated by James Mill. They talked not only of oriental despotism but also of the unchanging east. Montesquieu postulates immutability of laws, customs manners and religion in the eastern countries,[1] and Hegel speaks of unchanging Hindus,[2] their one unbroken superstition,[3] and stationary China and India.[4] Evidently the idea of oriental despotism occupied with the unchanging character of the east infected not only the western orientalists of the second half of the nineteenth and early twentieth centuries but also Karl Marx and Friedrich Engels. What Marx and Engels really did was to discuss the different features of oriental despotism in their scattered writings and to link them up with the Asiatic mode of production, which was put forth as a reasoned explanation for oriental despotism. It would be however wrong to attribute to the two thinkers any systematic and well thought out formulation of the Asiatic mode, for they kept on shifting their views not only on its components such as irrigation, absence of private property in land, autarchic villages, lack of towns, and such others but also on their relative importance. The problem of oriental despotism can be studied by isolating and analysing these ingredients and by examining their applicability to ancient India.

*Previously published as 'Theory of "Oriental Despotism": A Socio-Economic Critique' in R.S. Sharma, *Aspects of Political Ideas and Institutions in Ancient India* (New Delhi: Motilal Banarsidass Publishers, 1991).

We may begin, with an ecological explanation of oriental despotism given by Montesquieu. As he puts, it: 'In Asia they have always had great empires; in Europe these could never subsist. Asia has larger plains; it is cut out into much more extensive divisions by mountains and seas; . . . Power in Asia ought, then to be always despotic; for if their slavery was not severe they would make a division inconsistent with the nature of the country'.[5] This geographical factor leading to despotism cannot be applied to India. India, unlike Egypt, is not the gift of one river. Geographically several viable territorial units could be formed in pre-industrial India, and its history attests this process. If there are many units one would act as a check on the other. Montesquieu buttresses his theory of oriental despotism in emphasizing the unchanging character of laws, customs, manner and religion of India. He states that the Indians easily succumb to all kinds of impressions,[6] and once an impression is formed it cannot be easily wiped out. There is no change in laws, custom and manners because the Indians are indolent in both body and mind, and hence prone to inaction.[7] This again is attributed to the excessive heat of the climate, which deprives the body of all vigour and strength.[8] Montesquieu's ecological explanation of the inaction and submissiveness of the Indians should not detain us long.

But another explanation which is both ecological and sociological deserves more attention. The need for irrigation in arid zones is sometimes put forward as the main cause of oriental despotism.[9] It is stated that irrigation facilities could not be organized by individual families or local authorities but only by a strong central authority. The point has been developed in the theory of hydraulic despotism. Irrigation maintenance required a large number of officers so that bureaucracy became an important element in the Asiatic mode of production or of oriental despotism. The applicability of irrigation theory in medieval India has been rightly questioned.[10] Even theoretically irrigation is not considered to be a monocausal explanation for centralization and despotism by anthropologists and archaeologists who have examined its relevance in non-Indian contexts.[11] This has led some recent exponents of this theory to revise their stand,[12] and consider irrigation as one of the several factors leading to centralization.

Only the north-western part of the Indian subcontinent is arid, otherwise its major part has plenty of rain, which certainly must have been greater in ancient times when there was not much of deforestation. Irrigation would be needed still, but it could be a communal, provincial and central responsibility as was the case under the Mauryas. There is nothing to show that a large bureaucracy developed in Maurya times in response to the needs of irrigation. Kauṭilya mentions about 30 departmental heads and eighteen high officers, all of whom are needed for looking after various economic and administrative activities, but none is provided for irrigation. That governors of Saurashtra took steps to repair the embankment of the Sudarśana lake under the Mauryas, Rudradāman and the Guptas shows that irrigation was also a provincial responsibility. Evidence of family and communal construction of irrigation works is not lacking.[13]

Basing his argument on Colebrooke's *Digest of Hindu Law*, which emphasizes the sovereign's proprietary right to the land on the strength of conquest, Richard Jones (1830–1) made the point that right from brāhmaṇical times the sovereign had the right to the ownership of all the land[14] and that all subordinate peasant (ryot) rights were either rendered precarious on account of constant wars or else were completely nullified by the king who was the strongest person.[15] Since everybody depended for his livelihood on the sovereign who was the sole proprietor of land this perpetuated Asiatic despotism, which did not have any intermediate and independent classes.[16] The thread was resumed by Karl Marx, who at the initial stage accepted Bernier's theory regarding royal proprietorship of all land in India. Marx looked upon the absence of private property in land as the key to the understanding of the Asian system.[17] Later he came to stress the communal ownership of land, and eventually he seems to have realized that the question was not so simple. It has been ably shown that Marx recognized three forms of land tenure in India: (i) communal property, the 'original form' of tenure which had survived in certain Indian villages; (ii) 'Private property' in the region south of the Krishna which had not come under British rule; and (iii) feudal property in areas such as Oudh, where tax-collectors had developed into feudal landholders on account of weakness in the central government.[18] Of these the first two relate to ancient India, and there is some evidence for them in both texts and inscriptions[19]. However, in early medieval times there is strong evidence for the royal ownership of land[20] as well as some kind of feudal property in land.

Evidence for royal ownership of land in ancient times is weak. Under the all-powerful Kauṭilyan state royal ownership seems to have been enforced only in the waste lands in which new rural settlements were founded and peasants allotted arable lands for lifetime. However, the situation began to change in Maharashtra, in the second century AD and over a considerable part of the country in the Gupta period. The royal right to grant was extended to cultivable areas situated in the personal domain of the king. The term *rājakaṃ khetam* (cultivable land under the king's possession) occurs as early as the second century in a Sātavāhana grant.[21] Eventually the grants were extended to revenue-paying lands held by the peasants, so that the superior rights of the king covered all the three categories of land—waste royal domain and revenue-paying (the last two belonging to cultivable category).

The first important indication of the process by which the king claims ownership of the soil is found in Manu, who calls the king *mahīpati* or lord of the earth;[22] later Kātyāyana calls him *bhūsvāmin* or owner of the earth.[23] The synonyms for the term king found in Sanskrit and Jaina Sanskrit kāvyas are significant. The terms *kṣitīndra*, *kṣitīśa*, *kṣitipati*, *urvipati*, *pṛthvīpati*, *vasudheśvara*, *mahībhuk*, *mahīpati*, etc. represent him more as the lord of the land than the protector or lord of the people. The practice becomes common in early medieval law-books, which emphasize royal lordship over the land. The literary texts of early medieval times make the point that earth is like wife to the king, meant for enjoyment. Hence the principle of possession and enjoyment rather than that of royal service, sovereignty and protection becomes the basis of the king's claim to taxes, both proper and improper, in this period.

Royal ownership of arable and revenue-paying lands in early medieval times is supported by the fact that the king claimed *bhoga*, *bhogakara* or *rājakīya bhoga*.[24] Initially *bhoga* stood for periodical supplies of fuel, flowers, fruits and similar other things by the peasants to the king; then gradually it came to include eight or eleven types of *bhoga* embracing the enjoyment of all possible agrarian resources.[25] The absence of *bhoga* in Kauṭilya's enumeration of taxes to be collected from the rural areas is as striking as that of Kauṭilya's *sitā* (income from crown lands directly cultivated by the king's agents) in the land grants. *Bhoga* is invariably used in the sense of possession or enjoyment and repeatedly mentioned in the Smṛtis in that sense either singly or with other terms. It is, therefore, most likely that the king demanded *bhoga* from the peasant on the plea that the kind lay within his overall possession (*bhoga/bhukti*).

But in addition to royal rights in land there developed in early medieval times feudal property in land. The king's dominion over the soil was limited by the intermediate landlords he created. In the earliest grants the royal right to revenues was transferred, but in later grants the royal right to the enjoyment of all agrarian resources was transferred. What is more significant, the beneficiaries were given the right of evicting the existing cultivators and getting the lands enjoyed and cultivated by others. Naturally royal charters called *śāsanas* were bound to lead to land disputes between the beneficiaries and peasants, and in such cases the king respected his charters. Medieval legal texts enjoin that in trying a suit if there are differences between *dharma* (law), *vyavahāra* (agreement), *carita* (custom) and *śāsana*, the last should override all the three other sources of authority.[26] Most probably this rule applied to land disputes which out of peasant claims to the benefice lands. These could be decided mainly on the strength of royal charters or *śāsanas* and not so much on the basis of the other types of titles to the land. All the religious and secular beneficiaries who were granted lands by the king developed their own rights in these lands, as distinct from those of the king and peasants. So the fact that the king becomes the greatest landowner in the early medieval phase does not lead to royal despotism for his power is restricted by the lesser landlords he creates and by the revenue officials who turn into hereditary landlords. The king could possibly intervene in an effective manner in the conflict between the peasants and beneficiaries, or between rival beneficiaries. And then there were remnants of communal rights. Conflicts between these different types of land rights would pose problems for the stability of government. It is held that the combination of sovereignty and ownership of land in the person of the king led to oriental despotism. But there is nothing to show that this happened either in ancient or medieval India, for royal ownership had to contend with feudal property and peasant property.

An important ingredient of, and explanation for, oriental despotism, is the self-sufficiency of villages which led to the unchanging character of Indian society presided over by a despot. The idea was first advanced by Hegel. Hegel speaks of a fixed and immutable arrangement, subject to no one's will existing in the villages, with the result that all political resolutions become matters of indifference to the common Hindu, 'for his lot is unchanged'. The arrangement may be described in his words:

> The whole income belonging to every village is, as already stated, divided into two parts, of which one belongs to the Rajah, the other to the cultivators; but proportionate shares are also received by the Provost of the place, the Judge, the Water-Surveyor, the Brahmin who superintends religious worship, the Astrologer (who is also a Brahmin, and announces the days of good and ill-omen), the Smith, the Carpenter, the Potter, the Washerman, the Barber, the Physician, the Dancing Girls, the Musician, the Poet.[27]

As is well-known, on this basis as well as on the basis of the early nineteenth-century reports of some British officials, Karl Marx developed the theory of the self-sufficiency and autarchy of villages based on a happy combination of crafts and agriculture, which freed them from economic dependence on the outside world. Artisans did not have any 'market' outside their village. These microcosms led passive and vegetative life, and were incapable of combining horizontally with the result that the oriental despot reigned supreme over them.[28] Recently the theory has been taken over by anthropologists and refined into the *jajmānī* system. But it would be wrong to postulate that the Indian social structure was based on this system from ancient times. Only in the Maurya period some kind of oriental despotism with a sizeable bureaucracy can be noticed, but the system was not exclusively based on the taxes collected from peasants living in self-sufficient villages. The contribution of state production carried on with the help of slaves and wage labour in farms and elsewhere seems to have been significant. Although the surplus was collected from the countryside which also included state farms (*sītā*), urban settlements (*durga*) inhabited by artisans and traders formed a good source of income. In fact far more sources of taxes are mentioned under the urban head than under the rural head. These were supplemented by income from mining activities (*khani*).[29] The detailed laws of Kauṭilya against the undesirable activities of artisans[30] (*kāruka-rakṣaṇam*) and traders[31] (*vaidehaka-rakṣaṇam*) underline the importance of artisanal production. Obviously the commodities produced by state artisans and by guilds of artisans were used not only by people living in towns but also in the countryside.

Generally speaking till Gupta times artisans and traders were mostly associated with towns, as would appear from Kauṭilya's plan regarding the foundation of cities. In the settled, developed areas clusters of villages seem to have existed around towns which satisfied their artisanal and other needs such as cloth, salt and agricultural implements in return for raw material, food-grains, and cash payment. Kauṭilya provides for the establishment of various types of urban centres in the midst of villages. The theory that in India towns were princely camps superimposed upon a predominantly agricultural population without having any organic relation with it may not apply to ancient times. The continued existence of a good number of towns in north India from the fifth century BC to the third century AD and even later cannot be doubted. Archaeology, inscriptions and classical texts refer to several towns in western India, all connected with crafts and commerce, in the two centuries before and after Christ. Merchants from the Deccan evince a sense of pride in their cities inasmuch as they mention them along with their names. The decline of trade and town seems to have started in Gupta times and become marked in the post-Gupta phase.[32] It is in this period that we notice many princely military camps called *skandhāvāras*, nine of the Pāla and twenty-one of the Candellas, from where land charters were issued.

With the decline of trade and towns in early medieval times artisans dispersed to the countryside and contributed to the formation of autarchic villages. A good deal of peasant needs were supplied by village artisans who were remunerated at each harvest in fixed quantities of foodgrains. Big temples, and land magnates, living on rents collected from the peasant tenants obtained the services of artisans in return for grants of land with the result that artisans lost mobility and became encumbered with agriculture. Thus in early medieval times villagers obtained what they needed through the *jajmānī* system. However all economic activities were not exhausted by this system, and occasional market fairs (*haṭṭa*) run by pedlars were held to meet the needs of the countryside. The *jajmānī* system, therefore, has neither been typical of India in all ages and all periods, nor all-pervasive even in medieval times. Self-sufficient units seem to have originated and proliferated in medieval times, but they do not seem to have been so passive as they are depicted.

The concept of Asiatic despotism presupposes the absence of an exploiting class apart from the king and his bureaucracy.[33] Even those who argue for the limiting role of *dharma* ignore its class character. In the ancient Indian system the king was a member of the warrior-noble order. To us it seems that the exploiting orders were symbolized by *brahma* (priests) and *kṣatra* (warrior-nobles). The two upper orders may not have been in effective possession of land, the chief means of production, but the varṇa system was devised in such a way that taxes and tributes collected from the peasants, artisans and traders could be used to maintain them. The fact that the two upper orders did not pay taxes in the age of the Buddha is significant. Naturally the two orders were allied to the king for the protection of the rights and privileges conferred on them by the varṇa system as against the vaiśyas and śūdras. The two upper orders were opposed to the king when their rights and privileges were threatened from above. But by and large the texts stress the collaboration between these two. Constitutionally there may not have been a check on royal authority except the body of the brāhmaṇas which was called to interpret *dharma*, but socially the king dare not ignore the power behind the throne.

The Asiatic stereotype suggests the helplessness of the rural population in the face of royal despotism, but the Buddhist and brāhmaṇical texts mention several popular revolts led by the brāhmaṇas against the king. In the early Christian centuries slowly emerges a class of landed magnates, mostly brāhmaṇas, as a result of land grants. In post-Gupta times they were supplemented by secular grantees. Although the landed beneficiaries do not seem to have formed a well-articulated class, they did constitute an important segment of the ruling order and certainly a check on the power of the king.

The reason why the theory of oriental despotism was propounded by most western scholars is evident to students of the colonial history of India. It was meant to serve as a garb for colonial aggression. A disappointed French patriot and orientalist called Anquetil-Duperron writes: 'Despotism is the government in these countries, where the sovereign declares himself the proprietor of all the goods of his subjects: let us become that sovereign, and we will be the master of all the lands of Hindustan. Such is the reasoning of avid greed, concealed behind a facade of pretexts which must be demolished'.[34] Obviously in adopting the theory of oriental despotism Karl Marx was deeply influenced by Hegel and by colonialist writers on India. But significantly enough he tried to explain oriental despotism in terms of the mode of production and not in terms of the psychological make-up of the Hindus, as was done by Montesquieu and Hegel.

Ours is a preliminary examination of the socio-economic assumptions underlying the theory of 'oriental despotism' in the light of the existing historical evidence from early India.[35] We have touched upon such features as irrigation, royal ownership of land, self-sufficient villages, lack of towns, absence of intermediate classes, etc. It appears that generalizations regarding despotism in ancient India not only overreached the existing evidence but were even motivated. Of course it is easy to criticize theories of oriental despotism propounded in the eighteenth and nineteenth centuries on account of subsequent advance in historical research. But the theory is not yet a dead horse, and is now being resurrected by injecting a dose of religion into it. However, our understanding can advance if we examine the social and economic formations in early India. In this respect credit must be given to Karl Marx for posing the problem of Asiatic despotism in quite a different manner and thus making us think about the socio-economic bases of the state in India and other parts of Asia in ancient times. If orientalists, who have the advantage of keeping very close to the sources, get interested in the larger aspects of 'despotism', they can make an effective contribution to the subject.

NOTES

1. *The Spirit of the Laws*, p. 225.
2. *Philosophy of History*, p. 154.
3. Ibid., p. 167.
4. Ibid., p. 173.
5. *The Spirit of the Laws*, p. 269.
6. Ibid., ii, 224–5.
7. Ibid., p. 225.
8. Ibid., p. 224.
9. Karl Marx, *Historical Writings*, i, p. 593.
10. Irfan Habib, 'An Examination of Wittfogel's Theory of Oriental Despotism', *Studies in Asian History*, pp. 378–92.
11. William P. Mitchell, 'The Hydraulic Hypothesis: A Reappraisal', *Current Anthropology*, xiv (Dec. 1973), pp. 532–4.
12. Steward, who advanced the irrigation hypothesis in 1949 (Wittfogel first did it 1955), revised it later. Ibid., p. 532, fn. 2. For critique of Wittfogel's hydraulic despotism see Barry Hindess and Paul Q. Hirst, *Pre-Capitalist Modes of Production*, pp. 207–20; Brendan O'Leary, *The Asiatic Mode of Production*, Ch. 6.
13. R.S. Sharma, *Perspectives in Social and Economic History of Early India*, Ch. XI (New Delhi: Munshiram Manoharlal, 1983).
14. Rev. Richard Jones, *An Essay on the Distribution of Wealth and on the Sources of Taxation* (London, 1831), p. 114.
15. Ibid., pp. 114–15.
16. Ibid., p. 113.
17. *Capital*, iii, p. 771–2.
18. R.A.L.H. Gunawardana, 'The Analysis of Pre-Colonial Social Formations in Asia in the Writings of Karl Marx', *The Indian Historical Review*, ii (1976), p. 377.
19. R.S. Sharma, *Indian Feudalism*, *c*. 300–1200, Ch. IV.
20. Ibid.
21. D.C. Sircar, *Select Inscriptions*, Bk. II, no. 84, line 4.
22. VIII, 39.
23. Verse 16.
24. For references see U.N. Ghoshal, *Contributions to the History of the Hindu Revenue System* (Calcutta: University of Calcutta Press, 1929), p. 394.
25. Ibid.
26. *Kātyāyana* quoted in Laxman Shastri Joshi, *Dharmakośa*, vol. I, Pt. I, p.

103; Hārita quoted ibid., p. 106; cf. Bṛhaspati quoted ibid., p. 99. To me it appears that a similar verse in *AŚ*, III.1 is a later insertion.

27. Hegel, *Philosophy of History*, p. 154.
28. Karl Marx, *Historical Writlngs*, i, pp. 594–6; *Capital*, i, pp. 357–8.
29. *AŚ*, II.6.
30. Ibid., IV.1.
31. Ibid., 1V.2.
32. For details see, R.S. Sharma, *Urban Decay in India* (*c*. 300–*c*. 1000) (New Delhi: Munshiram Manoharlal, 1987).
33. For a theoretical critique see Hindess and Hirst, *Pre-Capitalist Modes of Production*, pp. 197–9.
34. *Legislation Orientale* (1778), p. 178, quoted in Perry Anderson, *Lineages of the Absolutist State*, pp. 465–6, fn. 9.
35. A detailed and convincing refutation of the theory of 'oriental despotism', appears in Brenden O'Leary, *The Asiatic Mode of Production*, Chs 6 and 7.

6

Writings on the Śūdras*

The modern study of the ancient Indian social order owed its inception to the efforts of the East India Company, which could not govern an alien people without some knowledge of their institutions. With the Mughal grant of Diwani rights in 1765 to manage the civil affairs, the East India Company faced the problem of governing the people from Bengal to Allahabad. This could not be done without some knowledge of the social institutions of the Hindus who formed the major population. The preface to *A Code of Gentoo Laws* (1776), one of the first English works which have some bearing on the early social history of India, states that 'the importance of the commerce of India and the advantages of a territorial establishment in Bengal' could be maintained only by 'an adoption of such original institutes of the country, as do not intimately clash with the laws or interests of the conquerors'.[1] In his preface to the translation of the *Manu Smṛti* (1794) Sir William Jones, the father of modern Indology, adds that, if this policy is pursued, 'the well-directed industry' of 'many millions of Hindu subjects' 'would largely add to the wealth of Britain'.[2] Four years later, on the basis of these sources, Colebrooke wrote an essay on the 'Enumeration of Indian classes',[3] which appeared to him among the most remarkable institutions of India.[4] Soon after, in 1818 these sources were utilized by Mill to describe the caste system in his *History of India.* Discussing the disabilities of the śūdras he came to the conclusion that the vices of caste subordination were carried to a more destructive height among the Hindus than among any other people,[5] and remarked that the hideous society of the Hindus continued in his times. But from the same sources Elphinstone (1841)

*Previously published as 'Historiography and Approach' in R.S. Sharma, *Sudras in Ancient India: A Social History of the Lower Order Down to Circa A.D. 600* (New Delhi: Motilal Banarsidass Publishers, 1990).

deduced that the condition of the śūdras 'was much better than that of the public slaves under some ancient republics, and, indeed, than that of the villains of the middle ages, or any other servile class with which we are acquainted'.[6] He also perceived that such a servile class did not exist any longer in his time.[7]

But there is no doubt that many age-old social practices continued into the nineteenth century. The glaring contrast between the rising industrial society of England and the old decaying society of India[8] attracted the attention of the educated intelligentsia, who were being permeated with the spirit of nationalism. They realized that the practices of sati, lifelong widowhood, child marriage, and caste endogamy were great obstacles to national progress. Since these practices were supposed to derive sanction from the Dharmaśāstras, it was felt that necessary reforms could be effected easily if they could be proved to be in consonance with the sacred texts. Thus in 1818 Rammohan Roy published his first tract against satī, in which he tried to show that, according to the śāstras, it was not the best way for the salvation of a woman.[9] In the fifties of the same century Ishwarchandra Vidyasagar ransacked Smṛti literature in order to make out a case for widow remarriage.[10] In 1879 Swami Dayanand, the founder of the Ārya Samāj, brought out a collection of original Sanskrit texts called the *Satyārthaprakāśa* to support widow remarriage, rejection of caste based on birth,[11] and the śūdras' right to Vedic education.[12] We do not know how far the early social reformers drew inspiration from the contemporary works of the British scholar Muir,[13] who tried to prove that the belief in the origin of the four varṇas from the primeval man did not exist in ancient times,[14] and from those of the German scholar Weber, who presented the first important critical study of the caste system on the basis of the Brāhmaṇas and the Śūdras.[15]

On the occasion of the introduction of the Age of Consent Bill in 1891, Sir R.G. Bhandarkar brought out a well-documented pamphlet citing Sanskrit texts to establish that a girl should be married only when she attains maturity. On the other hand B.G. Tilak, to whom any stick was good enough to beat the alien rulers, cited texts against this Bill.[16]

This tendency to quote ancient scriptures in support of modern reforms can be well summed up in the words of R.G. Bhandarkar (1895):

> In ancient times girls were married after they had attained maturity, now they must be married before; widow marriage was in practice, now it has entirely gone out. . . . Interdining among the castes was not prohibited, now the numberless castes . . . cannot have intercommunication of that nature.[17]

But the attempt of the Indian scholars to present early social institutions in a form more palatable to the modern mind did not always commend itself to western writers. Thus Senart (1896) pointed out that the castes are compared by the Hindus of English upbringing with the social distinctions that exist among Europeans, but that they correspond only very remotely to western social classes.[18] Similarly Hopkins (1881) stated that the position of the śūdra was not different from that of the American house slave before 1860.[19] Reviewing Hopkins' generalizations, Hillebrandt (1896) held that the position of the śūdras should be judged in comparison with the slaves of the ancient world and not in the context of developments in later times.[20]

Criticizing Hopkins, Ketkar (1911) complains that European writers are influenced by their ideas of racial discrimination against the Negroes, and hence unduly exaggerate this in their treatment of the caste system.[21] The main trend noticeable in the works of recent Indian writers such as Ketkar, Dutt, Ghurye and others is to present the system in such a way as may help to recast it in response to present requirements.[22] Thus it would appear that problems of ancient Indian society have been largely studied against the background of struggle between the reformist and the orthodox schools. The dominant motives of reform and nationalism have undoubtedly produced valuable works on India's early social life; but what appeared to be seamy and ugly in comparison with modern standards came to be either ignored or explained away unconvincingly. For instance, it has been argued that the disabilities of the śūdras did not reduce their happiness or well-being.[23]

It is this tendency to concentrate on favourable aspects of early social life that accounts for the almost complete absence of works on the position of the śūdras in ancient India. Even European writers gave their attention mainly to the study of the upper classes of Hindu society. Thus Muir devoted 188 pages to the legends of struggles between brāhmaṇas and kṣatriyas,[24] and Hopkins (1889) presented a comprehensive study of the 'Position of Ruling Caste in Ancient India.'[25] The admirable work of Fick (1897) on the social organization of northeastern India also mainly confined itself to the treatment of kṣatriyas, brāhmaṇas and gahapatis or seṭṭhis. It is difficult to explain these writers' lack of interest in the fortunes of the lower orders unless we suppose that their vision was circumscribed by the dominant class outlook of their age.

The first independent work on the śūdras was a short article by V.S. Śastri (1922), who discussed the philosophical basis of the term śūdra.[26] In another article (1923) he tried to show that the śūdras could perform

Vedic rituals.[27] In a paper published in 1947 Ghoshal dealt with the status of śūdras in the Dharmasūtras.[28] A valuable article was written by a Russian writer G.F. Ilyin (1950),[29] who, on the basis of the Dharmaśāstra evidence,[30] demonstrated that śūdra were not slaves. The only monograph on śūdras (1946) was published by a well-known Indian politician Ambedkar, who confined himself to the question of their origin.[31] The author was entirely dependent for his source-material on translations.[32] What is worse, he seems to have worked with the fixed purpose of proving a high origin for the śūdras, a tendency which has been very much in evidence among the educated sections of the lower caste people in recent times. A single passage of the *Śānti Parvan,* which states that the śūdra Paijavana performed sacrifice, is sufficient to establish the thesis that śūdras were originally kṣatriyas.[33] The author did not bother himself about the complex of various circumstances which led to the formation of the labouring class known as the śūdra. A recent work[34] (1957), allied to this subject, brings together scattered information on labourers in ancient India, but it does not make any significant addition to our knowledge. The main object of this book is to explore the field of Labour Economics in ancient India, and in doing so the author looks for past parallels to modern wage-boards, arbitrators, social security etc., with the result that this work suffers from undue modernism. Moreover, the book mainly draws on the *Arthaśāstra* of Kauṭilya, is sketchy, and lacks historical sense.

In my *Śūdras* I have tried not only to provide an adequate treatment of the position of the śūdras in ancient times, but also to evaluate their modern characterizations, either based on insufficient data, or inspired by reformist or anti-reformist motives. I have made an attempt to present a connected and systematic account of the various developments in the position of the śūdras down to *circa* AD 500.

Since the śūdras were regarded as the labouring class, particular attention has to be paid to the investigation of their material conditions and the nature of their economic and social relations with members of the higher varṇas. This naturally leads to the study of the position of slaves, with whom the śūdras were considered identical. The untouchables are also theoretically placed in the category of śūdras, and hence their origin and position needs to be discussed in some detail.

The position of the lowest order in ancient Indian society cannot be studied without raising a few questions. What led to the formation of the śūdra community? If the śūdras were meant for serving the three higher orders, can they be categorized as slaves? Was ancient Indian society a slave society? How far does the ritual status of the śūdras correspond to their economic status? Did the reforming religious sects bring about any fundamental change in the position of the lower orders or did they try to contain and stabilize the changes that had occurred on account of other factors? Did the role of the lower orders in the economic system undergo any change over the centuries? How is it that the twice-born vaiśyas came to be reduced to the level of the śūdra and śūdras placed on a par with the vaiśyas? How do we explain the proliferation of the servile orders towards the end of the sixth century? How did the śūdras react to their servility and disabilities? Why are social revolts comparatively absent in ancient India? All these and similar other problems have to be tackled.

This study has to be mainly based on literary sources, though their precise dating or the dating of their various parts has been a baffling problem. It may be better to adopt the generally accepted chronology of the literary texts, though in the case of different opinions the writer has to indicate his own reasons for adopting an unconventional dating.

Although the texts belong to different periods, they repeat *ad nauseam* the same formulae and terminologies, as make it difficult to detect changes in society; hence special attention has been paid to the study of variants. Many of these texts cannot be understood without the aid of the commentators, who not unoften project the ideas of their own times into earlier periods.

Further, the literary texts, brāhmaṇical and non-brāhmaṇical, seek to establish the supremacy of the brāhmaṇas or of the kṣatriyas, or of both, but they hardly show any sympathy for the śūdras. Ambedkar argues that the Dharmaśāstras and other treatises were written by the enemies of the śūdras and so they have no evidential value.[35] But the law books of other ancient societies also prescribe class legislation as the Dharmaśāstras do; unfortunately for lack of sufficient data we cannot definitely say about the implementation of the Dharmaśāstra laws.

Myths and rituals which dominate ancient texts are an important source for the reconstruction of social history. Recently because of the influence of some sociologists a few Western Sanskritists have started questioning the validity of directly using the myths and superstitions. They attribute various symbolical meanings to rituals and connect many of them with the creation processes. We cannot ignore fertility rites, but it should be noted that they underscore the importance of the production of plants, animals and human beings. The operation of rituals in day-to-day life shows that they originate in reality, and change with change in real life. Hence studies in rituals cannot be discarded by social historians. I would like to refer to a ritual related to my sacred thread ceremony performed seventy-seven years ago in my village Barooni. In that ceremony as a bābhan or brāhmaṇa I enjoyed eating in the houses of several śūdra families including those of potter, carpenter and hair cutter. But once I was invested with the sacred thread (*upanayana*) this practice was stopped forever. It is well known that śūdras were among the untouchables and that through the *upanayana* the śūdras were kept out of education. At present seats are reserved in the schools for their education.

The history of social classes cannot be followed in isolation from changes in material life, material changes in time sequence can be indicated on the basis of archaeology and inscriptions. We can notice the impact of animal husbandry, settled agricultural life, flourishing trade and land grants on the social formation at various stages, and its implications for the life of the lower order.

In order to explain and illustrate certain developments in the position of the śūdras it is necessary to make a comparative study of similar development in other ancient societies. We have also to study that relics of tribal life based on hunting and food gathering persist in the caste divided society till today.

NOTES

1. *Vivādārṇavasetu*, Translator's preface, p. IX. This work was translated from English into German in 1778.
2. *Institutes of Hindu Law*, Preface, p. XIX. Cf. Discourse of Colebrooke in the first general meeting of *RAS* (15 March, 1823), *Essays*, i, 1–2.
3. *Essays*, ii, 157–70.
4. Ibid., ii, 157.
5. *The History, of India*, ii, 166; i, 166–9; 169 fn. 1. It seems that Mill's generalizations about the history of India exercised the most dominant influence on later British historians.
6. *The History of India*, i, 34.
7. Ibid., 107.
8. In 1902 an old Indian writer laments that the brāhmaṇas should be made to take their place below Eurasian (Anglo-Indian) industrialists. J.C. Ghosh, *Brahmanism and Śudra*, p. 46.
9. *The English Works of Rammohan Roy*, i, Introd., pp. XVIII; ii, 123–92.
10. R.G. Bhandarkar, *Collected Works*, ii, 498.
11. *Satyārthaprakāśa*, 4th samullāsa, pp. 83–92, 113–22.
12. Ibid., 3rd samullāsa, pp. 39, 73–4.
13. *Original Sanskrit Texts*, i.

14. Ibid., 159–60.
15. *Indische Studien*, x, pp. 1–160.
16. R.G. Bhandarkar, *Collected Works*, ii, 538–83. Also see Bhandarkar's criticism of Jolly's article on the 'History of Child Marriage', ibid., pp. 584–602.
17. *Collected Works*, ii, pp. 522–3.
18. *Caste in India*, pp. 12–13.
19. *Mutual Relations of the Four Castes in Manu*, p. 102.
20. Hillebrandt, 'Brāhmanen und Śudrās, *Festschrift für Karl Weinhold*, p. 57.
21. Ketkar, *History of Caste*, p. 78, fn. 3.
22. Ketkar, op. cit., p. 9; Radhakrishnan's foreword to Valavalkar's *Hindu Social Institutions.* The works of Dutt and Ghurye display a better historical sense, but see Dutt, op. cit., Preface, p. VI.
23. On the basis of the *Śukranīti-sāra*, Sarkar, *Hindu Sociology*, pp. 92–5, cf. K.V. Rangaswami Aiyangar, *Indian Cameralism,* p. 85.
24. *Original Sanskrit Texts*, i, Ch. IV.
25. *JAOS*, xiii, pp. 57–376.
26. *IA*, ii, pp. 137–9.
27. 'The Status of the Śūdra in Ancient India', *Viswa Bharati Quarterly*, i, pp. 268–78.
28. *IC*, xiv, pp. 21–7.
29. Śūdras und sklaven in den altinclischen Gesetzbuchern' in *Sowjetwissenschaft*, 1952, 2 tr. from *Vestnik drevnei istorii*. 1950, No. 2, pp. 94–107.
30. Kane's compilation of the Dharmaśāstra extracts regarding śūdras provide valuable raw material for an historical study of their position. Chitra Tiwari's *Śūdras in Manu* (1963) does not add to our understanding.
31. Ambedkar, *Who were the Shudras*?
32. Ibid., Preface, p. IV.
33. It is to be noticed that in recent caste movements many śūdra castes claim to be kṣatriyas. Thus the Dusādhas claim to be the descendants of Duḥśāsamana, and the Goālās those of the Yadus.
34. K.M. Saran, *Labour in Ancient India.*
35. Ambedkar, op. cit., p. 114.

7

Historiography of the Ancient Social Order*

There is hardly any work exclusively devoted to the history of the social structure in ancient India, but there are many books on the different aspects of this subject, especially the caste system. A recent writer has listed 5,000 books on caste.[1] But historians can claim very little credit for this vast amount of literature, which is largely the work of ethnologists, sociologists, statisticians, economists, missionaries, and caste organizations. Most of this material deals with caste in recent times. Nevertheless, books dealing with the origin and growth of caste are not so few as to prevent an exhaustive survey. This essay indicates some broad lines of historiography as revealed from important works on caste and also on such allied subjects as family, marriage, the position of women, and such others in ancient India.**

The modern study of the ancient Indian social order owed its inception to the policy of the East India Company, which could not govern an alien people without some knowledge of their institutions. The preface to *A Code of Gentoo Laws*[2] one of the first English works which have some bearing on the early social history of India, states that 'the importance of the commerce of India and the advantages of a territorial establishment in Bengal' could be maintained only by 'an adoption of such original institutes of the country as do not intimately clash with the laws or interests of the conquerors'.[3] In his preface to the translation of the *Manusmṛti* (Calcutta, 1794), Sir William Jones, the father of modern Indology, adds that if this policy is pursued, 'the well-directed industry, of many millions of Hindu subjects . . . would largely add to the wealth of Britain'.[4] Four

*Published originally as 'Historiography of the Ancient Indian Social Order' in R.S. Sharma, *Perspectives in Social and Economic History of Early India* (New Delhi: Munshiram Manoharlal Publishers, 1983).

**This survey is limited to publications till the middle of 1950s.

years later, on the basis of these sources, Colebrooke wrote an essay on 'Enumeration of Indian Classes'.[5] 'which appeared to him among the most remarkable institutions of India'.[6] Soon after (1818) those sources were utilized by Mill to describe the caste system in his *History of India*. In discussing the disabilities of the śūdras he came to the conclusion that the vices of caste subordination were carried to a more destructive point among the Hindus than among any other people,[7] and remarked that the hideous society of the Hindus continued in his times. But from the same sources Elphinstone (1841) deduced that the condition of the śūdras 'was much better than that of the public slaves under some ancient republics, and indeed, than that of the villains of the Middle Ages, or any other servile class with which we are acquainted'.[8] He also perceived that such a servile class did not exist any longer in his time.[9]

From the beginning of the nineteenth century the sharp contrast between the rising industrial society of England and the decaying feudal society of India attracted the attention of the educated intellectuals and particularly of those who received western education, such as the students of the Hindu College, Calcutta. They realized that the practices of satī, lifelong widowhood, polygamy, child marriage, caste endogamy and purdah system were great obstacles to national progress. As Sir R.G. Bhandarkar put it in 1894; 'If we have to march along with the progressive races of the West . . . our social institutions must improve . . . There can be no advancement politically without social and moral advancement'.[10] But the weapons that the reformers employed to remove these obstacles and to lay the foundations of a better social order were not those of the progressive nations of the West but of the ancient Indian society. These were not weapons of reason drawn from the armoury of rationalism and utilitarianism, which moulded the minds of the western intellectuals in the eighteenth and the early nineteenth century, but those of authority taken from the armoury of the Dharmaśāstras.

The leaders of social reforms, who were mainly middle class intellectuals or scions of zamindar families educated in English schools, never tried to win public opinion by exposing the absurdity of the age-old social evils. But they tried to persuade the public to their point of view by convincing them that social reforms were in consonance with the sacred texts. This gave rise to an acrid controversy between the reformers who tried to justify social changes on the strength of passages from the Dharmaśāstra and the orthodox Hindus who tried to uphold the existing social practices by quoting from the same texts. Memoranda and memorials, meant for enlisting the support of the British bureaucrats, did not so much appeal to their reason and progressive social outlook as tried to impress upon them the desirability of these reforms in the light of the old texts. In part this revivalist attitude was the result of the policy of the British, who from the beginning of their rule did not like to meddle with the religious and social affairs of India, although the policy was set forth in so many words only in 1858.

The use of ancient texts can be seen in the movement for social reforms in Bengal, Punjab and Maharashtra. In Bengal the reform movement began with the agitation of Rammohan Roy against satī. In 1818 he published his first tract against satī, in which he tried to show that according to the Śāstras it was not the best way for the salvation of women.[11] On the other hand his opponents tried to prove that satī enjoyed the sanction of the old Hindu texts. They established in 1828 an institution called Dharmasabha. It was led by Raja Radhakanta Dev, who edited the famous modern Sanskrit Dictionary *Śabdakalpadruma* and naturally enjoyed the support of a large number of pandits who cooperated not only in the preparation of the dictionary but also in the compilation of the texts directed against the abolition of satī. We need not exaggerate the importance of ancient citations in bringing about the abolition of the satī system for many more could be produced in favour of its continuance. In this particular case the enlightened opinion of William Bentinck was of more moment than the texts marshalled by Raja Rammohan Roy. Here it may be stated that in accepting the abolition of satī in the nineteenth century the British were more responsive to the demand for changes in social practice than in administration. This was mainly because the changes touched only the outer fringe of the existing social structure and did not in any way affect the position of zamindars whom Bentinck considered the supporters of British Raj. Again the ultimate political implications of these social reforms in helping national integration were not realized by them. For when similar reforms came to be demanded by nationalist leaders in the present century, the British resisted these stubbornly.

In the middle of the nineteenth century ancient texts were quoted in favour of the abolition of polygamy, which prevailed among the kulīn brāhmaṇas of Bengal. The Association of Friends submitted to the Legislative Council a petition, in which it quoted verses from the ninth chapter of the law-book of Manu to explain the conditions under which a husband could have a second wife.[12] If the wife suffered from barrenness, adultery, garrulousness, and gave birth to only female children, etc., she could be superseded by another wife. The petitioners further showed on the basis of Yājñavalkya that if the wife was obedient, skilful in business, produced male children, remained loyal to her husband. etc., the husband had no right whatsoever to separate from her and take another wife.[13] They contended that the kulīn brāhmmaṇs were having more than one wife in violation of these instructions of the Dharmaśāstra, which they should not be allowed to do by law.[14]

The reformers further prayed that children born of polygamy should be considered illegitimate and should not be entitled to any share in property.[15] In the opinion of a contemporary paper all this was done by educated natives who did not command adequate influence in their community to effect the necessary reform and therefore resorted to those extraordinary measures.[16] On the other hand this alerted the orthodox Hindus who formed associations to thwart the movement for reforms. Awareness of the ancient texts caused some awakening among the high-caste Hindus, but despite their quotations from the ancient law-books and their argument that the original kulinism permitted marriage only within certain circles, the reformers did not succeed in abolishing polygamy by law.

The efforts of reformers met more success in their movement for the introduction of widow remarriage, in which the value of ancient texts were better propagated. It was Iswarchandra Vidyasagar who first ransacked the Smṛti literature to be able to establish that marriage of widows was sanctioned by the Śāstras.[17] The champions of the reform gave publicity to the text of Parāśara that a woman can take a second husband when her first husband is dead, destroyed, is impotent, has become an ascetic, or has fallen from the duties of his varṇa.[18] This was countered by the orthodox pandits on the ground that the text of Parāśara did not enjoy any authority in ancient times. In a way they were right, for the law-book of Parāśara, which was comparatively liberal, was finally compiled in about the eighth century AD and hence did not command much prestige before Gupta times. The crucial passage occurs only in Nārada and some later Purāṇas such as the *Agni* and the *Garuḍa*.[19]

Connected with the legislation of widow remarriage was the problem of the legal recognition of sons born of such marriages, so that they might inherit the property of their father. It was possible to produce texts in support of such sons as are known *paunarbhava* in the Dharmaśāstras but difficult to prove that they were entitled to a share in property like the sons born of regular marriage. Since the lower caste people did not possess much property worth the name they could afford the luxury of widow remarriage, but not the higher caste people in whose case it would create real complications. In fact this was one of the main reasons why certain high-caste Hindus opposed the reform strongly.

Thus the struggle for social reforms was a vital factor in the study of ancient texts. It consisted of a series of battles of precedents, which reminds us of the constitutional conflict between the King and the Parliament in the Stuart period. Each side tried to build its case on the past precedents, which were called to the aid of the present controversies.

It is not without significance that the leading advocates of reforms in the nineteenth century were without exception great scholars of Sanskrit College, Calcutta. This was true of Raja Rammohan Roy, but more so of Ishwarchandra Vidyasagar, who was principal of Sanskrit College, Calcutta. Swami Dayananda was a profound scholar of Vedic Sanskrit and based all his arguments for reform on the ancient Vedic texts. Similarly R.G. Bhandarkar, who was an active member of the All-India Social Conference was a renowned scholar of classical texts. His *First and Second Book*(s) *of Sanskrit* are the earliest textbooks prepared by an Indian for learning Sanskrit through the medium of English. Of these reformers Vidyasagar and Bhandarkar were primarily scholars, but they were deeply conscious of their social role and played an important part in the social movements of their times. Except Dayananda all these personalities lived in contact with the British in some way or the other. In fact it was not the study of ancient texts which originated modern reforms but the need for modern reforms that led to the study of ancient texts, which in its turn gave the reformers the tongue to speak to their people. Therefore although the primary impulse for reforms came from contact with the modern way of life, only a resurrection of what the reformers considered to be ancient values facilitated the course of the reforms.

Why the reformers harped on ancient texts is difficult to explain. When they tailored the texts to suit their ideas they continued the old tradition of adjusting them to the changing social conditions. They did not justify reforms on grounds of reason and utility because they did not find the mental climate receptive. Without any appreciable progress in science and industrialization, the country did not provide the requisite material conditions in which rationalist ideas could fructify. That the reformers talked about the texts to the credulous Hindu masses is understandable, but why they approached the British administrators on the same lines is not easy to appreciate. In any case they appear to be consistent in their arguments.

A detailed examination of the arguments adduced in support of social reforms in the nineteenth century might expose the unhistorical interpretations to which the ancient texts were subjected by the interested parties. But convincing the British rulers and changing the Indian mentality which obviously meant the opinion of the high-caste, kulīn, landed Hindus or of their members educated through the medium of English—ancient values played a great part. The procedure also set the pattern for preparing the case for fundamental changes in the social structure in subsequent times. The same line of argument was refurnished to buttress economic and political reforms in the twentieth century. Those who demanded the abolition of the Permanent Settlement pointed to the absence of landed intermediaries in the past, and those who fought for a better political order pointed to the presence of constitutional monarchy, republics and above all Ram Raj in the past.

In the seventies Swami Dayanand, the founder of the Ārya Samāj, brought out a collection of original Sanskrit texts called the *Satyārtha-prakāśa* to support widow remarriage, rejection of caste based on birth,[20] and the śūdras' right to Vedic education.[21] We do not know how far the early social reformers drew inspiration from the contemporary works of Muir,[22] who tried to prove that the belief in the origin of the four varṇas from the primeval man did not exist in ancient times,[23] and from those of Weber, who presented the first important critical study of the caste system on the basis of the Brāhmaṇas and the Sūtras.[24] In the eighties of the same century R.C. Dutt in his work *Civilization in Ancient India*, which enjoyed great influence and popularity,[25] carried forward the reformist approach to the study of ancient Indian society. While pointing out that modern Hindus lose sight of the spirit of the ancient faith, he regrets that the use of spirituous liquor and even crimes do not involve loss of caste in modern times, but penalties are reserved for widow marriage, intercaste marriage, social intercourse among people descended from the same vaiśya rank, and for voyages and foreign travel. He emphasizes[26] that in ancient times caste never divided and disunited the Āryan people, but rallied them as one man against the aborigines.[27] He regrets that in the course of time caste should have degraded the vaiśyas to the rank of the śūdras.[28] The writer boasts that no ancient nation held their women in such a high honour as the Hindus did. He complains that the Hindus have been misjudged and wronged by writers unacquainted with their literature. These writers used notions of the women of the East from Turkish and Arab customs.[29] Writing about a decade earlier (1867) than R.C. Dutt, a French woman writer, who wants her work to serve as a guide to the British in regenerating the conquered through the application of the practical spirit of Christianity, impresses upon the Indians the high position of women in ancient times in order that they may emulate the great characters and sublime actions as depicted in the epics.[30]

On the occasion of the introduction of the Age of Consent Bill in 1891, Sir R.G. Bhandarkar brought out a well-documented pamphlet citing Sanskrit texts to establish that a girl should be married only when she attains maturity. On the other hand B.G. Tilak, to whom any stick was good enough to beat the alien rulers, cited texts against this Bill.[31]

This tendency to quote ancient scriptures in support of modern reforms can be well summed up in the words of R.G. Bhandarkar (1895): 'In ancient times girls were married after they had attained maturity, now they must be married before; widow marriage was then in practice, now it has entirely gone out . . . Interdining among the castes was not prohibited, now the numberless castes cannot have intercommunications of that nature.'[32]

But the attempt of Indian scholars to present their early social institutions in a form more acceptable to the modern mind did not always commend itself to western writers. Thus Sénart (1896) pointed out that the castes have been compared by Hindus of English upbringing with the social distinctions that exist among Europeans, but that they correspond only very remotely to western social classes.[33] Similarly Hopkins (1881) stated that the position of the śūdra was not different from that of the American house slave before 1860.[34] Reviewing Hopkins' generalizations, Hillebrandt (1896) held that the position of the śūdras should be judged in comparison with the slaves of the ancient world and not in the context of development in later times.[35]

Criticizing Hopkins, Ketkar (1911) complains that European writers are influenced by their ideas of racial discrimination against the Negroes, and hence unduly exaggerate this in their treatment of the caste system.[36] Ambedkar (1917) also points on that, impregnated by colour prejudices, the European scholars have unduly emphasized the role of colour in the caste system.[37] There seems to be some force in this argument, for Risley (1908) stated that the conquering Āryans behaved towards the conquered Dravidians in the same way as some planters in America behaved towards the African slaves whom they imported.[38] Keith was of the opinion that the Āryan contact with the aborigines raised questions of purity of blood very like those which at present agitate the Southern States of the U.S.A. or the whole of the white people in South Africa.[39]

Risley advanced the view that in India races were transformed into castes, that the process of racial fusion was arrested long ago and that therefore no national type could develop as in Europe,[40] deducing therefrom that there were no prospects of the rise of nationalism in India.[41] This view was challenged in articles such as 'Varṇāśrama Dharma and Race Fusion in Ancient India' (1917).[42] 'Intercaste Marriage in Buddhist India' (1919),[43] 'Foreign Elements in the Hindu Population,'[44] which were written to demonstrate the assimilative character and resilience of ancient Indian society. Attempts were made to prove that Indian society had attained a large measure of ethnic–cultural unity,[45] which could form the basis of further national development.

But generally the reformist and nationalist school has derived support from the works of western writers, who evaluate ancient Indian society in a manner different from that in which they judge ancient Indian polity. They point out that oriental despotism was the chief characteristic of the political life of ancient India, a generalization which could very well justify the continuity of British rule. But on the whole they present ancient Indian society in a favourable light, which could naturally provide the basis for several social reforms, rendered necessary owing to the needs of administration introduced by the British during the nineteenth century. Apart from the belief in the community of race and language between the Indo-Āryans and Europeans, the idealization of ancient Indian society was due to the anti-Mohammadan attitude of the British, which is evident in some writings of the eighteenth and nineteenth centuries.[46] To this was added the admiration for primitive forms of society which is noticeable in eighteenth-century writers such as Rousseau.[47] Although after 1857, and especially from about the end of the nineteenth century, many members of the administration stressed divisions of caste, race, language, etc., as a shield against the growing nationalist demands,[48] this attitude appeared only in the Census Reports and very little affected western writings on ancient Indian society, which followed the old tradition.

The main trend noticeable in the works of recent Indian writers such as Ketkar, Dutt, and Ghurye is to present the caste system in such a way as may help to recast it in response to present requirements.[49] Works on the position of women in ancient India display the same tendency. In his work D.N. Mitter attempts to refute the generally accepted doctrine of the perpetual tutelage of women in Hindu Law.[50] A.S. Altekar indicates the general lines on which the various problems of Hindu women should be tackled in order to get a fairly satisfactory solution.[51] In a recent work it is argued that the scheme of *āśramas* was designed to give wide scope to individuals in the choice of a vocation in life which was best suited to their intellectual capacity and mental inclinations.[52] This is obviously projecting the modern idea of individualism on to ancient society, for, in fact, generally the varṇa system gave hardly any option to the individual to choose his occupation, and, as to the *āśramas*, the śūdra was entitled only to the life of a householder.

Thus it would appear that problems of ancient Indian society have been largely studied, especially by Indians, against the background of the necessity for social reform. The dominant motives of reform and nationalism have undoubtedly produced valuable works on India's early social life. They helped to establish that the four varṇas existed as social classes in the Vedic period and that *jātis* and caste restrictions developed in the period of the Dharmaśāstras. It was recognized that large numbers of foreign and tribal peoples were absorbed into brāhmaṇical society. It also came to be accepted that widow marriage and *niyoga* prevailed in earlier times when the practices of child marriage and satī were absent.

But what appeared to be seamy and ugly in comparison with modern standards came to be either ignored or explained away unconvincingly. For instance, it was argued that the disabilities of the śūdras did not reduce their happiness or wellbeing.[53] In justification of child marriage in the later period it came to be urged that this practice helps a girl to know whom she has to love, before any sexual consciousness has awakened in her.[54] Similarly, the permanent dependence of woman came to he justified by arguing that she would make herself ridiculous by claiming an identity of temperament and functions with man.[55] Again, since the need for such reforms as the abolition of satī, widow marriage, divorce, etc., was most pressing in the case of the members of the upper varṇas, due attention could not he paid to the nature of the social practices of the lower orders. Furthermore, the reformists found it difficult to explain and interpret the contradictory statements in the Dharmaśāstras, which constitute our main source for the social history of ancient India. They picked out and focused light on the passages which supported their case without bothering to determine the dominant features of society in different periods and regions.

The tendency to concentrate on favourable aspects of early social life accounts for the almost complete absence of works on the position of the śūdras in ancient India. Even European writers gave their attention mainly to the study of the upper classes of Hindu society. Thus Muir devoted 188 pages to the legends of struggles between brāhmaṇas and kṣatriyas.[56] Hopkins (1889) presented a comprehensive study of the 'Position of Ruling Caste in Ancient India'.[57] The admirable work of Fick (1897) on the social organization of northeastern India also mainly confined itself to the treatment of kṣatriyas, brāhmaṇas, and *gahapatis* or *seṭṭhis*. It is difficult to explain these writers' lack of interest in the fortunes of the lower orders unless we suppose that their vision was circumscribed by the dominant class outlooks both of their own age and of the age they studied. The only monograph on the śūdras so far published is by a well-known Indian politician, who confines himself to the question of their origin.[58] The author is entirely dependent for his source-material on translations,[59] and moreover, he seems to have worked with the fixed purpose of proving a high origin for the śūdras—a tendency which has been very much in evidence among the educated sections of lower caste people in recent times. A single passage of the *Śānti Parvan*, which states that the śūdra Paijavana performed sacrifice, is sufficient to establish the thesis that śūdras were originally kṣatriyas.[60] The author does not care to analyse the complex of various circumstances which led to the formation of the labouring class known as the śūdras.

Similarly our knowledge of the untouchables has not advanced much beyond what we learn from the school textbooks, quoting from Fahsien and Hsüan Tsang. The work on this subject by one of the present leaders of this class advances the ingenious theory that the roots of untouchability lay in the contempt for Buddhism and in the practice of beef-eating.[61] Further, the few articles on slavery do not improve much upon the findings of Rhys Davids on that subject. A work on the origin, growth, nature, and extent of slavery in ancient India still remains a desideratum.[62] Again, although it is argued that the disabilities and privileges of the varṇas should be looked upon with the greatest suspicion, no serious attempt has been made to inquire into the nature of economic and politico-legal relations into which members of the various varṇas enter with one another. Generalizations such as 'caste did not cause poverty and did not divide the city into two parts like the East End and West End of London'[63] or 'in ancient India there was no concentration of the prestige of birth, influence of wealth and political office which imparts an aristocratic tinge to social organization and sustains aristocratic government'[64] need a careful examination. Because of their reforming outlook the writers have not bothered themselves about unpleasant questions such as the repeated joint notices of woman and śūdras or of woman and property in ancient Indian literature. Such an attitude has also prevented an investigation into the traces of promiscuity, matriarchy, and the position of prostitutes in ancient India,[65] which may have also been the result of a disinclination to consider the theory almost universally held by nineteenth-century anthropologists, and still maintained by many, that marriage developed by way of hetaerism and matriarchate.[66] A pioneer attempt was made to examine such questions by S.C. Sarkar in his work *Some Aspects of the Earliest Social History of India*,[67] but that line of research has not been pursued further.

The study of the lower orders in ancient India has not only been ignored, but, strange as it may seem, in some cases they appear to have been held in the same contempt by modern writers as they were held by the members of the upper varṇas in ancient times. It is stated that child marriage originated among the lower classes, whereas the Dharmaśāstra rules leave no doubt that it first began among the three upper varṇas.[68] It is said that women held a higher position among the upper classes, whereas the opposite seems to have been the case. The climax is reached when on the basis of his study of ancient Indian society a writer prescribes sexual self-control and abstinence for the 'Brāhmaṇ' and the use of contraceptives for people of the lowest varṇa.[69]

Most available works neither identify nor explain the chief phases of social evolution. Jolly's *Hindu Law and Custom*,[70] which is a textbook in many Indian universities, presents a good analysis of family life and the position of woman in Hindu society, but it does not present an integrated picture. Although the author discusses the dates of his sources, he fails to introduce this historical perspective in the treatment of his subject, with the result that we get very little idea of changes in the social order.[71] The only distinction made in such books is the one between Vedic and post-Vedic periods. Thanks to the pioneer labours of Europeans, especially German Indologists, the basic facts about the social organization during the Vedic period are fairly well established. Indians have not progressed much in this field. Their main concern has been to establish that oil was good in the Vedic period and that degeneration set in post-Vedic times. The treatment of society in the *Cambridge History of India*, vol. 1, is not done chronologically but literature-wise so that the total picture of society in a particular phase is lacking. By now the material bearing on social aspects in the Pāli texts has been examined by Fick, Rhys Davids and R.N. Mehta, in the Jain texts by J.C. Jain and B.C. Law in the epics by Hopkins and Meyer, and in the Dharmaśāstras by Jolly, Jayaswal, Kane, R.C. Hazra and other scholars, but a complete sketch of the social structure on the basis of these sources is not to be found anywhere. The first important attempt of this kind has been made in the Bhāratīya Vidyā Bhavan series on *The History and Culture of the Indian People*, but it has suffered for three reasons. First, the Dharmasūtras and Gṛhyasūtras, which are definitely works of post-Vedic times, are included in the Vedic period. Secondly, writers have failed to distinguish between the didactic and narrative portions of the epics. And thirdly, since the sections on society have been done by several hands,[72] there is not much idea of development in the treatment of the theme. Probably the main reason for not stressing the process of social development has been the very widely held belief in the conservative and unchanging character of the Indian people.[73] Like the Chinese and the Egyptians, the Indians are believed to be an unchanging people.[74] Even those who subscribe to the materialist interpretation of history have paid very little attention to the fact of social development because of the basic formulation of Karl Marx about the unchanging character of Asian society before the advent of the Industrial Revolution. It is true that in the pre-Industrial period, unlike changes in dynasty, social changes could not have been rapid, but it would be wrong to proceed on the axiom that they were entirely absent.

Interest in the study of the ancient Indian social order in Europe and India has also been stimulated by a sense of revolt against the over-materialistic life which has been seen as the result of the progress of science and the Industrial Revolution. The old family life is being shattered and the bonds of the former control of man over woman are being loosened. Perhaps in order to restore the balance the old Indian ideal is invoked. In her book *Women in Ancient India* (1867), a French writer feels the necessity of refreshing 'ourselves' (that is, Europeans) from more life-giving and generous sources from India where society has a sense of duty dominating all affections, and a feeling of respect for family life, all presenting a nearly Christian atmosphere.[75] She points out that the moral elevation of the Greeks was much below that of the Indians.[76] To quote the author, 'in what century, in what country, in what literature, could there be found a more admirable type than that of Sītā?'[77] Similar ideas are repeated by the German Indologist Meyer in 1915.[78] In his opinion no literature could provide more lovely songs of the faithful wife's love for her husband than the poem of Damayantī and that of Sāvitrī.[79] He further states that as regards woman the old Indian books display a deeply ethical spirit, a wholesomeness in contrast to the often empty frivolity—the nauseating filthiness and vulgarity—that marks most of the literature of the Middle Ages, old and modern French literature, and even many highly praised later and latest German writings.[80] Naturally the belief in progress does not make any sense to Meyer.[81] He feels the necessity of 'feeding on the marvellous works of the Buddha, Jesus, etc.'[82] The tendency to prescribe precepts and practices of ancient Indian society as a panacea for the social evils of the West reaches its culmination in a work *Dharma and Society* by a minor Dutch Indologist G.H. Mees, published forty-seven years ago. The writer holds that the ideal of the varṇa system is of universal and permanent value and can be applied to all kinds of societies irrespective of time and place. He thinks that the varṇa ideal was a natural and organic hierarchy, which degenerated when artificial distinctions began to be made in the form of the caste system.[83] Scared by the exaltation of Labour and its desire to climb higher in the hierarchy of power,[84] he thinks that only the sense of varṇa (that is, natural hierarchy) can unite people, who are divided by class-consciousness, into a whole.[85] Therefore he recommends that the West should benefit by realizing the fundamental composition of human society as developed in India.[86] He also seems to have some leaning towards Fascism and National-Socialism, which, in his opinion, are movements of the ruling varṇa to make an end of 'mixture of varṇas' in matters of government, for according to the theory of varṇa, classes corresponding to lower varṇas should have no legislative powers and should not criticize the government policy.[87]

The views of Mees have been treated in some detail because they also find favour with some Indian writers, who glorify the old system of family and varṇa to stem the tide of social change. Thus the specious argument of equality in spiritual rights, irrespective of sex and caste considerations, is advanced to meet the demand for equality in material rights.[88] Some writers believe in certain intrinsic virtues of the old Hindu theory and conception of human life and organization,[89] which they boldly recommend for adoption by the whole world. Prabhu's work (a textbook in several Indian universities), which emphasizes such virtues and justifies varṇa on fundamental principles of ethics and psychology, has been criticized by P.V. Kane, a person of moderate views,[90] as a disappointing work from the practical point of view. K.V. Rangaswami Aiyangar seems to have made a study of the social structure as known from the Dharmaśāstras, and especially from Manu, in order to present the varṇa system as a shield against all equalizing tendencies let loose by modern industrial society. He looks back with horror upon the idea of 'a classless, sexless (?), equalitarian society, a "secular democracy" sustained and guided by frequent plebiscites of the proletarians'.[91] He sets forth the purpose of his books on the social and political aspects of Manu in these words:

If the Hindu scheme of life 'has no other value except as exposing the unstable foundations of many modern social and political beliefs—such as the equality of the sexes, the equal rights of men, and of equal weight to everyone in society; or the value of only a materialistic view of life and life's problems; of the superiority of environment of heredity; of the exclusively material basis of social betterment; of the belief that the proper standard for remuneration is material productive capacity, etc.—it will have served its purpose.'[92]

It is difficult to pass judgement on the merits of such books. The dominant motives of reform have produced valuable works, but probably the object of defending the social *status quo* has not made any significant addition to our knowledge of the early history of India's social structure; such books are too deeply saturated with prejudices.

An important point for consideration is an inquiry into the nature of the forces which, according to all these writers, influence social developments in ancient India. This can be best illustrated by examining their perception of the causes of the origin and growth of caste. Racial and occupational factors are ascribed to explain the origin of the castes, but this is also attributed to the 'essentially particularist instinct of the Indian people.'[93] It is suggested that the brāhmaṇas first extended the principle of exclusiveness to the śūdras and then to all the other varṇas, and this led to the growth of the caste system.[94] The *ultimate basis* of the caste system has been traced to two doctrines:[95] (i) the doctrine of the religious unity of the family, and (ii) the doctrine of the *svakarma* which lays on every man the obligation to do his duty in that state of life in which he is born,[96] suggesting thereby that these doctrines arose first and the caste system came next. It is significant that a common reason assigned for the origin of the caste system by both European and Indian writers such as Fick, Sṉart, Risley, Ghurye, etc., has been the Indian predilection for symmetry and their love for classification.[97] But they hardly indicate the premises from which they have drawn such an important deduction. Risley enumerates the pecularities of the Indian intellect which have promoted the growth of the caste system. These according to him are: 'its (i.e. the Indian intellect's)[98] lax hold of facts, its indifference to action, ts absorption in dreams, its exaggerated reverence for tradition, its passion for endless division and sub-division, its acute sense of minute technical distinctions, its pedantic tendency to press a principle to its farthest logical conclusion and its remarkable capacity for imitating and adapting social ideas and usages of whatever origin.'[99] Risley thinks that a superstructure of fiction has specially contributed to the growth of the caste instinct,[100] for, in his opinion, fictions of *I* various kinds have contributed largely to the development of early societies in all parts of the world.[101] Similarly, discussing the decay of social organization in India an Indian writer ascribes this decline not so much to external opposition or to any inherent weakness in the ideal but to a falling off from the ideal itself.[102] Thus it would appear that ideas and ideals are represented as playing an important part in the origin, development and decay of social organization.

Many writers believe that religious ideas have moulded the social history of India. Jolly holds that in India, as in other oriental countries, the law *(vyavahāra)* is an integral part of religion and ethics.[103] Winternitz points out that the structure of society is influenced through religious ideas, which are nowhere so deep in the life of the people, especially in the life of women, as in India.[104] This he derives from a general theory that the entire cultural development of mankind is shaped to an immense degree by religion.[105] In the case of India such a belief is also shared by Fick, who considers religious differences as an important cause of the origin of the caste. Indian writers also look upon religious injunctions as one of the reasons of the growth of the caste system. Thus there is a fundamental presupposition that ideas and ideals, particularly religious have played a vital part in shaping the course of social developments in ancient India. This discussion can be closed with the statement of an eminent scholar of ancient Indian civilization that the harmony of the three pursuits of life was the ideal which formed the background of social life in ancient India.[106]

As against the idealist conception applied to the study of ancient Indian social structure, its study, in recent times has been taken up by some writers who seem to have been influenced by the materialist conception of history. A.N. Bose,[107] S.A. Dange,[108] B.N. Dutt,[109] G.F. Ilyin,[110] D.D. Kosambi,[111] and Walter Ruben[112] may be placed in this group. In spite of their sharing a common outlook these writers not only differ on the dating of literary sources, such as the *Arthaśāstra* of Kauṭilya and the Jātakas, but they also differ fundamentally on several other questions. While some hold that ancient Indian society was a 'slave society', others argue that this is not true in the same sense as in the case of the other ancient societies. Again, while some argue that varṇa corresponds to the Marxian conception of economic class, others think that economic considerations cut across the hereditary social varṇas. But, excepting some articles by Kosambi, so far very little attention has been paid to the mode of production in ancient India, which, in the materialist view, determines the relations of production—economic, social, and political, Although some works by these writers appeared sufficiently early, it is significant that none has been mentioned in the bibliographies appended to the volumes on *The History and Culture of the Indian People* published by the Bhāritīya Vidyā Bhavan. It may be too much to assert that historical materialism can provide the only scientific approach to the investigation of the ancient Indian social structure, but its possibilities are still to be explored, and hence in any future study of ancient Indian society such a line of inquiry cannot be ignored.[113]

NOTES

1. Stated by J.H. Hutton, *Caste in India*, see ed. (Bombay: Oxford University Press, 1951), p. ix. This seems to be the work on W.H. Gilbert, *Caste in India*, cyclostyled copy (Washington, 1948). I have been able to see only Pt. I of this work which contains 1,970 entries.
2. London, 1976.
3. *Vivādārṇavasetu*, trans. into English by N B. Halhed, translator's preface, p. ix. This work was translated from English into German in 1778.
4. *Institutes of Hindu Law*, preface, p. xix. cf. Discourse of Colebrooke in the first general meeting of *RAS* (15 March 1823), *Essays* (London, 1823), I, 1–2.
5. *Essays*, II, pp. 157–70.
6. Ibid., 157.
7. James Mill, *The History of India* (London, 1820), II, 166–9, 169, fn. 1. It seems that Mill's generalizations about the history of India exercised the most dominant influence on later British historians.
8. *The History of India* (London, 1841), I, 34.
9. Ibid., 107.
10. R.G. Bhandarkar, *Collectd Works*, II, 513.
11. *The English Works of Rammohan Roy* (Calcutta, 1901), introduction, xviii, ii, 123–92.
12. *Intelligenster*, 16 July 1855.
13. Ibid.
14. Ibid.
15. *Eastern Star*, 8 December 1855.
16. Ibid.
17. Isvarchandra Vidyasagar, *Marriage of Hindu Widows*, reprint of the English version of two pamphlets written in Bengali in 1855, Calcutta, 1976. Around 1855, reprints of the first pamphlet reached a second number of 15,000 copies, ibid., pix.
18. IV, 30

19. 107. 28.
20. *Śatyārtha-prakāśa* (Ajmer, Samvat 1966), fourth *samullāsa*, 83–92, 113–22.
21. Ibid., third *samullāsa*, 39, 73–4.
22. John Muir, ed., *Original Sanskrit Texts* (London, 1872–4), I.
23. Ibid., 159–60.
24. *Indische Studien*, hrsg. Albrecht Weber, X, 1868, 1–160.
25. *A History of Civilization in Ancient India, based on Sanskrit Literature*, 4 vols (Calcutta, 1889–90). The first edition of 1,000 copies of the first two vols was out in 1890, and the work was translated into the vernaculars of Bombay, Madras, and the North Western Provinces (roughly modern U.P.). Another work of Dutt was adopted as a textbook in many schools in Bengal.
26. Ibid., II, 103.
27. Ibid., I, 240.
28. Ibid., 240–1.
29. Ibid., 256–7.
30. C. Bader, *The Woman in Ancient India* (London, 1930), 333–4.
31. R.G. Bhandarkar, *Collected Works*, II, 538–83. Also see Bhandarkar's criticism of Jolly's article on the 'History of Child Marriage' in *Collected Works*.
32. Ibid., II, 522–3
33. E. Sénart, *Caste in India* (London, 1930), 12–13.
34. E.W. Hopkins, *Mutual Relations of the Four Castes in Manu* (Leipzig, 1881), 102.
35. A. Hillebrandt, 'Brāhamaṇen and Śūdras', *Festschrift fur Karl Weinhold* (Breslau, 1896), 57.
36. S.V. Ketkār, *History of Caste in India*, 2 vols (New York, 1909; London, 1911), I, 9, 78, fn. 3.
37. *Indian Antiquary*, XLVI, 1917, 94.
38. H.H. Risley, *The People of India* (London, 1915), 275.
39. *Cambridge History of India*, I, 125.
40. H.H. Risley, op. cit., 5, 26.
41. Ibid., 293.
42. B.K. Sarkar, *Modern Review*, 1917, 211 ff.
43. R.P. Chandra, *Modern Review,* 1919, 595 ff.
44. D.R. Bhandarkar, *Indian Antiquary,* XL, 1911, 7 ff.
45. B.N. Dutt, *Studies in Indian Social Polity* (Calcutta, 1944).
46. J.Z. Holwell, *Interesting Historical Events Relative to the Provinces of Bengal and the Empire of Hindostan* (London, 1765–71), I, 5; 111, 13.
47. Holweil states that 'the primitive Hindoos . . . subsisted far a long series, of ages in holiness, peace, tranquillity and happiness', ibid., III, 218.
48. Several such statements are quoted in P.L. Narsu, *The Essence of Buddhism* (Madras, 1912), 154, and by G.S. Ghurye, *Caste and Class in India* (Bombay, 1950), 176–7.

49. Ketkar, op. cit., p. 9; Radhakrishnan's foreword to P.H. Prabhu's *Hindu Social Institutions* (London, 1939). The works of Dutt and Ghurye display a better historical sense, but see Dutt, op. cit., preface, xvi.
50. *The Position of Women in Hindu Law* (Calcutta, 1912), preface, *a*.
51. *The Position of Women in Hindu Civilization* (Banaras, 1938), preface, i.
52. R.C. Majumdar, ed., *The Age of Imperial Unity* (Bombay, 1951), 553.
53. On the basis of the *Śukranītī-sāra*, B.K. Sarkar, *Hindu Sociology Allahabad,* 1920), 92–5, cf. K.V. Rangaswami Aiyangar, *Indian Cameralism* (Madras, 1949), 85.
54. Ketkar, op. cit., 32–3.
55. H.C. Chakladar, 'Social Life in Ancient India', *The Cultural Heritage of India*, issued by Sri Ramakrishna Birth Centenary Publication Committee (Calcutta, 1937), III, 204.
56. Op. cit , I, chap. IV.
57 *Journal of the American Oriental Society*, 1889, XIII, 7–376.
58 B.R. Ambedkar, *Who were the Shudras?* (Bombay, 1946).
59. Ibid., preface, p. iv.
60. In recent caste movements many śūdra castes claim to be kṣatriyas and even brāhmaṇas. Thus the Dusādhas claim to be the descendants of Duḥśāsaṇa, and the Goālās those of the Yadus. The process, noted in Census Reports, is now called Sanskritisation, although many caste leaders do not know Sanskrit.
61. B.R. Ambedkar, *The Untouchables* (New Delhi, 1948), chap. IV.
62. D.R. Chanana's *Slavery in Ancient India* (New Delhi, 1960) is a valuable contribution, but it is based mainly on the Pāli texts.
63. S.K. Das, *The Economic History of Ancient India* (Calcutta, 1914), 185.
64. Majumdar, op. cit., 311; Beni Prasad, *The State in Ancient India* (Allahabad, 1928), 7–8.
65. J.J. Meyer, however, devotes chapter IX to this subject. *Sexual Life in Ancient India* (London, 1952).
66. Ibid., 398.
67. London, 1928.
68. *Viṣṇu Smṛti*, *SBE*, VII, xxiv, 41 (with fn. on 41). The commentator seems no have projected later ideas in the explanation of this passage.
69. G.H. Mees, *Dharma and Society* (The Hague, 1935), 189–90.
70. Calcutta, 1928 (trans. from the German ed. of 1896).
71. Jolly had reserved the treatment of classes and castes for his work, *State Antiquities*, but it was never published.
72. Y.M. Apte, R.K. Mookerji, R.C. Majumdar, and U.N. Ghoshal.
73. Majumdar, op. cit., III, 14.
74. Cf. E.J. Rapson, *Cambridge History of India*, I, 53–4.
75. Bader, op. cit., preface, viii–ix.
76. Op. cit., 223.
77. Op. cit., 222.
78. Op. cit., 215, 340.

79. Op. cit., 215.
80. Ibid., 5.
81. *Das Weib im altindischen Epos* (Leipzig, 1915), viii.
82. Ibid.
83. *Dharma and Society* (The Hague, London, 1935), 142.
84. Ibid., 180.
85. Ibid., 149.
86. Ibid., preface, xv.
87. Ibid., p. 188.
88. Chakladar, op. cit., 203–4.
89. P.H. Prabhu, *Hindu Social Institutions* (3rd ed., Bombay, 1948), 336; cf. 344; Chakladar, op. cit., III, 170.
90. Kane does not consider it feasible to destroy the whole edifice of the caste system in the near future, *History of the Dharmaśāstra* (Poona, 1930), II, part I, 22.
91. *Some Aspects of the Hindu View of Life According to time Dharmaśāstra* (Baroda, 1932), II.
92. *Aspects of the Social and Political System of Manusmṛti* (Luckow, 1949), 197–8.
93. Risley, op. cit., p. 79.
94. R.C. Majuindar, *Corporate Life in Ancient India* (Calcutta, 1922), 350.
95. 'Italics mine.
96. Rapson, op. cit., I, 54.
97. R. Fick, *Social Organization in North-East India* (Calcutta, 1920), 282; Ghurye, op. cit., 159; Majumdar, op. cit., 385.
98. Bracketed portion mine.
99. 'Risley, op. cit., 275–6.
100. Ibid., 273.
101. Ibid., 275.
102. Chakladar, op. cit., 208.
103. *Hindu Law and Custom,* 1.
104. *Die Frau im Brahmanismus* (Leipzig, 1920), 2; of 121.
105. '. . . die ganze Kulturentwicklung der Menschheit in ungeheuren Masse "on der Religion beeinflusst worden ist.' ibid., 1.
106. R.C. Majumdar, *The Age of Imperial Unity*, p. 581.
107. *Social and Rural Economy of Northern India,* 2 vols (Calcutta, 1942–5).
108. *India from Primitive Communism to Slavery* (Bombay, 1949). The book shows more schematicism than scholarship, but it has run into a third edition in a short time and has been translated into several languages.
109. *Studies in Indian Social Polity* (Calcutta, 1944).
110. Śūdras und Sklaven in den altindischen Gesetzbuchern' in *Sowletwissenschaft*, 1952, no. 2, trans. from *Vestnik drevnei istorii*, 1951, no. 2, 94–107; 'Osobennosti Rabstva v drevnei Indii', *Vestnik drevnei istorii*, 1951, no. 1, 33–52.

111. Articles in *Journal of the Bombay Branch, Royal Asiatic Society* and *Journal of the American Oriental Society; An Introduction to the Study of Indian History* (Bombay, 1956). His book, *The Culture and Civilization of Ancient India in Historical Outline* (London, 1965) became more popular. During the last twenty years since 1960 or so Kosambi, who died in 1966, has turned out to be the most influential historian of early Indian society and economy. Perhaps no other writer of the subject has been quoted, criticized and followed up so widely as he has been. Three memorial volumes issued from different places have been dedicated to him. The first to appear was R.S. Sharma in collaboration with V.N. Jha ed., *Indian Society: Historical Probing:*, New Delhi, 1974; its second edition came out in 1977. For various assessments of Kosambi's historiography see D.N. Jha, "A Marxist View of Ancient Indian History,' *Das Capital Centenary Volume,* ed. Mohit Sen & M.B. Rao, New Delhi, 1968, 166–80; Romila Thapar, 'The Contribution of D.D. Kosambi to Indology', *The Journal of the Asiatic Society of Bombay,* 52–3, 1977.78 (New Series), 365–84.
112. *Einfuhrung In die Indlenkunde* (Berlin, 1954).
113. This suggestion was made in 1956, but appeared in print in 1961. During the last 20 years or so some serious investigation has been carried on these lines. Suvira Jaiswal's 'Studies in Early Indian Social History Trends and Possibilities', published in *The Indian Historical Review,* VI, 1979–80, 1–63, devotes more than half of its nearly 40,000 words to the survey of works on social history published during the last 25 years. R.S. Sharma and D.N. Jha, 'The Economic History of India up to AD 1200: Trends and Prospects,' *Journal of the Economic and Social History of the Orient,* XVII, 1974, 48–80, touches on this problem to some extent.

8

Light on Satī System*

The Satī system seems to be a peculiar Indian practice. How it originated is difficult to explain. It is the product of a strong patriarchal society. Ancient people practised both matriarchy and patriarchy. Thus in ancient Egypt the throne went always to the daughter and not to the son of the Egyptian king called Pharaoh. But, the earliest Aryans practised both polyandry and polygamy. This can be said on the basis of the remnants of Aryan tribal practices recently reported from Ladakh in north Kashmir. In 1870 an Indo-Aryan tribe which settled in the Ladakh valley was identified. Its people numbered 2500 and lived in three small villages of Ladakh. They were called Dards or Brogpas. The Darda is mentioned in the *Mahābhārata.* The tribals took to both premarital and extra-marital sexual relations. They practised both polyandry and polygamy. The first suggests importance of female and the second that of male. But under pressure from modern contacts and reactions they gave up polyandry and took to polygamy. They kissed one another openly in public, but this was also given up under modern pressure. However, it is not indicated in the research reports whether they were buried or cremated after death. The satī system is connected with the cremation of the wife with the dead husband. It indicates so much of patriarchal dominance that the wife was compelled to accompany her husband even after his death.

It is suggested by K.M Shrimali that the satī system appeared in the age of Gautama Buddha. This may have happened because both polyandry and satī practices find place in the *Mahābhārata.* Till recent times polyandry was practised by an Aryan tribe in Ladakh in Kashmir. We

*Previously published as, 'Historical Aspects of Satī' in R.S. Sharma, *Perspectives in Social and Economic History of Early India* (New Delhi: Munshiram Manoharlal Publishers, 1995).

have referred to this at some places in this work. Further the brāhmaṇical law books create conditions for the satī system. Compiled from the fifth century BC they do not grant property rights to women. This creates the problem of feeding the wife after the death of their husband. Since the practice of cremation was widely followed in the brāhmaṇical society, women were also cremated along with their husbands. Burial with the dead was practised in parts of south India. But I have no information whether wives were buried with their husbands in those parts. In any case the servile position of women is based on law books. Both women and śūdras are denied property rights. Long ago I collected Sanskrit passages in which śūdras and women are placed in the same category. However, the exact time and place of the origin of the satī system needs to be examined.

The problem of the origin of satī and its continuity is closely linked with the history of marriage and family system. The immolation of the wife on the death of the husband originated in the patriarchal marriage system, which was not concerned with individuals but with the clan or the family or even the class-divided society. Hence in order to understand the dimensions of satī it is necessary to comprehend the nature of the social system which gave rise to it. Ancient India had two types of marriage traditions, matriarchal and patriarchal, as is also the case in modern times in certain parts of the subcontinent. The matriarchal system in which woman enjoys more importance is found in many primitive societies. Sometimes matriarchy is associated with the pre-Aryan peoples and patriarchy with the speakers of the Indo-European languages, though traces of matriarchy can be found in ancient Indo-European texts also. We have shown that recent research shows the practice of polyandry among the Aryans of Ladakh in India.

In the nineteenth century two scholars Bachofen[1] and Morgan[2] held that matriarchy preceded patriarchy. They also associated matriarchy with the egalitarian and communistic pattern of life. But this theory was questioned by anthropologists, particularly in the United States. However the old theory has been resurrected with modifications. There is good evidence to show that many tribes that have been studied are matriarchal. This exercise has been carried out by F. Murdoch with the help of a team of scholars who have investigated the position of women and marriage practices in five hundred and seventy-seven tribes.[3] But it appears that the matriarchal system is found among those tribes which are horticulturists; it is not found among full-fledged agriculturalists. Between horticulture and full-fledged agriculture lies the stage of shifting cultivation which is called *jhum* cultivation in India. In such a cultivation the role of women is fairly important. Although jungle clearance, terracing, ploughing and sowing are done by men, transplantation, weeding and many agricultural operations are done by women. So there is no doubt that women contribute considerably to agricultural operations in shifting cultivation. Of course in India we have no examples of strong mother rights in those tribes which practise shifting cultivation, but the relative importance of women in such tribes cannot be denied. Both anthropologists as well as archaeologists attribute the invention of agriculture, weaving and spinning to women. It is also held that they play a more important part in the reproduction of human life and consequently in making labour power available. So it is clear that in a particular stage of the development of human society women were more important than men. Gradually as agriculture developed and the domestic responsibilities of women increased they could not fully perform their earlier functions and lost their importance. In the developed agricultural stage matriarchy is not so widespread although traces of matriliny can be found now in many parts of India including north-eastern India and Kerala. Therefore one of the problems for a historical study of the position of women in the Indian texts is to look at the institution of matriarchy and patriarchy in tire context of the modes of subsistence pursued by the people.

Undoubtedly we have many illustrations of matriarchal practices in ancient times.[4] In Punjab, probably in the Madra area, *strī-rājya* or the rule of women prevailed; especially Madra women are considered to be self-willed and they could mate with anybody they liked.[5] It is because of the importance of women in early times that many proper names give the identity of the mother but do not say anything about the father. Such cases are those of Kaunteya that is the son of Kunti, which is generally applied to Arjuna. We have many other names such as Māmateya from Mamatā, Aitareya from Itarā, Daitya from Diti or Āditya from Āditi, etc. It seems that matriarchy in ancient times was associated with the practice of polyandry, traces of which are still to be found among the Khasis in north-eastern India and also among some Himalayan peoples in Uttar Pradesh. Since we do not have much information about the modes of subsistence of the people who lived under various shades of matriarchy in ancient times, this exercise is worth undertaking.

With the beginning of historical times in India around the sixth century BC caste or varṇa emerged as an important socio-economic factor, and came to be closely connected with all the eight forms of marriage enumerated in the Dharmaśāstras. Varṇa in early India should not be understood merely as a system of ranking based on rituals and notions of purity. Varṇa and jātī hierarchy really indicates the relations of production. In the ideal varṇa system the brāhmaṇas and kṣatriyas lived on the produce of the vaiśyas who were principal taxpayers and the chief givers of *dāna* and *dakṣiṇā* to religious functionaries. In this system both the upper varṇas together with the vaiśyas exploited the labour of the śūdras who worked as slaves, domestics, artisans and agricultural labourers. Until Gupta times the vaiśyas mainly paid taxes and the śūdras supplied the necessary labour power. Thus the two constituted the main earning hands or the backbone of society.

In this context we can appreciate the views of Kauṭilya regarding the varṇa orientation of the approved and unapproved forms of marriage. Kauṭilya points out that the approved forms of marriage (*dharmya*) are prescribed for the two higher varṇas and the unapproved forms (*adharmya*) are prescribed for the two lower varṇas.[6] This is done by him deliberately because approved forms of marriage, particularly *ārṣa* and *daiva*, mean many restrictions but unapproved forms of marriage allow comparative freedom and initiative to women; they also imply their role in negotiating and fixing marriage. The approved forms of marriage require only the consent of the father,[7] but the unapproved forms need the consent of both the father and mother for validating the unions.[8] It is significant that the forms of marriage in which the opinion of the mother counts are not recommended for the brāhmaṇas and the kṣatriyas. All this is done to perpetuate the state-based and varṇa-divided society. Since unapproved forms of marriage impose few restrictions and give wide latitude to men and women they can be easily performed by members of the lower orders. After all free union of men and women leads to more production of manpower which is needed for running the economy on which the state and varṇas are based. The law-book of Baudhāyana specifies that vaiśya and śūdra women are comparatively free because they are engaged in agricultural and servicing functions.[9] It will, therefore, appear that the marriage forms discussed in the ancient law-books are basically linked to the production system. Whoever wishes to study the subjection or otherwise of women cannot afford to ignore the mode of production and the alterations that it underwent from time to time.

In the class-divided patriarchal society of Rome women and slaves were placed in the same category. Certain forms of marriage in Rome were patrician in character and correspond to the approved forms of marriage. On the other hand the other forms were plebeian in character and they correspond to the unapproved forms of marriage of ancient India.

But the significant fact in India is the lumping together of women (through they may belong to higher orders) and labourers in the same position. Women and śūdras were placed in the same category in the varṇa-divided patriarchal society[10] as was the case with women and slaves in Rome. Many passages in Sanskrit texts treat śūdras and women equally. Both of them were deprived of the right to study the Veda and denied participation in Vedic rituals in post-Vedic times. Participation in rituals was a symbol of social status. Anybody who was kept out of rituals was denigrated in the dominant brāhmaṇical society. The earliest reference that we have to the bracketing of women and śūdras appears in the *Śatapatha Brāhmaṇa*,[11] which may be a work of about the sixth century BC. But numerous passages in pre-Gupta texts and more so its post-Gupta texts attest the subjection of women by ranking them with śūdras who were considered to be the serving class. So in both the pre-feudal and feudal stages the general subjection of women especially of those belonging to the higher varṇas, appears as a fact and an ideology.

We have contradictory mentalities and attitudes towards women in ancient texts to enable us to argue in favour of both the higher and lower status of women. All such passages have been repeatedly reproduced by social reformers and their opponents right from the days of Raja Rammohan Roy in the early nineteenth century. But if the relevant passages are sifted, on balance it would be more than clear that gender discrimination loomed large and that generally women were placed in a position of utter subjection. In many passages women are idealized as Laxmi and placed on a high pedestal, but these statements do not mean such. We may pick instances of individual women who were educated and who could successfully take part in theological disputations. But the ideology which tries to elevate women to higher position in relation to men is certainly a very weak trend in our ancient social philosophy. At best it only shows the desire of some people to improve the position of women, but this desire is never fulfilled.

Even Gautama Buddha who laid emphasis on *karma*, that is function, as the basis of determining the varṇa of a person in society and opened the doors of the sangha to śūdras and women, did not go far enough to accord the same place to women as they enjoyed in a matriarchal set-up, though he may have been influenced by traces of matriarchal traditions among the Kosalas and Sākyas. But his decision to admit women to the Buddhist church as nuns was certainly a forward step. This did not bring about any fundamental change in the dominant mentality towards women. Compared to men they were considered slow in attaining enlightenment.

A careful reading of the *Vinaya Piṭaka* shows many instances of derisive attitude towards women. The Buddha's low opinion of women is well known. He is said to have stated that since women were admitted to the sangha, the sangha would last only for five hundred years; otherwise it could last for one thousand years.

In ancient texts women were not only bracketed with śūdras but also with property. They were debarred from having a share in inheritance. Manu declares women and śūdras to be servile for ever,[12] and states that slaves and women have no rights to property. Generally women could not get a share in landed property. Women were entitled to *strī-dhana*, which meant that they could receive and retain gifts and presents consisting of dress, jewels and similar items of movable property given by their relations,[13] but really only women of upper and propertied classes could take advantage of such a provision. On the other hand as time passed women themselves came to be regarded as an item of property. Many passages in ancient texts place women and property in the same category.[14] In these passages women are treated as chattel. Such passages abound in texts belonging to Gupta and post-Gupta times, and their number goes on increasing in early medieval literature. It therefore appears that the subjection of women, particularly those belonging to upper classes or varṇas, becomes complete in early medieval times.

In India man's domination over woman and the idea of treating her as a chattel becomes prominent in early medieval times when we have feudal developments. It is this idea which eventually gives rise to satī system and leads to its spread. However the sacrificial slaughter of wife on the death of her husband is indicated by some burials in the fourth millennium BC in Poland and Baltic states and in the third millennium BC in the Danube region and Italy. We have reference to widow burning among the Scythians in Central Asia as early as the fifth century BC as pointed out by Herodotus.[15] But the practice of widow burning did not survive in Central Asia on any scale in subsequent times. Similarly, despite matrilineal traditions in the society of ancient Egypt, women were buried along with the Egyptian king called Pharaoh to give him company in the next world. The king's companions and various types of equipment were also buried with him in order to make his life comfortable in the next world. Obviously such ideas had grown out of a strong sense of private property and the overall despotic authority of the Pharaoh. There is nothing to show that outside the royalty the practice of widow burial was widespread in Egypt. At any rate it is very clear that such a practice did not survive in Egypt in subsequent times. It is only in India that satī developed as a regular practice, especially in Rajput families. We have instances of satī even in the *Mahābhārata* and in the Purāṇas also. The earliest instance is traced to the *Atharva Veda*,[16] though it is dismissed by many scholars.

It seems that the epic and the Puranic references were inserted in the texts only around Gupta, and post-Gupta times. The oldest inscriptional instance of satī is not older than the early sixth century AD (510). In subsequent times many instances are known from inscriptions. Satī memorial stones were discovered in the western part of Madhya Pradesh and also in Rajasthan. In our country we have two types of memorial stone inscriptions. In south India we have hero stones which are called *virakala*. They record the memory of those who laid down their lives in defence of land, cattle or in defence of the master. In north India, particularly in the early Rajput kingdoms, we have satī memorial stones. Some of these are found in the kingdoms of the Candellas and Kalacuris in Madhya Pradesh, but most of these appear in Rajasthan.[17] The custom of *jauhar* (derived from *yamagṛha* or *jamghar*), in which wives of the Rajput princes burnt themselves to death in the fort, started with the invasions of the Delhi sultans. Sometimes the prince burnt himself with his queens.[18] Satī stone inscriptions continue in Rajasthan up to the twentieth century. Many medieval satī stone inscriptions were noted and collected by the Italian Indologist L.P. Tessitori who worked in the former states of Bikaner and Jaipur in the second decade of the present century. Of course, many villages inhabited by upper castes in Bihar have also some satī shrines or *sthānas*. We have satī *sthānas* with which various types of legends of widow burning are associated. Some of these 'sacred' spots may have been really the places where widows were burnt either under social pressure or because of their entrenched belief in their eternal and exclusive loyalty to their husbands. Whatever may be the cause it is clear that the practice of satī was confined mostly to the Rajputs although its cases among the brāhmaṇas are not wanting. Why satī is peculiar to Rajput families in Rajasthan is a question which has to be investigated. We have also to identify the period when the practice becomes frequent and widespread.

The peculiar practice prevalent among the Rajput nobles was to burn a number of servants on the occasion of the funeral ceremony of the nobles. We hear of the case of Ramadas Kachhwaha along with whose dead body several servants were burnt to death. This was not a novel practice, because it also obtained among many ancient peoples, particularly among the members of the royalty. What makes it peculiar in the case of India is the lumping together of women and lower orders not only in matters of day-to-day life but also in matters concerning the next world. Socially women and śūdras were placed in the same category and similarly women and members of the lower orders who served their masters were burnt along with them at the time of their funeral. Thus it appears that the practice of burning both women and servants along with the master was confined to the Rajput nobles. Why it happened only in the case of Rajput nobles is a matter which needs inquiry. We may, however, add that the practice of satī became pronounced in the feudal phase in Rajasthan. Since this phase was marked by constant military activity, because of physical dominance men became all the more powerful. Complete with a strong sense of private property in land they relegated women more and more to the background and considered them items of property. The male domination spread the satī practice wider.

There is no doubt that emphasis on the unilateral and unquestioned loyalty of the wife to her husband was developed in the brāhmaṇic society. The earlier Smṛtis recommend the burning of brāhmaṇa widows also. But inscriptional evidence for such a practice is meagre. However, enquiries made in different parts of the country show that the practice of satī was not altogether absent among the brāhmaṇas, though it was not so widespread and glaring as we find in the case of the Rajputs. Some texts state that the practice of satī was valid for the kṣatriya.[19] As a militant community the Rajputs expected more fidelity and loyalty from their women, servants and others; this would not apply to the brāhmaṇas engaged in priestly and other religious activities. Whether society was feudal or pre-feudal the brāhmaṇa set the model for the social conduct of the members belonging to the lower castes. However an early medieval lawgiver, Aṅgiras, considers the satī committed in a brāhmaṇa widow to be suicide.[20] Again an early medieval Purāṇa, which praises the practice of widow burning, does not allow it to the brāhmaṇas.[21] Therfore why the brāhmaṇas did not practice much of satī appears to be intriguing.

Some explanation has been given for the practice of satī among the brāhmaṇas of Bengal. P.V. Kane[22] and A.S. Altekar[23] attribute it to the *dāyabhāga* system of inheritance prevalent in Bengal. According to this system of inheritance women were entitled to receive shares in the property. In the other parts of the widows were not allowed any share in property; they were entitled to only maintenance country. In Bengal the dāyabhāga, originally expanded by Jimūtavaha sometime between the twelfth and the fourteenth century, conferred proprietory rights on the wife after the death of her husband. Since the kṣatriyas or the Rajputs were not a numerous community in Bengal, the law affected mainly the brāhmaṇas who had primarily become a landed community because of the continuous practice of land grants. Kulīnism made things worse. To gain status brāhmaṇas of lower ranks gave their daughters to those of higher ranks which increased polygamy. By the end of the eighteenth century widow burning in Bengal had assumed such proportions that it attracted the attention of both the missionaries and Raja Rammohan Roy.

The practice of satī also spread among the Sikhs and Marathas and some other militant communities of south India. But at the time of its abolition in 1829 it was fairly widespread in Bengal and Rajasthan. It is held that 10 per cent of widows practised satī in Rajasthan, although in the country as a whole it may not have exceeded 1 per cent.[24] We have no means to check these figures, but the continued practice of widow burning is as peculiar to India as that of untouchability.

We can suggest some reasons for the occurrence of satī cases in Gupta and post-Gupta times. In pre-Gupta times literary evidence suggests case of levirate and widow marriage among members of higher castes.[25] *Niyoga* or levirate was permitted by the Dharmaśāstras to such women as were not capable of getting sons produced by their own husbands. If the husband could not produce children, this could be done by his younger brother or by his kinsmen or by his villagers. If nobody was available even a brāhmaṇa could be commissioned for this purpose. In the early centuries of the Christian era the practice seems to have been disallowed to the dvijas or the twice-born. In their context it is condemned as a beastly practice (*paśu dharma*) by Manu.[26] It came to be permitted only to the śūdras,[27] who formed the majority of the population in India in Gupta and post-Gupta times. This same was true of widow marriage, which came to be confined only to the śūdras.[28] Widows belonging to higher varṇas came to have a difficult time and the dominant brāhmaṇic society looked upon them with contempt and prescribed a puritan life for them. It seems that in such a situation when they were encouraged to burn themselves with their husbands they found this option to be better than that of living a miserable life as widow. It would, therefore, appear that the discontinuance of levirate and widow marriage among the upper castes created conditions for the widespread practice of satī among their members. On the otherhand lower caste people continued to practice levirate and widow marriage.

The law-book of Nārada provides that a woman can take another husband under five conditions. They consist of the loss of her husband, his death, his asceticism, his impotence and his excommunication from the caste.[29] This provision, first inserted around the fifth century, is repeated by Parāśara[30] in the seventh century. It does show the concern of a section of the brāhmaṇa ideologues to retrieve the situation, but does not seem to have worked in Bengal and Rajasthan.

It is needless to add that Indian society was basically a patriarchal society. With the growth of a strong sense of private property in land about which we have detailed provisions in the Dharmaśāstras, and also with the provisions for the inheritance of land through the male line a situation was created in which chastity of woman came to be considered far more important than that of man. Virgin land was considered to be suitable for gift to a brāhmaṇa; similarly only a virgin woman was held fit for marriage or making gift, that is, *kanyādāna*. Once a woman was married it was expected of her that she must remain faithful to her husband throughout life and after his death. This kind of idea about the chastity and loyalty of women developed as an autonomous force in society. Numerous stories of women who burnt themselves to death along with their husbands and thus attained salvation came to be propagated through the Purāṇas and by word of mouth. Consequently women themselves came to believe in the religious merits that would accrue to them as a result of burning themselves with their husbands' dead bodies. So it appears that the practice of satī was not only the eventual product of a class-divided property-based patriarchal society in militant communities but also the result of a deeply entrenched idea that the suicide ritual would confer great religious merit on widows. When Raja Rammohan Roy started the agitation for the abolition of satī in the first quarter of the nineteenth century he collected numerous texts to prove that the practice was not in vogue in earliest times in India. But the satī could not be easily removed only by marshalling such evidence. This task required both social and ideological action. The structure of the society in which women and lower orders were placed in the same category needed a radical change.

NOTES

1. 'Bachofen's book *Mutterrecht* was published in 1861. See F. Engels, *The Origin of the Family, Private Property and the State* (Calcutta, 1943), 4.
2. Lewis Henry Morgan, *Ancient Society* (New York, 1907)
3. Quoted in Maurice Godelier, *Perspectives in Marxist Anthropology* (Cambridge, 1977), p. 106.
4. S.C. Sarkar, *Some Aspects of the Earliest Social History of India* (1928, reprint, Patna, 1985); S.D. Singh, *Polyandry in Ancient India* (Delhi, 1978).
5. Karṇa Parva (Kumbkonam edn.) 37.22-23.
6. *Arthaśāstra,* III.2.

7. Ibid.
8. Ibid.
9. *ayantritakalatrā vaiśyaśūdrā bhavanti karṣaṇaśyśrūṣādhikṛtatvāt. Baudhāyana Dharmasūtra*, 1.20.14.15.
10. *Supra,* ch. 6.
11. XIV.1.1.31.
12. VIII.414; IX.2.
13. A.S. Altekar, *The Position of Women in Hindu Civilization* (Banaras, 1938), ch. VIII.
14. *Supra,* ch. 5.
15. S.C. Sarkar, op. cit., 82.
16. XVIII.2. 1–3.
17. Six instances of satī among the Chauhāns, the earliest belonging to AD 890, are given in Dasharatha Sharma, *Early Chauhān Dynasties* (Delhi, 1975), 289–90.
18. Ibid., 290–1.
18. *Bṛhaddevatā* quoted in A.S. Altekar, op. cit., 150.
20. P.V. Kane, *History of Dhavmaśāstra*, II, pt. I, 637, fn. 1468 quoted in D. Sharma, op. cit., 290, fn. 121.
21. *Padma Purāṇa,* Anandasrarma Sanskrit Series, V.49.72–3.
22. *History of Dharmaśāstra* (Hindi Version), I (Lucknow, 1980), ch. 15.
23. Op. cit., ch, IX, section 2.
24. Ibid.
25. S.C. Sarkar, op. cit., pp. 78–9, 82–3, 165–85.
26. IX.66.
27. Quoted in P.V. Kane, *History of Dharmaśāstra,* II, 604.
28. *Manu,* IX.66.
29. *naṣṭe mṛte pravārjite klīve ca patite patatu, pañcasu āastu nārīṇām patir anyo vidhīyate. Nārada*, XII.97.
30. *Parāśara,* IV.28.

9

Some Western Views on the State and Economy in Early India

In the last four decades most research work on early Indian history is being done in Indian institutions. It is really sad that despite its excellent library facilities the School of Oriental and African Studies in London, where considerable work on early Indian History was done at one time, has little to offer in this field. Obviously the loss of empire eventually led to the loss of interest in the history of south Asia. But some westerners find it difficult to reconcile themselves to the loss of dominance and console themselves by proving the superiority of European rule and heritage. Although they do not exaggerate the role of external influence in Indian history in the old imperialist manner they object to India being compared with European countries.[1] The common Indo-European heritage constructed on the basis of linguistic studies is discarded, and an explanatory framework based on the study of an African tribe is being applied by A. Southall and some others to the whole range of pre-modern Indian history.[2] Indian historians should welcome those methods and results of anthropological investigations which help in understanding developments in the predominantly tribal phase of Indian society. But it would be utterly wrong to think that throughout its ancient or medieval periods India remained basically tribal and that developments in this country cannot be compared with those in European countries. Proceeding on the assumption that India did not travel beyond the tribal stage and was incapable of forming a wider political entity, as Rome did, J.C. Heesterman assumes that the Maurya state did not have any element of centralization and the king was considered equal to many functionaries who were thought to be his peers.[3] He points out the absence of a chain of command, a system of reporting and the lack of supervision over numerous superintendents who appear in the *Arthaśāstra* of Kauṭilya. He adds that the Maurya state was interested merely in the distribution of taxes and there was no method of mobilizing and husbanding resources. It would be nobody's argument that resources were mobilized and transferred in the same manner as they are done now and that bureaucracy in Maurya times was organized on modem lines. But we cannot rule out a measure of control exercised by the Maurya rulers.

Centralization depends on the degree of central control exercised over the officials, and this control depends on the mode of payment to government officials. If the officials are paid in cash, central control is better ensured. Heesterman rightly thinks that monetization introduces a modicum of central control, but he ignores the evidence regarding the widespread use of money in Maurya times. Even if we leave aside the coins in Panini, Pali texts and references in the *Arthaśāstra* of Kauṭilya, how can we write off the physical presence of a large number of punch-marked silver coins during the Maurya period? Punch-marked coins were both local and pan-Indian, and those which were pan-Indian carried symbols of peacock and crescented hill. Pan-Indian coins are found in the whole of northern India and also beyond it. Evidently they were used for collecting taxes, paying officials, soldiers, and carrying on commercial transactions. It is difficult to use the whole of Kauṭilya's *Arthaśāstra* for the Maurya period, but a good part of this text can be studied for the functioning the state in ancient times. The rate of payment for various grades of officials are given in BK V of the *Arthaśāstra* of Kauṭilya, which also provides for rates of interest. Monetization was linked to a countrywide zone of exchange, a kind of pan-Indian economy, which facilitated the creation of a wider political entity.

The *Arthaśāstra* (BK II) enumerates taxes to be collected from the rural and urban areas. In its fiscal organization the collector (*samāhartā*) and treasurer (*sanniddhāta*) are important functionaries. The fiscal measures recommended by Kauṭilya leave no doubt about the pooling of resources. Of course taxes may have been collected and disbursed locally. But they were also taken to the *durga* or the fortified capital for payment to soldiers, officials, priests, artisans, etc., by the central authority.

It may not have been difficult to transfer taxes in cash to provincial or central headquarters. Taxes collected in kind may have been stored locally in local granaries, mentioned in the Sohgaura inscription in eastern Uttar Pradesh and the Mahasthan inscription in Bangladesh.

It would be wrong to think that because of difficulties in logistics men and material could not be moved from one place to another. Both river and land routes were used widely for transporting men and material, and the transportation of Asokan pillars, most of which were inscribed, is an important illustration. These pillars were quarried, chiselled and given cylindrical shape in the mines of Chunar situated on the bank of the Ganga near Varanasi,[4] and from there they were taken to various places in northern India. It is remarkable that an Asokan pillar of the Chunar buff sand stone has been found in Amaravati in Andhra Pradesh. Needless to add that Asokan inscriptions have been found at a dozen places in Andhra Pradesh and Karnataka, and they form a complete set of Rock Edicts. It appears that all these edicts were drafted at Pataliputra, the capital of the Maurya empire, and engraved at important places not only in India but also in Afghanistan.

These inscriptions, of which Heesterman seems to be ignorant, leave no doubt that there was a chain of command headed by the king; his orders went to provincial governors,[5] who also communicated it to lower officers.[6] The effectiveness of the system of reporting can be gauged from the fact that in case of difference of opinion in a council of high functionaries Asoka made himself available for receiving reports at all places and at all times.[7] Obviously the pre-industrial state under the Maurya or the Mughals[8] could not be as effective and centralized as the modern state, but a good deal of centralization in a limited area cannot be ruled out.

In fact transport facilities till the advent of the rule of the East India Company had not changed materially. The setting up of the caravan *sarais*, where the messengers and reporters could halt, and the introduction of the relay of messages through horsemen by Sher Shah Suri certainly meant improvement, but these did not alter the situation dramatically. Until 1830s, when steam ships began to be used, the East India Company used traditional modes of transport except that these were reinforced by hand guns.

Therefore Heesterman's attempt to write off the centralizing element in the Mauryan administration is based neither on logic nor on evidence. It however is consistent with his outlook reflected in the statement that the Indians never fought against British Raj and that they always fought among themselves. Such statements can be condoned because Heesterman is not a student of modern history. However since they emphasize the divisiveness of India during the whole span of the pre-British period and highlight the incapacity of the Indians to form wider political units they tend to serve a pernicious political purpose.

The characterization of the Maurya state as a decentralized political entity is linked with the theory of the segmentary state based on the idea of ritual polity.[9] Control and administration over territory is regarded not so important in the formation of the state as the ritual integration of various groups and peoples into one.[10] This formulation is being particularly applied to India. It means that the major part of territory under a king acknowledges his authority because he is considered to be endowed with certain divine powers which are articulated and exercised through the performance of rituals. Rituals enable him to establish and continue his control over various communities and interest groups living in his kingdom. The great economist, Marshall, held that religion and commerce moulded the history of mankind. But the nineteenth and the early twentieth century western orientalists and Indianists held that religion alone shaped the history of India and other eastern countries. In reaction Indian historians produced well researched monographs to demonstrate that in early India commerce and other economic factors played an important part. But the tradition of colonialist or orientalist historiography is so strongly entrenched that Indianists refuse to look at the evidence and assert that rituals confer legitimacy on rulers and are therefore far more important than the political authority derived from taxes, army and bureaucracy.

In our view rituals do communicate messages of social significance, but in their origin they are only outer manifestations of the way in which human beings organize their subsistence and manage their affairs. The rituals related to the daily routine of the presiding deity in the temple shows that the deity takes bath, eats, sleeps, clothes, listens to music, etc., in the same manner as a human being does, and accordingly all arrangements are made for the purpose. Indian myths and legends show gods and goddesses to be as immoral as human beings; this is also true of ancient Greece. This is very natural because gods are the divine counterparts of human beings, and they live their life in the manner the human beings do. However certain supernatural elements are attributed to gods. But generally gods placed in temples are supposed to lead the life of the royalty and the other privileged sections of society; they are not supposed to live like the common people. Even Gautama Buddha was credited with previous births in the families of the kshatriya and brahmans only and not of ordinary people. This is because gods and the legends associated with great men of antiquity are inventions of priests and rulers rather than of ordinary human beings and are manipulated to maintain the authority of the dominant interest groups.

It is true that rituals helped to strengthen the authority of the ruler. But they were deliberately created and elaborated for this purpose by privileged social and political power groups once they came into existence. Ancient thinkers and writers such as Kauṭilya and Bāṇabhaṭṭa were rational enough to reject the efficacy of rituals. Bāṇabhaṭṭa clearly exposed the hollowness of the divinity of kingship. Kauṭilya did not believe in the theory of destiny and he stated that if a person does not work then the state will not help him. For mobilizing and manipulating resources Kauṭilya lays down several measures to fully exploit the credulity and religious sentiments of the masses. Kauṭilya's measures show that the king and his officers were fully conscious of the fact that they are trying to befool people by taking advantage of their credulity.[11] If ancient thinkers, who cannot be credited with great rationalism, considered rituals to be non-real, it is strange that some modern western writers give primacy to the ritualistic factor at the cost of political and economic factors. Rituals were used for political purposes, but major rituals could not be performed without raising resources. Similarly law and order could not be maintained only through the prescription of penances as punishment for offences.

The ritualistic factor or ideology, depending on the time, place and circumstances, may move people to action. It may enjoy a measure of autonomy and can prove even crucial in certain situations but it would be wrong to think that rituals are not man made. The best course for a historian would be to investigate the social and material dimensions of rituals and to examine continuous process of interaction between the ritualistic factor on the one hand and the economic and political factors on the other. The legitimatizing aspect of the ritual cannot be ignored. But the need for legitimatization in most cases in history arises only when a ruler has usurped power or conquered some area. For doing; so it is necessary that he is able to mobilize both economic and military resources. The mere use of ritual does not lead to the formation of the state at any point of time in any part of the world.

Ritual plays an important part in the concept of the segmentary state. It is held that each segment recognizes the ritualistic authority of the king[12] which implies that his economic and political authority is not recognized. In pre-industrial times because of the difficulty of communications the authority of the central government could be effective mainly in the core area within a radius of 100 miles or so of the capital depending on the nature of the terrain. The areas situated away from the seat of central authority may not have been effectively controlled, and their allegiance to the central authority may have been merely symbolic and nominal. But it should be made clear that they offered allegiance to the central authority not because they associated any divine, ritualistic or supernatural elements with it. However such elements were attributed to the ruler by the priest who lived on royal grants of land. In some ways or other the people living on the periphery were overawed by the authority of a king living at a distance.

The term segment is never defined or even described clearly. Basically 'segmentary' is an anthropological term and relates to organizations based on kinship. But there is nothing to show that in early medieval India royal polities were mainly organized on the basis of kin groups. In a way the term segmentary is used to signify loose control exercised by the centre. But in the Indian medieval context this idea is better conveyed by the term feudal. Only in the case of early medieval Rajput states, specially that of the Chauhans, one can think of kin groups headed by their respective chiefs and owing allegiance to a central authority. But Dasharatha Sharma, who has a well-researched book on the Chauhans, holds that the Chauhan political and military system was feudal in character. Otherwise in most states found in early medieval times the link between the central authority and distant local units is maintained neither through the tie of ritual nor through the tie of kinship. It is the tie of land grant that comes out prominently. Pockets of political power are created by the assignment of lands to priests and temples which naturally work for consolidating the general social and political system under which they are made landed beneficiaries. A similar relationship seems to have subsisted between the central authority and heads of non-religious groups who are assured of the enjoyment of land and taxes by the centre.[13] Either the authority of the conquered kinglets over their smaller kingdoms is recognized by the conqueror or the agents appointed by the king are formally granted lands for their fiscal, military and administrative services.

One can readily agree with the view that the medieval state exercised loose control over its territory but the formulation that this control was mediated through rituals or ties of kinship rather than through ties of land grants cannot be accepted. Burton Stein's characterization of the Coḷa state as a segmentary polity in this sense had been rejected by scholars who are deeply read in sources and have examined the evidence carefully. Eventually Stein also gave up his thesis. The attempt of Southall, who is the originator of the idea of the segmentary state,[14] to apply this view to all pre-industrial states in ancient and medieval times in Asia[15] is not backed by any empirical evidence whatsoever.

Closely connected with the idea of the ritual polity is the idea of the temple town. It is being argued in some quarters that towns mainly originated at places which were centres of religion and pilgrimage. But the earliest Indian experience shows otherwise. Rituals and religious shrines do not play any important part in the rise of the early historic city. Kauṭilya provides for the location of brahmanical deities in the fortified capital area of *durga*, but this seems to be a later provision in the text and until Gupta times brahmanical temples are practically non-existent. In pre-Gupta times monasteries do appear and sometimes it is held that Buddhism contributed to urbanism, but in accordance with the rules of the *Vinaya* the monasteries were located at the outskirts of towns, as has been pointed out by John Marshall in his excavation report on Taxila. Pre-Gupta ancient Buddhist shrines appear and prosper because of the craft, commerce and political power of the city. When the city declined its shrines suffered. Thus ancient pre-Gupta towns were not the products of rituals.

Only in medieval times temples and places of *tirthas* arise in good numbers, but these had a special type of economic character. In their first phase they did not have much of crafts and commerce, as was the case with ancient towns. Monasteries such as Nalanda, and Jetavana in Sravasti, came to be maintained through land grants. The walls of the great temple of Tirupati are full of land grant inscriptions from about the eighth century onwards. With 10,000 monks Nalanda had the largest number of clerics in medieval times, and for their maintenance 200 villages were granted. In medieval times both in Anuradhapur in Sri Lanka and Kanchipuram in India networks of rituals were deliberately created by the ruling authorities to strengthen their own power. However, early medieval temple settlements had pontentialities for urban development. In course of time they changed their character and came to have a good number of craftsmen and traders as can be found in the case of Deoghar in Bihar and Varanasi in Uttar Pradesh. Professional variations in the population changed the nature of the temple settlements.

Finally, we may consider a view that relates to Indo-Roman trade. The well-known fact that Rome was drained of gold because of its trade with the east is now being contested by some scholars. Sidebotham argues that Rome was not being drained of gold and that the balance of Indo-Roman trade was not favourable to India.[16] In earlier times colonialist scholars argued that Indians did not take much interest in material matters and did not achieve anything significant in the economic field. But when examples of economic activities are presented by researchers including western scholars now the importance of economic activities undertaken by the Indians in ancient times is underrated. The view expressed about the nature of India's trade with Rome can be better appreciated in this context. Of course we have no difficulty in accepting that the concept of balance of trade was not known to the ancient people. But the ancient Romans could certainly see that what they consumed from India and other eastern countries cost them dearly. It is argued that no reliance can be placed on Pliny's complaint regarding the drain of gold from Rome because he was a liar. But even if this position is accepted we cannot ignore the measures that were adopted by the Roman senate to ban trade with India.[17] Rome lost heavily because of purchase of cutlery goods and silk, and to arrest the process of loss, restrictions were placed on trade in these items. More importantly, Roman coins, glasses, bullae and pottery appear in good numbers in the Indian peninsula. The total number of gold and silver coins from Rome found in India it is 6000,[18] which is evidently a very small fraction of the total amount that came to India from Rome. Therefore it is not incredible that Rome lost in gold on account of its trade with India.

Whether the western argument in favour of Rome is motivated by Euro-patriotism cannot be said. In the eighteenth and early nineteenth centuries India was drained of its resources on account of trade with Britain. Attempts are made to disprove the drain of Indian resources because of unequal trade and to paint the British political domination in a better light. Similarly in the case of Roman trade an attempt is made to assign a greater role to Rome and to show that trade did not go in favour of India. However, in the case of modern India it is argued that British rule and trade with Britain contributed to the economic development of the subcontinent. All these arguments seem to be of a piece, and their object is to laud all European activity, past or present.

Though western formulations on the nature of the Maurya state, medieval state, temple settlements and Indo-Roman trade are not supported by evidence, they cannot be ignored. They help us to realize that modern elements of centralization and bureaucracy were absent in early times, and that advanced ideas of modern trade cannot be applied to pre-modern times. However the exaltation of European and the deprecation of Indian achievements have to be discarded, for they spread prejudices and make it difficult to understand the past.

NOTES

1. A. Southall, 'The Segmentary State in Africa and Asia', *Comparative Studies in Society and History*, vol. 30, no. 1, January 1988, pp. 52–82.
2. Ibid.
3. *The Inner Conflict of Tradition*, OUP. Delhi, 1985. pp. 16–18, 129, 132–3, 139–40, 142–3, 260 with fns. 20 and 21.

4. P.C. Pant and Vidula Jayaswal, 'Chunar Stone Quarries: Raw Material for Sculpture and Architecture', *Marg*, XLII, no. 1, pp. 59–61.
5. Sep. Rock Edict I, MRE I, RE III, MPE II, SREI. PEVII.
6. MRE I (Brahmagiri and Siddapura Versions).
7. Rock Edict VI, lines 5–8.
8. Irfan Habib refutes A. Wink's views regarding lack of centralisation in the Mughal empire. *Indian Economy and Social History Review*, vol. XXV, no. 4, 1988, pp. 527–31; XXV, no. 3. 1989, pp. 363–72. See also his paper on Mapping the Maurya Empire submitted to Fifteenth Session of the Indian History Congress at Gorakhpur, 1989.
9. J. Heitzman, 'Ritual Polity and Economy: The Transactional Network of an Imperial Temple in Medieval South India'. *Journal* of *the Economic and Social History of the Orient*, XXXIV, pt. 1, 1991, pp. 22–54.
10. Ibid., p. 23.
11. R.S. Sharma, *Aspects of Political Ideas and Institutions in Ancient India*. Third Edn., Motilal Banarsidass, Delhi, 1991, Ch. XVII.
12. A. Southall, op. cit.
13. *Early Chauhan Dynasties*. Second edn., Delhi, 1975, p. 244.
14. D.N. Jha, 'Validity of Brahmana Peasant Alliance and the Segmentary State in Early Medieval South India', *Social Science Probings*, vol. 4, no. 2, June 1984, pp. 270–96; R. Champakalakshmi, *Indian Social & Economic History Review*, vol. XVII, nos 3 and 4, 1983, pp. 411–26; M.G.S. Narayanan, 'Review Article; South Indian History and Society', *Tamil Civilization*, vol. 3, no. 1, 1985, pp. 57–91; Vijaya Ramaswami in *Studies in History*, vol. 4, no. 2, 1982, pp. 307–19; Kesavan Veluthat, 'Power Structure of Monarchy in South India (*c.* AD 600–1300)', Ph.D. thesis University of Calicut, 1989.
15. Op. cit.
16. Steven E. Sidebotham, *Roman Economic Policy in the Erythra Thalassa*, 30 BC–AD 217, Leiden, 1986, p. 39 ff.
17. R. Pleiner, 'The Problem of the Beginning of Iron Age in India', *Acta Prehistorica et Archaeologica*, vol. 2, 1971, p. 17.
18. Paula J. Turner, *Roman Coins from India*, London, 1989, p. 23.

10

Mode of Production in Ancient India*†

In the Marxist view the mode of production includes the various types of resources which generate production; these are called means of production. It also includes relations of production which are established as a result of the distribution of the production resources or because of the sharing of the fruits of production. Means of production in the context of ancient India comprise land, pastures, labour power and tools used for artisanal and agricultural operations. Those who possess the means of production form the dominant class, and those who are dispossessed of these form the dominated class. Further distinction is caused by the sharing of the surplus.

The concept of surplus plays a vital role in the Marxist theory. If producers consisting of peasants, artisans and others produce something over and above their day-to-day needs, this extra produce is called surplus. In ancient India it used to be given to the state as taxes and tributes and to the priests and religious bodies as gifts, tithes, etc. Basically those who live on the surplus and do not take part in primary production constitute the ruling class or its allies, and those who are deprived of the surplus form the ruled class. The same applies to the possession of the means of production. However, in ancient India we notice the peculiar phenomenon of entitlement to surplus without much control over the means of production. The differences over the sharing of the production resources and the surplus lead to the class conflict. Some Marxists consider ideology to be a part of the mode of production. While the significant role of ideology

*Previously published as, 'Mode of Production in Ancient India' in D.N. Gupta, ed., *Changing Modes of Production in India: An Historical Analysis* (Delhi: Hindu College, 1995). The section 'Asiatic Mode of Production', in this chapter, has been added by the author specially for this volume.

in influencing production cannot be denied, it is best studied as a by-product of the operation of the productive forces.

We may review the application of the Marxist theory to the period from Rigvedic times to Maurya times. The Rigvedic people were confined to Afghanistan, Pakistan (mainly Punjab), and to Punjab and Haryana in India, especially in the upland or hilly areas in 1500–1000 BC. They practised both agriculture and stock-raising. *Yava* mentioned in the *Rigveda* means cereals though they are not specified. But the general impression created by the *Rigveda* is one of pastoralism. Animals served not only as a source of food but also of dairy products. The verbal term for milking occurs in most Indo-European languages. It seems that agriculture provided fodder which led to the expansion of pastoralism. Numerous terms indicating non-cattle institutions are derived from cattle. They are *gaveshana* (search for cows), *gavishti* (battle on the issue of cows), *gavyuti* (measurement for distance) *gopa* and *gopati* (head of cattle and therefore of people).

There is very little indication of private ownership of land. More than land, pastures such as *vrijana* provided free access to all. But chiefs seem to have possessed far more cattle than ordinary clansmen. This may have been the result of distribution of booty acquired from perpetual wars that were fought between tribes for possession of cattle. Horses may have been largely owned by the chiefs. The importance and ownership of the horse can be inferred from many horse-based names of Vedic chiefs.

Unequal distribution of horses and cattle worked for inequality in early Vedic society. The Puranas indicate grossly unequal distribution of cattle, which are shown in the possession of members of the two higher varṇas, but such references are lacking in Vedic texts. The Vedic chiefs claimed larger shares in booty as reward for their physical and mental qualities. Clansmen surrendered to the chief all the booty they captured. Occasional *bali* or voluntary tribute given by clansmen and defeated chiefs may have generated inequality.

The early Vedic society was neither fully egalitarian nor class-divided. The brāhmaṇas and kshatriyas are mentioned only a few times in the *Rigveda*, and only a late interpolated passage suggests the varṇa system. Basically it was a kin-based society in which close kin groups were engaged in cattle rearing, agriculture and war. The frequency of the terms *jana*, *vish*, etc., indicate the tribal or the kin-based character of the society.

In 1000–500 BC the Vedic people moved to mainly alluvial tracts lying in the Indo-Gangetic divide, and in the land lying between the Ganga and Yamuna. Though stock-raising continued to be important, the settlements marked by the use of the diagnostic pottery called Painted Grey Ware show that agriculture became far more important with the production of wheat, rice and lentils. The appearance of iron probably helped the chief in wars, for tribal analogies suggest the control of the head of the tribe over the mines. Though initially iron was not used on any large scale in agriculture, the peasants produced a modest amount of surplus to enable the chief to perform ostentatious sacrifices. However, there is no archaeological evidence of urban settlements prior to 500 BC in the later Vedic zone.

Land, the principal means of production, could not be alienated by the chief without the consent of his clansmen. But the chiefs certainly owned far numerous heads of cattle. Possibly they received regular *bali* though it had not been converted into taxes. Differentiation between the prince and the peasant had started, but it was not so wide and sharp. They ate from the same plate and used the same weapons though horses may have probably been used only by the chiefs.

Towards the end of the later Vedic period (500 BC) the varṇa system had become a reality. This was linked with production relations. The brāhmaṇas who received gifts and the kshatriyas who received voluntary payments had come to the forefront. The vaiśyas were mainly peasants and the śūdras were a small serving community. Certain groups of families took to war and administration, and received shares without working in fields and pasture grounds. Similarly other groups became confined to priestly functions and received gifts which they did not have to return. Although progress in agriculture made this possible, how and why the priests and warriors claimed a larger share in the surplus needs to be investigated. Differentiation is attributed to the difference between the senior and junior lineage, but why and how such lineages were formed needs to be explained. In our view the earliest social division may have been in the form of male dominance caused by plough agriculture and the use of horse. In the male society further differentiation may have arisen because of differences in age and experience coupled with mental and physical qualities. Whatsoever be the precise cause, the relations of production appearing at the end of the Vedic period were legalized as varṇa system when iron came to be used substantially in the upper and middle Ganga plains in artisanal and agricultural production.

The society that emerges in post-Vedic times in the middle Ganga plains can be called a peasant society in the sense that free peasants dominated it numerically. If the peasant mode of production means a mode in which the peasant meets the subsistence needs of his household and then provides sufficient surplus for the support of priests, warriors, administrators, artisans, merchants and urban people, this term can be used to describe and analyse the system of production that prevailed in pre-Maurya times. In this system priests and administrators act as managers of production, and merchants function as economic mediators between the peasants and artisans on the one hand, and the ruling groups on the other. Like peasants, artisans, slaves and agricultural labourers are also directly engaged in production and work for their subsistence.

The 'peasant mode of production' arose in the thickly forested but extremely fertile alluvial plains of the middle Ganga. The use of iron in clearing vegetation and breaking the hard soil of the new alluvium led to an enormous increase in the production of foodgrains. The beginning of paddy transplantation increased its yield nearly twofold or more. This scenario explains the burgeoning of settlements in the period of the North Black Polished Ware from 600 to 200 BC.

No doubt cereals were produced in parts of the middle Ganga plains around 2000 BC and in other parts from 1500 BC onwards. But the neolithic-chalcolithic settlements are much fewer in comparison with the NBPW settlements. It is wrong to think that the intensive use of bone and stone tools together with the practice of double cropping produced surplus. Double cropping was not practised in the middle Ganga plains till the 1930s or so, and there is no evidence of intensive use of bone and stone tools in promoting agriculture in the middle Ganga plains.

Archaeological finds leave no doubt that iron acted as a catalyst in transforming the agricultural and artisanal scene. Its increasing use multiplied not only the iron tools but also the objects made of copper, bone, stone, semiprecious stone, wood and glass. Iron tools facilitated the fabrication of metal money which boosted petty commodity production and long-distance exchange. But the most important consequence of the use of iron was the production of agricultural surplus which enabled the peasant to pay taxes to the state and provide gifts for the priests. According to the Sanskritist P.V. Kane the vaiśyas were the principal taxpayers, and according to the Pali scholar Richard Fick brāhmaṇas and kshatriyas were exempted from payment of taxes. Thus the two higher orders formed privileged varṇas. The śūdras acted as domestic slaves, hired labourers and artisans, but they were not engaged in production as slaves on any large scale. The relations of production formed towards the end of the Vedic period were formalized in the law-books or the Dharmasūtras between 500 and 200 BC.

Kauṭilya's model of the state visualizes state control of production. Whether centralization applies to the Maurya state has been under debate.[1] His *Arthaśāstra* may not be Maurya, but it is not much later than the third century AD. The Maurya model may have continued with modification under the Satavahanas and the Kushanas.

How does the Kauṭilyan model suit the Maurya state? Classical accounts mention that the Mauryas maintained either 400,000 or 600,000 soldiers. Megasthenes and Asokan inscriptions attest the presence of a good many state officials. The need for the support of the professional soldiers and bureaucracy led to the regulation of economic activities by the state. The taxes collected from the rural (*rashtra*) and urban (*durga*) sectors seem to have been insufficient. Hence the tax area was expanded by founding new rural and urban settlements (*janapadanivesha, durgavidhana* and *durganivesha*). Even then the taxes collected from the people could not satisfy the needs of the state. Therefore, Kauṭilya provides for emergency taxation under which the peasants are compelled to produce extra crops.

More importantly, the state ran its own farms on which slaves and hired labourers were employed under the supervision of *sitadhyaksha*. It also raised its stock of animals under a superintendent. But most superintendents were engaged in controlling and generating artisanal and commercial activities for the sake of income to the state. Altogether we hear of nearly 28 superintendents. According to Kauṭilya these and other officials were paid in cash but they may have been also paid in kind. Although a good many coins called punch-marked coins of the imperial series are attributed to the Maurya state, they cannot be assigned to any Maurya king with confidence.

There is no way to measure the effectiveness of the state control of production. We do not know whether it was real or symbolic. But if palace economies could be practised in Egypt and Mesopotamia in the Bronze Age, state control of production could be possible in the Iron Age. The effective jurisdiction of the Maurya state may have been confined to the middle Ganga plains. These plains had four to six million people, if we calculate on the basis of the figures of soldiers given by classical writers. If the East India Company controlled the Ganga plains from Allahabad to Calcutta, the Maurya state could also do it in pre-industrial times. By river and land route the Asokan pillars could be transported from Chunar to Allahabad, Meerut and Ambala and also to Sanchi and Amaravati, not to speak of Patna and other places in Bihar.

What does the Maurya state signify in terms of production relations? By Maurya times the varṇa system was well established and Kauṭilya and other lawgivers lay down that high functionaries shall belong to higher varṇa and noble families. The state apparatus was therefore dominated by the brāhmaṇas and kshatriyas who constitute privileged groups in the Dharmasūtras. Though the vaiśyas could also be recruited for high offices śūdras were totally excluded. The Kauṭilyan king is considered to be all-powerful, but really his power is limited by dharma or law which upholds the established social hierarchy.

Production relations seem to have been upset towards the end of the third and beginning of the fourth centuries AD. The earliest Puranic descriptions of the Kali age assigned to these centuries by the Sanskritist R.C. Hazra speak of chaotic conditions created by the refusal of the vaiśyas and śūdras to perform the functions prescribed for them.[2] The rulers are called tyrannical and grabbers of property (*vittapiharinah*) and the brāhmaṇas are shown as behaving like śūdras. The state tried to cope with the situation by using force which is lauded in many texts. They also seem to have adopted the practice of land grants which led to unequal distribution of land and eventually to the contraction of the area covered by the ancient mode of production.

The best way to study ancient India is to study the development of material culture and its impact on society and economy, for we cannot apply any single label to the ancient mode of production. The Asiatic mode applied to the economic systems of both ancient and medieval India by Karl Marx has lost its relevance because of the material and methods available to us 150 years after his study of India. Marxism certainly helps us understand better the economic and other aspects of ancient history, but the specific historical findings of Marx may not be always useful. The attempt to place the ancient Indian economy in the straitjacket of the slave mode of production is misplaced. The Kauṭilyan state used slaves and hired labourers on state farms, but neither the number of farms nor that of the slaves are known. Asoka's claim to have brought 100,000 captives from Kalinga to Pataliputra may be an empty boast, for the term one hundred thousand or *sata sahasa*, repeatedly mentioned in his inscriptions, is a cliche. The law-books state that the śūdras must be reduced to slavery, for which they are created by the Creator Himself. But the ancient texts mostly suggest domestic slavery and not slaves engaged in artisanal and agricultural production. Ancient Indian society can be called a slave owning society in the sense that people employed domestic slaves, but it cannot be characterized as a society based on the slave mode of production. The mode could however be called a peasant mode though such a generalization leaves out the śūdra labour employed in production. At any rate no single mode of production can be posited for the period from Rigvedic times to Gupta times.

ASIATIC MODE OF PRODUCTION

The Marxists speak of the Asiatic mode of production, and some of them also apply it to pre-modern India.

The Asiatic mode of production stresses not only the role of the slaves in production, but also oriental despotism which regards the king as an untrammeled agrarian emperor. But in ancient India and in later times the rules of the Dharmaśāstras and the continuity of tradition controlled the king. Therefore neither the theory of slavery nor that of the despotic agrarian emperor can be applied to the pre-modern history of India. Therefore the Asiatic mode of production has no place in Indian history.

The early mode of production could be called a peasant mode. Though such a generalization ignores the śūdra labour enjoyed in production the vaiśyas were mainly peasant producers who paid taxes in ancient India

We have no idea about the number of various varṇas. Though some śūdras were used as slaves, they did not outnumber the vaiśyas in ancient times. Bharatratna P.V. Kane, who wrote five volumes of the history from the Dharmaśāstras,[3] states that the vaiśyas were the principal tax payers in ancient times. This suggests that they were mainly peasants who produced and paid taxes. Hence it would be wrong to think that the śūdras were mainly used as slaves in the mode of production. It seems that the mode of production was far more managed by the vaiśyas than by the śūdras who only could be reduced to slavery according to Manu.

In developing the idea of the Asiatic mode of production some scholars stress the role of slaves in the mode of production and also em-phasized the presence of oriental despotism. Some Marxists apply this mode of production to pre-modern India. But the historical sources do not show that the agricultural production was mainly carried on by the slaves. Similarly the country did not experience the rule of an untrammeled agrarian emperor.

It is said that the king controlled both land and water. Control of water or hydraulic despotism does not appear in early India. The rules of the law books or the Dharmaśāstras governed the connections of the different castes with the management of production as well as the functioning of the rājā on the basis of Dharma. Further, the tribal traditions of equality did not completely disappear from society even when it was divided into castes. Only the śūdras were considered slaves. On the other hand the kṣatriyas represented varṇa of rulers. But the kings ruled with the support of the brāhmaṇas who created an ideological atmosphere through their teachings and various social and religious ritualism festivals.

NOTES

†For the earlier studies see Bhupendranath Datt, *Studies in Indian Polity*, Calcutta, 1944; S.A. Dange, *India from Primitive Communism to Slavery*, People's Publishing House, Bombay, 1949; and R.S. Sharma, *Some Economic Aspects of the Caste System in Ancient India*, Patna 1952. D.D. Kosambi, *An Introduction to the Study of Indian History*, Popular Prakashan, Bombay, 1956 was a pathbreaking work. Dev Raj Chanana *Enclavage dans l'Inde ancienne de' apres les Texts Palis at Sanskrits*, Pondicherry, 1957, was the first well-researched work on slavery; it appeared in English version as *Slavery in Ancient India*, People's Publishing House, Delhi, 1960. My own books include *Shastras in Ancient India*, Motilal Banarasidass, 1958, 3rd edn. 1990: *Aspects of Political Ideas and Institutions in Ancient India*, Motilal Banarsidass, 1959, 3rd edn 1991, *Material Culture and Social Formations in Ancient India*, Macmillan, Madras, 1983; *Perspectives in Social and Economic History of Early India*, Munshiram Manoharlal, New Delhi, 1983; and *Origin of the State in India*, Department of History, University of Bombay, Bombay, 1989. Also see Romila Thapar, *From Lineage to State: Social Formation in the Mid-first Millennium BC*, Oxford University Press, Delhi, 1984.

1. I.W. Mabbett, *Truth, Myth and Politics in Ancient India*, New Delhi, 1972; J.C. Heesterman, *Inner Conflict of Indian Tradition*, Oxford University Press, Delhi, 1985, pp. 16–18, 129, 132–3, 139–40, 142–3, 260 with his 20–1; Romila Thapar, *The Mauryas Revisited*, Calcutta, 1987.
2. R.S. Sharma, 'The Kali Age: A Period of Social Crises' in S.N. Mukherjee, ed., *India: History and Thoughts—Essays in Honour of A.L. Basham*, Calcutta, 1982, pp. 186–203.
3. R.S. Sharma, *India's Ancient Past*, OUP, New Delhi, 2005, p. 324.

11

Stages in Ancient Economy*

I

The economic history of India can be traced back to 3500 BC, which marks the birth of an urban civilization, based on the surplus produced by the peasants. This civilization became fully urban by 2600 BC. Although the two well known centres of Harappa culture were Harappa and Mohenjodaro, several other sites, including some towns, have been recently discovered, extending the outposts of the culture into Eastern Punjab, Rajasthan and the Narmada estuary in the Kathiawad peninsula; it is reported that Harappa pottery has been also unearthed at Kausambi near Allahabad. The means of transport was nothing better than the cart drawn on uncharted roads, but there does not seem to be any doubt about the close connection between the different Harappa areas, which are characterized by uniformity in several aspects of material life such as the use of the same chalcolithic implements, pottery, and weights and measures. The period of this civilization extends from *c*. 3500 to 1900 BC.

There is no doubt that thickly populated and congested nuclei of houses, which can be rightly designated as towns, were populated by the rulers (possibly priests), traders and craftsmen, who lived on the surplus produced by the peasant communities inhabiting the villages situated in the suburbs. Agriculture and domestication of animals such as bulls, dogs, elephants, etc. were practised, but the archaeological evidence suggests that the means of production were primitive. It was neither plough nor hoe agriculture, but cultivation was probably carried on by means of the celt, the use of which cannot be definitely attested on

*Previously published as, 'Stages in Ancient Indian Economy', *Light on Early Indian Society and Economy* (Bombay, 1966), pp. 52–89. The French version of the article was published in the *Journal of World History*, vol. VI, no. 2.

account of the difficulty of identification. It is suggested by Gordon that wooden ploughs may have been used,[1] but perhaps they were drawn by men and not by oxen. Of such cutting implements as could extend the area of cultivation, we hear of the stone axe, which could not be as effective as the socketed axe. The latter first appears in cemetry H, ascribed variously to the Aryans or to a still unidentified people known as the Ravi people. In spite of such primitive implements the peasants produced sufficient grain, thanks to their hard work and the efficiency of the economic organization, over and above their needs, and the excess could be diverted to meet the needs of the people living in towns and engaged in trade and commerce. Perhaps a part of the grains was received as taxes, which were stored in the two huge granaries at Harappa and Mohenjodaro.

We have no evidence of trade in grains, although a part of the excess grain may have been exported to the neighbouring backward semi-nomadic peoples. Cotton cloth and raw cotton in bales may also have been exported. There are good reasons to suppose the existence of commerce in copper, lead and tin, which were wanting in the area covered by the Harappa sites and probably imported by traders from Iran, perhaps by way of the sea. Probably trade in tin was not as brisk as that in copper, for the proportion of tin found in the Harappa bronze is less than that used in contemporary Mesopotamia. Besides these two metals of common use, the Harappa people also traded in several precious metals such as lapis lazuli, amazonite, jade, etc. These were apparently used as objects of ornamentation and refinement by the higher class people. In commerce the Harappa culture gravitated more towards the west than the east, for the Harappa seals belonging to the period between 2600 BC and 1900 BC, especially after 2400 BC, have been found in some quantity in Sumer or Lower Mesopotamia. Trade between Sumer and the Indus Valley seems to have been particularly thriving between 2400 BC and 2150 BC. Whether the Harappa traders set up in Sumer their regular trading agency just as the Semites did in Asia Minor is not known; in any case there must have been certain well defined laws to regulate such brisk commercial relations.

Unless the Indus Valley scripts are deciphered the nature of the organization, which made possible urban life on a scale incomparable in ancient India from the point of view of a limited area, will remain a matter of speculation. Obviously the laying out of towns with streets and perfect drainage systems and the erection of houses all made of burnt bricks, must have required a huge staff of bricklayers, masons, woodcutters, charcoal burners, smiths, surveyors, engineers and carters, a fact which bears testimony to the great organizing feat of the Indus Valley people. The industry of bricklaying and building was far more important and developed in the Indus Valley than in the land of the Euphrates and Tigris, where the bricklayers specialized in bricks baked in the sun. It is suggested that all economic activities were directed by some central authority, but the theory that slave labour was an important part of the economy and daily life of the Harappa civilization has not much evidence to commend it. Judged from Indian standards the two-room tenements should not necessarily be taken as coolie lines, for even now the average family cannot boast of more than two rooms, which are sufficient to serve the needs of an Indian household of five, mostly working outdoors.

From the material point of view the chief cause of the disappearance of Harappa culture seems to have been the stagnation which is evident throughout its existence. On its first appearance about 2600 BC it strikes us as a chalcolithic culture with static maturity, which perpetuates its monotonous, uniform character, with some minor local variations, for about 1000 years. At the end of this period it goes out of history practically unwept and unsung. During this long period the Indus people do not make any creative or original contribution to the further progress of material life. Their ultimate fall is ascribed to climatic enervation and lack of external stimulus. But when the Harappa culture came into contact with external elements, instead of getting invigorated it died an ingnominious death. The theory that the Aryans destroyed the sites of Harappa culture looks plausible, and is becoming increasingly popular.

II

Evidently the Aryans possessed certain technological and material advantages, which enabled them to overcome their opponents in India. The widespread use of the horse yoked to their chariots was a potent cause of the military success of the Aryans, who combined it with the knowledge of cultivation by the plough. Although the Rgvedic Aryans do not seem to have been acquainted with bronze weapons, for *ayas* means pure dark copper, this was more than compensated by their use of horses and chariots, which made them formidable from the military point of view. The Vedic period which can be called the period of *Plough Cultivation* extended from *c.* 1000 to 500 BC.

The striking contrast between the material life of the Aryans and the Harappa people does not lie in the use of metals, but in the almost complete absence of towns in the Rgvedic period. If we rationalize the exploits of Indra recorded in the earliest Indian hymns, the Aryans appear as the destroyers of towns and not their builders. At best the Rgvedic Aryans lived in fortified places protected by mud walls, mostly in times of flood, and these cannot be regarded as towns in the Harappa sense. Perhaps the absence of urban life among the Aryans should be ascribed more to their early migratory habits and the predominance of cattle-rearing than to any other weakness in the material basis of their culture. Besides, in the first phase of their expansion when they were surrounded by hostile aborigines, commonly known as Dasas and Dasyus, they could not afford to lead a settled life in towns.

But the destructive exploits of their hero-god Indra should not make us blind to the great constructive role of the Aryans in the economic history of India. Literary evidence shows that their chief contribution was the introduction of cultivation by means of the plough drawn by bulls, evidently not known to the Harappa people. In the later Vedic texts, while the *Vratyas* are described as not cultivating the soil, the Vedic Aryans are frequently credited with practising agriculture. That the non-Aryans, with whose practices the *Vratyas* were supposed to have been tainted, knew agriculture is beyond any doubt. Hence the condemnation of the *Vratyas* as non-agriculturists only implies that the non-Aryans did not practise the art of ploughing in the Aryan manner. The Vedic Aryans yoked the oxen to their plough, in contrast to the Harappa people, who seem to have dug the fields themselves. Another factor which promoted agriculture was the knowledge of seasons. Five seasons are mentioned in the *Rgveda*. The various operations connected with ploughing, sowing, cutting of the corn with the sickle, threshing and winnowing are found in the first and tenth books of the *Rgveda*, which suggests that agrarian economy become more stable towards the end of the Rgvedic period. References in the tenth book of the *Rgveda* also suggest that the Aryans used fire for clearing the forests and thus making the land fit for cultivation.

Despite their practice of ploughing the Aryans are known to have had only one variety of grain known as *yava*, which may be taken either as a generic name for the various kinds of grain or in its later meaning, barley. Perhaps cattle-raising was a more important occupation, especially in the beginning of the Rgvedic period. Its importance can be inferred from the fact that 'the search for cows', *gavisti*, was another name for war, that constant prayers were made for kine; and that the daughter was known as *duhitr*, which term literally meant the milker of the cow. In addition to cows, goats, sheep and horses were domesticated, since common words for these animals are found in Indo-European languages. Of these, kine and horses are mentioned in the *Rgveda* in the context of agricultural operations although the exact use of the latter in agriculture cannot be determined. At any rate horses were not yoked to the plough, although they may well have been used as pack animals for carrying grain and fodder. Cattle were tended by common herdsmen, thus suggesting common ownership of some kind, but this cannot be said of the ownership of land with the same certainty. Common ownership of land in the *Rgveda* is an arguable proposition. Several words for fields and the practice of measuring land suggest that at least in actual practice there was private ownership of land. But this was of a very limited nature, for even in the later books of the *Rgveda* we have no evidence of the sale, transfer, mortgage, or gift of land or its disposal by an individual in any other way. We do not know whether the German analogy of Tacitus, who refers to the communal ownership of land distributed periodically among individuals, holds good of the Rgvedic Aryans, but clearly private ownership of land had not become effective during this period.

Among the arts and crafts the most important seem to have been those of weavers, wheelwrights and smiths. Weaving seems to have been mainly confined to wool, which was derived from the sheep. Cotton, attested by archaeological evidence in the ease of Harappa people, is not known to the *Rgveda*. On account of the importance of chariots in war the *rathakaras* (wheelwrights) performed an important function; so also seems to have been the case with the smiths, who made tools, implements and weapons of *ayas*. How far they inherited and carried on the craft traditions of the Harappans, whom they succeeded, cannot be said, The Rgvedic word for potter, *kulala*, has no parallels in other Indo-European languages, which might suggest that the Aryans adopted the local traditions in pottery. R.L. Turner considers it a Dravidian word. The tentative results of recent excavations at Hastinapura credit them with the introduction of Painted Grey Ware.

Since the Rgvedic Aryans were mainly occupied with war, they hardly had any time to produce the necessary surplus for purposes of trade. Although literary evidence testifies to their comparatively advanced knowledge of agriculture, their migratory habits and pre-occupation with cattle-raising were serious handicaps in the development of trade. The cow being the medium of exchange, internal transactions of sale and purchase were mostly in barter, although at one place the price of what appears to be an image of Indra is stated in terms of an unspecified unit, suggesting an incipient money economy. It is reasonable to suppose that the Rgvedic Aryans did not possess any knowledge of the sea, and the word *samudra* is used in the sense of collection of waters lying at the month of the Indus river.

III

The later Vedic period (*c*. 1000-500 BC) witnessed the expansion of the Aryans from the Panjab and Western U.P. into Eastern U.P. and Northern Bihar. The texts of the period give some clue to the material basis of this expansion. The *Satapatha Brahmana* states how Videgha Mathava went on burning the forests till he reached the Sadanira in North Bihar, an event which probably took place towards the end of the Vedic period. Burning, which was now adopted on a considerable scale, seems to have been supplemented by the use of the axe for cutting forests and of the iron ploughshare for bringing virgin land under cultivation. Although according to one source the plough was made of *udumbara* (Ficus Glomerata) wood, the *khadira* (Acacia Catechu) ploughshare had now given way to the iron ploughshare. We have references to the yoking of six, eight, twelve and even twenty-four oxen to the plough, indicating deep ploughing which could be rendered possible only by the use of iron ploughshare. Literary texts indicate the advent of iron about 800 BC, for we have references to the iron smelter and blacksmith in the *Yajus* collection, but archaeological evidence is better. The presence of iron slag in a Hastinapura layer is attributed to about 800 BC. At several places iron appears archaeologically about 1000 BC.

Although the *Atharva Veda* contains innumerable prayers for the increase of cattle, agriculture had come to be the chief means of the livelihood of the people, cattle remaining the principal form of their movable property. The *Satapatha Brahmana* devotes one whole Brahmana (VII.2.2.) to rites in connection with ploughing. In addition to barley the chief crop produced during this period was wheat, which still continues to be the staple food of the people in the Panjab and U.P. But it is for the first time during this period that rice, known as *vrihi*, makes its appearance. Remains of rice, ascribable to about the eighth century BC, have been found at Hastinapura. At this stage, however, rice seems to have been a crop of secondary importance. Sugarcane, which is mentioned in the *Atharva Veda* (I.34.1-5), may have been valued as a wild product.

In this period we have clear evidence of the private ownership of land. It is stated that a person who has a dispute about a field or with his neighbours should make an offering to Indra and Agni on eleven potsherds.

For the first time we hear of attempts at grants of land. We learn that the ksatriya can grant a settlement to a man with the consent of the clan (*SB*, VII.1.4). This implies the existence of separate holdings under the general control of the ruling tribe, at the head of which stood the king. But we have no cases of actual grants, for when in one case land was granted to a brahmana, the goddess of the Earth refused to be transferred.

The Vedic economic organization was closely related to the varna-divided social organization, which had been firmly established during this period. The priests, who headed the social order, officiated at the various rituals, sacrifices, and festivals associated with agricultural operations and offered prayers for the success of their patron chiefs in war. The ksatriyas earned their livelihood by means of war and government. To the vaisyas was assigned agriculture, and to the sudras service of the three higher varnas. Thus the priests and warriors had hardly any connection with the primary aspect, of production. It is not clear whether they owned large areas of land during this period. Keith holds that during the period of the *Brahmanas* there had emerged large estates worked by slaves and serfs. But there does not seem to be any basis for such a theory, for we have hardly any instance of slaves being employed in production. Inequalities of wealth did not result so much from the direct exploitation of slave labour as from the collection of a part of the produce from the peasants in the form of taxes by the king and his officers. In the *Atharva Veda* prayer is made to Indra for the grant of a share in villages, kine and horses to the king (IV.22.2). The share in villages perhaps implies a share in the crops produced by peasants, who paid this to the *bhagadugha*, after which it was perhaps deposited with the *samgrahitr*.

An important development in the later Vedic economy was the rise of diverse arts and crafts, which are enumerated in the list of the sacrificers at the *purusha-medha* (human sacrifice). This indicates considerable progress in the differentiation of functions but not any qualitative change in economy. We hear of smelter (*dhmatr*) and smith or carpenter (*karmara*), but we are not quite sure whether they had anything to do with iron working, which had just begun. Numerous copper hoards found in Bihar and U.P., ascribable to this period, indicate the predominance of copper working, copper tools and implements. General words for weaving suggested that this craft was mainly confined to women and practised on a wide scale. Leather work, pottery, and carpenter's work, probably connected with building activities, had also made some progress. We also hear of jewel workers, who probably catered for the needs of people living in towns. The presence of towns during this period is attested by the use of such words as town (*nagara*), town-dweller (*nagarin*), and the mention of Kausambi, Kosala and Vidbarbha as great towns. Excavations prove the existence of at least two great towns Kausambi and Hastinapura, the origins of which can be attributed to this period. It is doubtful whether arts and crafts contributed in any substantial measure to the rise of these towns, they seem to have been rather seats of political power.

The texts of the period make distinct references to the sea, and sea voyages, which may have been made for the purpose of carrying on commerce, stimulated by the rise of new arts and crafts.

IV

The period from *c.* 500–322 BC may be taken as marking a significant change in the economy, which was strengthened by the widespread use of iron, the extensive cultivation of rice, sugar and cotton, the rise and growth of numerous towns in North-Eastern India, the further diversification of craft and their organization into guilds, and last but not the least the brisk inland and foreign trade.

The technological basis of the economic progress was the growing knowledge of the use of iron, which was further facilitated by the use of bellows. Although in one text it is stated by way of simile that a ploughshare is heated through the whole day, suggesting thereby that the bellows was not in use, several texts of the period clearly refer to the use of bellows.[2] The importance of its introduction has to be emphasized. It made possible production of iron tools and implements on a large scale, and this hastened the process of the clearance of jungles in Bihar. Various kinds of rice, known as *sali* during this period, and especially the cultivation of sugar, required deep ploughing, which in its turn needed the periodical sharpening of the plough-share by means of bellows. The evidence from *Panini* shows that fields were ploughed twice or thrice; they were also divided according to crops. Thus an improved knowledge of cultivation and the use of effective implements enabled the peasants to produce more surplus, which could be used in feeding the people of about sixty towns that are mentioned during this period, and also for promoting trade. Trade received further impetus from improvement in means of transport. A later Jataka (iv, 210) informs us that a sheath of iron, two inches wide, was put round the outer edge of the wheel to make it very strong. It seems that by this time iron products themselves had become an important item in trade. Herodotus, who flourished in the fifth century BC, refers to the iron-tipped arrows carried by Indian soldiers of the army of the Persian ruler Xerxes. Similarly his contemporary Ktesias pays tribute to the excellence of the two swords of Indian steel presented to Artaxerxes Mnemon. Thus it is rightly suggested that trade in Indian iron and steel had already commenced from this time. At any rate in spite of less archaeological evidence it is fair to infer that the use of iron in pre-Maurya times made an important contribution to the overall development of economy.

It seems that the Buddhist ideology of non-injury to living beings and reaction against Vedic sacrifices helped to protect the cattle wealth, which was indispensable for the progress of agriculture. A Buddhist text (*Sutta-Nipata*, PTS, 296-7, cf. 309) states that cattle constitute the source of grain, strength, beauty, happiness, and hence they should not be slaughtered. This value was also emphasized by a brahminical lawbook, which lays down the difficult penance of *candrayana* for slaying a milch-cow or a draught-ox (*Baudhayana*, 1.10.4). In view of many references to cow-slaughter in Vedic texts,[3] this must be regarded as a very healthy development from the economic point of view. Cattle were probably owned individually, but as in the Vedic period, grassland or woodland was owned in common.

Efforts for the extension of the arable land by clearing woodland continued in pre-Maurya times. It is laid down by a lawgiver that the king may injure trees that bear fruits or flowers in order to extend cultivation and for sacrifices.[4] There prevailed the practice of burning forests for this purpose, as can be inferred from the comment of Abhayasuri on a passage of a Jain canonical text.[5] Initiative for bringing virgin soil under cultivation was obviously taken by the state or the community, to the pioneering or collective efforts of which can be ascribed the rise of plots of 500 or 1000 *karisas*, cultivated by slaves and hired labourers. But individuals did not lack such initiative. We have the instance of the sale of forest land cleared by the proprietor or his ancestors.[6] It seems that in Eastern India a considerable portion of land lay in the hands of the two upper *varnas*, who were free from taxes, but perhaps a greater part of the land was in possession of *gahapatis* (peasant proprietors) or *kutumbikas* (well-to-do-peasants). The number of such independent peasants was substantial, and their holdings were just sufficient to maintain them. According to *Baudhayana*, a lawgiver of about the fifth century BC, an ideal economic holding, necessary to support a family, seems to have been a holding of land measuring six *nivartanas*. This may have been the average size of a holding with regional variations. In any case the holdings of individuals were well-demarcated, for *Panini* refers to a systematic survey of agricultural land undertaken by special officers called *ksetrakaras*, corresponding to the *rajjugahaka-amaccas* of Buddhist sources. We have no idea of the rate of tithe, which may have varied from 1/6th to 1/12th, but in cases of emergency taxes in cash were also levied upon the people.[7] In spite of individual ownership two things are very clear about the land system of pre-Maurya times. First, although land revenues were assigned to the brahmanas, there was no sizable class of intermediaries between the king and the tillers of the soil. The peasants paid taxes directly to the king and were sometimes compelled to perform corvée. Second, there was a definite anti-alienating and communal feeling, subsisting from old tribal days, which did not allow free and easy disposal of land by way of sale, gift or mortgage.

The distinctive feature of pre-Maurya times is the development of urban economy, which reappears in India after a lapse of about one thousand years. In connection with the begging round of a monk the Jain canonical texts mention different kinds of urban settlements such as a scot-free town, a town with an earthen wall, a town with a small wall, an isolated town, a large town, a sea-town, and a capital.[8] We further learn that Aristobulus, when sent on a commission by Alexander to a region left a desert by a shifting of the Indus to the east, saw the remains of over a thousand towns and villages once full of men. Unfortunately these towns of the Indus Valley have not been excavated so far. Taking the country as a whole, to this period are assigned sixty well-known towns, spreading from *Campa* in the east to *Bhrgukaccha* in the west, from *Kaveripattana* in the south to *Kapilavastu* in the north.[9] Big cities such as *Sravasti* were twenty in number, and six of them were considered sufficiently important to be the scene of the Buddha's passing away. These were *Campa, Rajagrha, Saketa*, Kausambi, Banaras and *Kusinara*; the greatness of *Pataliputra* was still to come. Really the towns owed their importance to arts and crafts. Thus in the case of *Rajagrha* later texts refer to the existence of eighteen guilds. Of the conventional eighteen guilds referred to in the Buddhist texts only the names of four, woodworkers, smiths, leather-workers and, painters are mentioned. Every guild was presided over by a head, and had its own laws to observe. In two Buddhist birth-stories, the royal procession on two important occasions is said to have included the eighteen guilds, which implies that the king exercised some general control over them. Probably the *bhandagarika*, who held the office of the treasurer at Banaras, exercised such a supervision over all the guilds on behalf of the king. Industry and trade were handled by *setthis*, who generally lived in towns but also maintained connections with their counterparts living in the countryside. There were different grades of *setthis*, high and low, and the title of the *setthi* was conferred as a mark of distinction by the king. Such *setthis* were also granted *bhogagamas* or revenues of the villages for their upkeep. But we are not sure whether the *setthis* had any connection with the guild. At any rate, the king's supervision did not destroy the initiative of the guilds, for while administering justice he was required to take into account the laws of the guilds, castes and regions. Similarly although localization and heredity came to be associated with crafts on account of the prevalence of the guilds, they did not suffer from lack of mobility. We know the story of a whole village, of carpenters who overnight emigrated to a different place because they found it impossible to comply with the wishes of the king.

We do not know the exact relation between the village and the town. Villages, which, because of better means of production, produced seven kinds of grain and seven kinds of pulses, obviously supplied surplus food for the large number of artisans, merchants, and soldiers and for the household establishments of the king and nobles living in the town. Panini indicates that the king and richer sections of people employed as many as a dozen varieties of attendants to look to their personal comforts.[10] Whereas the king collected his taxes in kind, some *setthis* collected grain from their *bhogagamas* in the countryside, which enabled them to live comfortably. In return for surplus grain the towns probably supplied cloth to villages, for we hear of the cultivation of cotton in the neighbourhood of Banaras which manufactured cloth from it.

Like town life, trade revived on a considerable scale after a lapse of 1200 years. Cloth seems to have been an important article of trade, for the early Pali texts suggest that cotton came into general use in the age of the Buddha, but trade was mainly confined to luxury articles. Nevertheless, traders laden with commodities frequented the distant and difficult trade routes in the country. We have frequent references to caravans of 500 carts each in the Buddhist birth-stories. Traders also visited such distant countries as Babylon. Shore-sighting birds were employed to facilitate navigation.

Trade was facilitated by the advent of money economy, which was ushered in by the use of punch-marked coins. Vedic evidence for the prevalence of coins is not corroborated by any finds belonging to that period. Our earliest finds of coins cannot be dated beyond the age of the Buddha, when they were used by groups of merchants who punched their marks on them. During this period money economy had become so important that even the price of a dead mouse is stated in terms of money. We repeatedly hear of *setthis* or others possessing eighty *kotis* (crores) of wealth living in towns. Moneylending was practised, and although it was not encouraged by Buddhism, as by Calvinism, those who had not cleared off their debts were not permitted to join the Buddhist *Sangha.*

It would be fair to conclude that in pre-Maurya times urban and rural economy developed on even lines in North-Eastern India, although the Precise role of the state in this connection cannot be indicated. Coins first appear in the northwest. But in regard to the Ganga region, it has been suggested that the punch-marked coins were issued by the ruling dynasties of Magadha and Kosala; the possibility cannot he ignored, but identification of coins with particular rulers still awaits final solution. The rulers showed interest in other economic activities such as the clearance of forests, regulation of the land system and supervision of guilds.

V

In Maurya times we witness an unprecedented expansion of the economic activities of the state. The distinguishing feature of Maurya economy (c. 322-200 BC) is the state control of agriculture, industry and trade, and the levy of all varieties of taxes on the people. Evidently the state was in dire need of a great amount of surplus in kind and cash, which had been rendered necessary because of several factors. No other state in ancient India, either earlier or later, maintained such a huge standing army as the Mauryas did. The process had begun with the Nandas (354-324 BC), who had raised their army from 5,000 elephants, 20,000 cavalry and 50,000 footsoldiers to 60,000 elephants, 1,00,000 cavalry and 2,00,000 foot-soldiers. Perhaps these figures accord well with the traditions about the enormous wealth of the Nandas. But by the time of Candragupta Maurya this figure multiplied almost twice, for Plutarch and Justin inform us that this first Maurya emperor overran the whole of India with 6,00,000 men. Megasthenes puts the total number of Mauryan army at 4,00,000. To maintain this large army, which was essential to defend the different parts of the farflung empire, must have meant terrific economic strain, which could not be met without finding new sources of income. Secondly, the Mauryas followed the policy of maintaining sufficient surplus in the treasury against emergencies. The normal taxes were not considered sufficient to meet all the needs of the state, and hence the state undertook and regulated numerous economic activities, which formed a profitable source of income to it. These enterprises necessitated the employment of a vast, numerous bureaucracy, consisting of the superintendents and subordinate staff in some thirty departments; this further burdened the state exchequer, which had to be replenished by new sources of taxes.

The Mauryas made an important contribution to the development of rural economy by founding new settlements janapadanivasa, and rehabilitating the decaying ones by drafting surplus settlers from overpopulated areas. The sudras, who were hitherto regarded as the collective property of the three higher varṇas, meant for their service as slaves and hired labourers, were encouraged to settle down as farmers in these settlements, made possible by the aid granted to them by the state. In order to bring virgin soil under cultivation, they were allowed remissions of taxes and other concessions by way of supply of cattle, seeds and money, in the hope that they would repay when they were in a position to do so. In the new settlements land was granted to retired village officials and priests, but such land could not be sold, mortgaged or inherited. Even the ordinary peasants could not pass on their land to the non-taxpaying peasants. If the farmers failed to cultivate the plots allotted to them, these were transferred to others for better use. Although the extent of these new settlements is not known, it would be reasonable to suppose that by means of sudra labour a considerable portion of the Ganga basin was brought under cultivation.

The state farms working under the supervision of the *sitadhyaksa*, or superintendent of agriculture, formed a major source of income to the state. We do not know the origin of these farms, but they seem to have been the natural culmination of the largescale farming with units of 500 or 1,000 *karisas* carried on by the '*kulaks*' in pre-Maurya times. Megasthenes refers to the absence of slavery, but under Candragupta a considerable number of slaves and hired labourers were employed in working these farms. Besides, the superintendent made use of an advanced knowledge of agriculture; thus *Kautilya* refers to six seasons, whereas we find only five seasons in the earlier period.

What helped agriculture most was the provision of irrigation facilities by the state and the regulation of water supply for the benefit of the agriculturists. Megasthenes informs us that in the Maurya empire the officer measured the land as in Egypt, and inspected sluices by which water was distributed into the branch channels, so that everybody might enjoy his fair share of the benefit. We learn from *Kautilya* that irrigation cess amounted to a fifth, a fourth or a third of the produce of the irrigated soil. As in Egypt, the regulation of irrigation may have contributed to the centralization of the state power, especially in Western Bihar, U.P. and Panjab where only a regular supply of water could ensure the normal yield of crops.

The Maurya state regulated trade and industry by means of a number of superintendents. The superintendent of commerce (*panyadhyaksa*) corresponded to Megasthenes's 'great officers of state of whom some held the charge of the market'. The superintendent of weights and measures (*pautavadhyaksa*) was responsible for enforcing correct weights and measures. The superintendent of ships regulated communications by water and realized ferry dues. But the customs on commodities for internal and external commerce were mainly collected by the superintendent of tolls (*sulkadhyaksa*), who realized customs varying from 1/5 to 1/25 according to the nature of commodities. The state derived further profit from the supervision of several industries. The superintendent of weaving (*sutradhyaksa*) looked after the weaving industry, which was mainly run by woman labour. The superintendent of liquor managed the breweries and state wine shops, which flourished at the cost of private breweries, encumbered with the payment of heavy duties to the state. Thus the state enjoyed almost unrestricted monopoly in trade in liquor, as in salt.

In our opinion the main base of royal power, and all agriculture, trade and industry, was mining and metallurgy. Speaking of the Kathaians in the time of Alexander, Strabo states that the Indians are unacquainted with the mining and the smelting of ores and hence do not know their wealth and traffic with simplicity[11] but this can apply to the Kathaians and not to the Indians as a whole. In the Maurya period *Kautilya* provides for the superintendent of mines (*akaradhyaksa*), who was expected to possess a thorough knowledge of the technical aspects of mining, including metallurgy. He was to prospect for new mines and discover old and disused ones by various signs. The literary evidence suggests that gold, silver, copper, lead, tin, iron and bitumen were worked. But except for the mining of copper and gold the archaeological evidence is scanty. It has been suggested that the copper and gold mines in Dhalbhum in Chotanagpur were worked from the time of Candragupta Maurya. The nearest copper mines to the Maurya capital *Pataliputra* are those of Baragunda in the Hazaribagh district and Singhbhum, and probably they furnished at least some copper vessels, used at the court.[12] Since numerous small heaps of iron slag are to be found scattered all over the iron belt in south Bihar, these may have been the refuse of local iron smelters.[13] But whether these workings are as old as the Maurya period cannot be stated. Literary evidence, however, does not leave any doubt about the working of iron, for *loha* (iron) in its various forms is mentioned far more frequently in the *Arthasastra* than *tamra* (copper). The *lohadhyaksa* seems to have been the officer in charge of iron working. Other officers employed in connection with mining and metal work were the superintendent of digging (*khanyadhyaksa*), the officer who distinguished between different elements (*laksanadhyaksa*), and the superintendent of salt (*lavanadhyaksa*). Thus the state enjoyed a monopoly in the working of mines and in trade in mineral products. This was not only a source of great income but was also of great help in strengthening the central power for only the state could equip the soldiers with metal arms and furnish agriculture and industry with necessary tools and implements. *Kautilya* was fully conscious of the importance of metals and mining. He points out that the treasury has its origin in mining, and force (*danda*) in the treasury, and it is by means of the treasury and force that earth is acquired (II.2).

The income derived from economic undertakings was supplemented by a large number of customary and new taxes. The chief tax was the royal share in the produce of the peasants, amounting to perhaps 1/6th. But the Greek accounts suggest that this was levied at the rate of 1/4th of the produce. One Greek source indicates that the levy amounted to 1/4th, whereas the other states that the peasants received one-fourth of the produce as their share. Perhaps the second is due to some confusion, and both mean the same thing. However, we hear of sharecroppers, who were supplied with seed, oxen, etc., by the state and received arable land for cultivation. Those who were in a position to invest their own capital in the land allotted to them by the state received half the crop as share. Thus the state derived income from both the fixed royal share of the 1/6th of the produce as well as from sharecropping. Besides the regular *bhaga* (royal share of 1/6th), the peasants were required to pay the *pindakara*, which was lump assessment made on the groups of villages. We do not know the nature of another tax, known as *bali*, which was as old as Vedic times but may have been a religious tax during Maurya times. *Kara* was probably a part of the produce, from the fruit and flower gardens paid to the state. *Senabhakta* probably involved an obligation on the part of the villagers to supply provisions to the royal army when it passed through their territories. *Hiranya* seems to have been a payment in cash. In addition to these the peasants had to pay irrigation cesses, to which reference has already been made.

We have seen how customs and ferry dues constituted important sources of income to the state. Taxes were also levied on the guilds of artisans living in the capital (or *durga*), which may imply that the artisans living in the countryside enjoyed exemption. Thus the list of taxes in Maurya times is impressive, and reveals a deliberate attempt on the part of the state to extract as much surplus produce from the people as possible. But what is remarkable, even these numerous taxes, levied normally, could not meet the mounting expenditure of the state. And hence, although we hear of emergency tax in Panini, for the first time the *Arthasastra* provides such taxation measures of a large scale. One such measure was the imposition of *pranaya*, which has been interpreted as the gift of affection, but this meaning seems to be as illusory as that of the term *bali* in the sense of voluntary offering in Maurya times. *Pranaya*, however, could be levied only once and amounted to 1/3 or 1/4th of the produce according to the nature of soil. Another extraordinary measure laid down by the *Arthasastra* is the compulsory raising of a second crop by the cultivators. We learn from Patanjali that the Maurya rulers also derived income from the images of gods. This may have been done either by selling them or establishing them for worship. The latter device was recommended by the *Arthasastra*. According to the Jain tradition *Canakya* issued eight hundred million debased silver coins called *karasapanas* to fill the treasury. All these were emergency measures to meet extraordinary situations in Maurya times. Moreover, a major portion of the ordinary taxes seems to have been set apart for this purpose, for the Maurya policy was to deposit half the income as an insurance against emergencies. Had they not followed this policy, the incidence of normal taxation on the people would have been lower. But as it is, the numerous ordinary and extraordinary taxes, and the undertaking and control of important economic activities of the country, show that the whole economy of the country was geared to the financial needs of the state.

Perhaps most of these taxes were realized in kind and deposited in the central store house under the supervision of its superintendent (*kosthagaradhyaksa*). But as would appear from payment to government employees in cash (their highest salary being 48,000 *panas* and the lowest 60 *panas*) and from the duties of the superintendent of the mint, money economy had made considerable headway. This can be also inferred from several hoards of the punch-marked silver coins, certain types of which are specifically ascribed to Maurya rulers. Nevertheless, further development of money economy was thwarted by the Maurya policy of freezing half of the collected taxes in the treasury and not putting them to any productive use. Besides, the irksome customs levied on all varieties of commodities may have acted as another deterrent to the progress of money economy. In spite of this the country registered substantial economic progress in the Maurya age, which witnessed giant strides in the development of agriculture and the mining industry.

VI

The state control over all sectors of economy established by the Mauryas did not last for more than a century. In post-Maurya times (*c.* 200 BC–AD 200) we no longer hear of state farms worked by slaves and hired labourers under the supervision of the superintendent of agriculture. But land seems to have been mainly in possession of individual farmers. As regards the extension of the area of cultivation state efforts seem to have been replaced by individual efforts. The *Milinda-panha* refers to the individual who clears the forest and takes other steps for making the land fit for cultivation. And because he brings the land under use, he is called the owner of the land.[14] This Is also corroborated by *Manu*, according to whom sages declare a field to belong to him who cleared away the timber, and a deer to him who first wounded it (IX.44). Thus theoretically the investment of physical labour in a piece of unclaimed property was supposed to confer on the individual the title to that property. The principle was probably enunciated to give a fillip to the extension of cultivation. This can be also inferred from a passage of *Manu*, according to which the acceptance of an untilled field by a brahmana is less blamable than that of a tilled one (X.114). Although, as we shall see presently, the practice of making grants of cultivated land had already come into vogue, the underlying idea of making grants of untilled land to the brahmanas was to make it arable. *Gautama* and *Manu*[15] encourage separate households for brothers on the ground that it increases religious: merit; this implies promotion of individual ownership of land. The *Divyavadana* refers to individual farmers in large numbers working hard and engaged in cultivation.[16]

This period provides us the first epigraphic evidence for the grant of land by merchants, lay worshippers and rulers to Buddhist monks for their support and allied religious purposes[17] in the Satavahana dominions. Grants made by the rulers carried freedom from taxation and full and unrestricted enjoyment of the resources of the village which was granted. Some inscriptions refer to the size of plots of 2, 3, 4, 8, 12 and 25 *nivartanas*,[18] one *nivartana* being roughly equal to an acre and a half. These plots do not necessarily give any idea of the fragmentation of land, except suggesting that there also existed smaller plots of land. We have, however, also a reference to a grant of 100 *nivartanas* of land of a royal field.[19] Remarkably enough none of the inscriptions from northern India refer to the grant of land during this period, although the epigraphic reference to the *aksayanivi* (perpetual endowment) system in connection with money donations may suggest that the grant of land according to this tenure, which became fashionable in Gupta times, had already begun during the first two centuries of the Christian era.

Stringent punishments, including death, laid down by the law-books for those who cause any harm to water reservoirs and destroy embankments, and the glorification of the virtues of constructing wells and tanks, indicate that the importance of irrigation was fully realized. Irrigation facilities continued to be provided by some rulers on regional basis. Thus *Kharavela* not only repaired and enclosed a tank in *Kalinganagari*, but also extended an old canal, opened by king Nanda, at the cost of a hundred thousand *panas*. A work of similar importance was undertaken in Saurastra by *Rudradaman* (A.D. 150), who repaired a major breach in the dam of the lake, by spending enormous wealth out of his own pocket, without burdening his subjects with taxes, forced labour and emergency impositions. The happy tradition of constructing tanks in Western India was maintained by the successors of *Rudradaman*. Tanks seem to have been constructed by *Saka* and *Kusana* chiefs in North-Western India. Evidence of the popularity of tanks in this part as well as U.P., during the first two centuries of the Christian era, is furnished by the practice of offering ritual tanks, which have been discovered at Taxila, Hastinapura, Udaipur, Ahicchatra (in Bareily), Kausambi and Bhita near Allahabad. Whereas tanks may have been constructed by rulers, initiative for such undertakings was also shown by individuals, whose house, tank, orchard and fields were protected against seizure by others.[20] Tanks were also dug by co-operative efforts made by the villagers. There is however not much evidence for the use of canals in the first two centuries of the Christian era. This might suggest that comparatively smaller plots of land had come to be the order of the day, and irrigation by wells or tanks may have been employed as an aid to the intensive cultivation of these plots.

Although the state did not undertake agricultural operations as it did in the Maurya period, it probably enforced laws to protect agriculture, which was apparently disturbed by repeated foreign invasions. Thus Manu enjoins the king to punish people for the theft of agricultural implements (IX.293) and provides mutilation for selling false seed corn, for taking up seed already sown, and for destroying boundary marks

(IX.291). Perhaps this was one of the most tangible economic benefits, in return for which the state levied taxes on the agriculturists. The *Milinda-panha* refers to the village headman (*gamasamika*), who summoned all the village householders through his messenger to the front of his house for the purpose of levying taxes on them on the king's behalf (p. 147).

The state hardly exercised any control over arts and crafts, which witnessed a remarkable growth during this period. We do not come across so many kinds of artisans in the earlier Buddhist texts or the *Arthasastra,* as during this period. The *Digha Nikaya* mentions about two dozen traders,[21] but the *Mahavastu* gives a list of thirty-six kinds of workers living in the town of *Rajagrha.*[22] The list is not exhaustive, for it is said at the end of it that there are others besides these mentioned. The *Milindapanha* enumerates as many as seventy-five occupations (p. 331), about sixty of which were connected with various kinds of crafts. Of these eight crafts were associated with the working of mineral products, such as gold, silver, lead, tin, copper, brass, iron and precious stones or jewels (p. 331). A variety of brass (*arakuta*), zinc, antimony and red arsenic are also mentioned.[23] All this betokens considerable advance and specialization in the working metals. In particular, technological knowledge about the working of iron had made considerable progress.[24] It is because of this that Indian iron and steel are mentioned in the *Periplus* as imports into the Abyssinian ports.

Cloth-making, silk-weaving, and the making of arms and luxury articles[25] seem to have made progress during this period. Five processes of cloth manufacture were undertaken by Gotami, the aunt of the Buddha.[26] Mathura had acquired special celebrity for its manufacture of *sataka*, a special kind of cloth.[27] Manu levies taxes on the produce of the weavers, who probably owed their affluence to trade in textiles produced in Mathura. We do not know whether there was any special progress in the manufacture of oil, but the *tailkacakra* or oil wheel is mentioned in the *Divyavadana* (p. 70). In the inscriptions of the period weavers, goldsmiths, dyers, workers in metal and ivory, jewellers, sculptors, fishermen, smiths, and more frequently perfumers, figure as donors of caves, pillars, tablets, cisterns, etc., to the. Buddhist monks, which suggests that their crafts were in a flourishing condition.

In post-Maurya times we get the earliest epigraphic evidence regarding the existence of the guilds of artisans. Artisans were organized under their headmen, who probably enjoyed the favour of the king.[28] During the second century AD in the Satavahana territory money (in silver *panas*) was deposited by the lay devotees of Buddhism with the potters, the oil millers and the weavers for the purpose of providing robes and other necessities for the monks.[29] In the same century a sum of money was deposited by a chief with the guild of flour makers at Mathura, out of the monthly interest of which a hundred brahmanas were to be served daily.[30] Thus the craftsmen organized in guilds could function independently. Evidently they could purchase raw materials and implements with money deposited with them and could pay interest on it out of the proceeds from the sale of their commodities. Literary evidence indicates that the number of guilds had increased during this period. Besides the traditional eighteen guilds the *Mahavastu* (iii, 442f.) mentions eleven kinds of artisans, all working under their respective heads (ii, 463–78). A comparison of the two lists of this text attests the existence of at least two dozen guilds of artisans during this period. Many of these artisans functioned both as producers and small traders. Although the Buddhist texts refer to Rajagrha and Sakala as centres of arts and crafts, most artisans known from inscriptions were confined to the Mathura region, and to the Western Deccan where their prosperity was stimulated by the growing trade with Rome.

From the economic point of view the most important development of the period was the thriving trade between Southern India and the Roman Empire. In the beginning the major part of this trade seems to have been by land. But the movement of the Sakas, Parthians and Kusanas which followed from the first century BC put an end to this trade. The Parthians of Iran, however, imported iron and steel possibly from China or India. But from the first century AD, trade was carried on mainly by sea. The discovery of monsoons by Hippalus in AD 46 gave a great impetus to this trade, which may have existed in driblets in earlier times. The sailors now became armed with better knowledge of navigation, which enabled them to call at the Indian ports of *Bhrgukaccha* (Broach), Arikamedu (Pondicherry) and Tamralipti. But the trade between India and Rome was not carried on in articles of daily or common use. The details show a brisk commerce in luxury goods but no extensive production by large industries.[31] It seems that the Romans mainly imported spices for which Southern India was famous. They also imported muslins, pearls and jewel-stones from Central and Southern India. All this may be taken as constituting 'terminal trade', for these products were directly supplied by India.[32] Besides, there was also some 'transit trade', especially in silk, which diverted by Parthian hostility from the more direct continental routes, sometimes found its way from China via the east coast of India to the ports of the Malabar coast from where it went to the West. In return the Romans exported to India wine-amphorae and red-glazed Arretine ware, which have been discovered in recent excavations at Arikamedu. But what is more important the Romans exported to India large-number of coins, invariably of gold and silver. Sixty-eight hoards of Roman coins of the first century AD have been unearthed in the sub-continent, and no fewer than fifty-seven come from south of the Vindhyas.[33] This justifies the complaint of Pliny who bewails the fact that Rome was being drained of gold on account of her trade with India.

It has been suggested that the Indians in peninsular India did not know the use of gold or silver currency,[34] and that, for the most part, the imported coins can only have been used as bullion. But we have some silver coins ascribable to the Andhras, and the epigraphic evidence suggests the use of silver *panas*. Hence Roman gold coins may have been valued for their intrinsic worth, but may also have circulated in big transactions. In the North, the Greek rulers issued a few gold coins, but the *Kusanas* issued them in considerable numbers. It is difficult to subscribe to the theory that all *Kusana* gold coins were minted out of the Roman gold. As early as the fifth century BC the Indian satrapy paid a tribute of 320 talents of gold annually to the Persian empire. The source of the metal may have been the gold mines, reported to have existed in Sind in the time of Alexander.[35] This territory and the gold mines of Dhalbhum lay under the sway of the *Kusanas*, who enjoyed the benefit of the knowledge of melting and mining transmitted by the Mauryas. But on account of contact with Rome they began to issue the *dinara* type of gold coins, which became abundant under the Gupta rule. Nevertheless, in day-to-day transactions silver, and especially gold coins, could hardly be used by the people. *Patanjali* refers to payment in *niskas* to the wage earners (*karmakaras*), but these do not seem to have been gold coins at this stage. In this connection the issue of lead or potin coins by the Andhras is significant, for it indicates that in the Deccan and in the coastal area money economy had come to be prevalent. The same inference can be drawn in respect of Northern and North-Western India from the coinage of the *Kusanas*, who perhaps issued the largest number of copper coins. Copper coins were also issued in large quantities by the Naga rulers, especially *Ganapati Naga*, and by several indigenous dynasties such as those of the *Yaudheyas* and the Mitra rulers of Kausambi, Mathura, Avanti and Ahicchatra and other dynasties. This would suggest that perhaps in no other period had money economy penetrated so deeply into the life of the common people of the towns and suburbs as during this period, a development which fits well with the growth of arts and crafts and the country's flourishing trade with the Roman Empire. In spite of this progress of money economy, if we rely on Manu it would appear that royal officers were not paid in cash. Revenue officials, who were in charge of one, ten, twenty, a hundred or a thousand villages, were remunerated by grants of land,[36] which indicates the dominance of natural economy in rural areas.

VII

The main interest of the economic history of Gupta age (*c.* AD 200–500) lies not so much in its foreign trade and money economy as in the partial feudalization of the land system and the rise of local units of production. An important development was the grant of cultivated land to temples and brahmanas in Northern and Eastern Bengal, and in the eastern part of modern Madhya Pradesh. But the land grants in Madhya Pradesh differed from those in Bengal in two important respects. The Bengal grants were the results of sale transactions effected by individuals and involved the transfer of land, but the Central India grants were made by feudatories who gave away villages. The Bengal grants were made with the consent of the officers of the central government and carried immunity from taxes only, but the Central India grants provided administrative immunities as well. Nevertheless, in the case of both these regions, terms denoting uncultivated land were used in a conventional sense. The same seems to have been true of the grants dated in the Kalacuri-Cedi era, found in Gujrat and Maharashtra during the fifth to the seventh century AD. The usual phraseology in most of such grants is that villages and plots of land were granted together with *udranga* and *uparikara*, inclusive of all dues and exempt from all gifts, forced labour and special rights, and not to be entered by soldiers and policemen, which indicates that those areas were settled areas. It has been suggested that the practice of granting land in Bengal and other parts of India extended the area under cultivation and rural settlement. This may have been true of some plots of land in Northern and Eastern Bengal, but generally in Madhya Pradesh, Gujrat and Maharastra settled villages and cultivated plots of land were the objects of gifts. In some cases the order regarding the grant of a village to the brahmanas was conveyed to the brahmanas and other inhabitants of the village, which shows that the brahmanas were not introduced into the village as pioneering cultivators.

The terms of transfer indicate that generally plots of land were cultivated not by the brahmanas but by temporary peasants. It seems that the number of independent and permanent peasant proprietors paying land tax directly to the king was falling off. Fa-hsien states that 'only those who till the king's land pay a land tax' and that they are free to go or stay as they please.[37] This probably excludes a large number of other people, who did not pay land taxes to the state but to priests, temples, monasteries and other intermediaries. For in the succeeding paragraph Fa-hsien clarifies the position by stating that monasteries are given fields and gardens with husbandmen and cattle to cultivate them.[38] Land grants from the fourth to the sixth century AD in Maharastra and Gujarat clearly establish that the recipient was given the right of enjoying the land, cultivating it or getting it cultivated on lease.[39] The number of the brahmanas who were actual cultivators may not have been insubstantial, for the law-books of the period provided that brahmanas might legitimately take to cultivation. But the brahmanas and temples often got their lands cultivated by others.

The law-books show that similar arrangements were made in relation to secular holdings, with the difference that the owner of the land had to make some payment to the state. *Kautilya* provides that in new settlement land fit for cultivation should be given to the peasants by the king,[40] but *Yajnavalkya* lays down that land should be assigned to the cultivator by the landowner (*ksetrasvami*), who, of course, was entitled to the fruits of improvement made on the land in the case of the absence of the owner (II.157). In the organization of the land system *Yajnavalkya* (II.158) introduces three stages, *mahipati* (king) *ksetrasvami* (landowner) and *karsaka* (cultivator), which is roughly corroborated by *Brhaspati* (XIX. 54–5). The intermediaries leased out land to cultivators, who were liable to penalties if they neglected cultivation.[41] So these cultivators were in the nature of temporary peasants. The same seems to have been true of the peasants under donees, who could replace old peasants by new and thus might oust their tenants.[42] Besides, the economic advantages, which hitherto accrued to the state, were completely transferred to the donees, thus cutting asunder the ties between the central government and the peasants. The state, however, maintained its control over the free peasants through the imposition of taxes. The villagers had to make not only various kinds of contributions to royal troops and officials when they passed through their areas, but they were also subjected to forced labour of all varieties (*sarva-visti*), probably for military purposes. Local officers were gradually assuming economic power. Vatsyayana informs us that peasant women were compelled to fill up the granaries of the village headman, take things into or out of his house, clear or decorate his residence, work in his fields, and spin yarn of cotton, wool, flax or hemp for his clothes (V.5.5), so that clothes might be supplied to him locally.

Some of the commodities thus produced were also put on sale, apparently to cater for the simple needs of the villagers. The Maurya state regulation of trade and industries was giving way to the management of these affairs by the chiefs of local economic units, independent of the central control.

There is further evidence to show that an important development in Gupta times was the rise of local units of production. Irrigation tended to be a local responsibility. In the Gupta period we have a reference to the repair of the famous Sudarsana lake in Saurastra, carried out by the local provincial government. But already from the beginning of the Christian era the local population had begun to take initiative in irrigation. The law-books of Brhaspati lay down that the guilds should look after irrigation dams (XVII.11–12).

Elaborate laws about corporate activities can also be linked with the rise of local and 'autonomous' units of production. The law-books of Gupta times lay down detailed rules regarding partnerships in business and functioning of guilds. These corporate bodies not only performed important economic functions such as carrying out joint contracts, plying trade and receiving money deposits, but also performed judicial and executive functions in relation to their members. Epigraphic evidence of the period shows that the guilds not only issued coins and seals; but also maintained their militia, which, according to the Kalacuri inscriptions, was known as *srenibala*. The increasingly autonomous character of the guilds, as virtually independent units of production and political power, can be inferred from the rules which govern the relation between the guilds and the state. Whereas the earlier texts enjoin the king to pay respect to the customs of the guilds (*srenidharma*),[43] those of the Gupta period instruct the king to enforce the usages prevalent in the guilds.[44] Brhaspati lays down that whatever is done by the heads of guilds towards other people, in accordance with prescribed regulations, must be approved by the king, for they are declared to be the appointed managers of affairs (XVII.18). He also warns that if the usages of localities, castes and families (*kulas*) are not maintained, the people will get discontented and wealth will suffer thereby (I.126). Thus it seems that the guilds were free to act in whatever way they liked, and the king was bound to accept their decision.[45] It is true that on certain occasions the king could interfere in the affairs of the guilds. Narada ordains that the king should prevent a combination of different guilds, probably of a hostile nature, the arming of these corporations without sufficient grounds, etc. He should also prevent them from embarking on anti-state or immoral or criminal actions (X.4–7). But these regulations clearly show that during this period the guilds were considered capable of threatening the authority of the state. Probably some of these guilds dominated the economic life of the towns such as Vaisali and Mandasor, and thus functioned as independent units of production.

That local units of production were coming into existence can also be inferred from the paucity of coins of common use from the Gupta period onwards. Whereas the Indo-Bactrians, and especially the Kusanas, issued a considerable number of copper coins, which were evidently in common use in the Punjab, and occasionally are found even as far east as Buxar in Bihar the Gupta emperors, other than Kumara Gupta, hardly issued any copper coins. Thus Fa-hsien seems to have been correct when he stated that cowries formed the common medium of exchange. Even allowing for the fact that copper is mow susceptible to corrosion than more precious metals, the comparative rarity of Gupta copper coins suggests that money economy was becoming weaker at this time. Coins in general become still rarer from the time of Harsavardhana onwards, which leads us to the conclusion that from the seventh century AD onwards trade suffered a decline and urban life began to disappear, a feature which can be compared with a similar development in Iran.

Reference has been made to the issue of copper coins by several indigenous dynasties of Northern India in post-Maurya times. There also began the practice of issuing coins by the *nigamas* during the post-Maurya and Gupta periods, which seems to provide further evidence of the rise of self-sufficient economic units. This accelerated the process of political disintegration, for issuing coins was an important function of the sovereign power. Besides, the issue of the seals by Nalanda villages, which glorify themselves as *janapadas* even in Gupta times, indicates that they were emerging not only as politically independent hut economically self-sufficient units. At least four such seals were issued from villages, some of which were issued by the *nigsmas*, but not by rural units as we find in post-Gupta times.

The rise of the local units of production undermined central authority, but some allied developments such as the strengthening of guilds helped to improve the position of artisans, who, instead of working a day in a month for the king, were now required to pay taxes. This was obviously an indication of further progress in arts and crafts. As in the previous period, during this period also the basis of economic progress lay in the extended and better technical use of metals. The *Amarakosa* furnishes us a long list of commonly used metals. We get two names for bell-metal (*pittala*) (II.9.96), four names for lead (II.9.105) three names for mica, four names for antimony (II.9.100), four names for blue vitriol (II.9.101), three names for vitriol of copper (*rasanjana*) (ibid., 102), four names for calx of brass (II.9.103), five names for yellow orpiment (*haritala*) (ibid.), five names for red chalk (*silajatu*) (ibid., 104), seven names for red arsenic (ibid., 108), three names for nitre or saltpetre (ibid., 108), and five names for natron or alkali (ibid., 109). Thus these furnish us not only the names of metals, natural and artificial, but also various kinds of ingredients used in making alloys. Copper, mica, manganese or glass, and mines of which the king was regarded as the owner, are mentioned in the works of *Kalidasa.*

From the point of view of common use the most important metal was iron, for according to a Mahayanist text the *yogi* was permitted the use of earthen or iron pots, but not of gold, silver, bronze or copper pots. The *Amarakosa* gives seven names for iron and two names for iron rust.[46] The same text provides five names for ploughshare (II.9.13), which may indicate ready supply of this most important agricultural implement and intensive cultivation of land. It seems that during this period there had also taken place some improvement in the ploughshare itself. In connection with the performance of the ordeal ceremony it is stated that the ploughshare, 4 lb in weight and eight *angulas* or four inches in breadth, was used in cultivation.[47] The weight seems to be reasonable, although the breadth may have been actually less. At any rate this indicates the use of a heavy ploughshare intended for deep ploughing or bringing virgin soil under cultivation. As is evident from the Mehrauli Iron Pillar of *Candra*, the technical knowledge in iron working had reached its high watermark during this period. The manufacture of bronze articles, which became more abundant from this period onwards, became widespread on account of the increasing and easy use of iron implements. Metal workers formed an important and sizable class of artisans, but hardly owned metals. It was laid down that a metal worker in iron, copper, lead, tin, silver or gold, has to pay to the owner of these metals, who gives these to him to prepare utensils for the loss in smelting which exceeds the usual loss.[48]

Besides metal workers, we learn of the presence of garland makers, washermen, potters, bricklayers, weavers, tailors, painters, armourers, leather workers, blacksmiths, and shell-cutters, for each of whom *Amara* gives two names (II.10.5.10). He, however, gives four names for goldsmiths and five for carpenters (II.10.8–9), which shows that their crafts were considered more important in society. The inscriptions show that in Central and Western India the crafts of silk-weavers and oilmen flourished well, for they were organized in guilds, made endowments for religious purposes; and especially the silk-weavers of Malwa showed considerable mobility and initiative.

Despite flourishing arts and crafts foreign trade does not seem to have been as extensive as in post-Maurya times. Trade with Rome, which was the main source of earning bullion for India, was undermined by the Roman reaction against the drain of gold, and was completely stopped because of the barbarian invasions of the Roman and Gupta Empires. Trade was, however, revived between India and the Byzantine Empire, as we learn from the account of Procopius, and the balance was still in favour of India. As usual the chief article of import by foreign traders was spices, to which we may add silk produced and manufactured in India; for Chinese silk was probably obtained by Byzantium directly from China rather than through India. The coastal people of Southern India carried on trade with the countries of South-East Asia, where they had planted colonies, but this did not seriously affect the economy of the interior of the country. Really the comparative absence of copper coins issued by the central authority during this period shows that there was hardly any medium through which the ordinary folk of one town could enter into exchange relations with those of the other. The gold coins issued by the Gupta rulers could be useful only for big transactions such as the sale and purchase of land, in which *dinaras* were used. Smaller transactions were evidently conducted through the barter system or cowries. It will be therefore fair to hold that Indian economy in Gupta times was based on self-sufficient units of production, in villages and towns. The bond of state control which kept these units together in Maurya times and that of copper currency which unified it in post-Maurya times no longer operated during this period. This is, however, not to suggest that production declined. On the other hand, it seems to have shown substantial rise, leading to some improvement in the position of the lower orders.[49]

The above survey of the economic history of ancient India, covering a period of about 3,000 years, would show that changes in economic life were not so swift and rapid as in political life, but they were not altogether absent. We can mark certain well-defined stages in this long history, namely, the urban economy of the Harappa culture; the pastoral and plough-cultivation economy of Vedic times; the wider use of iron, the extensive cultivation of rice, sugar and cotton, and the rise of towns in pre-Maurya times; the Maurya state control of all sectors of economy; expansion of money economy and thriving trade with the Roman Empire in post-Maurya times; and the partial feudalization of land system and the rise of local units of production in Gupta times. Many of these changes could not have been rendered possible without periodical improvements in the tools, implements and knowledge of production. It has been held that in India there has been practically no change in the means of economic production for more than 2,000 years,[50] but as far as ancient India is concerned there can he no basis for such a view.

NOTES

1. D.H. Gordon, *The Pre-historic Background of Indian Culture*, Bombay, 1958, p. 71.
2. *Panini*, VII.3.47; *Uvasagadasao*, ed. A.F. Rudolf Hoernle, Calcutta, 1890, p. 108.
3. S.K. Das, *The Economic History of Ancient India*, Calcutta, 1944, pp. 110–11.
4. *Vasistha*, XIX, 12.
5. *Uvasaga*, 51.
6. Rhys Davids, *Buddhist India*, pp. 46–7.
7. V.S. Agarwala, *India as known to Panini*, Lucknow, 1953, pp. 414–15.
8. *Antagada-Dasao* (tr. L.D. Barnett), pp. 44–5; *Ayaranga Sutta* (PTS), I.7.6.4; *Kalpasutra* (ed. H. Jacobi), p. 88; *Suyagadam* (ed. P.L. Vaidya), II.2.6.
9. S.K. Das, op. cit., pp. 175–83. *Kavirapattana* is mentioned in a past-story in *Jat.*, iv.238.
10. V.S. Agrawala, op. cit., pp. 97–8.
11. McCrindle, *Ancient India as described in Classical Literature*, p. 86.
12. Murray, *JRASB*, 3rd series, vi, 101.
13. Ibid., 79.
14. *Milinda*, Trenckner's edn, p. 219.
15. XXVIII, 4 and IX, 111 respy.
16. Cowell's edn, p. 463
17. *Lüder's List*, nos 1000, 1024, 1030, 1158.
18. *Arch. Surv. Western India*, iv, 97.
19. Ibid., p. 160.
20. *Manu*, VIII.264.
21. PTS, ii, 50.
22. Senart's edn, iii, 442–3.
23. *Mahavastu*, ii, 106.
24. It is stated that even when beaten, black iron carries weight and that it does not vomit up the water it has once soaked in (*Milinda*, p. 415).
25. *Milinda*, p. 331.
26. Ibid., p. 240.
27. *Patanjali*, I.1.2; Kielhorn, i.19.
28. *Luder's List*, no. 346.

29. Ibid., nos. 1133, 1137.
30. *EI*, xxi, Incr. no. 10.
31. E.H. Warmington, *Commerce between India and the Roman Empire*, Cambridge, 1928, p. 300.
32. Wheeler, *Rome beyond the Imperial Frontiers*, Pelican, p. 164.
33. Ibid., p. 165.
34. Ibid., p. 167.
35. Strabo, XV, 1.34 in Hamilton and Falconer, iii. 96.
36. *Manu*, VII.115–20
37. Legge, *A Record of Buddhistic Kingdoms*, pp. 42–3.
38. Ibid., p. 43.
39. *CII*, iv, no. 2, line 6; no. 11, line 13 etc.
40. *AS*, II.1.
41. *Yaj*., II.151–8; *Br*., XIX.19, pp. 53–5.
42. *CII*, iv, Introd., p. clxxi.
43. *Gaut.,* XI.21–2; *Manu,* VIII.41 and 46.
44. *Yaj*., II.192. Cf. I.361; *Narada*, X.2.
45. R.C. Majumdar, *Corporate Life in Ancient India*, Calcutta. 1918, p. 62.
46. II.9.98–9
47. *Brhaspati*, IX, pp. 79–80.
48. Jolly, *Hindu Law and Custom*, p. 236.
49. R.S. Sharma, *Sudras* in *Ancient India*, Delhi, 1958, pp. 234–41.
50. S.N. Dasgupta, *A History of Sanskrit Literature*, Calcutta, 1947, Introd., p. xciv.

12

Transition from Ancient to Medieval*

The concept of modernism is more or less clear to us. It is associated with the advent of capitalism in developed countries and colonialism in 'developing' countries. But the same cannot be said of medievalism, which may not mean the same thing in Asia and Europe. In western Europe, medievalism is associated with the feudal age roughly from AD 500 to AD 1500. But feudalism did not obtain in all non-European countries in pre-colonial times. The concept of what constitutes antiquity is even more complicated. If we leave out prehistory, ancient history extends roughly from 3500 BC to AD 500. Formerly antiquity meant Greece and Rome. Now we have to take account of Bronze Age civilizations such as those of Crete, Egypt, Mesopotamia, Elam, India, central Asia and China among others. It is very difficult to take a combined view of the cultures in the Bronze Age and antiquity and then to identify the common features of ancient life. In classical Greece and Rome, slavery appears as the dominant mode of production, and the transition to feudalism/medievalism is seen in terms of the transformation of a slave society into a serf-based society, caused by a combination of the decomposed slave mode of production with the deformed primitive modes of production introduced by the Germanic invaders in the Roman empire.[1] Social and cultural transformations cannot be viewed similarly in India, for ancient Indian society was neither dominated by the slave mode of production nor overwhelmed by foreign invasions. But there is no doubt that certain basic changes occurred in polity, economy, society and other aspects of Indian life between the fourth and seventh centuries AD. In our search for these changes we cannot lose sight of the elements common to antiquity

*Previously published as, 'Transition from Ancient to Medieval' in R.S. Sharma, *Early Medieval Indian Society* (New Delhi: Orient Longman, 2004).

and the Middle Ages. Thus, the social order based on state, varṇa and jati and the patriarchal family appears in both ancient and medieval India. Similarly, iron-based plough share agriculture continues in both antiquity and the Middle Ages. This also applies to bricks, pottery and structures and methods of fabricating them. The same is true of a number of rituals, varṇa reform movements and the bhakti movement. Notwithstanding the existence of all these elements in both the pre- and post-seventh century periods, there are certain striking differences between the two.

The advent of Turkish Muslim rule in India is generally seen as marking the end of the ancient period, and textbooks on ancient Indian history by eminent scholars such as R.D. Banerji, R.C. Majumdar, K.A. Nilakanta Sastri and K.S. Tripathi carry the narrative roughly down to AD 1206. This position is based on the British scheme of dividing Indian history into Hindu, Muslim and British periods and is broadly accepted by the Indian History Congress. Thus, ancient India is confused with Hindu India and medieval India with Muslim India. The obsession with Muslim rule has been so strong with the earlier generation of Indian historians, both Hindu and Muslim, that they equate medievalism with Muslim rule. If the establishment of Muslim rule is taken to mark the beginning of medieval India, then Turkey, Egypt, Iraq, Iran, Pakistan and Indonesia, will have to be permanently placed in the medieval period and Hindu Nepal in the ancient period. And what of the onset of the medieval age in those countries which were not conquered by Islamic forces?

Sometimes the language of source materials is used as a ground for identifying a new period in Indian history. Arabic and Persian sources are taken as representing the beginning of a new period. But how can a period be identified with the use of one particular language? The same period has radically different languages that are used in the reconstruction of its history in one region, several regions or the subcontinent as a whole. Variation in sources and languages makes identifying and understanding the history of ancient India extremely difficult. We have to use not only Vedic and classical Sanskrit together with Pali and Prakrit but also tackle Greek, Latin, Iranian and Chinese sources. If the languages of the source for modern history are counted we will have to think of more than two dozen periods of modem Indian history simultaneously.

What criteria have then to be adopted in differentiating antiquity from the Middle Ages in India? Will it be correct to fix the watershed on the ground of political and dynastic history alone? The dates proposed on this ground are AD 646, 712, 750, 916, 985, 1174, 1206 and 1325. But none of these dates signifies any basic change in polity, society, economy and culture. Processes of change in these fields take long to fructify and cannot be assigned to a single fixed date. We have to find out whether these processes converge in any time bracket.

H.C. Raychaudhuri's *Political History of Ancient India* ends with the fall of the Gupta empire, but he does not assign any reasons for bringing the ancient period to an end in the sixth century; he may have been guided by the periodization in European history which he taught for a long time. It is argued that after the fall of the Gupta empire the country did not have a similar level or kind of political unification for centuries, but this is not sufficient ground for determining the end of antiquity. The imposition of Maurya and Gupta rule over the greater part of India did not make the ancient period an age of lasting unification, nor was the medieval period an age of permanent divisiveness. Despite giving the Mauryas credit for a centralized government modelled on the Hellenistic form, the difficulties of communication in a preindustrial society would have restricted effective Maurya control to the middle Ganga plains. The Gupta empire was much smaller and the central authority much weaker. The Gupta period saw the feudalization of the state apparatus, which is not to be found in Maurya times.

The central factor that ultimately transformed ancient Indian society into medieval society was the practice of land grants. Why did this practice originate? The charters say that the givers, mainly kings, wanted to acquire religious merit, and the receivers, mainly monks and priests, needed the means to perform religious rites. But the practice seems to have originated because of a serious crisis that affected the production relations on which the ancient social order was erected. Varṇa society was based on the production activities of the peasants called vaiśyas and of the labourers called śūdras. The taxes collected by the royal officers from the vaiśyas enabled the kings to pay salaries to their officials and soldiers, make gifts to their priests, and purchase luxury and other articles from merchants and big artisans. But between the third and fourth centuries AD Puranic texts complain of a situation in which varṇas or social orders discarded the functions assigned to them. The lower orders attempted to arrogate to themselves the status and functions of the higher orders. In other words, they refused to pay taxes and render labour service. This led to *varṇasaṃkara* or the intermixture of social classes. Varna barriers were attacked because the producing masses were oppressed with heavy taxes and impositions, and denied protection by the kings. This state of affairs is known as Kali Yuga in the Puranic passages of the third and fourth centuries AD[2] and seems to have appeared in the Deccan and central India which were less brahmanized.

Several measures were adopted to overcome the crisis. The almost contemporary law book of Manu advises that the vaiśyas and śūdras should not be allowed to deviate from their duties. This may have led to coercive measures. But a more important step to meet the situation was to grant land to priests and officials in lieu of salaries and remuneration. Such a practice passed the burden of tax collection and law keeping in the donated areas to the beneficiaries. They could deal with the recalcitrant peasants on the spot. The practice could also bring new lands under cultivation. Moreover, by implanting brāhmaṇas in the conquered tribal areas the tribal people could be tamed and taught to obey the king and pay taxes to him.

Although Aśoka's edicts deal with religion and administration, they do not speak of any land grants. The earliest epigraphic evidence belongs to the first century BC. But administrative power was not transferred to the beneficiary. This was done for the first time in the grants made to the Buddhist priests by the Sātavāhana ruler Gautamīputra Śātakarṇi in the second century AD. The land granted to them is described as *apraveśyam* (not to be entered by royal troops), *anāvamarśyam* (not to be molested by government officials) and *arāṣṭrasaṃvinayikam* (not to be interfered with by the district police).[3] This amounts to devolution of power.

From the middle of the fourth century AD onwards such grants in favour of the brāhmaṇas became frequent. They transfer all sources of revenue and delegate police and administrative functions. The grants of the second century AD abdicate royal control only over salt, which implies that the king retained certain other sources of revenue. But in Berar the Vākāṭaka princes gave up their control over almost all the sources of revenue. These sources include pasturage, hides and charcoal, use of palmyra and other trees for obtaining salt, liquor, sugar, etc., forced labour and all hidden treasures and deposits.[4] More important, the donor abandoned his right to govern the people inhabiting the donated villages. During the Gupta period in Madhya Pradesh, at least six grants of villages were made by the big feudatories to the brāhmaṇas, in which the residents including cultivators and artisans were expressly asked by their respective rulers not only to pay their customary taxes to the beneficiaries but also to obey their commands. In two other land grants royal commands were issued to the government officials employed as *sarvādhyakṣa* and also to regular soldiers and umbrella bearers asking them to leave the brāhmaṇas undisturbed.[5] All this is good evidence to show the transfer of administrative power of the state to the beneficiaries. In the inscriptions of the fifth century AD the ruler generally retains the right to punish thieves, which is one of the main bases of state power, but in later times he empowers the beneficiaries to punish all offences against family, property and person. Thus, the landed beneficiaries are given powers of taxation and coercion, leading to the creation of a new source of authority or state power.

D.R. Bhandarkar thinks that in Gupta inscriptions *daṇḍanāyaka* was a title of the nobility, and its holder was similar to the Mughal mansabdar.[6] According to him four grades *of daṇḍanāyaka* rendered military and other services to the king when called upon to do so.[7] The different meanings of the term *daṇḍanāyaka*[8] suggest that the official performed police, magisterial, judicial and military functions. More importantly, he maintained forces comprising horses, elephants and foot soldiers. For this he may have received land grants.

Fiefs are usually granted as long as the sun and the moon, the earth and ocean exist. This implies the break up of the state and creation of smaller nuclei of power. Although fiefs were conferred on the brāhmaṇas for their religious and spiritual services, they created secure and sacrosanct political pockets that were not to be disturbed by the royal agents. In all probability secular parties were also granted fiscal rights, although direct evidence is very weak. All told, we have in the Gupta period, a polity which is basically different from the Maurya polity. Megasthenes, Books II and III of Kauṭilya's *Arthaśāstra* and the Aśokan inscriptions show that the state officials assessed and collected taxes, levied forced labour, regulated mines and agriculture and maintained law and order. All this may have been confined to a core area covering the middle Ganga plains. Later, all these functions were abandoned step by step, first to the brāhmaṇas and then to others.

Though Maurya centralization could have been effective in a limited area,[9] such centralization was waning in the Gupta polity. The provincial or *bhukti* governor called *uparika* was appointed by the Gupta emperor, but he was autonomous enough to appoint district heads called viṣaya-pati;[10] it was only in the region of his capital the king appointed viṣayapati directly.[11] It is significant that *bhukti* means an era of enjoyment, rather like a grant. A Damodarpur plate describes the *uparika* as running the administration 'with the enjoyment (of the rule) consisting of elephants, horses and soldiers.'[12]

Kauṭilya provides for census to be made of all the households recording the number of inmates and amount of property owned by them. The obvious objective was to determine the amount of taxable property and to obtain and estimate of the labour power needed by the state. From the Gupta period onwards the state shifted at least part of the function of collecting taxes to the beneficiaries, which made the census unnecessary. This can be inferred from the accounts of the Chinese pilgrims in the AD fifth and AD seventh centuries. Writing about the conditions in Madhya-deśa, which formed the heart of the Gupta empire, Fa-hsien observes: 'They have not to register their households or attend to any magistrates and their rules'.[13] Similarly Hsüan Tsang writes: 'As the government is generous, official requirements are few. Families are not registered and individuals are not subject to forced labour contributions.'[14] These two observations imply that the state bothered neither about the direct collection of taxes from the peasants nor about the strict enforcement of its executive orders. Many of these functions were evidently taken over by the intermediaries between the tillers of the soil and the government; some of these may have been religious beneficiaries and others may have been non-religious vassals. In the Gunaighar grant (AD 507–508) of Vainyagupta, who was the ruler of a large part of Bengal, his agent Viajaysena, the *dūtaka* or executor of this grant, is described as *mahārāja śrī mahāsāmanta, patyuparika* and *purapāloparika.*[15] Evidently executive, military and police functions were conferred upon or seized by the feudal vassal. Similar developments seem to have taken place about the same time in northern and western India. The land grants of Harsavardhana associate the titles *sāmanta mahārāja* and *mahāsāmanta* with high-ranking officers. All this gives considerable indication of the feudalization of the state apparatus.[16]

The post-Gupta period saw a significant change in the mode of payment to government officers. If we rely on Kauṭilya, in pre-Gupta times all the officers of the state from the highest to the lowest were paid in cash, the maximum salary being 48,000 *paṇas* and the minumum 60 *paṇas*, although in some cases a paltry salary of 20 *paṇas* could be paid. Payment in cash fits in with the discovery of the largest number of punch-marked coins, mostly silver, belonging to Mauryan times. There was no dearth of coins, especially copper, under the *Kuṣāṇas*, who also initiated the issue of gold coins on a large scale. The largest number of ancient coins found so far, belong to the *Śātavāhanas*. The period 200 BC to AD 300 was the most prolific in the production of coins, as known from actual finds. Monetization presupposes a measure of centralization. The discovery of several Gupta gold coins shows that high-ranking officers may have been paid in cash. But the Gupta kings issued very few copper coins and, Bṛhaspati, a lawgiver of the sixth century, recommends reward of services with land.[17] In any case under the Harsavardhana public officials were not paid in cash. According to Hsüan Tsang, a quarter of the royal revenues was earmarked for assignment to great public servants.[18] The Chinese pilgrim adds that the governers, ministers, magistrates and officers were given portions of land for their personal support.[19]

The state which appears in the time of Harsavardhana in north India or under the Pallavas and the Cāḷukyas of Badami in south India is different in nature from the state which is to be found in pre-Gupta times. The role of the bureaucracy was considerably important in the pre-Gupta states which generally paid their employees in cash. No doubt a large number of tributary states surrounded the Maurya state, and were in the nature of feudatories, but the pattern of the state cannot be called feudal. In Gupta times, and more so later, religious and administrative services were remunerated through grants of land, and even in the core area, administrative powers devolved on landed beneficiaries or on functionaries who were granted certain taxes for their maintenance. This naturally took away much authority from the head of the state. The weakness of the central authority is also indicated by the existence of several capitals. The fortified capital or *durga* is considered an organ of the state in ancient texts. But in early medieval times a king came to have several capitals called *skandhāvāras*. Fortresses, obviously meant for protecting the king, vassals and big landed magnates, against their rivals and peasants, became a part of the early medieval landscape.[20] The practice of constructing forts became even more widespread under the sultans.

Thus, under the new political system in every important kingdom the central government lost considerable authority. Such a loss was made up by deifying the king and building his image. All kinds of achievements, especially military, were attributed to him. His edicts may have bolstered the image of Aśoka as a peaceful ruler wedded to the welfare of his people, but he was neither divinized nor credited with all-around achievements. In contrast hyperboles are used in Gupta and post-Gupta inscriptions to build the image of the king as the greatest conqueror. A telling example is that of Samudra Gupta followed by those of Candra, Dharmapāla and others. Inscriptions generally speak of the victories of the king and hardly ever of his defeats.

The pattern of the four varṇas comprising brāhmaṇas, kśatriyas, vaiśyas and śūdras in a hierarchical order continued at least up to Gupta times and it was not merely a ritualistic gradation. All social and economic legislation took note of this model. In early medieval times the place of kśatriyas was taken by the Rajputs. The *rājanya* is mentioned in the *Rg Veda* and repeatedly in other Vedic texts, but he was in a way replaced by the kśatriya in the varṇa system propounded in the Dharmasūtras. In medieval times we notice the Rajputs, a social category connected with *rājan*. The replacement of the kśatriyas by the Rajputs or *rājaputras* may be considered a new phenomenon. In the feudal age, war became far more important, and the various types of warriors and rulers came from different stocks— indigenous aboriginals, Indo-Aryan and central Asian peoples. Even some brāhmanas preferred to take to arms. They all combined to produce a new social order which performed the functions of the kśatriyas but were known as Rajputs. This does not mean that the category and concept of being a kśatriyas lost its importance. It was stated that a kśatriya is called raja or a raja is called kśatriya: *kṣatriyo rājā ucyate*. Early medieval rulers claimed descent from the solar and lunar dynasties in order to gain antiquity and respectability for their families; this could legitimize their position in the eyes of the people. The fabrication of family trees is a striking feature of medieval times. Genealogy was turned into ideology. People were fed on legends and superstitions which glorified miracles attributed to the ancient rulers of the solar and lunar races and which were enshrined in the *Ramayana*, *Mahabharata* and the Puranas.

Advances in agriculture and the outbreak of social conflicts changed the character of the śūdra community. In order to have rent and other benefits the landed beneficiaries had to get their lands cultivated. I-tsing (seventh century) states that most Indian monasteries possessing lands had them cultivated by servants and others. He adds that the monasteries provided the oxen and the fields and generally received one-sixth of the produce,[21] which was the same as the conventional share payable to the state. However, unlike the monasteries the state did not provide the cultivators with oxen. Probably, the tillers of the soil were not slaves or wage labourers, as is indicated by Kauṭilya in some cases; they were peasant tenants who paid a share of their produce to the landlord. Hsüan Tsang describes the śūdras as agriculturalists[22] which suggests that they cultivated the land as they did in the past and also occupied it temporarily. In all earlier sources only the vaiśyas clearly appear as agriculturalists. In the earlier Dharmaśāstras, Kauṭilya's *Arthaśāstra* and other texts, the śūdras appear mainly as landless labourers, engaged in cultivation either as slaves or hired wage-earners by the higher classes. Land being the main source of revenue and the śūdras being landless, they were not taxed by the state. Kauṭilya speaks of śūdras as agriculturalists[23] in new settlements founded by the state. Apart from Hsüan Tsang, for the first time Asahāya, a legal commentator of the seventh century, describes the śūdras as cultivators.[24] Evidently by the seventh century temporary tenancy was given to the vast masses of people, who were mostly śūdras. This happened in old settled areas in northern India, and recalls in some ways the transformation of slaves in Europe into serfs. How and why the śūdras, slaves and agricultural labourers were transformed into tenants and agriculturalists in Madhyadeśa can be linked to the crisis in production relations associated with the Kali age.

In the tribal areas agriculturalists were placed under the control of the religious beneficiaries, especially the brāhmaṇas, who began to be granted land on a large scale from the fifth and sixth centuries onwards. Although the earliest example of sharecroppers being transferred along with the land is found in a late third century Pallava inscription from Andhra, in backward and mountainous regions such as Orissa and the Deccan, sharecroppers and peasants were particularly asked to stay with the land granted to the beneficiaries from the sixth century onwards.[25] The practice later spread to Madhyadeśa, where one seventh-century charter, forged in the name of Samudra Gupta, asks the beneficiaries not to introduce artisans and peasants from another village into gift villages. It implies that the beneficiaries had to depend on the inhabitants of the village to cultivate and provide rent and services. This became fairly common in subsequent times, and the villages transferred to the grantees were called *dhana-janasahita, janatā-samṛddha*, and *sa-prativāsi-jana-sameta*.[26] All this worked for a closed economy.

The system according to which artisans are attached to the service of big and small landowners in exchange for a part of the produce at the time of harvest seems to have originated around the fourth century AD. The Nalanda land grant of Samudra Gupta specifically attaches tax-paying artisans and peasants living in the donated village to the beneficiaries. Such peasants may be treated as semi-serfs because of restrictions placed on their mobility. Later several such instances appear, particularly in Orissa and eastern Madhya Pradesh. The grant of Samudra Gupta attests to attachment of artisans in a developed area such as Nalanda. The artisans may have been either paid in kind at harvest time or granted pieces of land for their maintenance. Such a system has now been popularized as jajmani by social anthropologists.

From the sixth century AD onwards long-distance trade began to decline. Trade with the western part of the Roman empire ended in the third century, and silk trade with Iran and the Byzantium stopped in the middle of the sixth century.[27] India continued some commerce with China and Southeast Asia, but its benefits were reaped by the Arab middlemen. In the period before the eleventh century, the Arabs practically monopolized the export trade of India.[28] The decline of commerce for well over three hundred years after the sixth century is demonstrated by the near absence of gold coins and the paucity of other types of coins not only in north India but also in the south.

The decline of trade led to the decay of towns.[29] Towns flourished in west and north India under the Sātavāhanas and Kusāṇas. A few cities continued to thrive in Gupta times. But the post-Gupta period witnessed the downfall of many old commercial cities in north India. Excavations show that several towns in Haryana and east Punjab, Purana Qila (Delhi), Mathura, Hastinapura (Meerut district), Śrāvastī (Uttar Pradesh), Kauśāmbi (near Allahabad), Rajghat (Varanasi), Chirand (Saran district), Vaiśālī and Pāṭaliputra began to decline in the Gupta period, and mostly disappeared in post-Gupta times. The Chinese pilgrim Hsüan Tsang visited several towns considered sacred on account of their association with the Buddha but found them almost deserted or dilapidated. A restricted market forced artisans and merchants living in these towns into the countryside to take up cultivation. In the late fifth century a group of silk weavers from the west coast migrated to Mandasor in Malwa, gave up their occupation and adopted other professions. On account of the decay of trade and towns the villagers had to meet their needs in respect of iron, oil, salt, spices and cloth either by themselves or through weekly fairs. This gave rise to smaller units of production, with each unit meeting its own needs.

The mode of production which emerges as a result of land grants and the decline of towns, both of which tie up with the Kali crisis, creates a kind of self-sufficient economy. Karl Marx sees in it a typical blending of agriculture and artisanal activity at the lowest level and considers this feature to be the main cause of a vegetative, stagnant economy. He named this kind of economy the Asiatic mode of production. In fact, however, this appears to be the main characteristic of a feudal economy, especially in its classical phase, when it is difficult to detect the forces that work for its disintegration. But once relations of production are organized in a feudal manner they give rise to many sources of conflict which revolve around the possession of land. This could certainly be a factor for social and economic change. In any case if the Asiatic mode is the same as a changeless economy and society, it cannot be applied to medieval India. And what is regarded as the Asiatic mode of production should be considered a feudal mode of production which was linked with a self-sufficient economy in its initial stage.

The Asiatic mode of production implies an undifferentiated village community in which landowning families are considered to be more or less equal to one another. This may apply to some tribal communities which own land and other resources in common, but not to many villages mentioned in land grants and also in literary texts. The law books of Gupta and post-Gupta times leave no doubt that the king enjoyed superior rights regarding land. He granted it to the svāmī, who assigned it to the *kṣetrika* or *karṣaka* (cultivator), and sometimes the cultivator assigned it to the sub-cultivator. Therefore, on the basis of land, society was divided into three or even four classes. This division is clearly attested by the land grants.[30] From the Gupta period onwards the varṇa and jati differentiation based on functional and ritualistic grounds is aggravated by a new type of differentiation caused by the possession of land and the acquisition of power in the management of village affairs. Different parts of northern India show the rise of a class of rich substantial peasants called *mahattaras* who included the śūdras. They are repeatedly mentioned in land charters, which are addressed not only to the various castes inhabiting the village but also to a class of elders. These village elders enjoyed a high status and played an important role in the management of rural affairs. The term *mahto*, which means head, is derived from *mahattara.* Today this title is borne by various castes, high and low, which shows that at one time their ancestors enjoyed authority in the village. But once the family multiplied the title came to be held by all the descendants irrespective of their fiscal or social status.

Further, from the Gupta period onwards inscriptions mention the existence of cultivating groups called *kuṭumbin*, although in the sense of householder the term occurs in earlier inscriptions. This term does not seem to be of Sanskritic origin. It may be derived from the Prakrit root *kuḍ.*[31] It is interesting that *kudi* means both land measurement as well as a container for drawing water either from the well or from some other reservoir of water. In Dravidian languages the term for land tax is *kuḍimai.*[32] Perhaps *kuḍi* has something to do with *kulya* which is a measure of grain, from which the measure of land called *kulyavāpa* is derived. Therefore, the *kuṭumbins* were certainly connected with land measurement and irrigation, and they were clearly cultivators. They included both Indo-Aryans as well as Dravidians. From the term *kuṭumbin* have been derived many cultivating caste names such as the Kurmis and Koeries of Bihar and Uttar Pradesh and the Kunbis of Maharashtra and Gujarat. Most seem to have been śūdras, who emerged as the principal paying peasants in medieval times. It appears, therefore, that apart from the landed beneficiaries or the agents of the king who were entitled to rent or tax, as the case may be, the rural areas came to have two strata consisting of the *mahattaras* on top and the *kuṭumbins* below. Of course, the land assignees formed a higher rung in the rural ladder. This pattern prevailed in northern and western India and a large part of the Deccan and eastern India.

The medieval period is also marked by the appearance of forced labour imposed on the villagers as a whole. *Viṣṭi* was imposed on the common people for the construction of lakes, although in the middle of the second century AD a king claims to have exempted the people in Saurāṣṭra from this levy. But many inscriptions in central India, Maharashtra and Gujarat speak of the imposition of forced labour on the villagers by the king or beneficiary. In these areas peasants were not generally forced to labour on the fields of their masters; forced labour was levied for the construction of roads, palaces, fortresses and also to help transport the royal army and officials in the countryside. But in south India the situation seems to have been different. *Veṭṭi*, which is very frequently used in Coḷa[33] and Pāṇḍya land charters and also in those of the other south Indian dynasties, especially in Andhra, refers to bonded labour used in agriculture. *Veṭṭi*, therefore, in the context of south India may signify the lowest agricultural stratum engaged in ploughing for a pittance or for maintenance. That there was differentiation in the peasantry and villages in south India is confirmed by the presence of the class of Vellals who were substantial peasants. A large number of graded intermediaries in land were treated through the grant system not only in the north but also in the south. Under the Coḷas the king was above the assignee and the assignee above the occupant in the hierarchy. The occupant leased land to the sub-occupant who had it tilled by the cultivating tenant.[34] It would, therefore, appear that the social and economic stratification of the rural population was much more marked in medieval times, and the land charters from the fourth to the seventh centuries AD clearly show this trend.

The early Middle Ages in India saw a great spurt in agrarian expansion. This was partly due to the decline of towns in which soldiers, administrators, artisans, merchants, brāhmaṇas and others were concentrated. Inscriptions speak of brāhmaṇa migration from towns to rural areas. Perhaps the artisans, who deserted towns, disseminated technological knowledge in rural areas. Iron technology became widespread, and black metal was used in huge quantities in medieval times. Iron tools made it possible to produce a large quantity of bronze objects, which far surpassed those of the Harappan Bronze Age in number and quality. Moreover, iron came to be used for non-utilitarian purposes. The Mehrauli iron pillar, set up to mark the conquest of a king called Candra, is an example of such non-functional use. This tradition was followed by several Rajput rulers.

The older forces of production were made available in new areas and were also reinforced by new ones. It seems that the *arahaṭṭa*, identical with the Persian wheel for drawing water, first appeared around the seventh century AD.[35] It became popular in Rajasthan from the ninth century onwards, and also spread over a large part of northern India. In addition, the use of tanks and wet rice cultivation spread in the peripheral areas, particularly in south India. All this contributed to agrarian expansion, which is corroborated by the rise of numerous states in outlying areas and by the creation of many fiscal units called *nāḍus* in peninsular India.

The *Āryabhaṭiya* written in AD 499 is a landmark in the progress of mathematical and astronomical knowledge. It is a distinct contribution to trigonometry[36] on the basis of which all shapes and sizes of plots involved in gift making and inheritance partition could be measured and assessed for the purpose of rent or tax in Gupta and post-Gupta times. This knowledge could also be used for various kinds of measurements in erecting temples and palaces and in engineering work. The use of the zero and the decimal system finds place in the *Āryabhaṭiya.*[37] But it was not put to any significant use in the country. Once it spread westward through the Arabs it came to be used for bookkeeping by the Italian traders in the tenth century.[38] The fact that India did not have much trade between the sixth and the tenth centuries can perhaps be linked to the neglect of the zero and decimal system. More accurate knowledge relevant to measurement and also to agro-astronomical calculations was made available by the algebra developed by Brahmagupta during the first half of the seventh century.[39] Meanwhile Varāhamihira, the younger contemporary of Āryabhaṭa, had written his *Bṛhat Saṃhitā* in the sixth century.[40] His plant and animal classifications are in keeping with the importance given at that time to agricultural knowledge. Although his predictions relate to numerous social matters, the instructions given by him regarding the selection of sites for building houses tie up with the founding of new villages. Similarly, Varāhamihira's observations on seasons and the weather could be useful for the agricultural calendar. He emphasizes that the calendar should be constantly updated to keep pace with the change in seasons. We may add that the importance of the office of *jyotiṣī* or *daivajña* (astronomer-cum-astrologer) began in early medieval times,[41] as shown by the numerous land charters. At the lower level in many parts of the country the priest-*jyotiṣī* became an integral part of the jajmani system. Altogether, the forces of production underwent considerable change in Gupta and post-Gupta times.

However, the reproduction of human beings or the supply of labour power which is essential to economy and society, did not undergo much change. This was ensured in ancient times by marriage rules and family customs according to which members of lower varṇas such as the vaiśyas and śūdras were comparatively free to take and discard wives; freedom of marriage was also enjoyed by their women to some extent. In the interest of social inequality, the higher varṇas practised social distancing by placing various kinds of restrictions on their marriage practices which made them privileged groups in contrast to the vaiśyas and śūdras who respectively formed the peasantry and labouring masses. It seems that the practice of the reproduction of labour was continued by keeping the old marriage practices intact. However, in the medieval period the practice of polygamy increased in the upper classes. In order to preserve their inherent purity and high social status they encouraged satī and child marriage and discouraged widow marriage and levirate or *niyoga.*

Oddly enough the increasing practice of dowry in medieval times contributed to the unequal distribution of land. The Jain epics show that this practice was widespread among the princely classes. A dowry which included numerous villages, along with men, women and artisans, was given to the bridegroom.[42] It appears that in the higher sections of society *bhūmidāna* went along with *kanyādāna.* Hence the practice of this type of *kanyādāna* also helped shape new production relations. The transfer of artisans to distant areas would help in the diffusion of technological knowledge.

Between the fifth and seventh centuries important changes occurred in the social organization. In the Ganga basin the vaiśyas seem to have been peasant proprietors for long, but land grants created landlords between the peasants on the one hand and the king on the other, so that the vaiśyas became servile peasants. Large numbers of tribal peasants were enrolled as śūdras. Consequently the śūdras, who served as slaves, domestics, agricultural labourers and low grade artisans in earlier times, now emerged as farmers, like the vaiśyas. Literature shows a pronounced tendency to lump together the vaiśyas and śūdras from the Gupta period onwards. Thus, the old brāhmaṇical order was modified.

This modified brāhmaṇical order spread from Madhyadeśa into Bengal and south India as a result of land grants to the brāhmaṇas, many of them migrating from the north between the fifth, sixth and later centuries. This order was marked mainly by the brāhmaṇas and śūdras. Although the Rajputs emerge as a significant factor in the politics and society of northern India from the seventh century onwards, landed brāhmaṇas appear to have taken this position in Bengal and peninsular India. In the older inhabited areas the traditional theoretical fourfold varṇa system did not fit in with the new feudal and social ranks created by the unequal distribution of land and military power. In the sixth century attempts were made to square up feudal ranks with ritual ranks. The earlier texts make many economic regulations on the basis of the varṇas. But the sixth century *Bṛhat Saṃhitā* of Varāhamihira prescribes varying sizes of houses both according to the varṇas and also according to the grades of the ruling chiefs. This tendency becomes marked in later times in several medieval texts on architecture.

A striking social development from about the seventh century onwards was the proliferation of castes along with the division of the śūdras into pure and impure castes. Manu notes sixty-one castes, but the *Viṣṇudharmottara Purāṇa*, a text of about the eighth century, states that thousands of mixed castes are produced by the connection of vaiśya women with men of lower castes.[43] In fact, proliferation affected brāhmaṇas, Rajputs and above all the śūdras including the untouchables. Increasing pride of birth, characteristic of a feudal society and the accompanying self-sufficient village economy, which prevented both spatial and occupational mobility, gave rise to many castes. The guilds of artisans, which appear in inscriptions from the first century AD onwards, were gradually converted into castes for lack of mobility in post-Gupta times. The tribal people were absorbed into the brāhmaṇical fold through conquests coupled with large-scale religious land grants. Cultural interaction assumed enormous dimensions and considerably added to the varieties of the śūdras and the so-called mixed castes whose deities were adopted in the brāhmaṇical pantheon.

The sixth and seventh centuries saw the faint beginnings of the formation of regional cultural units such as Andhra, Assam, Bengal, Gujarat, Karnataka, Kerala, Maharashtra, Orissa, Rajasthan and Tamil Nadu. The Gurjaras, who came in large numbers to India, founded various kingdoms in Rajasthan and Gujarat in the sixth century and paved the way for the formation of the future Gurjaradeśa. The Rajputs, who emerged as a result of the improvisation of local tribes and the absorption of the Huns and other foreign tribes into brāhmaṇical society in the sixth century, cleared the ground for the rise of Rajasthan. The beginnings of regional and cultural personality consciousness can also be traced in other parts of the country. Bengal was divided into two main units, Gauḍa and Vaṅga, and later the whole region was named after Vaṅga. Sub-national groups are recognized by both foreign and indigenous sources. Hsüan Tsang mentions several nationalities. The *Mudrārākṣasa* of Viśākhadatta speaks of the different regions whose inhabitants differ in custom, clothing and language.[44] The *Kuvalayamālā*, a Jain text of the eighth century, notes the existence of 18 major nationalities and describes the anthropological character of sixteen peoples, pointing out psychological features and citing samples of their languages.[45] Thus the sixth century seems to have marked a watershed in the ethnic history of India.[46]

What is more significant, around the seventh century, Apabhramsa began to differentiate into proto-Hindi, proto-Bengali, proto-Rajasthani, proto-Gujarati and proto-Maithili. Although it is difficult to fix the beginnings of regional languages, on the basis of the Vajrayāna Buddhist religious writings from eastern India, proto-Bengali, proto-Assamese, proto-Oriya, proto-Maithili and proto-Hindi can be traced back to the seventh century.[47] Similarly, on the basis of Jain religious Prakrit works proto-Gujarati and proto-Rajasthani are traced back to the same period. The parent stock of languages in eastern India was certainly different from that of languages in western India, but the pace of linguistic variation quickened in the country from the sixth and seventh centuries mainly on account of the lack of sufficient mobility and inter-regional communication. Contacts were mainly confined to the march of soldiers and the migration of monks and brāhmaṇas from northern India and the Deccan into the peripheral areas for enjoying land grants. The first proved to be ephemeral but the second produced important consequences. In the tribal areas the brāhmaṇas imposed various forms of Sanskrit on the substratum of the existing Indo-Aryan and pre-Indo-Aryan dialects. The consequential interaction gave rise to regional languages. The migrating brāhmaṇas from mid-India enriched the vocabulary of the regional languages. They also helped to develop and systematize local dialects into languages through the introduction of writing and eventually the composition of grammar based on Sanskrit.

The local element in language was strengthened by the insulation of many fiscal and political units formed by the rise of states and feudal principalities. In each case the ruling class comprising the assignees was deeply attached to its territory. Between the sixth and tenth centuries diminishing communication between different regions was indicated by the decline of long-distance trade, which is shown by the striking paucity of coins in this period. It is, therefore, evident that too many principalities, little trade, and decreasing inter-zonal communication created congenial conditions for the origin and formation of regional languages from the sixth and seventh centuries onwards.

The emergence of regional languages was paralleled by that of regional scripts. From Maurya to Gupta times the script changed mainly as a result of the passage of time, and an epigraphist who has mastered the Gupta Brahmi can decipher inscriptions from different parts of the country dating to the end of the Gupta period. But from the seventh century onwards regional variations become so pronounced that one has to learn several scripts to be able to read inscriptions. Obviously the regional script was produced by regional insulation and the availability of locally educated scribes to meet the needs of local education and administration. The country did not have any wide political authority such as that of the Mauryas, Sātavāhanas, Kuṣāṇas or Guptas to enforce the same script in a very large area. The rise of states in new areas meant the creation of scribes to keep land and other records and of priestly writers for religious and theological purposes.

In the history of literature the sixth and seventh centuries are equally important. Sanskrit continued to be used by the ruling class at the highest administrative level. But in keeping with the emergence of the new social hierarchy marked by pomp, show, vanity and splendour, which were reflected in the court style of higher and lower *sāmantas* or vassals, the style of Sanskrit prose and poetry underwent a distinct change. Writing was full of metaphors, imagery, adjectives and adverbs which made it difficult for the reader to locate the real purport of what the author wanted to communicate. A typical example is to be found in Bāṇa's prose. In poetry many metres were invented and elaborated to meet the requirements of the new ornate, verbose, high-flown style. This is found in both inscriptions and literary texts. In tune with the dominance of landed magnates over the social hierarchy, artificial prose and poetry became fashionable with the elitist authors, whose writings widened the chasm between the landlords and peasants.[48] Kosambi considers the combination of sex and religion to be a distinctive feature of feudal literature.[49] The growth of a leisured landed class which sought the support of the Sanskrit-knowing priesthood for its legitimization and stability gave rise to this feature which became prominent under the influence of tantrism.

Sexual union came to be interpreted spiritually as union with the supreme divine power. According to the Vajrayānī tantrikas the realization of supreme knowledge, which amounted to supreme bliss, lay in the sexual union of the male and female.[50] Inverted spiritualism was thus used to justify eroticism in both art and literature.

The medieval period is noted for the production of a large corpus of commentaries on ancient texts. They cover Sanskrit, Pali and Prakrit texts, and fall mainly into the period between the fifth and eighteenth centuries. They include not only the Dharmaśāstras and Smṛtis but also Pāṇini's grammar, Gṛhyasūtras, Śrautasūtras, Sulvasūtras, and medical and philosophical texts. Commentaries on the Pali texts are called *aṭṭhakathā*, and those on Prakrit texts are called *cūrṇi, bhāṣya* and *niryukti*. The commentarial literature greatly strengthened the authoritarian trend in intellectual life, but the reiteration of the old was considerably modified by the introduction of the new. All this was done to preserve the state- and class-based patriarchal society, and to adapt it to new situations. Several law books were composed between AD 600 and AD 900 to meet the needs of early medieval times. In order to emphasize continuity and make themselves acceptable, several lawgivers called themselves Vṛddha Manu or Bṛhat Parāśara. Together with the law books, the commentaries helped perpetuate the essentials of social inequality and adjust law and rituals to the new inequalities arising out of the unequal distribution of land and power. Commentaries and digests emphasized continuity, and the dominant trend in medieval times was that of a closed mind linked to a closed economy. In a way, creativity was blocked. It is significant that in spite of contact with the Europeans in the sixteenth century there was neither any instance of learning European languages nor of adopting printing or any other European technology in India.[51]

It seems that beginning with the sixth century litigations over land became frequent. Cases were obviously argued to settle claims to the disputed land. This seems to have led to the development of logic. Before the fifth century logic was not a well established discipline. The *Nyāya Sūtra* seems to have been compiled around AD 400.[52] It mentions four proofs or *pramāṇas* comprising perception, inference, comparison and testimony. Detailed discussions regarding valid and invalid knowledge, and aspects of each kind of proof are treated in detail.[53] Although debating devices were used in theological disputes,[54] they could not have been developed in isolation from land disputes.

Art and architecture entered a new phase of development because of the emergence of regional styles in sculpture, which became particularly prominent from the eighth century onwards. Although the birth of regional styles is attributed to regional psychology and consciousness, the reasons which led to the origin and formation of regional languages also applied to art.

In medieval times the temple came to play an important part, especially in south India, where it served as a centre of social, economic and cultural activities. Temples and monasteries were mainly supported by land grants. Centred on the temple there emerged a new type of architecture in which the main shrine came to be surrounded by smaller temples. We find the appearance of the *pañcāyatana*, that is, a complex of five temples. In such an arrangement the main temple, in which the chief god was installed, was a large structure in the middle, in contrast to four small temples situated at each corner of the rectangle; these temples were meant for the subsidiary gods. This kind of temple architecture suited the hierarchy of gods in the pantheon. Both temple architecture and pantheon iconography followed the general social differentiation in which landed magnates were graded in a system of subinfeudation.

Post-Gupta iconography pointedly displays a divine hierarchy which reflects pyramidal ranks in society. Vishnu, Shiva and Durga appear as supreme deities, lording over many other divinities of unequal size and placed in lower positions as retainers and attendants. The central cult diety was the largest in size and was considered high, middle or low in rank according to the number of subordinate deities that surrounded it. The pantheons do not so much reflect syncretism as forcible absorption of tribal and lower order deities. The reality of unequal ranks appears in the Shaivite, Jain and tantric monastic organizations, in which as many as five pyramidal ranks are enumerated. The ceremonies recommended for the consecration of the acharya, the highest in rank, are practically the same as those for the coronation of a prince.

The religious rituals and practices underwent important changes in the early centuries of the Christian era and afterwards. Domestic worship and the *mahāyajñas*, which started with the establishment of private smaller households, secure family property in land and the use of money from about the fifth century BC, ceased to be popular beyond the second century AD. Although the Sātavāhana rulers dispensed thousands of *kārṣāpaṇas* as gifts in these sacrifices, in subsequent times this was done by a few princes and practically ceased in the case of less affluent people. In Gupta and post-Gupta times the Puranas lauded the virtues of visiting sacred places and making gifts. These Puranic practices overshadowed the cult of sacrifices. On the other hand, the growing practice of offering and surrendering land, other property and various services to the lord and then receiving fiscal rights, land and protection in return as prasada or favour, promoted the growth of the puja system. Puja was interlinked with the doctrine of bhakti. The earlier concept of bhakti had something to do with the idea of sharing[55] although *bhakta* also means boiled rice. In any case the earlier bhakti arose in a society in which the king and his officials were very important, and the number of gods was small. The early medieval bhakti meant complete surrender of the individual to his or her god. This became a distinctive feature of medieval religion, especially in south India from the seventh century onwards. Bhakti reflected the complete dependence of the tenants or semi-serfs on the landowners in medieval times.

Both puja and bhakti became integral ingredients of tantrism, which arose outside central India in the aboriginal, peripheral areas on account of interaction between the brāhmaṇas and tribal people through large-scale religious land grants. Brāhmaṇical authority in the new territories could be maintained by adopting tribal rituals and deities, especially the mother goddess. Between the fifth and seventh centuries many brāhmaṇas received lands in Nepal, Assam, Bengal, Orissa, central India and the Deccan, where tantric texts, shrines and practices appeared at about this time. In a large part of Tamil Nadu brāhmaṇas settled in great numbers from the eighth century onwards, and the *Āgamas* were compiled around the ninth century. Tantrism permeated Jainism, Buddhism, Shaivism and Vaishnavism and from the seventh century onwards continued to hold ground throughout the medieval period. Many medieval manuscripts deal with tantra and astrology, the two being inextricably linked together.

There is no doubt that growing brāhmaṇical influence and property rights in the hands of men gradually elevated patriarchy over matriarchy. Patriarchy became important to the tribals when temples and brāhmaṇas were granted lands in the aboriginal tracts. It appears that among tribals, women played a more important part, but under the new land system and with the introduction of iron-share plough agriculture women became less important in agriculture. In order to assimilate the tribals into the feudal brāhmaṇical society the mother goddess was recognized and given an honourable place in brahmaṇical texts and iconography. Though the matriarchal element was widely suppressed at the social and economic levels in the Middle Ages, the tribals were compensated at the ritualistic and religious levels. Mother goddesses came to be worshipped widely under the influence of tantra, but in reality women suffered in importance in tribal society as a result of interaction with the bṛahmanical feudal order.

Magic rituals to fulfil material desires and to cure everyday diseases and injuries afflicting human beings, animals and physical possessions were as old as the *Atharva Veda*. But now they were officially sponsored, fostered and distorted by the educated brāhmaṇas and their rich clients. The medieval *tantrika* functioned as priest, physician and astrologer. Nobles, chiefs and the richer folk practised occultism to obtain the elixir of life and gold when it was scarce.

The medieval social system was rife with new types of conflicts and contradictions. In ancient times, peasant protests and popular anger were directed against the king and sometimes his priest. Both were considered responsible for the sufferings of the people. Complaints were also made against provincial governors and bureaucrats who fleeced the people. We also hear of varṇa conflicts in which the vaiśyas and śūdras refused to perform the tasks assigned to them in an ascriptive society. In the new social and agrarian order, conflicts centred mainly around the possession of land. Land disputes seemed to have become frequent between the king and the beneficiaries, between the beneficiaries themselves, and particularly between the beneficiaries and the peasants. Such disputes also occurred between landed temples and priests on the one hand and secular parties on the other. Obviously, to solve them the supremacy of the royal charter overriding the other sources of title to property was propounded in the law book of Nārada and repeated in several Gupta and post-Gupta texts. *Rājaśāsana* or the royal charter became the decisive source of title to landed property in cases of dispute between different parties including the peasants. Those who based their titles on religion, agreement or custom were placed at a disadvantage. The Pala land charters show that officers, such as the *daussādha sādhanika*, were employed to deal with refractory elements. Since the number of *dusādhs*, considered to be criminal by the British, is considerable in eastern India, these peasants and agricultural labourers must have been in constant conflict with those who demanded rent and labour service from them. Thus, new institutions had to be evolved to deal with new conflicts.

Undoubtedly, the establishment of the Muslim Turkish rule introduced significant changes in the social, economic and political organization of the country. But most features such as the feudal state organization, control of the landlords over production, proliferation of castes, regional identity in art, script and language, puja, bhakti, *tirtha* and tantra, which came to the fore in medieval times and continued later, can be traced back to the sixth and seventh centuries. More importantly, land assignments first appeared between the fourth and seventh centuries and became widely prevalent under the Turks and Mughals when they were called *iqta*, jagir, *mansab, madad-i-maash, milk, inam, lakharaj, nazrana*, etc.[56] Older practices of giving *brahmottara, devottara*, etc., were continued by the Muslim rulers. Further, the old commentarial tradition, which relied on authority as the main source of knowledge, was pursued with vigour. The system of law introduced by the Muslims was fundamentally similar to that of the Hindus inasmuch as the latter was based on the Dharmaśāstras and the former on the Koran. Neither system made provision for legislation; only authorities and commentaries were quoted.[57] In both cases we find the largest number of digests written under the sultans and Mughal emperors.

It would then appear that between the fourth and seventh centuries ancient Indian life was in a stage of fermentation and transformation. Momentous changes appear in polity, society, economy, language, script, art and architecture, and in religion and intellectual life. It is very difficult to take their total view and locate and explain their convergence. But it is necessary to make an attempt in this direction. The concept, content and origins of medievalism need to be analysed and clarified. This can be done not through a survey of political and dynastic developments but through an integrated study of all the strands in Indian life in different parts of the country.

NOTES

1. Perry Anderson, *Passages from Antiquity to Feudulism*, London, New Left Books, 1974, p. 18.
2. See R.S. Sharma, *Śūdras in Ancient India*, 3rd edn, Delhi, Motilal Banarsidass, 1990, pp. 233–9; B.N.S. Yadava, 'The Accounts of the Kali Age and the Social Transition from Antiquity to the Middle Ages', *IHR*, vol. 5, nos. 1 and 2, 1978, pp. 31–63.
3. D.C. Sircar, *Select Inscriptions Bearing on Indian History and Civilisation* (*Sd. Inscrr.*), 1, 2nd edn, Calcutta, University of Calcutta, 1965, pp. 198–9.
4. Ibid., pp. 432–4.
5. R.S. Sharma, 'Politico-Legal Aspects of the Caste System', *Journal of the Bihar Research Society* (*JBRS*), vol. 39, pt. 3, 1953, p. 325.
6. *CII*, III, Introduction, pp. 95–7.
7. Ibid., p.96.
8. Ibid., pp. 95–6. Various meanings of the term *daṇḍanāyaka* appear in D.C. Sircar, *Indian Epigraphical Glossary*, Delhi, Motilal Banarsidass, 1966, pp. 80–1.
9. R.S. Sharma, *Aspects of Political Ideas and Institutions in Ancient India*, 4th revised edn, New Delhi, Motilal Banarsidass, 1996, p. 392ff.
10. Bhandarkar's Introduction, *CII*, III, 1981, p. 93.
11. Ibid.

12. Ibid.
13. Samuel Beal, tr. Travels of *Fa-hian and Suang-Yun*, London, 1869, chapter 16, p. 37; reprint, New Delhi: Oriental Publications 1971.
14. T. Watters, *On Yuan Chwang's Travels in India*, ed. T. Rhys Davids and S.W. Bushell, London, 1904–5; Indian reprint, New Delhi, Munshiram Manoharlal, 1974, p. 176.
15. Dinesh Chandra Bhattacharya, 'A Newly discovered Copper Plate from Tippera (The Gunaighar Grant of Vainyagupta: The Year 188 Current [Gupta Era]', *Indian Historical Quarterly* (IHQ), 4, 1930, p. 55.
16. For more instances see R.S. Sharma, IF, 1980, pp. 20–4.
17. Quoted in *Vyavahāramayūkha of Bhaṭṭa Nilakaṇṭha*, ed. P.V. Kante, Poona, Bhandarkar Oriental Research Institute (BORI), 1926; tr. P.V. Kane and S.G. Patwardhan, Bombay 1933, pp. 25–7.
18. T. Watters, *On Yuan Chwang's Travels*, p. 176.
19. Ibid., p. 177.
20. R.S. Sharma, *IF*, 1980; Appendix II.
21. T. Takakusu, tr. *A Record of the Buddhist Religion as Practised in India and the Malay Archipelago by I-tsing*, Oxford, Oxford University Press, 1886, p. 61.
22. T. Watters, *On Yuan Chwang's Travels*, p. 176.
23. The term *śūdra-karṣaka* in Bk 2.1 of *Kauṭilya's Arthaśāstra* (*AS*), ed., tr. and a study, R.P. Kangle, Bombay, University of Bombay, 1960–5, may also mean śūdra and agriculturist.
24. *Nārada Smṛiti*, ed., tr. and commentary, Richard W. Lariviere, Philadelphia, University of Pennsylvania, 1989, 1.181.
25. R.S. Sharma, *IF*, 1980, pp. 44–5.
26. Ibid., p.46.
27. R.S. Sharma, *Urban Decay in India*, pp. 135–8.
28. Lotika Varadarajan 'Indian Participation in Trade of the Southern Seas *circa* 9th to 13th Centuries'. Paper submitted to the International Seminar on the Indian Ocean, New Delhi, 1985.
29. On this, see R.S. Sharma, *Urban Decay in India*, chs. 2–5; M.K. Dhavalikar, *Historical Archaeology of India*, New Delhi, Books and Books, 1999, ch. 4.
30. A. Laxmanshastri Joshi, ed. *Dharmakośa* (*DK*), vol. 1, Pt. II, Wai District, Satara, Prājña Pāṭhaśālā Maṇḍala, 1939, pp. 954, 961.
31. Mohan Chand, *Jain Sanskrit Mahākāvyon mein Bhārtiya Samāj*, New Delhi, Eastern Book Linkers, 1989, pp. 134–42.
32. R. Tirumalai, *Land Grants and Agrarian Reaction in Coḷa and Pāṇḍya Times*, Madras, University of Madras, 1987, pp. 5–6.
33. P. Shammugam, T*he Revenue System of the Cholas, 850–1279*, Madras, New Era Publications, 1987, p. 16.
34. R. Tirumalai, *Land Grants and Agrarian Reaction*, p. 60.
35. D.M. Bose, S.N. Sen and B.V. Subbarayappa, ed. *A Concise History of Science in India*, New Delhi, Indian National Science Academy, 1971, pp. 609–10.

36. Ibid., pp. 92–5, 165–6, 609.
37. Ibid., p. 165.
38. I owe this information to Gunakar Muley.
39. D.M. Bose, et al., ed. *A Concise History of Science*, p. 166.
40. Ibid., pp. 93–4, 609.
41. In certain parts of the country, especially in the Konkan, the *pañcāṅga* or calendar is taken annually in procession, and sometimes there is a dispute over ceremonial claims for receiving it.
42. Mohan Chand, *Jain Sanskrit Mahākāvyon mein Bhāraīya Samāj*, pp. 504–6.
43. *Viṣṇudharmottara Purāṇa*, II, Bombay, Venkatesvara Press, 1912, pp. 81–2.
44. *Mudrārākṣasa by Viśākhadatta,* ed. Alfred Hillebrandt, pt. 1, Breslau, M. and H. Marcus, 1912, p. 103.
45. Quoted in Yu. V. Gankovsky, *The Peoples of Pakistan*, Moscow, Nauka Publishing House, 1978, p. 103.
46. Ibid.
47. Shahidullah holds that some Caryāpadas are as old as AD 700; J. Bloch, *L'Indo-Aryan*, Paris, 1934, p. 15.
48. A.K. Warder discusses the impact of feudal polity and society on Sanskrit literature in his *Indian Kāvya Literature*, vol. 3, *The Early Medieval Period* (*Śūdraka to Viśākhadatta*), 2nd revised edn, Delhi, Motilal Banarsidass, 1990, paras 1153, 1273 and 1620. He continues it in vol. 4, *The Ways of Originality* (*Bāṇa to Dāmodaragupta*), Delhi, Motilal Banarsidass, 1983, paras, 1940, 1945, 1980, 2298, 2397 and 2636.
49. D.D. Kosambi and V.V. Gokhale, ed. *The Subhāṣitaratnakoṣa Compiled by Vidyākara*, Cambridge, Massachusetts, Harvard University Press, 1957, Introduction, 6. 'The Basis of Feudal Sanskrit Literature', pp. xlv–xlix.
50. Niharranjan Ray, *History of the Bengali People* (*Ancient Period*), tr. John H. Hood, Calcutta, Orient Longman, 1994, pp. 432–3.
51. I owe this information to Professor Surendra Gopal.
52. It contains passages quoted from several Buddhist works of about the third or fourth century AD. S.C. Vidyabhusana, *A History of Indian Logic*, reprint, Delhi, Motilal Banarsidass, 1988, p. 46.
53. Surendranath Das Gupta, *A History of Indian Philosophy*, reprint, Delhi, Motilal Banarsidass, 1975, pp. 332–60.
54. Ibid., pp. 360–6.
55. On the origin of bhakti see Suvira Jaiswal, *Origin and Development of Vaiṣṇavism*, 2nd edn, New Delhi, Munshiram Manoharlal, 1981.
56. I owe some of these terms to Professor Qeyamuddin Ahmad.
57. Robert Lingat, *The Classical Law of India*, tr. and with additions by J. Duncan M. Derrett, California, University of California, 1973, pp. 259–60.

13

Introducing Early Medieval Indian Society*

I first dealt with early medieval Indian society in my book, *Indian Feudalism*, which was primarily concerned with polity and economy. Published in 1965 as the elaboration of a paper I brought out in 1958,[1] it generated considerable debate among Marxist and other scholars. About the nature of early medieval social formation[2] they raised questions of both fact and judgement. In the present book I have tried to clarify the concept of feudalism and extend my discussion of polity and economy, I have also included material on the social and cultural aspects of the early medieval period.

In my understanding of feudalism I give the greatest weight to the economic factor. Gross disparity between various classes of people in their control over land and their appropriation of its product is the motive force behind social transformation. Since land is the chief means of production in preindustrial societies, unequal access to its use and its surplus product gives rise to a rent collecting landocracy and a subject peasantry. The dominant class of landlords and the servile peasantry, therefore, are essential; elements in the structure of feudalism presented in Marxist writings.[3] In his *Feudal Society*, Marc Bloch expounds a similar concept.

Marx did not examine the social and political aspects of feudalism. He looked upon it as a mode of production from which arose the capitalist mode of production. His views on the feudal mode of production may be summed up on the basis of John Pryor. According to Marx, craft and agricultural production in the feudal mode was carried on by a non-free labour force on large estates, which were 'owned' or effectively

*Originally published as 'Introduction' in R.S. Sharma, *Early Medieval Indian Society* (New Delhi: Orient Longman, 2001).

possessed by non-labouring landlords. In this mode the 'transfer of surplus labour or product of labour was effected not by economic means as in capitalism but rather by the exercise of direct political, legal and military force or coercion necessitated by the effective property rights of the producing labour force'.[4]

Marx accounts for the origin of the feudal mode of production in Europe. He was the first to perceive and underline the mingling of the Roman and German modes of production. He stated that for the Germanic barbarians, who lived on the land, 'agriculture with bondsmen was the traditional production', while in the Roman provinces 'the concentration of landed property which had taken place there had already entirely overthrown earlier agricultural relations'.[5] It was easy, therefore, for the Germanic barbarians to impose their conditions on the Romans. According to Marx, the mingling of the two elements gave rise to the feudal mode of production. In this mode, that is, the Romano-German feudalism, land could not be alienated to the commoners. In my view, in many preindustrial countries concentration of land in the hands of a few landlords, who got the land cultivated with the help of dependant rent-paying agriculturists, was the essence of the feudal mode of production. The political superstructure that grew out of this system is often noted by scholars who ignore the mode of production on which it was based.

In the Indian context, the ideas of Marx on feudalism appear in his criticism of the nineteenth century Russian scholar Kovlevsky's application of the feudal model to the sultanate and the Mughal rule. Kovlevsky draws attention to the prevalence of the benefice system. But Marx does not consider it an essential trait of feudalism.[6] He regards serfdom as an essential feature of feudalism, though Engels does not hold this view.

In my view, underlying the feudal structure is the subjection of the peasantry by the landed intermediaries. This matter on the whole deserves far more attention than any particular method by which the intermediaries ensured subjection. Serfdom was designed to organize agricultural and craft production on the estate or manor of the lord. The peasants were forcibly attached to the large land holdings and given small pieces of land for their support. The practice was meant to keep them under control and to ensure that land was not held in any large measure by the commoners. But serfdom cannot be regarded as the sole method of mobilizing peasants for carrying on production; it was not the only way of exploiting the labour of the peasants. The peasants could be made to render services and payments through other methods also. Both

Marc Bloch and the Marxist Russian historian E.A. Kosminsky regard the servility of the peasantry to be the crucial element of feudalism but they do not assign the same importance to serfdom.

As a mode of production feudalism has a dominant class of landlords who are not directly engaged in production. Production is carried on by the peasants who occupy land and work on it. But the landed interest extracts surplus product and labour from them by legal, military, ideological and other extra-economic means. Though the peasant may effectively occupy the land, taxes, tributes and labour services imposed by the landlord substantially undermine his control over production and reduce him to servitude. Therefore, in feudalism the vital element is the nature of property relations. As Robert Brenner states, feudal societies are 'social-property systems characterized by peasant possession and surplus extraction by extra-economic compulsion. . . .'[7]

Institutionally the Western feudal system is identified by benefice including the military fief, commendation, vassalage, immunity from the operation of police and judicial authority of the state, subinfeudation and serfdom. These institution resulted in the servility of the peasantry, but even without some of them we notice the subjection of the peasants to the landocracy.

Neo-Marxist scholars do not regard the fief or land grant meant for military service as the cornerstone of feudalism. They do not consider it even the most important element. They argue that a feudal mode of production prevailed in Europe in the Middle Ages and would have continued throughout this period even if the military fief had never existed. In their view 'the fief could never have existed without a pre-existing socio-economic structure of estate production'.[8]

Many institutions that developed in early medieval India to keep the peasants under control and make them pay recall the European types. These include religious, administrative and military fiefs, vassalage, freedom of the beneficiaries from the operation of the police and judicial authority of the state and the practice of subinfeudation. Institutions peculiar to India include hierarchy in the religious systems and the well-organized caste hierarchy. These are linked to feudal property relations in land, and effectively support and perpetuate those relations.

The causes of the origin of feudalism should not be confused with the traits of its structure. The ways in which the nature of property relations in land was altered may differ from area to area. In Europe the Hun invasions in the fourth and fifth centuries played a vital part in this process, but in India internal convulsions seem to have been the main reason behind the widespread practice of land grants. Grants gave rise to landlords, and also to feudatories who owed their origin to war, diplomacy and other factors. However, all the feudatories had to perform the same set of obligations in the feudal set up. The Allahabad Inscription of Samudra Gupta tells of five feudatory kingdoms and nine feudatory tribal states under that great conqueror. All these feudatories were obliged to pay tribute, obey orders, attend court for personal obeisance, and offer their daughters in marriage. Whether the feudatory headed a varṇa-based community or a broadly egalitarian tribal group, he paid the overlord out of his collection from the peasants who were burdened with supporting both the immediate lord and the distant overlord.

Therefore, once the feudal system was established, its economic traits were more or less the same in India and other countries. Whether a lord was a tribute-paying feudatory, or a landlord created through a royal charter or one developed out of tribal chief or royal agent, his relation with the peasants was one of collector of rent and labour service. It also did not make much difference whether the lord was hereditary or not and whether he belonged to the caste or kin group of his peasants.

Chattopadhyaya has criticized me for considering the land grants as the cause of political fragmentation and the rise of states,[9] but I discounted this possibility in peripheral states as early as 1960. I stated that in Orissa the transition to organized state/class society took place in the post-Gupta period and that the possibility of political fragmentation 'from above' did not exist.[10] However, land grants did lead to parcellization of power. The concentration of land control in the hands of the beneficiaries who were also delegated fiscal, judicial and military functions created pockets of state power, with the potential for autonomy. Gross unequal distribution of land and its products created conditions for social antagonism and political segmentation. However, the advocates of the segmentary theory postulate ritual ridden and kin-controlled polities in which peasants and brāhmaṇa landlords live harmoniously. Though such polities are not altogether absent in early medieval India, they are based on land grants and beset with the problems that the grants create. I have shown elsewhere that the segmentary model does not fit the Indian experience.[11]

Fragmentation or segmentation should not be regarded as a lasting feature of Indian feudalism. According to Marc Bloch, parcellization of sovereignty is a trait of feudalism in the first or the classical phase. In the second phase or in the phase of dissolution it shows centralization and royal absolutism. He observes this in the context of western Europe, but it may apply to India. Even under the absolute rule of the Mughals the feudal mode of production persisted in a large measure. It seems that fragmentation of political authority at the local level was a divide and rule device to maintain the overall authority of the state over its landed beneficiaries and also the mass of the peasantry in a tenuous manner. Therefore, fragmentation should not be considered to be a permanently disintegrating feature.

The integrating role of land grants is underlined by Kulke, particularly in the case of Kaliṅga, at social, religious and ideological levels. In the land grants rulers appear as deputies of divinities. The land-receiving brāhmaṇas were loyal and inculcated loyalty in others. But Kulke also stresses the 'sāmantisation' of the medieval realm and the consequent erosion of the power of its ruler.[12] I pointed out the integrative role of land grants through acculturation in 1965. In my view, the land grant, made by large and small states irrespective of their origins, proved to be a great transforming factor. It led to the restructuring of polity, society and economy on feudal lines. The new establishment also moulded religion, art and literature and promoted regionalism. Land grants, therefore, played a crucial role in the transition from the ancient to the medieval.

One of the ways of looking at early medieval society could be through the perspective of regional developments and various regional entities. 'Localism' in history and 'processualism' in archaeology have won some advocates. Scholars from Cambridge, Cornell[13] and other places apply the theory of localization to preindustrial South Asia and Southeast Asia. This has yielded some good results like Chattopadhyaya's case for the regional approach.[14] However, I am wary of those who look for roots of Indian nationalism in frivolous local grievances of individuals against British officials and thereby underplay the countrywide colonialist exploitation. In the medieval context regionalism is not incongruous with feudalism. Feudal developments may differ region-wise, but these differences relate not so much to the traits of the feudal structure as to its origin. I have shown elsewhere[15] that regionalism could encourage voluntary integration and land controllers of a region could combine against peasant resistance, as in the case of the Kaivarta revolt which was put down by a group of two dozen Pāla feudatories. The spatial reconstruction of the social order may reveal its specificities and intricacies. It may enrich and modify the pan-Indian perspective, but because of obsession with regionalism we may miss the wood for the trees.[16] Though the micro and particularist approach has its own value, no study of socio-economic development can be complete without the macro and universal approach. In early medieval India basic changes in the polity, society, economy and culture of a region cannot be satisfactorily explained without a synthesis of the two types of approach. To understand the pre-colonial history of a region it is necessary to reinforce the regional perspective with the pan-Indian and world perspective.

The problem of feudalism from below is connected with the locality approach. In my paper on the origins of feudalism published in 1958, I did not consider Kosambi's theory of feudalism from below,[17] which appeared in his book in 1956. We may look for feudalism from below not only in the later stage, as Kosambi does, but also in the initial stage. The king or high functionaries record their land grants in epigraphs, but grants from lower officials, village elders and heads of tribes, clans or families are not recorded. However, the possibility of the rise of landlords even without the blessings of the state cannot be discounted. Large landowners who employed slaves and agricultural labourers in their fields in pre-Gupta times may have developed into landlords like the owners of the Roman latifundias.

The Gupta inscriptions mention *kulika* and *kutumbin*. D.R. Bhandarkar regards the first as the zamindar and second as the peasant.[18] Though the second was really a peasant, he did not live whole on rent. However *kula* also means land cultivated by two ploughs with six bulls on each.[19] This suggests that a *kulika* owned more land than could be directly tilled by one family. Therefore the *kulika* could be easily turned into a landlord living on rent and services rendered to him. Again, the *bhojaka* mentioned in an Orissa charter of the fifth century is taken as a village proprietor or a *jagirdar* of the medieval Muslim rule.[20] Contemporary surnames such as Patel in Gujarat and Maharashtra, Mahto in Bihar, Nayak in Orissa, Gowda in Karnataka and Andhra Pradesh, and Pradhan in Bihar and Orissa held by the landowning families suggest that their ancestors were either substantial peasants or rent-receiving landlords. The early inscriptions of the Deccan mention the *mahajana* who seems to have been a village elder. He appears as land-donor and also as receiver, approver and a witness of the land grant.[21] Perhaps fiscal functionaries selected from the rural areas used their authority and influence to grab more land than could be cultivated by their family members. They may be compared with *jeth* raiyat or the head tenant chosen by the zamindars under the Permanent Settlement.[22]

Out of nearly 70 states between AD 400 and 650 several seem to have been set up by the tribal chiefs. Even ordinary tenants could become landlords. Since private property in land was well established by Gupta times, peasants could enlarge their property under congenial conditions.

According to Kalhana, an eighth century king from Kashmir states that villagers should neither be left with more food than required for one year nor with more oxen than necessary for the cultivation of their fields, because if this is not done in a single year they would become formidable landlords and disobey the king.[23] This view is consistent with the principle of taxation which recommends bare subsistence for the taxpayer. D.C. Sircar, who drew attention to this reference,[24] cites examples of *ḍāmaras* or landlords who rise from below in Kashmir without any contact or contract with the king.[25]

How tribal chiefs were transformed into landlords and feudatories needs investigation. I have given ethnographic examples elsewhere to show how, as pioneer settlers or discoverers of new resources, chiefs of clans or their individual members come to acquire special rights and privileges in the community land.[26] The elevation of the tribals may have been promoted by contact with state and varṇa society. Most probably, privileged family heads imitated the state functionaries in acquiring land through muscle power and ancestral influence.

The distinction between the landlords created by the state and those who became landlords on their own should not be over-emphasized. Even those who were granted land by the state were preferred because of their functions and importance. However, in the initial stage, religious and ideological functions were considered far more important. On the other hand, those who arose on their own seem to have been without much religious association. But the precise process by which village elders or heads of kin-based families turned into local landlords[27] requires further research.

André Wink charges me with applying the findings of Henry Pirenne on the decline of trade and towns in Europe to Indian history. But he reveals an ignorance of the research on early medieval India. As early as the 1940s Niharranjan Ray pointed out the decline of trade and towns[28] and D.D. Kosambi did so in the fifties.[29] They were not familiar with the writings of Pirenne, but they could not ignore the evidence from the primary sources. Wink's work contains so many inaccuracies[30] that a serious consideration of it is difficult.

Models promote research in history and other social sciences. But a model should not be considered the patent and monopoly of a country or a group of scholars. Its viability depends on the nature of supporting evidence and the logic used in interpreting it. In my opinion, models developed on the basis of the historical experience of one country help bring out the specificities of another country. Historians are free to create the Asiatic or the Indian model, but if it is divorced from practice and overplays geographical, political and cultural factors at the cost of changes in the social and economic mode of production, it does not advance our understanding of the social formation. Some writers talk of 'received models' and, ironically enough, do so in a 'received language'.

Recent studies do not view feudalism in one country as an autonomous entity. Its interaction with similar and even different socio-economic formations is considered. It has been shown how the feudal systems of France and England influenced each other. It seems that Indian feudalism influenced the polity and economy of the neighbouring areas in Southeast Asia. The spread of Indian art, religion, language and form of writing in Southeast Asia was probably accompanied by the diffusion of its feudal socio-economic organization. In Thailand, the idea of feudalism is conveyed through the use of the term *śaktina*, which literally means discriminatory distribution of rice fields (*na*) because of the possession of power (*śakti*). *Śaktina* first appears in the language of Thailand in the fifteenth century.[31] Thai researchers claim to have collected sufficient data to demonstrate the prevalence of a feudal system in their country in the pre-colonial era.[32] Scholars from Myanmar make a similar claim.[33] We may note that the Indonesians were familiar with the land grant system of India. Bālaputradeva, king of Sumatra, persuaded the Pāla king Devapāla (ninth century) to donate five villages to a Nalanda monastery erected by him.[34]

The best way to follow early medieval developments is to look at them in relation to the mode of production. In the early medieval context we have to bear in mind the craft technology and agricultural knowledge of the period. Further, we have to investigate the ownership pattern of agrarian, pastoral and water resources and also of the sources of metal of which tools were made. We have to determine the extent to which a peasant could freely produce and enjoy his products. We have to identify the relations of production, that is, the bonds between the state and its landed beneficiaries, and also between the peasants and the beneficiaries. We need an idea of the revenue and services collected by the state from the beneficiaries. Similarly, the various ways in which the beneficiaries extract rent and labour services from the peasants have to be noted. Moreover, the availability of market facilities to the peasants and artisans and others has to be explored. I have tried to explain these aspects of the mode of production in chapter three of *Early Medieval Indian Society*. In the light of the mode of production, including production relations, we have tried to understand developments in early medieval polity, society, religion and ideology. If we consider the continuous interplay that goes on between the mode of production on the one hand and the social, political and cultural trends on the other we achieve a superior historical perspective.

Although the basic traits of the mode of production remain constant throughout the development of feudalism, the institutions associated with them vary according to time, place and interactions with other socio-economic formations.

The first phase of feudalism in India, to my mind, coincides with the decline of towns, less use of metallic coins and the decay of long-distance trade. This phase shows a non-market or subsidiary market economy in which feudalism flourishes. My book, *Indian Feudalism*, attributes the origin of feudalism to the decline of trade and towns. After its publication I wrote a separate paper on the decline of towns after AD 300 which I wanted to include in this volume. But when I started revising the piece it turned into a book entitled *Urban Decay in India* (*c.* 300-*c.*1000).[35] Therefore, instead of the decline of ancient towns I have written a chapter on the paucity of metallic coinage in the post-Gupta period from *c.* 500 to *c.* 1000. For this I checked collections of coins in important museums. Though I did not have access to all the collections, the data I gathered is a fair index to the overall monetary situation.

Land grants fit well with the shrinkage of towns. But the decline of trade and towns may not fully account for the widespread practice of land grants. We have, therefore, considered the nature of internal social dynamics suggested by the Puranic passages on the advent of the age of Kali in the third and fourth centuries. Though the passages cannot be confidently attributed to specific areas they suggest serious dents in the varṇa-based social order. Less towns, trade and cash money suggest economic stagnation leading to land grants. Although grants promoted agrarian expansion and agricultural production, trade continued to suffer because agricultural surplus was mainly diverted to support religious constructions and the production of idols.

The impact of land grants on the caste system is treated in a chapter which also discusses the consequences of the spread of the brāhmaṇa beneficiaries in tribal areas. I have tried to show how feudal factors affect the position of the vaiśyas, śūdras and tribals. The issue of subinfeudation along with that of differentiation in the peasantry[36] is discussed in my earlier writings, although the categorization of the landed intermediaries does not receive the same attention from me. This chapter tries to understand the problem of correspondence between the caste hierarchy and the rungs in the rural ladder created by land grants. It also touches on the place of kinship structure in the feudal context.

Given the pressure of dominant landed intermediaries *vis-à-vis* the subservient peasants burdened with taxes, tributes and labour services, rural society was beset with perpetual tension and conflict. Similarly, quarrels between the various categories of the landed intermediaries and also between them and the state were bound to be endemic. I have, therefore, discussed the role of th:e *rājaśāsana* or the royal land charter which superseded all the other sources of evidence in case of dispute. U.N. Ghoshal and K.A. Nilakanta Sastri built up the theory of the royal absolutism of the Mauryas on the basis of *rājaśasana* found in Kauṭilya's *Arthaśāstra*. But the theory of absolutism does not explain the repeated occurrence of this term in the Gupta and post-Gupta texts which belong to a period of political fragmentation. While royal charters helped the landlords to retain their property, appropriate inheritance laws were framed to prevent the partition of the landed estates. I have dealt with these laws in a separate chapter in *Early Medieval Indian Society*.

Legal provisions and ideological propaganda could not always keep the peasants under control. Though we do not find organized peasant revolts, except in the case of the Kaivartas, there are several instances of peasant protest. The characterization of such protests remains a problem. I have tried to explore whether protest was inspired by any religious ideology or led by those who were thinly brāhmaṇized.

The close link of the brāhmaṇa beneficiaries from the tribal area with the origin and orgnization of tantrism has been examined. Tantrism provides the best example of the integration of tribal cults into a pan-Indian brāhmaṇical cult based on the worship of the mother goddess. The hierarchical organization of tantrism has been examined in the light of the feudal, economic and political hierarchy. Finally, the book explains the ideas and attitudes of the landocracy, and the feudal mind is seen as influencing the development of art, architecture, literature and religion. The elements of destiny, bhakti and 'gurudom' are also treated at some length.

The essays included in this book are written within the broad framework of the materialist approach to history. Change and continuity are treated accordingly. In the Marxist view, the succeeding stage in a society is generally related to the one preceding it, and change is continuous. Out of the existing order arises a new one. On account of the unequal access to control over sources of subsistence and production, ancient society became varṇa-based and generated ideas and institutions supporting unequal economic rights. It also produced attitudes of superiority and inferiority. Mental attitudes emanating from the institutions of private property, male dominance and varṇa society continued in early medieval times. So did some community practices of sharing pastures, water resources, fuels, religious offerings, etc. But despite the phenomenon of continuity ancient ideas and institutions underwent a qualitative change because of land grants. I have tried to illustrate this change by showing the emergence of landlords, erosion of peasant control over production, decline of ancient towns and trade, multiplication of states, parcellization of power, proliferation of castes, rise of tantrism and appearance of feudal ideology in early medieval times. The essays presented here trace these elements which appeared gradually because of internal upheaval and external influence embedded in economic factors.

I have tried to examine the origin and growth of the traits of early medieval society on the basis of the feudal model, but I do not think that feudalism is an essential prelude to the rise of capitalism or to the advent of colonialism. Capitalism arose out of feudalism only in England and Holland. However, for the study of preindustrial India, the model of feudalism is useful in several ways. If we accept the presence of the dominant landocracy and the subject peasantry bonded together by extra-economic methods, we can clearly understand the developments in art, religion, literature, polity and society. We can also better appreciate certain practices surviving in the modern social formation. We can get a better contextual and historical view of such pejoratives as 'feudal forces', 'feudal behaviour' and 'feudalistic outlook' used in day-to-day discourse.

NOTES

1. R.S. Sharma, 'Origins of Feudalism in India', *Journal of the Economic and Social History of the Orient, (JESHO)*, vol. I, 1958, pp. 297–328.
2. V.K. Thakur gives an idea of this debate in his *Historiography of Indian Feudalism: Towards a Model of Early Indian Economy.* AD *600–100*, Patna, New Delhi, Janaki Prakashan, 1989.
3. The Marxist scholar Halil Berktay gives the following definition of feudalism: Feudalism is the juxtaposition of a rent-collecting aristocracy (including effective aristocracies disguised as bureaucracies or 'state classes' by the convolutions of relatively strong state apparatuses), in an exploitative and contradictory relationship with a class of peasant direct producers in possession of their small economies, who for that reason have to be tied to the land and otherwise coerced extra economically to make possible the appropriation of all or part of their surplus labour. Halil Berktay, 'The Feudalism Debate: The Turkish End: Is 'Tax-vs-Rent' Necessarily the

Product and Sign of a Model Difference?', *Journal of Peasant Studies, (JPS)*, vol. 14, no. 3, April 1987, p. 311.

4. John Pryor, 'The Historical Foundations of a Feudal Mode of Production', in Edmund Leach, SN Mukherjee and John Ward, ed. *Feudalism: Comparative Studies*, Sydney, The Sydney Association for Studies in Society and Culture, 1985, pp. 66–86.
5. Karl Marx, *Grundrisse: Foundations of the Critique of Political Economy* (Rough Draft), tr. M Nicolans, Harmondsworth, Penguin Books, 1973, p. 98.
6. See Appendix II.
7. Robert Brenner, 'Agrarian Class Structure and Economic Development in Pre-Industrial Europe: The Agrarian Roots of European Capitalism', *Past and Present*, no. 97, November 1982, p. 18.
8. John Pryor, Historical Foundations of a Feudal Mode of Production, p. 82. In India the military fief systems existed in Orissa, Karnataka and elsewhere from the eleventh century onwards.
9. B.D. Chattopadhyaya, *The Making of Early Medieval India*, New Delhi, Oxford University Press, 1994.
10. R.S. Sharma, 'Land System in Medieval Orissa (*c.* 750–1200)', *Proceedings of the Indian History Congress (PIHC)*, Aligarh Session, 1960, pp. 89–96.
11. R.S. Sharma, 'The Segmentary Theory and the Indian Experience', *Indian Historical Review* (*IHR*), vol. xvi, nos 1–2, July 1989 and January 1990, pp. 80–108.
12. Hermann Kulke, 'Royal Temple Policy and the Structure of Medieval Hindu Kingdoms', in Eschmann, Anncharlott, Hermann Kulke and Gaya Charan Tripathi, ed. *The Cult of Jagannath and the Regional Tradition of Orissa*, Manohar, New Delhi, 1978, pp. 125–37; cf. Hermann Kulke, 'The Early and the Imperial Kingdom: A Processual Model of Integrative State Formation in Early Medieval India', in Hermann Kulke, ed. *The State in India 1000–1700*, New Delhi, Oxford University Press, 1995, pp. 233–63; Hermann Kulke & Dietmar Rothermund, *A History of India*, London, Routledge, 1998, pp. 121–3.
13. Kenneth R Hall, 'The Textile Industry in Southeast Asia', *JESHO*, 39, 1996, p. 90, fn. 7.
14. B.D. Chattopadhyaya, *Making of Early Medieval India* (New Delhi: Oxford University Press).
15. R.S. Sharma, *Urban Decay in India (c. 300–c. 1000)*, New Delhi, Munshiram Manoharlal, 1987, pp. 168–9, 175, 184–5.
16. For the strengths and weaknesses of the locality approach to the study of early medieval India, see Vishwa Mohan Jha, 'Settlement, Society and Polity in Early Medieval Rural India', *Social Science Probings*, vols 11 and 12, Special Issue, March 1994 –December 1995, pp. 35–65.
17. This has been pointed out by several scholars, and recently by B.D. Chattopadhyaya in his Introduction to *Making of Early Medieval India*, 1994.

18. *Corpus Inscriptionum Indicarum, (CII)* vol. III, revised by Devdatta Ramakrishna Bhandarkar, ed. Bahadurchand Chhabra and Govind Swamirao Gai, New Delhi, Archaeological Survey of India, 1981, Introduction, pp. 102–3, 106.
19. *s.v. kula in SED.*
20. Snigdha Tripathi, *Inscriptions of Orissa*, vol. I (*c.* Fifth to Eighth Centuries AD), New Delhi, Indian Council of Historical Research and Motilal Banarsidass, 1997, p. 20.
21. Aloka Parashar-Sen, Introduction, in Aloka Parashar-Sen, ed. *Social and Economic History of Early Deccan: Some Interpretations*, New Delhi, Manohar, 1993, p. 50.
22. A jeth *raiyat* or chief tenant selected from the richest and most influential family. He did not collect rent, but all the tenants were expected to deposit the rent with him. It was collected by the agents of the landlord.
23. *Rajatarangini, 1900*, iv, 347–8.
24. D.C. Sircar, *Landlordism and Tenancy in Ancient and Medieval India as Revealed by Epigraphical Records*, Lucknow, University of Lucknow, 1969, pp. 62–3.
25. Ibid., p. 37.
26. R.S. Sharma, *The State and Varṇa Formation in the Mid-Ganga Plains: An Ethnoarchaeological View*, New Delhi, Manohar, 1996.
27. B.P. Sahu, 'Arguing for Feudalism from Below: A Study in Orissa Setting, *c.* AD 400–1000, *PHIC*, Calcutta Session, 1990, pp. 141–50; 'Aspects of Rural Economy in Early Medieval Orissa', *Social Scientist*, vol. 21, nos 1–2, January–February 1993, pp. 48–68.
28. Ray, Niharranjan, *Bangalir Itihas (Adi Parva)*, Calcutta, Book Emporium, 1949.
29. D.D. Kosambi, *An Introduction to the Study of Indian History*, Bombay, Popular Prakashan, 1956.
30. These inaccuracies have been pointed out by Vishwa Mohan Jha in his review article entitled, 'The Artless Pirennion', *IHR*, vol. 18, nos 1–2, July 1991–January 1992, pp. 93–103.
31. Craig J. Reynolds, 'Feudalism as a Trope or Discourse for the Asian Past with Special Reference to Thailand' in Edmund Leach, et al., *Feudalism: Comparative Studies*, 1985, p. 141.
32. Ibid., pp. 146–51.
33. Ibid., p. 138.
34. D.R. Patil, *The Antiquarian Remains in Bihar*, Patna, KP Jayaswal Institute, 1963, p. 333.
35. R.S. Sharma, *Indian Feudalism*, Calcutta, University of Calcutta, 1965; 2nd edn, New Delhi, Macmillan, 1980. Also see R.S. Sharma, *Urban Decay in India*.
36. Ibid., p. 85. Also refer to R.S. Sharma, *Urban Decay in India*, pp. 175–6.

14

How Feudal was Indian Feudalism?*

Several scholars have questioned the use of the term feudalism to characterize the early medieval socio-economic formation in India.[1] But the points raised by Harbans Mukhia[2] deserve serious attention. He rightly suggests that, unlike capitalism, feudalism is not a universal phenomenon. But in our view tribalism, stone age, metal age, advent of food producing economy are universal phenomena. They do indicate some laws conditioning the process and pattern of change.

Tribalism may continue or be followed by different forms of state and class society, but it appears universally. Tribal society has many variations. It can be connected with any of the modes of subsistence such as cattle pastoralism, other types of pastoralism, hoe agriculture, plough agriculture, etc. The advent of agriculture requires cooperation and settlement at one place, and creates a lasting base for the tribal set-up. Many tribal societies practise shifting cultivation or swidden cultivation. But an advanced type of agriculture produces substantial surplus and creates dents in tribal homogeneity. Conditions appear for the rise of classes based on status and wealth and above all on the large-scale exploitation of the bulk of the kinsmen by a few people on top. In such a situation the tribal system gets heavily corroded.

Similarly, although the tribal society is organized on the principle of kinship, this organization could have large variations. Some form of organization, inherited from the band society, would be developed further in the tribal stage. Cooperation in production efforts would be needed; division of labour would be required. But this could be on the matriarchal basis, patriarchal basis, on the basis of a combination of the two, and in fact could rest on an organization based on all kinds of kinship

*Previously published as, 'How Feudal was Indian Feudalism?' in *Social Scientist*, vol. 12, no. 2, Marx Centenary no. 3 (February, 1984), pp. 16–41.

combinations and permutations. Marriage practices and laws of 'property' inheritance might differ from one tribal society to the other, and may differ even in the same tribe. But, in spite of these variations, tribal society has been found on a universal scale. Therefore the concept of tribe is useful even for the understanding of social formations known from written texts.

It is not necessary to posit diffusion of tribal society although this may have taken place in certain cases. Although feudalism does not seem to be as universal as, tribalism, in the Old World it was undoubtedly more widespread than the slave system. The concept of peasant society is still in a nebulous state. But if peasant society means a system in which the orders of priests and warriors live on the surplus produced by peasants and augmented by the activities of the artisans, such a society existed in a good part of the Old World. Tribalism, peasant society or slave system could originate due to internal or external fectors or due to both. Similarly it is not necessary to think in terms of the diffusion of the feudal system, although this happened in certain cases. For instance, the Norman feudalism in England was a result of the Norman conquest.

THE ESSENCE OF FEUDALISM

But just as there could be enormous variations in tribal society so also there could be enormous variations in the nature of feudal societies. It is rightly stated by Marx that feudalism 'assumes different aspects, and runs through its various phases in different orders of succession'.[3] But certain universals remain the same. This is admitted even by critics of Indian feudalism who think of the variants of feudalism.[4] Feudalism has to be seen as a mode of the distribution of the means of production and of the appropriation of the surplus. It may have certain broad universal features and it may have certain traits typical of a territory. Obviously land and agricultural products play a decisive role in pre-capitalist class societies, but the specific situation about land distribution and the appropriation of agricultural products will differ from region to region. It could be nobody's argument that what developed in pre-capitalist Western Europe was found in India and elsewhere. Historical laws, as far as they are known, do not work in this manner, nor could one say that feudalism was the monopoly of Western Europe. It is not possible to have any neat, cut and dried formula about feudalism. The most one could say about the universals of feudalism could be largely on the lines of Marc Bloch and EK Kosminsky.[5] Feudalism appears in a predominantly agrarian economy which is characterized by a class of landlords and a class of servile peasantry. In this system the landlords extract surplus through social, religious or political methods, which are called extra-economic. This seems to be more or less the current Marxist view of feudalism, which considers serfdom, 'scalar property' and 'parcellised sovereignty' as features of the West European version of the feudal system. The lord-peasant relationship is the core of the matter, and the exploitation of the estate by its owner, controller, enjoyer or beneficiary as its essential ingredient. With these minimum universals, feudalism may have several variations. The particularities of the system in some West European countries do not apply to the various types of feudalism found in other areas. For example, evidence for peasant struggles against landlords in other countries has not been produced in sufficient degree. Similarly, artisan and capitalist growth within the womb of feudalism seems to be typical of the West European situation where agricultural growth and substantial commodity production created major structural contradictions. The nature of religious beneficiaries, who grabbed a major portion of land, also differed from country to country. Thus the Church was a great landlord in Portugal. Buddhist and Confucian establishments controlled land in Korea. Buddhist monastries were also important in eastern India. Temples emerged as estates in south India, and many brāhmaṇas enjoyed a similar position in upper and middle Gangetic basins, central India, the Deccan, and Assam. Non-religious landed intermediaries also appear in different forms in different parts of India and outside this country. In certain parts of the country, for example in Orissa, we find tribal chiefs, being elevated to the position of landlords. In other parts many administrative officials enjoyed land taxes from the peasants. But in spite of all these variations the basic factor, namely, the presence of a controlling class of landlords and a subject peasantry, remains the same at least in early medieval times.

Again the degrees of the servility of the peasants to the landlords might differ from region to region; so also the composition of the cultivating class. The development of agriculture, handicrafts, commodity production, trade and commerce and of urbanization could create conditions for differentiation in the ranks of the peasantry. Those peasants who produce a little over and above their needs of subsistence might buy their freedom by payment of money in lieu of labour service provided such a practice was favoured by the state and provided a reasonable extent of market economy was available. Several peasants might be reduced to a state of further penury and rich peasants might grow at their cost. But where such developments do not appear, a more or less homogeneous peasantry might continue. However, differences in the techniques of farming and the nature of the soil might affect the agricultural yield and create variations.

Similarly peasants might be compelled to work as serfs on landlords' farms in Western Europe. But serfdom should not be considered to be identical with feudalism.[6] It was after all a form of servility, which kept the peasant tied to the soil and made him work on the farm of his lord. Those peasants who were compelled to pay heavy rents in cash and kind to the landlords or required to provide both rent as well as labour were as servile as those who supplied only labour. It also makes some difference to his servility if a peasant has to bear allegiance only to the landlord. If he has to be loyal to both the state and the landlord then it could be either a case of double servility or divided loyalty. But the fundamental point at issue is the subjection of the peasantry, and that subjection is found in all the possible situations to which we have referred earlier. There is no doubt that this subjection is a characteristic of early medieval Indian social structure.

It is argued that the peasant in medieval India enjoyed autonomy or production because he had 'complete' control over the means of production.[7] What is the significance of owning the means of production ? Is it not meant for using the fruits of production? Do the fruits stay with the peasant or are these substantially appropriated by the landlord? How does this appropriation become possible? What is the mechanism that enables the landlord to appropriate the surplus, a part of that fruit? Is it merely because of his control over the means of production or because of his coercive power? Or is it extracted through the ideological weapon such as the peasant's belief that he is duty bound to pay? The latter ideology that the landlords are the parents of the peasants[8] is reminiscent of the tribal outlook. But this idea may have been further fostered by the priestly landlords in medieval times. At present we will not try to answer all these questions but take up the problem of the distribution of the resources of production in early medieval India.

THE DISTRIBUTION OF RESOURCES IN EARLY MEDIEVAL INDIA

Obviously land was the primary means of production. But the real difficulty about the understanding of distribution of land is caused when we think in terms of exclusive control over land by one party or the other. It should be made clear that in early medieval times in the same piece of land the peasant held inferior rights and the landlords held superior rights. One may possess land, labour, oxen, other animals and agricultural implements. But we have to find out how effective is this 'control' over the means of production. Do other conditions such as taxes, forced labour, constant interference by on-the spot beneficiaries, who were ever present, make the peasant's control really operational? Obviously nobody would kill a hen that lays eggs. So peasants would be allowed to stay alive. But that should not be understood as their effective control over the means of production.

In fact land grants leave hardly any doubt that the landlords enjoyed a good measure of general control in the means of production. Why did the landlords claim various types of rents from the peasants and how could they collect their demands? Clearly they did so on the strength of royal charters which conferred on them either the villages or pieces of land or various types of taxes. Why did the king claim taxes? Formerly the king claimed taxes on the ground that he afforded protection to the people. In early medieval law-books he claimed taxes on the ground that he was the owner of the land.[9] Numerous epithets indicate that the king was the owner of the land in early medieval times.[10] Now by the charter he delegated this royal authority to the beneficiary, and on this strength the beneficiary claimed taxes. The king was *bhumidata*, giver of land. It was repeatedly said that the merit of giving land accrues to him who possesses it.[11]

Generally the early charters give the beneficiary usufructuary rights. But the later charters grant such concessions as render the beneficiary the de facto owner of the village land. The donated village/villages constitute his estate. For example, the beneficiary is entitled to collect taxes, all kinds of income, all kinds of occasional taxes, and this 'all' (*sarva*)[12] is never specified. Similarly he is entitled to collect proper and improper taxes,[13] fixed and not fixed taxes,[14] and at the end of the list of the taxes the term et cetra (*adi, adikam*)[15] is used. All this adds enormously to the power of the beneficiary. These extraordinary provisions could serve as a self-regulating mechanism as and when production increased,[16] but they could also interfere with the expansion of production. Some provisions clearly created the superior rights of the beneficiary in the land of the peasants. For example, the land charters of Madhya Pradesh, northern Maharashtra, Konkan and Gujarat in Gupta and post-Gupta times empower the beneficiary to evict the old peasants and introduce new ones; he could assign lands to others. Now such concessions leave no doubt that the beneficiary was armed with superior rights in land, which of course was in actual occupation of the cultivator. Most grants after the seventh century AD give away the village along with low land, fertile land, water reservoirs, all kinds of trees and bushes, pathways and pasture grounds. In eastern India grants the village was granted along with mango trees, *mahua* (Bassia datifolia) trees and jack-fruit trees and various other agrarian resources. Cotton, hemp, coconut and arecanut trees are also given away in grants, but this happens mostly after the tenth century when cash crops assume importance. Such provisions connect the agrarian production directly with the beneficiary and, more importantly, transfer almost all communal agrarian resources to him. If a peasant does not have free access to various agrarian resources his autonomy in production is substantially crippled. Only a free exercise of the agrarian rights mentioned above can make his unit effective in production. Till recent times the powerful landlords barred and blocked the access of the weak and helpless peasants to such rights and could make their life impossible. Of course the caste system helped this process. The untouchables had no access to public tanks, wells, etc. Even if they possessed their bits of land, how could they function independently in production?

Most charters ask the peasants to carry out the orders of the beneficiaries.[17] These orders may relate not only to the payment of taxes which will be concerned with the fruits of production but they may also relate to the means and processes of production. In a way the blanket authority to extract obedience places the peasant at the beck and call of the beneficiary. It implies general control over the labour power of the peasants, and undoubtedly labour is an assential ingredient of the means of production. This labour may be used either in the fields cultivated by the peasant or in those directly managed by the beneficiary. The beneficiaries may insist on having certain types of produce for their ostentatious and unproductive consumption, and with all the seigniorial rights that they possess they can compel the peasans to produce those cereals or cash crops which they need.

We may also note that the law-books of Yajnavalkya, Brhaspati and Vyasa specify four graded stages of land rights in the same piece of land. Thus we hear of *mahipati, ksetrasvamin, karsaka* and the subtenant or leaseholder.[18] It is important that the medieval jurists understood *svamitva* in the sense of ownership and *svatva* in the sense of property, and this was considered to be a significant distinction in Hindu law.[19] The *svamin* therefore could be equated with the landed beneficiary and the *karsaka* or the *ksetrika* with the rent-paying tenant peasant. Multiple, hierarchical rights and interests in land, which was the chief means of production, can be inferred even from Gupta land sale transactions. These transactions mention the interest of not only the king but also that of the local administrative body (*adhikarana*) dominated by big men; we also hear of the beneficiaries and of the rights of the occupant of the plot.[20] Of course in several Gupta transactions no occupant is mentioned, and it further appears that money for the purchase of the land is paid not only to the *adhikarana* but also probably to the occupant. These typical land transactions are found is Bangladesh. But in the grant system which became widespread in post-Gupta times the local *adhikarana* disappeared, and was generally not consulted in matters of land grants.

Hierarchical control over land was created by large-scale sub-infeudation, especially from the eighth century onwards.[21] Subinfeudation gave rise to graded types of landlords, different from the actual tillers of the soil. Such a process seems to be in line with a significant generalization made by Marx about feudalism. According to him 'feudal production is characterized by division of soil amongst the greatest possible number of subfeudatories'.[22]

The peasantry was divested more and more of its homogeneous and egalitarian character. Many indications of unequal distribution of land in the village are available. We hear not only of brāhmaṇas but also of the chief brāhmaṇa, *mahattama, uttama, krsivala, karsaka, ksetrakara, kutumbin* and *karuka*, land endowed brāhmaṇas and *agrahara*s. We also hear of *ksudra prakrti* or petty peasants, not to speak of Meda, Andhra and *candala*. It is obvious that certain people in the villages had a greater share in the sources of production and apparently possessed more than they could manage directly. It is also obvious that such people got their lands cultivated by petty peasants either through lease holding or through sharecropping or through the system of serfdom. We have therefore no means to establish that most peasants living in the villages were in 'complete' control of the means of production.

Terminological studies throw interesting and revealing light on the relation of the peasant to the land in early India. The English term peasant, which literary means rustic or countrymen, can be translated into *janapada*, which means an inhabitant of the countryside. That the *janapada* or the territorial unit formed by the countryside was considered to be a source of revenues is well known. Among the other qualities of a *janapada* are those of possessing active peasants capable of bearing taxes and fines (punishments).[23] Naturally when the peasantry was oppressed it led to the revolt of the peasants (*janapada-kopa*), which term occurs in the *Arthaśāstra* of Kauṭilya.[24] Curiously the term *janapada* is not in much use in medieval Sanskrit literature although it occurs in early medieval inscriptions. In medieval times *jana* came to mean a dependent who was valued and acquired because of his labour power. Thus he could be a servile peasant. What is more significant, in several Indo-Aryan dialects of Bihar the term means field labourer. In practice some of these labourers are given small patches of land to earn their subsistence. This practice is apparently a survival of the medieval system according to which *jana* or field workers were possessed by and transferred to landed magnates, as can be inferred not only from inscriptions but also from works on horoscopy.[25] This would show that the tribal *jana* with egalitarian ethos is reduced to almost a serf.

The terms for the peasant used in medieval texts, and particularly in inscriptions, indicate the change in the nature of the peasant's relation to the land he cultivated. From the age of the Buddha to the advent of the Gupta period taxpaying vaiśyas continued as an omnibus order, comprising mostly peasants. But by early medieval times they were reduced to the position of the śūdras who, in spite of having acquired peasanthood, continued to bear the hallmark of servitude.[26] *Gahapati*, literally head of the household, was the term used for the landowning peasant in early Pali texts[27] typical of the middle Gangetic plains which witnessed the rise of the first large states. He seems to have enjoyed substantial autonomy in his unit of production. But the term almost disappears in land grant inscriptions. *Gahapati* or *grahapati* becomes village headman in later texts.[28] A clear term for peasant is *ksetrika* or *ksetrin*,[29] which means controller of land, but even this is sometimes understood as an agriculturist or cultivator in later texts and lexicons. From *ksetrika* in Assamese is derived *khetiyaka*,[30] which means cultivator or husbandman, and is not necessarily the owner of the field. A common term used for the peasant in many grants, especially in those from eastern India, is *ksetrakara*,[31] which literally means cultivator. The term *shetkari* in Marathi is probably derived from it,[32] and does not always mean the owner of the land. Some other terms used in inscriptions are *karsaka*[33] and *kutumbin*.[34] The term *kutumbin* gives some indication of an autonomous peasant family, but it occurs mainly in early land records from eastern India and Madhya Pradesh. In later grants from eastern India it is replaced by *ksetrakara* or *karsaka*. In Gujarat and Rajasthan the *kutumbika* loses his status, for he is sometimes transferred to the beneficiary along with the land.[35] According to Yajnavalkya (*c*. AD 300) the *karsaka* is a mere cultivator in the service of the landowner or *ksetrasvamin*, whose field lay under the general control of the king (*mahipati*).[36] In the Candella grants in eastern Madhya Pradesh the *karsaka* was made over to the assignee along with the village.[37] Land grants also use the term *halika*[38] or ploughman. Sharecroppers are indicated by *arddhika, arddhasirika* or *arddhasirin.* In literature the word *kinasa* is also used.[39] Evidently these terms have nothing to do with control over land. The term *kisan*, so common now in India, is derived from *krsana* or one who ploughs. The word *krsivala*[40] or cultivator is also frequently used in medieval texts. The term *langalopajivin* or one who lives by ploughing is used in *Brhat Samhita.*[41]

A review of the terms used for the peasant in medieval inscriptions and literature fails to present the peasant's image as a controller of land. On the other hand we have such technical terms as *bhokta, bhogi, bhogika, bhogijana, bhogapati, bhogapatika, bhogikapalaka, bhogirupa, mahabhogi, brhadbhogi, brhadbhogika* etc, used generally for those who enjoyed landed estates.[42] Here we have not taken into account many other terms connected with *raja, ranaka, samanta, mandalesvara*, etc, who happened to be large landed intermediaries. The contrast between the two types of terms is obvious. Some people are meant for cultivating, and some meant for enjoying the fruits of production. There is nothing to show that the peasants who produced were in firm and independent control over their holdings. And finally there was the state symbolized by the king, whose general authority over land was recognized by numerous epithets used for him in early medieval records.[43]

CONTROL OVER LAND AND SEIGNIORIAL RIGHTS

The point that there were superior and inferior rights in the same piece of land was made much earlier,[44] but the common phrase 'means of production' was not used in that context. It may be added now that the practice of granting a village with all possible taxes and impositions and with all its resources created a kind of feudal property in contrast to peasant property and communal rights. The new phenomenon caused headache to medieval jurists and law commentators, who found neither much of a sanction nor a precedent in the early law-books. Therefore Vijnanesvara, the famous athor of the *Mitaksara*, which enjoyed authority in a large part of the country in legal matters, propounded the principle of the popular recognition of property. He and his followers, including Mitra Misra, maintained that property had its basis in popular recognition without any dependence on the *Sastras*.[45] Commenting on a passage of Gautama,[46] Haradatta of about the twelfth century expressed a similar view. According to him even short enjoyment of *bhumi*, which is explained as cultivated field (*ksetra*) and orchards, gardens, etc. (*aramadika*) confers property-rights on the enjoyer.[47] Short enjoyment probably means a period of less than ten years.[48] The complexities caused by the superimposition of new rights on the means of production hitherto effectively controlled by the peasants, also because of their free access to various village resources, baffled the medieval jurists who had to recognize the multiplicity of rights in the same piece of land. It is worth reproducing a question, which was used by me earlier. 'The Indian jurists took it for granted that the incidents of particular manifestations of ownership might differ, while the *svatva* (rights)[49] of the king, the *svatva* of the landowner, the *svatva* of the tenant-farmer, and in an extreme case, even the *svatva* of the mortgagee in possession (as against a trespasser) were all comprehensible under the single term of property.'[50] It has been shown that in law as well as in actual practice these rights were graded. In the Indian context one could therefore talk of the varying degrees of control over land, which was the primary means of production, and not of exclusive rights of either the landlord or the peasant. But the grants show an increasing tendency to establish the superior rights of the landlord at the cost of both the king and the peasantry so much so that ultimately assignments are converted into virtual estates.

More effective control over the means of production obtained in such cases as transferred plots of land to the beneficiaries. Many big plots of lands in Vidarbha and Maharashtra were assigned to gods and brāhmaṇas under the Vakatakas and also under the Rastrakutas. For example, eight thousand *nivartanas* of land was granted to one thousand brāhmaṇas by Pravarasena.[51] Similarly four hundred *nivartanas* of land was granted to a single brāhmaṇa.[52] Again the same measure of land was granted to a god.[53] Further 2052 *nivartanas* of land was granted to brāhmaṇas.[54] We learn from earlier authorities that in the Deccan land measuring 6 *nivartanas* was considered to be sufficient for maintaining a family of a brāhmaṇa which may have consisted of 5 to 8 members. But the instances given above refer to large stretches of land, which could not be cultivated by the brāhmaṇa beneficiaries themselves. Even if labour in a brāhmaṇa family was available for smaller pieces of land, they would not actually cultivate it because of social inhibitions. But, more importantly, grants of large plots introduced an element of direct control of the beneficiary over the means of production.

An important factor which gave the beneficiaries general control over the means of production was the conferment of seigniorial rights on them. The charters authorized the beneficiaries to punish people guilty of ten offences,[55] including those against family, property, person, etc., and to try civil cases.[56] Further royal officers were not allowed to enter their territory[57] and cause any kind of obstruction in their functioning.[58] All these are as good as manorial rights, and might even enable the beneficiary to force the peasant to work in his field. It would appear that the right to try cases on the spot involving the imposition of fines could seriously interfere with the process of production. It is therefore obvious that the political and judicial rights, which were non-economic rights, helped the beneficiaries to carry out the economic exploitation of the peasants in an effective manner living in his estate. This may have been a successful way of governing the vast population because the crimes could be nipped in the bud on the spot. But at the same time these non-economic rights served to enforce the general economic authority of the beneficiaries over both the means and the processes of production. It may further be noted that in many cases the beneficiary was empowered to adopt all measures to enjoy the village, and the term used for this was *sarvodaya-samyuktam*.[59] He was also authorized to enjoy the fruits according to his sweet will. If we carefully examine the phrase *sambhogya yavadichcha kriyaphalam*[60] it would mean that the donee could even intervene in the process of production. If a person is entitled to the enjoyment of the fruits of the process of production according to his discretion, he may develop a natural tendency to control the process (*kriya*) itself on which the nature and the amount of yield depend. Sometimes whatever belonged to the village (*svasambhoga sametah*) was to be enjoyed by the beneficiary.[61] The beneficiary was also granted the village along with all its products (*sarvotpattisahitah*).[62] The Candella charters from eastern Madhya Pradesh name the crops that were produced in the donated villages. Does it mean that the peasant could not alter the pattern of crops? At any rate all such provisions could create the interest of the landed beneficiary in the means and process of production. It would be really extraordinary if the beneficiary does not keep an eye over the resources, processes and fruits of production in such cases.

It is not clear how the peasants were provided with agricultural implements. The charters authorize the beneficiaries to enjoy all that is hidden under the earth. This will amount to giving the mining rights to the beneficiaries. It is well known that the mining rights belonged exclusively to the king. The king may have acquired this monopoly at the initial stage as the head of the tribe or the community. Once this exclusive control over iron and other types of mines passed into the hands of the beneficiaries, they could also control the supply of agricultural implements to the peasants. But in pre-feudal times the big landowners did not have such rights in lands. Mining rights belonged to the king who symbolized the community, and the peasants may not have experienced difficulties in procuring agricultural implements.

Not only are the successors of the king and people in power asked to observe the terms of the grants[63] but also all those who would upset the grant are threatened with the use of force.[64] In some warnings corporal punishment (*sariradandam*) is clearly mentioned.[65] The threat to use force is found mostly in the grants from Madhya Pradesh, Maharashtra, Andhra and Karnataka, and the earliest example belongs to the fourth century in a Pallava grant from Guntur district. In addition, the enemies of the land grant were invested with all kinds of cures and most heinous sins. The idea tht a peasant was the complete master of the means of production is also belied by the philosophical teachings found at the end of most grants. The grants underline the instability of life. Apparently this instability of life is based not merely on the idea of death which overtakes everybody ultimately but also on the fickleness of fortune. The concept of the fickleness of fortune (that is, mobility of Lakshmi) is mainly derived from the frequent transfer of control over the means of production from one hand to the other. It would therefore appear that ideology, derived from the relations of production, strengthened the general control of the beneficiaries over the means of production. Ideology was used for indoctrinating the producers in ancient times also. Through ideology and administration, the priests and warriors regulated production and distribution in prefeudal times, but now they acquired an effective hand in the mode of production because of their general, superior control over land, which was the chief means of production. The beneficiary started with the state-sanctioned title to various types of dues delivered by the peasants to the state, but in course of time his claims were made so comprehensive that because of his local presence and delegated administrative powers he could convert his title into possession and could treat the donated village as his estate. It is clear that the peasants had to reckon with the control of the donee over the village resources.

The real problem therefore is not to demonstrate the autonomy of peasant production which in any case was drastically curtailed in the land grant areas. But it is more worthwhile to determine the extent and impact of peasant population working in the land grant areas and that of similar people working in the non-land grant areas in medieval times.[66] Since references to palm-leaf (*talapatra*) and birch-bark (*bhurjapatra*) *sasana* charters even for religious purposes are found in Assam and Madhya Pradesh, it is likely that many such grants were issued in favour of both religious and secular parties. We learn how these *patra* grants were burnt and replaced by copper plate charters in Assam[67] and Madhya Pradesh.[68] Another important problem is to identify and plot on maps the donated villages or plots of land regionwise within a short time bracket (say within half a century or so). We have shown earlier that in the donated villages the beneficiaries enjoyed superior authority in the means of production. Donated fields, many of them very large in area, were without doubt under the direct and complete control of the beneficiaries, who manipulated its production resources and processes.

SURPLUS COLLECTION AND THE PATTERN OF PRODUCTION

It is argued that landed beneficiaries were mainly concerned with the problem of surplus collection. But the question of surplus collection/distribution cannot be viewed in isolation from that of the pattern of production. In a feudal system of production we expect the lord's share called rent, in labour and cash/kind, and this is coupled with a patron-client system of distribution, primarily between the peasant and the landlord. For surplus collection superior rights in the land of the peasants become the pre-condition. More surplus seems to have been extracted because of more product. In pre-Gupta times the surplus was mainly collected by the agents of the state in the form of taxes, or by priests in the form of gifts. There were a few landowners working with the help of slave and hired labourers in the age of the Buddha. We hear of state farms in the *Arthaśāstra* of Kauṭilya. But state control could operate only in small areas. By and large the settled part of the country had independent units of production and was also blessed with some amount of market economy. But market economy was not so strong as would enable the rich landowner to invest his capital in new enterprises and work for profits, and would thus eventually lead him to the capitalist path. At best a millionaire such as Anathapindika would purchase land for donation to the Buddha. There could be other such examples. Payment in cash could be made for the sale of cereals and for the purchase of petty commodities by the peasants. Generally, in pre-feudal times the priests, warriors and administrators were entitled to the surplus in the form of taxes and gifts for services rendered, but a good deal of these payments was made in cash. Peasant units of production first appeared in the age of the Buddha and not in post-Maurya times. Slavery was neither preponderant nor negligible in production. Large holdings, including Maurya state farms, were worked by slaves and hired labourers, in the middle Gangetic plains, but big landowners were swamped by peasants. The vaiśya, who was almost identical with the peasant, was the principal taxpayer. His counterpart in the Buddhist idiom was a peasant householder who contributed to the increase in cereals and paid taxes to the state (*gahapatiko karkarako rasivaddhako*). Thus the peasant units of production functioned more or less effectively in pre-Gupta times. But after that the authority of the peasants over these units suffered erosion because of the appearance of landed beneficiaries supplemented by large disappearance of trade and urban centres. In India the problem of the rise of the landed magnates is not connected with 'the decomposition of the slave mode of production' but with the decreasing control of the peasant over his unit of production, coupled with his restricted access to the communal agrarian resources. As will be shown later, overtaxation and imposition of forced labour by the state created such problems as called for new remedies.

To think that the fight for a share in the cake does not necessarily affect the production of the cake is to ignore historical examples. It is true even of capitalist societies in which such fights eventually lead to structural changes. In conditions of early medieval times the beneficiary demanded his pound of flesh because he claimed superior rights in land. If the object of the grant was the maintenance of the beneficiary and the provision of requirements either for worship or for domestic purposes the peasant could be compelled to produce certain cereals which were badly needed by the donee.

If parts of the products, are placed at the disposal of the grantee, what is the difference between enjoying the means of production, that is, land, and the fruits of production? Land does not mean anything without its products. Whoever seizes land rich with crops (*sasyasamrddam vasundharam*) is guilty of great sins, so goes the medieval saying. Thus land carried meaning in the context of its products. Surplus was collected not only after production but also in the course of production. On-the-spot collection and quick administration could be the most effective way of managing a large population.

THE QUESTION OF SERFDOM

On the basis of the land charters we can say that in the donated areas the landed beneficiaries enjoyed general control over production resources. Of course they did not enjoy specific control over every plot of land that the peasant cultivated. But there is nothing to question their control over the plots of lands that were directly donated to them by the king, sometimes along with the sharecroppers[69] and weavers and sometimes along with the cultivators.[70] This raises the problem of serfdom. It is thought that feudalism was identical with serfdom, and there seems to be an assumption that serfdom was the only potent method of exploiting the peasants. It may be very effective, but other forms of servitude imposed on the peasantry did not prove inoperative and unproductive. After all what is the essence of serfdom? In this system small farm units are attached to big farm units, and the two are interdependent for purposes of production. Big farms are directly managed by manorial magnates but cultivated by those who possesses small plots. Therefore serfdom means giving more of surplus labour than surplus produce. But in the Indian case surplus produce is extracted more through the general control exercised by the landed intermediaries than by their employment of serfs. A serf also occupies some land and provides his family with subsistence. But he not only pays rent in cash or kind for exploiting his unit of production but also spends extra hours labouring on the field of his lord. However, if these extra hours of his are used on the field occupied by him the extra yield does not necessarily stay with the cultivator. On the other hand, it enables him to pay more rent in cash or kind to his lord.

It has been argued that serfdom is an incidental feature in the case of India.[71] But the evidence cited so far would show that it is more than incidental.[72] In any case if the lord gets his share without reducing too many people to serfdom, what basic difference does it make to him or to the social pattern? Both systems are concerned with extracting the lord's share; in both the cultivator is a dependent peasant under the exploitation of his lord, and in both cases the social structure is beset with the internal contradiction between the landlord and the actual tiller. A beneficiary may not possess big plots but he possesses too many plots which make management difficult. In fact laws of partition of land became effective in Gupta and post-Gupta times[73] and they may have contributed to the fragmentation of land. Fragmentation of land is also indicated by epigraphic sale transactions found in Bangladesh.[74] Therefore if a landlord possess too many plots, tenanting and sharecropping may be more convenient than getting the land cultivated through the deployment of serfs.

It is argued that because soil in India was very fertile, there was no scope for the rise of serfdom or forced labour.[75] But we have indications of forced labour in the middle Gangetic basin where the soil is the most fertile. Till recent times poor tenants, belonging to lower castes, were forced by landlords from upper castes to work in the fields at meager wages.[76] Peasants were compelled to plough the land of the landlords and do various kinds of odd jobs for the sake of the landlords in other fertile areas. This is known as *hari* and *begari* in the whole Gangetic basin area. The medieval term for the first is *halikakara*,[77] and for the second is *visti*, from which *bethbegari* is derived. The Pala charters found in Monghyr, Bhagalpur, Sahara and Nalanda districts, all forming parts of the middle Gangetic plains, mention the term *sarvapidaparihrta*. This means that the peasants were subjected to all types of forced labour and oppressions, but when the village was transferred to a beneficiary he became entitled to these advantages without the interference of the state. Forced labour may have originated in less populated areas but not necessarily in less fertile parts. In any case, once its usefulness was recognized it spread to more populated parts.

Feudalism flourished in paddy producing areas. Paddy production requires 50 per cent more man hours than wheat production. According to a popular saying in Patna and Gaya districts, wheat cultivation can be undertaken even by a widow, who represents an image of helplessness in the countryside. Evidently wheat requires less and barley requires least labour. Therefore paddy transplantation would mean scarcity of labour in peak season; and it could be necessary to take to forced labour. We need not add that the term *satpadyamanavisti* is used frequency.[78] It has been translated to mean the use of forced labour as occasions arise. But since the term qualifies the donated land or village, it might mean the labour generated or produced by the village in future.[79] This was a significant development in a good part of the country. It would imply that besides customary sources of forced labour new sources could be exploited by the beneficiaries according to their needs. Unfortunately these sources are not specified in medieval records. That there were various types of forced labour is clear from the use of the term *sarvavisti*[80] in many land grants, particularly in Vakataka grants. It is obvious that these many types may have included the use of labour in the fields. The evidence from the *Skanda Purana* produced by B.N.S. Yadava leaves little doubt that hundreds of people were compelled to do forced labour and this was evidently meant for production.[81] Hence serfdom cannot be dismissed as an incidental feature.

If serfdom is understood as compulsive attachment of the peasants to the soil, it prevailed in good parts of Madhya Pradesh, eastern India, Chamba and Rajasthan. In many cases the charters clearly transfer the peasants, artisans and even traders to the beneficiaries.[82] In most charters they ask the villagers, the peasants and other inhabitants of the villages to stay in their villages and to carry out the orders of the beneficiaries. This fact of immobility of peasants and artisans has not been contested by anybody so far. However, it is argued that even if these people were allowed to move, what purpose it would have served. If such a view is taken, then what is the point in underlining the absence of serfdom in the Indian context? After all, in conditions of serfdom a peasant has to be tied to his piece of land and when that piece of land is transferred the peasant is automatically transferred. This practice prevailed widely in early medieval times. Nevertheless, they were not engaged widely in agricultural operations in the fields of their landlords. If it is argued that peasants were not employed in production but in building forts, roads, temples, massive and impressive structures, then we may say that all such grandiose projects were undertaken by the landed aristocracy, chiefs and princes, to strike the people with their awe and majesty. They could be of great indirect help in collecting taxes and presents from the peasantry. Some of them such as building of roads, could be eventually useful from the point of production. The employment of forced labour therefore did not depend on the fertility of the soil but on the realization of its usefulness by the landlords. There is no doubt that the rural aristocracy led an ostentatious and luxurious life requiring much consumption. Although we cannot measure the rising expectations of the landlords we notice indications of growing luxurious living.

The practice of forced labour, sharecropping or the leasing of land was promoted and supported by social institutions and inhibitions. The law-books ask the brāhmaṇas not to take to the plough. It seems that the upper caste people could not transplant paddy.[83] Naturally even in a small holding which could be managed by their family labour, such people would need some labour which could be either forced labour or sharecropping. In such a case it is immaterial whether the soil is less fertile or more fertile, for at any rate labour will have to be drafted from outside the family unit. Lack of labour power and plenty of land create conditions for introducing an element of compulsion. But this can happen only in a particular socio-economic formation. We have lack of labour in socialist and even capitalist countries, but that does not necessarily lead to forced labour.

The idea that the gap between the labour potential of the family and the land it has leads to feudal conditions may be far from true. Underutilization of labour capacity may not necessarily produce demand for such labour in the form of forced labour. This labour can also be invested in auxi liary crafts in response to agricultural and domestic demands. But, what is more important, if the needs of the landlord are met otherwise through rents and presents, why should he assume direct and onerous responsibility for cultivation and mobilize labour power for that purpose? At present we have no means to measure the needs, demands and expectations of the landlord, which may vary regionwise. These needs could be easily met by the landlords because of the provisions of the charters empowering them to depart from customary and established taxes and impose and introduce new levies and new forms of forced labour.

SOCIAL CRISIS AS THE ORIGIN OF LAND GRANTS

It is repeatedly stated that no new mode of socio-economic formation can appear as a result of political, administrative and juridical measures,[84] little realizing that the colonial system in India owed its origin largely to such measures. The king in ancient India symbolized state authority, and the state was backed by priests and warriors who lived on the surplus produced by the peasants and further supplied by the artisans. This kind of state and society appeared in the age of the Buddha. It continued to function more or less smoothly till the third century AD. But there are many passages in the epics and the Puranas, which speak of a kind of social crisis symbolized by the Kali age. These passages are ascribed to the second half of the third century AD and the beginning of the fourth century AD. They depict a state of affairs in which rural people were oppressed with taxes and forced labour,[85] which was considered an important element of the military power. The oppressions of the state coupled with the havoc caused by natural calamities created a state of chaos, and the lower orders, particularly the vaiśyas and the śūdras, refused to perform the functions assigned to them. On top of it the peasants refused to pay taxes.[86] The *Manu Smṛti, Santi Parva* and other texts suggested two measures to overcome this social crisis. One was the use of force or *danda*, which is glorified in these texts. The other was the restorationof the *varṇa-sramadharma* which was considered to be the bedrock of the class-based and state-based society. Obviously these measures alone could not cope with the critical situation. Since it became difficult to collect taxes it was not possible to run the state and to pay the priests, administrators, the army and numerous officials. Apparently, as an alternative, the practice of land grants, which was not unknown in early times, was adopted on a wide scale in a major part of the country, particularly from the fourth to fifth century AD onwards. It will therefore appear that we have an indication of a crisis in production relations, which may not be unconnected with changes in the mode of production. The fact cannot be discounted that trade[87] and urbanism[88] suffered a distinct decline, and the absence of gold coins for three centuries between the 7th and the 10th and paucity of other types of coins[89] are well known. There is practically no indication of the use of slaves in production. All these are presages of change in the methods and relations of production. Hence the production system as a whole was afflicted with certain maladies, which compelled the state to convert land/land revenues into a general mode of payment for religious and administrative services. The grant system relieved the state of the heavy responsibility of getting the taxes collected all over the countryside by its agents and then of disbursing them in cash or kind. On the other hand, priests, warriors and administrators were asked to fend for themselves in the villages assigned to them for their enjoyment. The system also relieved the state of the responsibility of maintaining law and order in the donated villages which now became almost the sole concern of the beneficiaries. Therefore it would be wrong to assume that political, administrative and juridical measures, which created new property relations in land, were undertaken by the state entirely on its own.

The social crisis apparently led to the withdrawal of slaves from production, and to the provision of land for them as tenants and sharecroppers. This explains to a good extent the elevation of śūdras to peasanthood and their participation in rituals. It seems that landowners converted śūdra labourers into peasants and themselves became landlords living on rent. The substantial *gahapatis* of the age of the Buddha probably turned landlords. That the village headman tended to become landlord has already been shown,[90] although the causes for this transformation need investigation.

CONFLICTS WITHIN THE NEW FORMATION

The new socio-economic formation that emerged as a result of the appearance of a class of landlords and that of a subject peasantry had its own limitations. The peasants were accustomed to give certain taxes and services to the state, and if the demand of the beneficiary was confined to those claims, in normal times the routine payment could continue. But the beneficiary would impose proper and improper taxes, fixed and unfixed taxes, would collect all kinds of taxes and, what is worse, they could make additional impositions which were covered by the term *adi*, i.e. et cetera. In certain areas they could also introduce new forms of forced labour. On top of this all communal and agrarian resources hitherto enjoyed by the peasants were transferred to the landed beneficiaries who were ever present on the spot. This situation caused constant conflict between those who claimed rent on the strength of their royal charters and others who claimed immunity on the basis of customary and immemorial rights which would be certainly known to local people but because of their illiteracy could not be shown in black and white. Hence there was bound to be constant friction, tensions and struggle between the landed beneficiaries and the servile peasantry. This might lead to litigations between the beneficiaries, and also between the beneficiary and the peasants.[91] Because of the common practice of land grants and the enormous advantages derived from them the brāhmaṇas forged many charters (*kuta-sasana*) and claimed enjoyment of villages on that basis. But there were so many valid charters that the conflict between the landlord and the peasant was an ever present possibility. In order to settle this conflict Narada, Brhaspati, *Agni Purana* and other authorities give the final authority to the royal charter in case of dispute. They lay down that if there is a conflict between the religious right (*dharma*), contract right (*vyavahara*), customary right (*carita*) and the right derived from the royal charter (*rajasasana*) the royal charter will override all the other sources of the law or authority.[92]

But it seems that this overriding power of the royal charter did not work in all cases. We have the case of the Kaivartas, a fishing and cultivating community in Bangladesh, who rose against Ramapala in the eleventh century AD. They fought with bamboo sticks riding on baffaloes. So powerful was their revolt that two dozen vassals had to be mobilized by Ramapala in order to put down the Kaivarta rebellion. This is an important example of peasant revolt.[93] The possibility of clash is also indicated in some Bengal grants which mention the term *karsanavirodhi sthana*.[94] At least two grants take pains to show that they do not clash with the existing cultivating rights of the peasants. Therefore the possibility of clash between the peasants and the incoming beneficiaries is clearly visualized. Similarly in many grants from Madhya Pradesh and Maharashtra the people are warned that if they tried to upset the grant in any manner then they would be punished with force.[95] This point is stated repeatedly[96] in many inscriptions. In some cases this threat is directed towards royal officials, but mostly it is a general threat meant for all.

Again in the texts of this period, *brahmahatya*, that is, killing of brāhmaṇa, is considered to be a great sin and it occurs in many Puranas. Why does the murder of brāhmaṇa become so important in early medieval times? Apparently it is because of his becoming a landed beneficiary and therefore an oppressor. If we look at the distribution of hero stones in Karnataka and other parts of South India it would appear that some of them are found in the *agrahara* areas.[97] This would again suggest that open frictions appeared between the beneficiary of the *agrahara* and the peasants living there. In the case of Karnataka, R.N. Nandi has collected certain evidence which suggests some kind of collaboration between the brāhmaṇas and the peasants in the beginning, but eventually shows open conflict between the two.[98] D.N. Jha refers to several instances of conflict between the peasants and the beneficiary landlords in Cola inscriptions, particularly after AD 1000.[99]

Although we can see and visualize polarity between the central state and smaller states, polarity between various types of beneficiaries, and polarity between landed magnates and the cultivator, the human factor operating in these polarities does not come out clearly in our sources. It is thought that the peasant's independent control over his process of production prevented acute social tensions.[100] But as shown earlier, this control was more dependent than independent. The multiplication of the existing units of production in new areas could obviate occasions for open conflicts leading to changes. But to a good degree the seeming stability was prompted by other factors which were closely linked with the system of production, especially with production relations. First, the caste system with the features of hierarchy and superiority, not to speak of untouchability, provided ritualistic sanction for the production and distribution system. It seems that the *jajmani* system developed in this period and was part of a more or less self-sufficient economy. At the end of harvesting, on the threshing floor, portions of paddy were given to gods, brāhmaṇas, rulers and the various kinds of labourers, indicated by the term *bhrtyavargaposanam*.[101] The brāhmaṇas, who controlled many 'estates', played a crucial ideological role in penetrating the consciousness of the peasantry and making them behave as they liked them to do. Some medieval religious reform movements apparently sought to improve the status of those who really produced and suffered, but those movements were manipulated to contain the conflicts and scotch the tension; they could not rouse the peasantry to realities. In certain parts of the country, survivals of the bonds of kinship also helped to keep people together. This may have particularly happened in Rajasthan and Himalayan areas.

Classes with conflicting interests were kept together through the performance of *puja, japa, vratas, tirthas, samskaras, prayascittas* and through prospects of heaven and hell. The all-pervasive influence of astrology (*jyotisa*) and that of the doctrine of Vedanta kept the people reconciled to their lot. All these factors brought the people of opposite interests together.

AGRICULTURAL EXPANSION

It is held that lack of 'concentrated social effort' blocked changes in the means, methods and relations of production.[102] We may not have much idea about the social effort, but we can certainly identify significant changes in the mode of production in early medieval times. This period was undoubtedly an age of larger yield and a great agrarian expansion. It is possible to count hundreds of states, particularly in those areas which had never witnessed the rise of full-fledged states. A state presupposes an assured source of income which will enable it to maintain a good number of managerial staff. This could not be possible unless the agrarian base was strong enough to pay for the priests, officers, army men, etc.

A few technological innovations contributed to rural expansion. Apart from the use of the *araghatta*, the Persian wheel, the early Middle Ages saw several changes in agriculture. The importance attached to agriculture in this period is indicated by the fact that several texts were composed on it such as *Krsiparasara* in the north and Kamban's book in the south. Kasyapa's *Krsisukti* has been found in the south,[103] but it may have belonged to some paddy producing area either in the north or south. It prescribes three methods of lifting water (that is, using the *ghati-yantra*) by men, oxen and elephants.[104] That certain persons were engaged in working the 'Persian' water-wheel can be inferred from the use of the term *arahattiyanara* in a lexicon of the twelfth century.[105] The *Vrksa Ayurveda* of about the tenth century recommends recipes for treating the diseases affecting the plants.[106] Apart from special attention being given to horses,[107] because they were used by chiefs and princes, animal husbandry was improved because of the care given to the treatment of cattle diseases.[108] In addition, detailed instructions regarding agriculture appear in the *Brhat Samhita* of Varahamihira, the *Agni Purana* and the *Visnudharmottara Purana*.[109] Three crops, first mentioned by Panini, were known widely,[110] and better seeds were produced.[111] Meteorological knowledge, based on observation, was far advanced in the *Krsiparasara*. The knowledge of fertilizers improved immensely and the use of compost was known;[112] and, what is more important, irrigation facilities were expanded. The law-books lay down severe punishments for those who cause damage to tanks, wells, ponds, embankments, etc.[113] The construction of *vapi* became very popular in Rajasthan and Gujarat. Its importance is also underlined in the work of Kasyapa.[114] In his doctoral thesis V.K. Jain has prepared a map in which he has shown the distribution of the *vapis* (step wells) in western India in the eleventh to thirteenth centuries.[115] It is interesting to note that the term *vapi* is derived from the Sanskrit root *vap* which means to sow. So it is clear that step wells were meant for irrigating the fields. Of course the use of iron implements attained a new peak in this period. In the *Paryayamuktavali*, a medieval lexicon whose manuscripts have been found in West Bengal and Orissa, as many as half a dozen types or grades of iron are mentioned.[116] The use of iron became so common that it began to be employed for non-utilitarian purposes. Several pillars, including the Mehrauli pillar in Delhi, were erected to mark the conquests of victorious princes. The increase in the number of the varieties of cereals including rice, wheat and lentils as well as in fruits, vegetables, legumes, etc, is striking. These can be inferred not only from the *Amarakosa* but more so from the *Paryayamuktavali.*[117] According to the *Sunya Purana* more than 50 kinds of paddy were cultivated in Bengal.[118] Apart from the foundation of numerous states the various medieval texts suggest an enormous increase in agricultural production. Therefore, agricultural technology in terms of a single major break may not be striking,[119] but the overall effect of various measures and improvements seems to have been substantial. However mere increase in production may lead neither to stability nor to structural changes. For this certain other conditions including the rousing of the necessary consciousness may be needed.

CONCLUDING OBSERVATIONS

Feudalism in India therefore was characterized by a class of landlords and by a class of subject peasantry, the two living in a predominantly agrarian economy marked by a decline of trade and urbanism and by a drastic reduction in metal currency. The superior state got its taxes collected and authority recognized by creating a number of inferior power blocs or even states (that is, landed priests, *mathas, viharas, basadis*, temples, *agraharas, brahmadevas*, etc.) who generated the necessary social and ideological climate for this purpose. Unlike the European system most of the power structures within the state did not have to pay taxes. West European feudal lords granted land to their serfs in order to get their own occupied land cultivated. But Indian kings made land grants to get the taxes (surplus) collected. In their turn the grantees collected rents from their tenant-peasants who could be evicted and even subjected to forced labour.

Our comments are couched sometimes in terms of probabilities and reservations, because the nature of sources does not admit of clear and categorical statements. Nevertheless they raise some theoretical issues. The position of class is to be located in the overall systems of production. But if a class covers those who either exclusively control the means of production or those who are completely deprived of such control, such a thing can happen only in a full-fledged capitalist system. The application of such a concept to pre-capitalist societies is riddled with difficulties, for even in the feudal society of Western Europe the serf enjoyed day-to-day control over his bit of the means of production.[120] In such a society class is best seen in the context of the unequal distribution of the surplus, which was eventually given a lasting basis by the unequal distribution of the means of production and strengthened by ideological and juridical factors. Second, ecological factors influence the development of material culture. But we find several countries with similar climatic conditions but dissimilar social structures. Therefore to attribute such structural phenomena as the absence of serfdom or the longevity of peasant autonomy to the carrying capacity of the soil would be going too far.

NOTES

(*This paper was written for publication in the forthcoming number of the* Journal of Peasant Studies. *We thank the editors of that journal as well as the author for allowing us to publish it here as well.*)

1. D.C. Sircar, *Landlordism and Tenancy in Ancient and Medieval India as Revealed by Epigraphical Records*, Lucknow, 1969. Also see *Journal of Indian History*, XLIV, 1966, pp. 351–7; LI, 1973, pp. 56–9, *Journal of Ancient Indian History*, VI, 1972–3, pp. 351–7; D.C. Sircar (ed.), *Land System and Feudalism in Ancient India*, Calcutta, 1966, pp. 11–23. Irfan Habib discusses 'Indian Feudalism' in *The Peasant in Indian History*, Presidential Address, the Indian History Congress, 43rd Session, Kurukshetra, 1982.
2. 'Was There Feudalism in Indian History?', *The Journal of Peasant Studies*, Vol. 8, no. 3, April 1981, pp. 273–310. In this paper the whole medieval period is discussed but I will confine myself primarily to early medieval times (fifth to twelfth century), about which I have some idea.

My task has been made easy because Dr Mukhia's criticisms have been effectively met by B.N.S. Yadava in *The Problem of the Emergence of Feudal Relations in Early India*, Presidential Address for Ancient Indian Section of the Indian History Congress, 41st Session, Bombay, 1980. In a similar address delivered at the 40th Session of the Indian History Congress held at Waltair in 1979 D.N. Jha anticipated and answered many of these objections in *Early Indian Feudalism: A Historiographical Critique*. Also see Suvira Jaiswal, 'Studies in Early Indian Social History', *Indian Historical Review*, VI, 1979–80, pp. 18–21.

3. Marx-Engels, *Pre-Capitalist Socio-Economic Formations*, Moscow, 1979, p. 23.
4. Muthia, op. cit., p. 310, fn. 225. In the discussion on variants Indian feudalism is seen as a distinct possibility.
5. Kosminsky's views based on Marx and expressed in his *Studies in the Agrarian History of England in the Thirteenth Century*, Oxford, 1956, are summarized and discussed in Barry Hindess and Paul Q Hirst, *Pre-Capitalist Modes of Production*, London, 1975, pp. 222–3, 234–5.
6. Marx considers tenants to be an object of feudal exploitation. According to him the feudal lord differs from the bourgeois in that he 'does not try to extract the utmost advantage from his land. Rather he consumes what is there and calmly leaves the worry of producing to the serfs and tenants', Marx-Engels, op. cit., p. 20. In the 1880s Engels also concluded that serfdom is not solely a 'peculiarly medieval-feudal form', ibid., p. 23. This implies that the feudal formation could have other features.
7. Mukhia, op. cit., pp. 275, 290, 291, 293.
8. I owe this to Ranjit Guha.
9. The king is called *bhusvamin* by Katyayana, a law giver of about the sixth century (P.V. Kane, ed, verse 16).
10. R.S. Sharma, 'From Gopati to Bhupati' (a review of the changing position of the king), *Studies in History*, II (2), 1980, pp. 6–8.
11. *Vasya yasya yada bhumih, tasya tasya tada phalam*, D.C. Sircar (ed.), *Select Inscriptions Bearing on Indian History and Civilization*, vol. I, University of Calcutta, 1965 (abbrev. As *Sel. Inscrr.*) Bk III, p. 49, line 26.
12. The terms used are *sarvoparikarakaradanasametah, sarvakarasametah, sarvakaravisar jitah*, etc. See Balachandra Jain, *Utkirna-Lekha*, Raipur, 1961, pp. 56–7. The terms *samastapratyaya* and *sarvayasameta* also occur (Sharma, *Indian Feudalism*, 2nd edn, p. 100). Also see *sarvadanasamgrahya, Epigraphia Indica* (*EI*), V, no. 5, line 41.
13. Sharma, *Indian Feudalism*, 2nd, edn., p. 98.
14. The phrase used is *niyataniyatasamastadya*, all specified and unspecified dues, *EI*, no. 21, line 26.
15. *Epigraphia Indica*, XXIX, no. 7, line 42; Jain, op. cit., p. 52.
16. Mukhia rightly postulates that the village potentates would be the first to notice the rise in productivity and the first to demand a greater share in the peasant's produce. Op. cit., p. 309, fn. 214.

17. The phrase *a jnasravanavidheyibhuya* is common in north Indian grants.
18. The point has been discussed in R.S. Sharma, *Indian Feudalism*, 2nd edn., Delhi, 1980, pp. 38–9.
19. The distinction is brought out clearly in P.N. Sen, *The General Principles of Hindu Jurisprudence*, Tagore Law Lectures, 1909, University of Calcutta, 1918, p. 42.
20. *Sel. Inscrr.*, Bk III, nos. 16, 18, 19, 41, 42, 43, etc.
21. Sharma, *Indian Feudalism*, 2nd edn., pp. 73–5, 185–7.
22. Marx-Engels, *Pre-Capitalist Socio-Economic Formations*, p. 22.
23. . . . *sadandakarasahah karmasilakarsako' balisasvamyavaravarnaprayo janapadasampat, Arthaśāstra* (of Kauṭilya), R.P. Kangle's edn., VI, 1.
24. *As*, I. 13. The term *prakrtikopa* or revolt of the subjects is used in V.6 and VII. 6.
25. B.N.S. Yadava, *The Problem of the Emergence of Feudal Relations in Early India*, p. 7, contains several references to the acquisition of *jana.*
26. R.S. Sharma, *Sudras in Ancient India*, 2nd edn., Delhi, 1980, Ch. III.
27. The term used is *kassako gahapati*, cultivating family head. *Angustara Nikaya* (Pali Text Society, London), i, pp. 239–40. But *gahapati*, in the sense of substantial peasant, is used in Pali texts at many places.
28. s r *griha*, Monier-Williams, *A Sanskrit-English Dictionary*, Oxford, 1951.
29. R.L. Turner, *A Comparative Dictionary of the Indo-Aryan Languages*, Oxford, 1973, no. 3736.
30. Ibid.
31. R. Mukherji and S.K. Maity, *Corpus of Bengal Inscriptions bearing on History and Civilization of Bengal*, Calcutta, 1967, no. 18, line 45; no. 22, line 46; no. 28, line 52; no. 30, line 48; no. 36, line 36; no. 37, line 32.
32. Turner, op. cit., no. 3736.
33. Mukherji and Maity, op. cit., no. 47, line 50.
34. Ibid., no. 7, line 3; no. 9, line 3 (p. 59).
35. Sharma, *Indian Feudalism*, 2nd edn., pp. 188–9.
36. Ibid., p. 38.
37. Ibid., p. 188.
38. Ibid., p. 98, fn 3, 99.
39. It is taken in the sense of a ploughman. See B.N.S. Yadava, *The Problem of the Emergence of Feudal Relations in Early India*, p. 25.
40. *sv Krsivala*, Monier-Williams, op. cit.
41. B.N.S. Yadava '*The Problem of the Emergence of Feudal Relations in Early India*', p. 32.
42. Sharma, *Indian Feudalism*, 2nd edn., pp. 12–13, 216.
43. These terms are *avanisa, avanindra, ksitipati, ksitendra, ksitisa, ksiteradhipa, parthiva, prthivipati, parthivendra, prthivinatha, bhupa, bhupati, bhubhuj, bhumipa, bhumisvara, mahipa, mahipati, mahipala, mahindra, mahamahendra, urvipati, vasudhadhipa, vasudhesvara, samanta-bhumisvara*, etc. R.S. Sharma, 'From Gopati to Bhupati', *Studies in History*, II (2), 1980, p. 8 with fns 81–2.

44. R.S. Sharma, *Indian Feudalism*, Calctta, 1965, Ch. IV.
45. P.N. Sen, *The General Principles of Hindu Jurisprudence, Tagore Law Lectures*, 1909, University of Calcutta, 1918, pp. 42–3, 46. The theory of popular recognition, which gives preference to unwritten laws, is known as *laukika svatvavada*, (ibid., p. 42). Several logicians such as Guru, Kumarila Svami and Parthasarathi Misra, who interpreted the Dharmaśāstras according to the canons of *mimamsa* also supported the popular recognition theory Jimutavahana, Dharesvara etc., supported the *sastric* view (ibid., p. 42). The difference does reflect conflicting claims to land control in early medieval times.
46. *Gautama Dharmasūtra* (Varanasi, 1966), 11-3-36. The passage reads *pasu bhumiṣtrinamanatibhogah.*
47. *Alpenapi bhogena bhoktuh svam bhavati.* Commentary on *Gautama* 11.3.36. By this interpretation cattle and women slaves are also covered. It is interesting that a ten-year limit of enjoyment is set for acquiring ownership over the property of others in several cases by the commentator. Comm. On *Gautama*, 11.3.34–5.
48. Commentary on *Gautama* 11.3.34–5.
49. *Svatva* should be taken in the sense of property rights, as has been done by P.N. Sen, op. cit., p. 42.
50. J.D.M. Derrett in *Bulletin of the School of Oriental and African Studies*, XVIII, 489.
51. V.V. Mirashi, *Inscriptions of the Vakatakas, Corpus Inscriptionum Ind carum*, Vol V, Ootacamund, 1955, no. 6, lines 19–20.
52. Ibid., no. 12, lines 20–1.
53. Ibid., no. 13, lines 22–3.
54. Ibid., no. 14, lines 22–32.
55. Sharma, *Indian Feudalism*, 2nd edn., 3; the common term used is *sadandada-saparadhah.*
56. Ibid. The term *abhyantarasiddhi* is used.
57. Ibid., p. 2.
58. *Sel Inscrr*, Bk III, no. 62, lines 21–2.
59. Mukerji, and Maity, *Corpus of Bengal Inscriptions*, no. 47, line 62.
60. Ibid., line 63.
61. Ibid., no. 46, line 22.
62. *Epigraphia Indica*, V, no. 20, line 54. The village, situated near Nagpur, was granted by Krsna III in 940–1.
63. *Sel. Inscrr.*, Bk III, no. 49, lines 18–28; no. 50, lines 15–24.
64. . . . *sadandanigraham karisyamah*. This phrase is found, with slight variations in many charters, ibid., 61, 11.22–4; no. 62, 11.32–4; no. 64, 11.21–4; no. 65, 11.39–41; no. 67, 11.24–5.
65. Ibid., no. 67, 11.24–5.
66. In the context of slave society it is held that if 20 per cent of people are engaged in production as slaves in a society, it should be considered a

slave society. Five such societies have been identified. Keith Hopkins, *Conquerors and Slaves*, Cambridge, 1978, pp. 99–100. But the qualitative place of slaves or other categories of servile people in the total mode of production deserves equal consideration.

67. D.C. Sircar, *Indian Epigraphy*, Delhi, 1965, p. 97, fn 2.
68. Balchandra Jain, *Utkirna-Lekha*, Raipur, 1961, no. 3, 11.6–11, (p. 8).
69. *Sel Inscrr.*, Bk III, no. 65, 11.38–9.
70. Ibid., no. 61, 1.15.
71. Mukhia, op. cit., p. 286.
72. R.S. Sharma, *Indian Feudalism*, Delhi, 1980, pp. 19, 31, 40–3, 56, 60, 67–8, 99–101, 109, 195–8; B.N.S. Yadava, *Society and Culture*, pp. 164–9; 'Immobility and Subjection of Indian Peasantry in Early Medieval Complex', *The Indian Historical Review*, I, 1974, pp. 18–27. A good deal of evidence can be obtained from G.K. Rai, *Involuntary Labour in Ancient India*, Allahabad, 1981, but the passage from Vatsyayana's *Kamsutra* (V.5.5) is inaccurately construed and translated.
73. Sharma. *Indian Feudalism*, 2nd edn., pp. 118–19.
74. Ibid., p. 49.
75. Mukhia, op. cit., pp. 286, 289, 303, fn. 124.
76. This was the case in my own village Barauni (District Begusarai, Bihar) till 1950 when the Permanent Settlement was abolished.
77. Y.B. Singh, 'Halika-kara: Crystallization of a Practice into a Tax', paper (unpublished) presented to the 43rd Session of the Indian History Congress, Kurukshetra, 1982.
78. Sharma, *Indian Feudalism*, 2nd edn., pp. 99–100.
79. The term *utpatsyamana* would suit this interpretation better, although even *utpadyamana* means the same thing. I owe this suggestion to Professor R.C. Pandeya. Palaeographically there is very little difference between the two terms.
80. *Sel Inscrr.*, Bk III, no. 61, line 19; no. 62, line 28.
81. *Society and Culture in Northern India*, pp. 164–6.
82. Sharma, *Indian Feudalism*, 2nd edn., p. 199 with fn 6.
83. The passage *pankisah panktiso bhrtyaih vinyaset samabhumike* (verse no 431) occurs in the context of paddy transplantation in the *Kasyapiyakrsisukti*, (ed.) Gy Wojtilla, *Acta Orientalia Huno*, XXXIII (2), 1979, pp. 209–52. The frequent use of the term *krsivala* for the peasant shows that the text belongs to some paddy producing area either in south India or in some other part of the country, and contains much medieval material. Verse no. 450 speaks of the employment of the classes of agricultural labourers *panktisah kramat, bhrtyavargaih, praty aham va vairicchedah prasasyate*. If we look at the survival of the transplantation practice, it would appear that this use of labour was made by the upper caste people in medieval times.
84. Mukhia, op. cit., pp. 274, 286.

85. This Kali passage in the Cr edn of the *Mahābhārata* (III. 188. 71) amended by me on the basis of the Gita Press edn reads: *nirvisesa janapada karavistibhirarditah*. Apparently taxes (*kara*) affected the vaiśyas and forced labour (*visti*) the śūdras.
86. I discussed the Kali problem in some detail three years ago in a paper 'The Kali Age: A Period of Social Crisis' meant for the A.L. Basham Volume, which has not been published so far. But see my *Sudras in Ancient India*, 2nd edn., Delhi: Motilal Banarsidass, 1980, pp. 233–9.
87. In addition to the material presented about the decline of trade in my *Indian Feudalism*, 2nd edn., Chs I and III, further evidence appears in B.N.S. Yadava, *Society and Culture in Northern India in the Twelfth Century*, pp. 270–5. Speaking of early medieval Bengal Dr M.R. Tarafdar says: 'The period between the eleventh and thirteenth centuries shows distinct signs of the decay of trade and urban centres, a process which must have started earlier' ('Trade and Society in Early Medieval Bengal', *Indian Historical Review*, IV, January 1978, p. 282). However in western India trade shows revival in this period (V.K. Jain, 'Trade and Traders in Western India', PhD thesis, Delhi University, 1983); so also seems to be the case with south India (Kenneth R. Hall, *Trade and State Craft in the Age of the Colas*, New Delhi, 1980). We postulate decline of trade mainly in the seventh to tenth centuries.
88. Although the decline of urbanism has been sometimes doubted (B.D. Chattopadhyaya, 'Trade and Urban Centres in Early Medieval North India', *Indian Historical Review*, I, 1974, pp. 203–19) progress in historical archaeology in the Gangetic zone and elsewhere since 1971, coupled with further research in literary texts, confirms what I stated earlier ('Decay of Gangetic Towns in Gupta and Post-Gupta Times', *Journal of Indian History*, Golden Jubilee Volume, 1973, pp. 135–50). Almost all Satavahana towns decay and disappear after the third century AD. Professor A.H. Dani informs me of a similar fate of the Kusana towns in Pakistan, and the Soviet archaeologist Professor V. Masson tells me that five central Asian urban centres of about 1–4th century AD became either villages or castles afterwards. In two Patna University doctoral theses (Om Prakash Prasad, 'Towns in Early Medieval Karnataka', 1978, and B.P.N. Pathak, 'Society and Culture in Early Bihar', 1983) the phenomenon of decay comes out very clearly. Dr R.N. Nandi convincingly shows that many of these decaying towns were converted into *tirthas* or places of pilgrimage in early medieval times ('Client, Ritual and Conflict in Early Brāhmaṇical Order', *Indian Historical Review*, VI, 1979, pp. 80, 100, 103–9). Additional evidence has been collected on the decay of towns (ibid., 74–80).
89. R.S. Sharma, 'Indian Feudalism Retouched' (review paper), *Indian Historical Review*, 1, 1974, pp. 320–30. For additional evidence regarding paucity of coinage, see M.R. Tarafdar, op. cit.
90. Sharma, *Indian Feudalism*, 2nd edn., pp. 41–2.

91. In 1214 a temple in Karnataka claimed the land of its neighbours, but the local authorities decided against the temple. S. Settar and G.D. Sontheimer (ed.), *Memorial Stones*, Dharwar, 1982, p. 303.
92. R.S. Sharma, '*Rajasasana:* Meaning, Scope and Application', *Proceedings of the Indian History Congress*, 37th Session, Calicut, 1976.
93. R.S. Sharma, *Indian Feudalism*, 2nd edn., Delhi, 1980, p. 220.
94. Mukerji and Maity, *Corpus of Bengal Inscriptions*, no. 6, line 18; no. 7, line 19.
95. *Sel Inscrr*, Bk II, no. 61, lines 22–4.
96. Ibid., no. 62, lines 32–4; no. 634, lines 21–4; no. 67, lines 24–5.
97. S. Settar and Gunther D. Sontheimer (ed.), op. cit., p. 223.
98. His manuscript entitled 'Class, State and Family in Early South India' is yet to be published.
99. D.N. Jha, '*Section I: Ancient India Presidential Address*', Indian History Congress, XL Session, Andhra Unversity, Waltair, 1979, p. 18.
100. Mukhia, op. cit., p. 293.
101. Gy Wojtilla (ed.), *Kasyapiyakrsisukti*, op. cit., verses 491–2.
102. Mukhia, op. cit., p. 292. However this statement is qualified by the phrase 'change completely' (ibid).
103. Gy Wojtilla, *Kasyapiyakrsisukti, Acta Orientalia Academiae Saentiarum Hung*, XXXIII, Fax. 2, 1979, pp. 209–52. The usual term for cultivator in this text is *krsivala*, which occurs in early medieval texts and inscriptions. Most material in this text probably belongs to medieval times.
104. Gy Wojtilla, op. cit., verses 167–8. The *ghati-yantra* operated by oxen is considered to be the best, that by men to be worst and that by elephants to be of the middling quality.
105. B.N.S. Yadava, *Society and Culture in Northern India in the Twelfth Century*, p. 259.
106. D.N. Bose and others (ed.), *A Concise History of Science in India*, New Delhi, 1971, p. 362.
107. Ibid., p. 255.
108. Ibid., pp. 363–4.
109. Ibid., pp. 358, 361, 365.
110. Ibid., pp. 356, 361.
111. Ibid., pp. 358–9.
112. Ibid., pp. 358–60.
113. These texts belong to the early centuries of the Christian era. See, R.S. Sharma, *Light on Early Indian Society and Economy*, Bombay, 1966, pp. 90–111.
114. Gy Wojtilla, op. cit., pp. 219–20.
115. 'Trade and Traders in Western India', PhD thesis, University of Delhi, 1981.
116. The text was edited by T. Chowdhury in *Journal of Bihar Research Society*, XXXI (1945) and XXXII, (1916). The earliest ms used by him belongs to

1851–2. Composed by Haricaranasana the text is based on the *Paryayaratnamala* of Madhavakara (*JBRS*, XXXII, 1945, Introduction, p. i). Since it is strikingly indebted to Amara in chs. 22 and 23 (ibid.) and since potato and tobacco are not mentioned in it, it seems to be pre-Mughal. The synonyms for iron and other metals are found in ch. (*varga*) 6 (*JBRS*, XXXI, 1945).

117. Ch. 18 (*JBRS*, XXXI, 1945, 31–3) speaks of 24 types of *simbisukadhanya-gana* (p. 33), but the varieties, when counted, come to nearly 110 types of cereals including wheat, barley, lentils, etc. Ch 19 (ibid., 33–4) speaks of 10 types of *salidhanya* (transplanted paddy) and 19 types of *trnasalidhanya* (untransplanted? paddy), but on counting various types of paddy and allied cereals come to nearly 64.

118. T.C. Dasgupta, *Aspects of Bengali Society*, Calcutta, 1935, pp. 219–50 quoted in B.N.S. Yadava, op. cit., pp. 258, 305 fn. Yadava has cited several other pieces of evidence, op. cit., pp. 251–9.

119. Mukhia, op. cit., p. 292.

120. Yadava, *The Problem of the Emergence of Feudal Relations in Early India*, p. 46, fn. 1, draws attention to the position of the serf as stated by E.J. Hobsbawm on the basis of Karl Marx: 'The serf, though under the control of the lord, is in fact an economically independent producer', Karl Marx *Pre-capitalist Economic Formations*, London, 1964, p. 42.

15

Historical Archaeology and Urban Decay*

The systematic excavation and exploration of historical sites is a little more than a century old. Students of urban history should feel grateful to early diggers and explorers for their work on the important cities and towns mentioned in ancient texts. They dug extensively and exposed many impressive structures. Alexander Cunningham, who worked as Archaeological Surveyor (1862–6) and again as Director General, Archaeological Survey of India (1870–85), identified several ancient sites, viz., Vaishali with Basarh and Nalanda with Bargaon. This process was continued by his successors. But because of the general orientalist image of India as a land of religion and spiritualism, strengthened by the publication of the accounts of the 'Buddhist' cities by the Chinese pilgrims, the diggers focused their attention on stupas, *caityas,* temples, monasteries, ete. They also doubted the creative ability of Indians to contribute to material culture. Writing on some ancient cities of India in 1945, Stuart Piggott spoke of the unchanging institutions and material culture of India. He says: 'We do not find, and should not look for an inherent element of progress in Indian history—no organic evolution of institutions to changing human needs, no development of material culture nor the gradual spread of higher standards of living to a constantly increasing proportion of the inhabitants.'[1] British archaeologists naturally looked for Iranian,[2] Greek[3] or Roman influence on Indian material culture, particularly on art and architecture. Moreover, because of their obsession with political and military history they

*Previously published as, 'Historical Archaeology and Problems of Urban History' in R.S. Sharma, *Urban Decay in India, c. 300–c. 1000* (New Delhi: Munshiram Manoharlal Publishers, 1987).

searched for palaces and defence ramparts. Of this the report of L.A. Waddell in 1896 on Pāṭaliputra and that of D.B. Spooner in 1913–14 on Kumrahar are good examples.

Early European, mainly British, archaeologists were keenly interested in recovering sculptures and art objects of exotic and aesthetic value; many of them were removed to enrich the British Museum and other foreign collections. The Indian museums were considered to be storehouses of wonderful relics of the past. Little archaeological interest was shown in 'minor finds'[4] which, if carefully preserved and analysed, could have become of major importance for the study of urban life. Temples and monasteries were indeed preferred to the habitations of the ordinary town dwellers.

In the twenties and thirties of the present century Indian archaeologists became quite active, but working under British guidance they could not completely liberate themselves from the colonial stereotype. Through extensive excavations they salvaged a great deal of the country's cultural legacy, though much of it consisted of religious structures. Some archaeologists rightly argued against foreign influence, but together with historians they created some myths including the myth of the golden age of the Guptas.

Under Mortimer Wheeler (1944–8) the technique of area excavation was superseded by stratified excavation, in which the preparation of an overall, schematic view of the material culture assumed importance. Although Arikamedu was a single-culture site, Wheeler's search for Roman influence led to its stratawise excavation.[5] Similar diggings were started by his Indian disciples, and one could clearly see a town in terms of its origin, growth and decline.

During recent years historical archaeology has been de-emphasized because of a shift in orientation and direction for archaeological work. In the last twenty-five years there has developed a craze for prehistory and protohistory. Greater antiquity is supposed to vest the object and its discoverer with greater prestige and respectability. There is also the problem of making up for the loss of the main Harappan sites on account of the creation of Pakistan. Additionally there is the desire to establish the original home of the Aryans in India which has led to endless archaeological search.[6] These efforts have considerably added to information about the Stone Age, the stone-copper phase, the Harappan culture and the users of the Painted Grey Ware.

But this has been achieved at the cost of historical archaeology, which has been denied its due share in the limited resources and expertise available in the country. In the case of those sites which yield both prehistoric and historical remains, the former receives more attention in reports and discussions. Thus the importance of the neolithic-chalco lithic material including bone tools found in a few trenches at Chirand is blown out of proportion. Several Deccan and central Indian sites show both the chalcolithic and historical phases with a gap of nearly six hundred years between the two. Although the two phases are covered in the same report, more importance is given to the chalcolithic phase.

Whereas ancient cities have received consideration in historical archaeology, the digging of rural sites lying in their periphery or elsewhere has been minimal. Since the difficulties of pre-industrial transport placed a town at the mercy of its hinterland, excavation at an urban site, unless backed by explorations and trial diggings in the adjacent areas, cannot disclose the nature of connection between a town and its supportive agrarian base.

The archaeology of medieval sites is sadly neglected, with the result that little is known about the life of the medieval settlements. In *Indian Archaeology* 1982–3: A *Review* the terms 'early historic', 'early medieval', 'medieval' and 'late medieval' are used. This is certainly an advance on previous attempts at periodization, and brings archaeology closer to history. But what these terms mean by way of chronology, concept and content of material culture, remains to be clarified.

Finally, we may consider the relevance of horizontal excavations to urban history. Large-scale excavations can tell us about the size and population of a town. Of the Bronze Age sites, Mohenjo-daro was subjected to a large horizontal excavation; it was five times the size of Harappa. Considering the large number of early historic sites in the subcontinent, only Taxila, Kauśāmbi, Ahicchatrā and Nagarjunakonda were excavated on a large scale. Atranjikhera, Rajghat, Khairadih and Chirand have also been considerably excavated. But even a key site such as Mathura has not been adequately excavated.[7]

Despite these limitations, on the basis of earlier extensive excavations and recent vertical and horizontal diggings attempts have been made to write urban history. In an able monograph published in 1973 Amalananda Ghosh tried to tackle the problem of urbanization in early historical times.[8] He considered an administrative and mercantile organization to be the prerequisite for a city.[9] Ghosh was preceded by Y.D. Sharma, who had competently surveyed the remains of towns in 1953 and 1964.[10] Notwithstanding these laudable attempts, the problem of urban decline,[11] needs research.

Whether we study urbanization or de-urbanization, towns have to be identified. What could be the archaeological criteria for this? The classical definition of Childe lists monumental buildings, large settlements with dense population, non-food producing classes (including rulers, artisans and merchants) and the cultivation of art, science and writing as traits of the urban revolution[12] which took place in the Bronze Age. Childe laid great stress on the presence of craft specialists and the role of the surplus which supported non-food producers living in cities. According to Adams, increased size and density of population are crucial to urbanism, and the contribution of the specialized crafts to the primary urban needs is negligible.[13]

These ideas are largely useful even in the context of Iron Age towns in early historic India. But the presence of monumental buildings and the insignificance of crafts do not apply to early historic towns. Heavy rains, moist conditions and perennial floods rule out the presence of large constructions in many river plains. Indeed, there has been no dearth of towns with mud houses. In our view what really marks out a town is not merely size and population but the quality of material life and the nature of occupations. Though agrarian surplus derived from the hinterland is vital to the existence of a town, merely a settlement of non-agriculturists cannot be regarded as an urban centre. Concentration of crafts and prevalence of money-based exchange are equally important features of urban life. In texts on architecture a *nigama* or town is rightly defined as inhabited by people of all classes and numerous artisans.[14] According to Kaiyata, a grammarian of the eleventh century, a city (*nagara*) is defined as a settlement surrounded by a wall and a moat, and marked by the prevalence of the laws and customs of the guilds of artisans and merchants.[15]

We may now spell out in some detail the identity marks of a town primarily on the basis of archaeological data. The size of a settlement is an important consideration. A single mound or several contiguous mounds measuring one square mile may indicate a dense and large population. Since such measurements are generally not given in the reports, neither the size nor the population can be estimated. As far as I know nobody has estimated the population of an early historical town although several estimates are made about the protohistbric Painted Grey Ware sites.[16]

The congestion of houses indicates dense population, but because of the limited area of excavation such exposures are very few. If the town is not situated on the river bank, the abundance of tanks and ring wells might suggest that water was needed by a large population. Ring wells used as soak-pits might suggest dense habitation. However excavations, carried out so far do not help us much in this respect.

The numerical dominance of non-agriculturists is the distinctive feature of the urban population. The nature of iron and other artefacts, that have been discovered in vertical excavations can provide some clue to the occupation of the people who used them. The artefactual assemblage holds the key to artisanal and other activities. Artefacts include not only axes, adzes, chisels, etc., but also crucibles, ovens, furnaces, dyeing vats, etc. Their social and economic implications have to be worked out. Fewer agricultural tools would mean a minor role for agriculture. Of course, hoes, axes, sickles, and, adzes can be used in both crafts and agriculture. But far more importance needs to be given to the absence or the presence of the ploughshare. Town may have been inhabited by some agriculturists, but their number would not be very large. However, as centres for manufactures of iron tools meant to cater to the primary needs of agriculturists, towns are expected to yield such artefacts. But much would depend on luck in vertical diggings.

Limited excavations make it difficult to locate craft and other specialists living in towns. But wherever kilns, ovens, furnaces, iron slag, coin moulds, moulds for beads, seals and sealings, jewellery, terracottas, etc. are exposed, they signify the presence of considerable craftsmen of different types. The same inference could be drawn from the finds of varied plentiful pottery.

Some signs of urbanism associated with early historic towns are not found in Harappan towns. Apart from the decipherable seals and inscriptions indicating the existence of organized and individual artisans and merchants (seals in Bhita, Vaishali and Paharpur), we also come across coins in excavated layers. The discovery of metallic money, when linked with the presence of artisans and traders, certainly lends a clear urban colour to such sites. Finds of coins indicate exchange of commodities through metallic money, and the occurrence of coin moulds are reported from about three dozen early historic sites. The urbanism of seaside sites where dockyards or warehouses are discovered is obvious. Arikamedu and Kaveripattanam are good illustrations.

Costly, prestige or luxury objects such as precious and semiprecious stones, sophisticated terracottas, thin-walled and shining pottery were apparently used by members of the upper class in historic towns. The same seems to be true of glassware, ivory objects and various types of Roman pottery discovered mainly in the sites situated south of the Vindhyas. Even the use of tiles for roofing may have been confined to richer sections of population. All this can be suggested on the basis of vertical excavations: which indicate the presence of a class of conspicuous consumers typical of pre-industrial towns. But what was luxury in ancient towns may have become necessity for the superior rural classes of early medieval times. Excavation of rural sites belonging to the early medieval period may throw light on this problem.

In Childe's view monumental buildings symbolize the consumption of the surplus, although they can also overawe commoners with the power and prestige of the rulers. But strangely such buildings have not been found in early historic towns. Burnt brick structures appeared around *c.* 300 BC and became important a century later. But it would be wrong to associate towns only with brick structures. In Central Asia a mud structure town was found in Afrasiyab. In India monumental structures of brick or stone became widespread in early medieval times, and they comprised forts, temples and monasteries. It is not known how populous they were. How they were supplied with food, artisanal goods and services is to be investigated. Considering the moist, rainy climate of many alluvial plains such as the middle Gangetic plains, baked brick structures on a good scale assume special importance and become a trait of towns. They can stand the moist much longer than unbaked brick constructions preserved in the dry climate of Central Asia, where mud structures alone can form towns.

At several places in the Deccan and elsewhere silos and granaries occur at historical sites. Apparently these silos were meant to store surplus foodgrains for feeding the urban people. We have no means to verify whether cereals were procured by the merchants or received as tax by the state agencies. At Dhulikatta (Andhra Pradesh) coins are recovered from the granaries, which can connect them with the sale and purchase of foodgrains. At any rate, granaries indicate the dependence of the towns on the countryside from where such cereals were brought for storage.

Streets, shops, drains, granaries and fortifications could give a good idea of the urban settlement. Fortifications are traced to some length in a few cases, but even the existing mud walls and baked ramparts indicate the need for security and partly satisfy the instructions given in the sections on *durganiveśa* or *durgavidhāna* in the *Arthaśāstra* of Kauṭilya. However in ancient times only seats of power and administration may have been enclosed.

Drains appear in many and streets in a few sites. Drains as well as sanitary arrangements suggest congested population. Brick-lined or cutcha roads and streets flanked by houses, as in Khairadih in Ballia district in eastern Uttar Pradesh, might indicate shops and the market. Clear indications of shops are found in Bhita.

Moving roughly from east to west to south, our criteria help us to identify many urban sites such as Chirand, Buxar, Khairadih, Mason,

Sohgaura, Bhita, Atranjikhera, Kondapur, Vadgaon-Madhavapur, Arikamedu, ete. These have been excavated but are difficult to locate in texts. Moving in the same order, the texts mention many important towns such as Vaishali, Pataliputra, Varanasi, Kausambi, Sridgaverapura, Sravasti, Hastinapura, Ahicchatra, Mathura, Indraprastha, Ujjain, Bhoga-vardhana, Kaveripattanam, ete. These have not been excavated fully. Many of them are described by the Chinese pilgrims.

Those who consider size and density of population crucial to the urban set-up may find vertical excavation insufficient for identifying towns. But for us the quality of life revealed by specialized artefacts and objects used by the inhabitants is far more important than mere size. In a single-culture site, as in the case of many Kuṣāṇa, Kṣatrapa and Śātavāhana mounds, the vertical excavation could be a good clue to the nature of ancient life lived in the whole area covered by the mound. The same could apply to major culture sites: But here again a line has to be drawn between the types of material life lived in the rural areas and that lived in the urban areas. This can be delineated only if we make some progress in the archaeology of rural sites of the early historical times. Villages mentioned in epigraphic land grants and identified in many cases could be taken up for excavation and exploration.

Meanwhile we may make the best of vertical excavations. If they suggest similar crafts and technology at sites which are far distant from one another, the phenomenon assumes a supra-local significance. Though not a happy method, an aggregate of the findings from vertical excavations at distant sites in the same cultural sequence would provide a general idea of urbanism. Again, if the traits of urban life revealed by vertical excavations at various sites tally with the traits exposed by horizontal excavations, this should be regarded far more significant.

By now nearly 140 urban sites have been excavated. Those dug according to Wheeler's method have been mostly reported in *Indian Archaeology: A Review*. But even at the end of their endeavours the excavators hardly care to favour the readers with an overall view of the site through schematic sections. The number of the available sections and the existing reports that clearly indicate urban decline in Gupta or post-Gupta times is not large. To infer de-urbanization from the desertion shown by vertical excavations may be criticized on the ground that the unexcavated parts of the mound could show habitation. But we have to rely on the digger who has a feel of the site. More importantly, when decline and desertion recur repeatedly at numerous sites they assume a pattern that cannot be ignored. Whether excavated vertically or horizontally, the overall outcome of vertical excavations is confirmed by the observations of Fa-hsien and Hsuan Tsang, who do not describe any particular part of the town but the town as a whole. The Chinese pilgrims speak of the decline of most Buddhist cities they visited in the fifth and seventh centuries.

The growth and decay of towns is intimately linked with the history of trade. The archaeological evidence for Indo-Roman trade is one-sided inasmuch as in sharp contrast to Roman goods found in peninsular India, only a few stray Indian objects are reported from the Roman empire. Hardly anything is reported from Roman Egypt and Western Asia with which India traded mainly. Of course Indian ivories of the first-second centuries AD have been unearthed in Begram (Afghanistan).[17] Similarly, though scientific examination of material remains can tell us about the existence of textiles, foodgrains, etc., commodities used in the two-way traffic between India and Central Asia under the Kuṣāṇas are not known.

A similar archaeological situation exists regarding India's trade with South-East Asia. The kaolin ware made of fine soft clay found in south Indian urban sites may have been of Chinese origin, as is certainly the case with the grey–green coloured Chinese celadon ware belonging to the ninth century or a later date. But only Indian beads of glass and of other materials have been found in excavations at some places in South-East Asia.[18] If South-East Asia actively traded with India between the fourth and tenth centuries we will need some proof in the archaeological record. As far is known, South-East Asian, and particularly the Indo-Roman trade, contributed substantially to the growth of towns in the peninsula till the AD third century. Once long-distance overland and overseas trade suffered, urban centres began to decline.

It is not necessary to define de-urbanization. If the concrete signs of urbanism that have been pointed out above are either wanting or found in considerably diminished form at an urban site, we visualize urban decline. It raises several issues. How to account for this widespread phenomenon? Can it be explained only on the basis of internal dynamics of the Indian society? Towns were inhabited not only by rulers, soldiers and men of religion and learning but also by artisans, merchants and numerous servicing groups. If they declined what happened to townsmen and how did they earn their livelihood? Did urban decline affect the character of the ruling class and the state? What use was made of the skill of the artisans and how were they paid? How far did de-urbanization help agrarian expansion? To what extent and how long did merchants and traders replace their traditional callings with new ones? In what ways did such centres of non-agriculturists as temples, monasteries and fortified garrisons differ from early historic towns? Above all, what was the nature of linkage between urban decline and the classical feudal set-up that emerged in the early medieval period? We will try to identify the signs of decline for every excavated site and also answer some of these questions.

NOTES

1. Stuart Piggott, *Some Ancient Cities of India*, pp. 1–2.
2. For instance see D.B. Spooner, 'The Zoroastrian Period of Indian History', *The Journal of the Royal Asiatic Society of Great Britain and Ireland*, 1915, pp. 63–82.
3. Sir John Marshall's *Taxila*, 3 vols, overemphasizes Hellenistic influence although otherwise it is an excellent report.
4. Reporting on Bulandibagh (Patna), Spooner says 'The site is evidently rich in minor antiquities', *Annual Report of the Archaeological Survey of India, Eastern Circle, for 1914–15*, Superintendent's Report, Bankipore, 1915, p. 49; but he does not pay any attention to them.
5. R.E.M. Wheeler with contributions by A. Ghosh and Krishna Deva, 'Arikamedu: An Indo-Roman Trading Station on the East Coast of India', *Ancient India*, no. 2, 1946, pp. 17–124.
6. R.S. Sharma, *Material Culture and Social Formations in Ancient India*, chs 2,4 and appendix III.
7. In view of the vastness of the country ancient Indian towns do not seem to be too many. The Roman empire had nearly 1500 towns spread over Italy, the Iberian peninsula, the eastern provinces and the north African littoral excluding Egypt (Keith Hopkins, 'Economic Gowth and Towns in Classical Antiquity', *Towns in Societies*, Philip Abrams and E.A. Wrigley, ed., p. 70) Although this index is considered imperfect, even a lesser number appears to be staggering when compared with India. It is likely that if we go only by archaeology the number of Roman towns will be much smaller. The Indian literary evidence is not helpful. Artistobulus, sent on a commission by Alexander to a region left desert by the shifting of the Indus to the east, saw the remains of over a thousand towns and villages full of men. The number may be exaggerated; but India and Pakistan will have to redouble their efforts to identify remains of those settlements. Indian archaeology also suffers from poor preservation. 'Paved streets, life-size statues, shady colonnades, temples, gymnasia, baths, fountains, theatres, amphitheatres, and aqueducts' constitute 'the monument ruins of classical towns'. But in contrast to these India's ancient urban monuments are pitifully poor.
8. A. Ghosh, *The City in Early Historical India.*
9. Ibid., pp. 20–1.
10. Y.D. Sharma, 'Exploration of Historical Sites', *AI*, no. 9, 1953, Special Jubilee Number, pp. 116–69; 'Remains of Early Historical Cities', *Archaeological Remains, Monuments and Museums*, A. Ghosh, ed.

11. The problem receives some attention in R.S. Sharma, 'Decay of Gangetic Towns in Gupta and Post-Gupta Times', *Proceedings of the Indian History Congress*, 33rd session, Muzaffarpur, 1972, pp. 94–104; B.D. Chattopadhyaya, 'Trade and Urban Centres in Early Medieval India', *IHR*, I, 1974, pp. 203–19; 'Urban Centres in Early Medieval India: An Overview', *Situating Indian History*, ed., S. Bhattacharya and Romila Thapar, 1986, pp. 8–33; R.N. Nandi, 'Client, Ritual and Conflict in Early Brāhmaṇical Order', *IHR*, VI, 1979–80, 103–9; V.K. Thakur, 1982, *Urbanisation in Ancient India*; Kameshwar Prasad, 1984, *Cities, Crafts and Commerce under the Kuṣāṇas.*
12. V. Gordon Childe, 'The Urban Revolution', 1950, Gregory L. Possehl, ed., *Ancient Cities of the Indus*, pp. 12–17.
13. Robert McC Adams, 'The Natural History of Urbanism', 1968, Possehl, ed., *Ancient Cities of the Indus*, pp. 18–26.
14. *Mayamata*, X, pp. 34–5; the term is *bahukarmakarayuktam*. Also see *Māṇasāra*, X, p. 42, which reads as *bahukarmakarairyuktam nigamam tadudahrtam. Nigama* means a market-place or a company/caravan of merchants, s.v. *nigama*, Monier-Williams, *Sanskrit-English Dictionary.*
15. *Prākāraparikhānvitaṃ sreṇidharmasaṃyuktaṃ saṃsthānam.* Kaiyaṭa on Pāṇini, VII 3.14. I owe this reference to B.N.S. Yadav.
16. Brehman Dutt, 'Settlements of the Painted Grey Ware in Haryana', unpublished Ph.D. thesis, Kurukshetra University, 1980.
17. Jeannine Auboyer, 'Ancient Indian Ivories from Begram Afghanistan', *The Journal of the Indian Society of Oriental Art*, XVI, pp. 34–46.
18. H.B. Sarkar, *Cultural Relations between India and Southeast Asian Countries*, ch. 11, p. 248. Numerous beads found in Malaya, eastern Java and northern Borneo are assigned to Roman, Hittite, Phoenician and south Indian sources from the pre-Christian centuries. The Indian bead trade continued in the early centuries of the Christian era, as the finds from Arikamedu or Virapatanam near Pondicherry and Oc Eo in Cochin China attest. What the Indian merchant received in return is not known.

16

Social Changes in Early Medieval India (*circa* AD 500–1200)*

I consider it a great privilege and honour to have been called upon to deliver the first lecture in the Devraj Chanana Memorial Series. Learning Sanskrit in the traditional manner at Hardwar, Chanana completed his formal education in Paris. He imbibed the best elements of traditional and modern cultures and contributed to their deeper understanding through lectures and publications. Participation in nationalist and progressive movements gave realistic dimensions to his studies. Chanana's varied interests covered Sanskrit, Hindi, Panjabi, Bengali, social and economic history, social anthropology, etc. A gifted linguist, he wrote with felicity in several languages. He produced his book *Slavery in Ancient India* in French and translated it into English; the book was also rendered into Russian.

Devraj Chanana was a devoted teacher and educationist. His family carried on fairly prosperous business, but he resisted pressures for joining his ancestral profession and chose to be a teacher. Although he was not given is due place in the academic hierarchy he gave his best to his students and colleagues. Chanana rendered valuable services to the University of Delhi in planning its development. It is fitting that Dr C.d. Deshmukh, with whom he was closely associated in this work and under whom he served as teacher, should preside over the first memorial lecture.

It is not possible to touch upon the wide range of scholarly contributions made by Devraj Chanana. But I wish to draw your attention to his penetrating analysis of the ancient slave syste. It is a thorough and careful examination of the various Pali and Sanskrit terms used for

*Previously published as 'Social Change in Early Medieval India (*circa* AD 500–1200)' in R.S. Sharma, *Early Medieval Indian Society: A Study in Feudalisation* (Hyderabad: Orient Longman, 2001).

slaves, and their skillful piecing together has resulted in a revealing work on the social structure of ancient India. It is a pity that Chanana did not live long to carry forward is researches into post-Gupta times. A discussion of some social changes in this period should be the best tribute to his memory.

CLOSED ECONOMY: LOSS OF MOBILITY

The background to social changes in early medieval India is provided by certain economic developments. The most significant change in the economy of the period is the large-scale transfers of land revenues and land to both secular and religious elements by princes and their vassals. The process is attested by a large number of charters generally recorded on copper-plates which mostly grant villages with fiscal and administrative immunities to priests in the initial stage but also to vassals and officials in the later stage. In the eleventh and twelfth centuries vassals and officials were granted villages and land revenues, especially in the Rajput kingdoms of northern India.[1] In the Deccan and South India they were assigned villages for military service. Although the country was split into numerous principalities, especially after the fall of the Pālas, Pratīhāras and Rāṣṭrakūṭas, the process of land grants made royal authority ineffective even in these small kingdoms. The economic and political tie between the central government on the one hand and local beneficiaries on the other was disrupted by the grant of fiscal and administrative autonomy to the beneficiaries, which gave rise to so many fiscal and administrative islands existing by themselves. Subinfeudation further reduced the size of these economic units and created conditions for the development of a kind of social hierarchy based on unequal distribution of land or land revenues, as the case may be.

The identity of the benefice of a village, or of groups of villages which were not included in it, was strengthened by the decline of trade in this period. The heyday of Indian foreign trade lasted for about 100 years or so in the first and second centuries when India exported spices, silk, and precious metals to the eastern part of the Roman empire. The export of Indian silk to the Byzantium continued till the middle of the sixth century AD. But once the Byzantines had learnt from the Chinese the art of growing silk worms they no longer required silk from China or India.[2] The coastal areas of India perhaps carried on some trade with South-East Asia and with China, though this had little impact on the internal economy of the country. But the overall decline of trade weakened the economic links between the coastal towns and the towns situated in the interior and again between towns and villages.

Commercial decline in this period is clearly indicated by the paucity of coins. Although the Pālas, the Gurjara-Pratiharas and the Rastrakutas ruled continuously for about three centuries and more, over the whole of the country except the deep South, we cannot attribute with confidence any series of coins to them. The absence of gold coins in post-Gupta times is in sharp contast with their abundance under the Kuṣāṇas and Guptas. In the absence of actual coins it is not possible to make much of the references to coins in inscriptions of medieval dynasties. Although gold coins were revived under the Kalacuris, Candellas, Gāhaḍavālas, etc., in the eleventh to twelfth centuries it was on a small scale, and at any rate in the period *c*. AD 650–1000 this coinage was almost conspicuous by its absence. It is obvious that the dearth of coins hampered both internal and external trade and left the villages to meet their needs by themselves either singly or collectively. The existence of too many kingdoms meant payment of customs at numerous checkposts which further undermined trade. The *Kathasaritsagara* speaks of traders who moved through forests to escape payment of duties *śulka*.[3]

The decline of trade and commerce practically stopped the movement of artisans and traders from one part of the country to another. Real urban centres which demanded the service of artisans declined, and their place was taken mostly by *skandhāvāras*, military and administrative centres or feudal courts which did not have much use for trade. Artisans had to be tied down to the villages or towns where they lived to serve local clients or masters without any break. Whenever a village was granted the inhabitants of the village, which naturally included artisans, were asked to carry out the orders of the beneficiaries. This could not be possible unless they stayed in the village. Two forged charters of the seventh century AD, ascribed to Samudra Gupta, ask tax-paying peasants and artisans not to leave the village and not to settle in tax-free villages.[4] Some Candella grants name the various categories of artisans who are transferred to the beneficiaries along with the villages which they inhabit.[5] In the Deccan and South India we have several instances of artisans being made over to temples and monasteries.[6] In the coastal area of the western Deccan they were also transferred to the guilds of merchants.[7]

We have no clear case of merchants being transferred to beneficiaries along with the land but medieval artisans who produced and sold their goods were not much different from merchants. Sea voyage would mostly affect merchants, and though this rule may not have been observed it reflects the stagnant economy of the period. A few charters of the sixth to eighth centuries from the western Deccan do not permit the merchants to congregate in the same market in the city,[8] which eliminates the element of competition and points towards the localization of traders.

That the peasants were expected to stay in the village made over in gift can be inferred from the wording of the land charters which commonly enjoin the villagers to pay all dues to the beneficiaries and carry out their orders. From the sixth century AD onwards, in backward and mountainous areas such as Orissa, Deccan, etc., sharecroppers and peasants attached to the land are specifically instructed to stick to the soil.[9] Once this practice was considered useful by the landowners it was also introduced into settled and agriculturally advanced areas. In northern India many land charters clearly transfer the peasants along with the soil to the beneficiaries, and the terms used for the purpose are *dhana jana-sahita*,[10] *janatā-samṛddha*,[11] or *sa-prativāsi-jana-sameta*.[12] This was done obviously to eliminate all ambiguities in the relation of the peasants with the donees; but its chief result was to preserve the existing character of village economy.

Since peasants, artisans and merchants were attached to their respective habitations, this fostered a closed economy and generated a sense of strong localism. Their masters—princes, priests and various kinds of beneficiaries—might change, but there would be no change in the position of labourers, artisans, cultivators, etc., who were attached to the soil whoever happened to be its master. Peasants and artisans found it difficult to go independently from one place to another. They stayed on at the same place unless they were compelled by intolerable oppression or removed for the benefit of the grantees under the terms of the grant, as in central and western India.[13] The only mobility worth the name in medieval period is that of soldiers for fighting, of priests for acquiring new lands, and of pilgrims for visiting religious shrines. Altough it was a period of war troop movements did not promote commerce. Part of the provisions meant for feeding the army was carried by the soldiers themselves, and the remainder was forcibly collected by them from the villages lying on their route, which were also compelled to supply forced labour for transport and other allied purposes. This system therefore did not generate any mobility of merchants, as was the case with the Muslim army whose provisions were supplied by the roving merchants (*banjārās*). Probably priestly donees induced some artisans and peasants to migrate to new settlements, as has been the practice in recent times, but the immigrants remained attached to their masters, and the new settlements assumed the pattern of closed economy prevalent in the original settlements. The migration of priests from one part of the country to another cannot be compared with the migration of discontented nobles and enterprising traders in ancient Greece. In India priests were invited by the princes to inhospitable tracts to strengthen their power against hostile populations, and generally brāhmaṇas were granted land within not more than 100 miles of their original homes.

The picture of immobile brāhmaṇas in the medieval Dharmaśāstras is in keeping with the growth of closed economic units in post-Gupta times. The *kalivarjyas* (things prohibited in the Kali age) limit the movements of the brāhmaṇas, and what is prescribed for members of the highest social order has to be emulated by others if they want to rise in status. Although brāhmaṇas are permitted to undertake journey for performing sacrifices, they are no allowed long journeys on the ground that this would interfere with keeping their Vedic and domestic fires burning.[14] The regulations regarding sea voyage are rather severe. The *Auśanasa Smṛti* states that those who undertake sea voyage are fallen from caste and not fit to be invited to funeral feasts (*śrāddha*).[15] Even after a brāhmaṇa performs the penance prescribed for going on sea voyage, intercourse with him is not considered desirable. Albiruni informs that the area within which a brāhmaṇa could live is fixed, and that a Hindu is not generally permitted to enter the land of the Turks or of the Karṇāṭas.[16] The law book of Brhatparasara recommends that no man would give his daughter to one who lives at a great distance,[17] and this is intended to cover persons of higher varṇas, especially the brāhmaṇas. Pilgrimages to very distant holy places, beyond the sea or on the border of Bharatv arsa, are prohibited.[18] All this makes sense in the context of feudal localism, which ruled out economic and other types of connections between one region of the country and the other. It is significant that the earlier texts talk in terms of *desadharma* or district customs, but several medieval works refer to *gramadharma*,[19] or *gramyadharma* as it is mentioned in the *Abhidhanacintamani*[20] of Hemacandra (1088–1172), and some texts also mention *gramacara*[21] and *sthanacara*.[22] They reflect the growing importance of villages as self-sufficient economic and administrative units.

FEUDAL RANKS AND THE VARṆAS

Land grants and subinfeudation led to unequal distribution of land and power on a large scale and created new social groups and ranks which did not quite fit in with the existing fourfold varṇa system. The medieval law-books ignore this development, but several texts on architecture try to reconcile the ranking based on birth with that based on the possession of land and power. A beginning is made Varāhamihira, who prescribes varying sizes for the houses of the different grades of ruling chief and also of members of the four varṇas; in such a context the natural thing for the earlier texts would have been to discuss the cases of only the four *varṇas*. The *Mayamata*, an early medieval text, lays down that the king of the whole earth should have an eleven-storeyed house, the *dvijāti* a nine-storeyed house, the ordinar king (*nṛpa*) a seven-storeyed house, the vaiśyas and military captains a four-storeyed house, the śūdra a house ranging from one to three storeys, and the *sāmantapramukha*, etc., a five-storeyed house.[23] Here along with members of the four varṇas different categories of princes and *sāmanta*s are introduced into the housing scheme more clearly than in the *Bṛhatsaṃhitā*.

However, some texts ignore considerations of varṇa and are solely guided by the relative status of the feudal lords or nobles. The *Aparājitapṛcchā* of Bhaṭṭa Bhuvanadeva (twelfth century) specifies the size of the residence of nine categories of nobles including *mahāmaṇḍaleśvara, māṇḍalika, mahāsāmanta, sāmanta* and *laghusamanta*. It also prescribes the size of the houses of some others who are lower in the scale.[24] It speaks of eight categories of feudal vassals when it describes a typical feudal court. It recommends that the emperor, that is, *samrāṭ*, who holds the title of *mahārājādhirāja parameśvara*, should have in the court 4 *maṇḍaleśvaras*, 12 *māṇḍalikas*, 16 *mahāsāmantas*, 32 *sāmantas*, 160 *laghusāmantas* and 400 *caturaśikas*, below whom all the others are known as *rājaputras*.[25] It further lays down that the income of the *laghusāmanta* should amount to 5,000, of the *samanta* 10,000, and of the *mahāsāmanta* 20,000.[26] Whether these various ranks of feudal chiefs are thought to be kṣatriyas or also belong to the other varṇas is not clear. But another contemporary text, the *Mānaśāra*, shows that at least a few feudal ranks were open to members of all the varṇas. In Chapter 42 it classifies the princes in descending order and status into nine categories, the highest being the *cakravartin* and the two lowest being the *praharaka* and *astragrāhin*; it also describes nine kinds of throne differing according to the status of the prince or chief.[27] The significant thing in this text is that everybody, irrespective of his varṇa, could get the two lower military ranks in the feudal hierarchy, the rank of *prahāraka* and that of *astragrāhin*. Although lowest in rank, the *astragrāhin* is entitled to have 500 horses, 5,000 elephants, 50,000 soldiers, 5,000 women attendants and one queen.[28] This text therefore clearly transcends considerations of varṇa and thus provides the basis for the emerging social and political organization based on new distribution of land and power.

Social hierarchy based on four gradations was reflected in the Vajrayāna system of Buddhism, which was popular in north-eastern India during this period. Its pantheon was conceived as a pyramidical structure having at the base twenty-five Bodhisattvas. These were headed by seven *mānuṣī* or mortal Buddhas, who in their turn were presided over by five *dhyani* or meditating Buddhas. And finally at the apex of the pantheon stood like paramount power the richly dressed and ornamented Vajrasattva.[29] The whole thing obviously represented a divine social ladder providing for four rungs of Buddhist gods.

The social identity of the higher sections of landed gentry was established by means of several outer symbols and insignia of power. In the Deccan, along with the land grants they were sometimes given a badge of honour on the forehead. In the country as a whole vassals were generally invested with fly-whisk, umbrella, horses, elephants, planquins, etc., and the mightiest of them was empowered to use five musical instruments,[30] which was a rare privilege enjoyed by the sovereign only. The *cakravartin, mahāsāmanta* and *sāmanta* were permitted to erect the chief gate (*simhadvara*),[31] which could not be done by lesser vassals. All these marks of social status seem to have been conferred without much consideration of varṇa; only those who enjoyed high military and political status on account of their landed possessions were entitled to these symbols of social rankings.

During the medieval period artisans and merchants were given feudal titles indicating military and administrative ranks. The Deopara inscription of Vijayasena informs us that Śūlapāṇi, head of the artisans of Varenda, held the title *raṇaka*,[32] which must have added to his social status. Certain titles such as those of *ṭhākur, rāut, nāyaka*, etc., were confined not only to the kṣatriyas or Rajputs but were also conferred on kāyasthas and members of other castes who were granted land and who served in the army. It is this which explains the survival of the title *thakur* in modern times among various categories of brāhmaṇas, among the Rajputs, kāyasthas, and among barbers and similar so-called lower castes.

The constant transfer of land or land revenues made by princes to priests, temples and officials led in early medieval times to the rise and growth of the scribe or the kāyastha community. A large number of writers and record keepers had to be employed to draft documents of assignment of land and to maintain records of the lands and villages, and of the gradually increasing items of revenue which were given in grants. The beginning of fragmentation of land on account of the laws of the partition of landed property from Gupta times made the maintenance of the details of individual plots necessary. Boundary disputes form an important section in the law books, and they could not be easily settled without the help of records. Further, on account of subinfeudation sometimes as many as four and five parties could lay claims to the same plot of land. Somebody would claim it as the sovereign of the land, another person might claim it as the vassal of the sovereign, a third person might claim it as a sub-vassal, and still a fourth person might claim it as the actual cultivator.[33] Therefore village and land records had to be carefully maintained in order to avoid and settle land disputes which arose frequently.

This whole work was done by a class of writers who were known by various names such as *kāyastha, karaṇa, karaṇika, adhikṛta, pustapāla, citragupta, lekhaka, divira, dharmalekhin, akṣaracaṇa, aksaracañcu, akṣapaṭalika, akṣapaṭalādhikṛta*, etc. Just as the brāhmaṇas formed only one class of priests out of sixteen kinds of priests in Vedic times so also in the beginning the kāyasthas formed only one class of about a dozen kinds of writers and record keepers. In course of time all the other record keepers came to be known as kāyasthas. In the initial stage literate members from the higher varṇas were recruited as kāyasthas or scribes to meet the fiscal and administrative needs of the community. Kalhaṇa notes that the brāhmaṇa Śivaratha was appointed as a kāyastha[34] official: we also hear that Lokanātha of brāhmaṇa ancestry on the father's side was a *karaṇa*.[35] But gradually the scribes, recruited from different varṇas, cut off marriage and other social connections with the parent varṇas and confined all their social intercourse to the new community; they practised class endogamy and family exogamy. Faced with the problem of finding a place for the kāyasthas in the varṇa system the brāhmaṇa lawgivers fell into a dilemma and connected them with both the śūdras as well as the dvijas (twice-born). Since the Dharmaśāstra texts on the origin of the kāyasthas are ambiguous and historical examples not confined to one varṇa, in recent times the Calcutta High Court called them śūdras and the Allahabad High Court called them brāhmaṇas.

The rise of the kāyasthas as a professional literati caste naturally undermined the monopoly of the brāhmaṇas as writers and scribes. Kāyastha ministers served the Candella and Kalacuri princes in Madhya Pradesh and the kings of Karṇātaka and Orissa. This was naturally resented by the brāhmaṇas who mostly manned such high offices. They were also angry with the kāyasthas because they maintained records of land grants with which the former were mainly concerned. As scribes and record keepers the kāyasthas must have caused constant trouble to the brāhmaṇas who formed a considerable class of assignees. The kāyasthas therefore never appear in favourable light in brāhmaṇical texts. Although they are first mentioned as early as the fourth century AD by the lawgiver Yājñavalkya,[36] they are represented as oppressors of subjects. By the twelfth century AD the tendency to denounce the kāyasthas had reached its culmination. Their condemnation was a favourite theme in the *Rājataraṅgiṇī* of Kalhaṇa,[37] and is repeated with modifications in several subsequent texts.

In the countryside in northern India there emerged a class of village elders and headmen called *mahattaras*, who had to be informed of the land grants and transactions. They had considerable share in the land of the village, and were apparently responsible for its administration. If we consider the evidence of the *Bṛhatkathākośa* of Hariṣeṇācārya, composed in about AD 920, it would appear that the *mahattara* of a village occupied the pastoral land adjoining the village on condition that he gave 1,000 pitchers of ghee to the ruler.[38] This substantial class, found in village settlements from Gupta times onwards, cut across varṇa and caste boundaries, and while it seems to have held land in each village it did not always enjoy the same ritual status. Such modern survivals of the title as *mahto, mehtā, mahathā, malhotrā, mehrotrā, mehtar*, etc., are found among both the higher and lower castes in modern times, and even making allowance for vicissitudes in the fortunes of these families it would appear that at least in some cases their medieval ancestors enjoyed the headship of the village and were substantial people. The same thing can be said of the *paṭṭakilas*, village headmen, in western India. Mentioned in inscriptions of the eleventh and twelfth centuries they did not always belong to the same caste, and their modern descendants *pāṭils* or *paṭels* do not constitute one single caste. Similarly *gavuṇḍas*, village elders and headmen who were assigned lands and given fiscal administrative rights in the medieval Deccan, did not belong to one single caste, and their modern representatives called *gauḍas* in Mysore are regarded as śūdras.

DECLINE OF VAIŚYAS AND ADVANCE OF ŚŪDRAS

The varṇa system was modified not only by the rise of the various strata of landed gentry connected with administration but also by the change in the relative position of the vaiśyas and śūdras. In post-Gupta times the śūdras no longer appear mainly as slaves, artisans and agricultural labourers; they take the place of vaiśyas as cultivators. Hsuan Tsang clearly states that the śūdras were agriculturists.[39] Albiruni notes the absence of any significant difference between the vaiśyas and the śūdras, who lived together in the same town and mixed together in the same house.[40] This change is reflected in some medieval texts, which represent the śūdras as farmers and agriculturists. The *Skanda Purana* describes the śūdra as giver of grain (*annada*) and householder (*gṛhastha*).[41] The *Abhidhanacintamani* of Hemacandra defines farmers and cultivators as *kutumbins*.[42] In our times śūdra castes called kurmins in Uttar Pradesh and Bihar and kunbis in Maharashtra are apparently the descendants of the medieval *kutumbins*.

From the beginning of the Christian era the Smṛtis approximate the vaiśyas to the position of the śūdras. By the sixth century AD the vaiśyas practically loose their identity as a peasant caste. The *Skanda Purana* predicts that the traders would decline in the Kali age, that some would become oilmen and winnowers of grain (*taṇḍulakāriṇaḥ*), and that some would seek refuge with the *rājaputras*, and others with all kinds of varṇas.[43] By the eleventh century they came to be treated as śūdras ritually and legally, for Albiruni notes that both vaiśyas and śūdras are punished with the amputation of the tongue for reciting Vedic texts.[44] As traders the vaiśyas seem to have been well off till the fifth century AD when Fa-hsien speaks of their charities in glowing terms. But in post-Gupta times they suffered in position on account of decline in trade. There is good evidence to show that from the eighth century AD trade and commerce declined in Bengal and that traders lost in importance. Professor Niharanjan Ray draws attention to a significant passage in this connection. In the reign of Lakṣmaṇasena, in connection with the unfurling ceremony of the trader's banner called *śakradhvaja*, a writer says: 'O where are the traders who once held you aloft. You are now being used as plough or animal-post'.[45] Commercial decline naturally undermined the position of those who practised commerce.

Although Hinduism spread over the distant parts of the country in medieval times, it did not mean diffusion of the fourfold varṇa system which had originated and developed in the central part of the Gangetic plains. In northern India many castes are grouped under kṣatriyas and vaiśyas from early times, but in South India and Bengal we find mainly brāhmaṇas and śūdras to the exclusion of intermediary castes. This peculiar phenomenon can be traced to the early medieval period.

Brāhmaṇism advanced in Bengal and South India in Gupta and post-Gupta times when the distinctions between the vaiśyas and śūdras had got blurred and the advent of the Rajputs had thrown the original kṣatriya varṇa into the background. The progress of Brāhmaṇism was not in the nature of the mass migration of Vedic Aryans, whose bulk was formed by the *vis* or vaiśyas. Hence the tribal and non-Hindu people in the peripheral regions were admitted to the brāhmaṇical system mainly as śūdras. The autochthonous inhabitants of these areas may have been conquered by the kṣatriya or Rajput princes, but their acculturation was really carried out by the brāhmaṇas who functioned as literate and enlightened landowners in these areas. Anthropometric studies suggest that in Bengal the śūdras are indigenous inhabitants, but the brāhmaṇas are not. According to Mahalanobis various śūdra castes in Bengal belong to the same stock and resemble their neighbours in Bihar. But the brāhmaṇas of Bengal resemble their counterparts from northern India.[46]

It is true that in this period the incorporation of foreign invaders and immigrant tribes added new castes to the kṣatriya fold. But Bengal and South India were never seriously affected by foreign invasions. In these areas only the ruling chiefs of local tribes were admitted as kṣatriyas, and the vast majority of their tribal kinsmen were condemned to the position of śūdra. In the absence of intermediary castes there was more of social polarization in Bengal and South India that in any other part of the country. It is perhaps this which accounts for extremist movements in these regions in subsequent times.

PROLIFERATION OF CASTES

The early medieval period was a period of proliferation and fragmentation. The existing varṇas were split up into many castes, and numerous new tribes and castes were annexed to and incorporated within them. A village named Brhat-Chattivanna,[47] inhabited by 36 varṇas, is mentioned in an tenth-century Bengal copper-plate, and several villages bearing similar names in present-day Bihar may have originated in medieval times.

The process of proliferation appears to be most striking among the brāhmaṇas. Many brāhmaṇa castes were named after the type of ritual they practiced or the branch of Vedic learning they cultivated, but the most important factor in the multiplication of their castes was the growth of strong localism. In land charters the brāhmaṇas are identified by their *gotra*, by the male ancestor's names sometimes extending up to four generations, by the branch of Vedic learning, and finally by the original home—the village—from where they come. In course of time they came to be recognized only by their *gotra* and *mūla*, family and territorial affiliations. At present it is difficult to be certain about the purity and continuity of their *gotras*, for members of non-Aryan tribes, especially in the Deccan and South India, seem to have been given Aryan *gotras* and thus made brāhmaṇas, but on the basis of field work one can find out their territorial antecedents. In most land charters the original homes of the brāhmaṇas are proudly mentioned, and from the Gupta period a brāhmaṇa is recognized by the village or the villages to which he belongs. In post-Gupta inscriptions praises are showered on several villages because of their being the native lands of the brāhmaṇas. A typical example of attachment to the village is provided by the description of the village Siddhala, which in an eleventh-century inscription is called the best of villages, the ornament of Āryavarta, the goddess of fortune presiding over Rāḍha.[48]

By late medieval times the brāhmaṇas of Rāḍha, West Bengal, had come to be divided into 56 subcastes based on their original villages (*gamis*),[49] several of which are mentioned in inscriptions of the eleventh to thirteenth centuries. In the fourteenth-century Harisiṃhadeva determined the relative status of the Maithil brāhmaṇas, who came to be divided into about 180 original homes (*mūlas*), and eventually their total original homes or subcastes shot up to about 1,000. If the total Maithil population is taken as 1500,000 (unfortunately the caste census has been now given up), it will roughly mean one subcaste for every 1500 Maithils. An eleventh-century Pāla grant shows that sometimes a brāhmaṇa was identified by his connection with as many as three villages, and the practice became more widespread later. Every Maithil subcaste based on one, two or three villages as its original home feels proud of itself and refuses to have social intercourse with subcastes considered to be inferior in the Maithil caste hierarchy. Similarly the kāyasthas came to be divided into territorial subcastes. At present the karaṇa kāyasthas of Bihar maintain lists of their numerous *mulas* like the Maithils and the ambaṣṭha kāyasthas are divided into more than 100 subcastes, based on their homes in different villages, and all this is taken into account in settling marriages. It is obvious that the concept of *grāmadharma* was more popular with the brāhmaṇas, kāyasthas and other literate Hindus who could maintain their genealogies. Lower castes such as goalas and kurmis, who are far more numerous, are also divided into territorial groups forming subcastes, but because of lack of written records feelings of family and village have not been accentuated among them. The *Brahmavaivarta Purāṇa* dictum that difference in the country (*deśabheda*) leads to difference in the caste worked strongly in the case of medieval brāhmaṇas,[50] but it also explains the multiplication of castes among the other varṇas.

In the kṣatriya community proliferation was caused mainly by the emergence of a new people called the Rajputs. No other community developed so much of racial and family pride as the Rajputs did. Some of them may have descended from the original kṣatriya stock. The practice of ascribing solar and lunar origins to ruling dynasties in inscriptions started from about the seventh century. Probably the Cālukyas, Candellas, Pālas, etc., were local tribes who were given respectable kṣatriya lineage by the brāhmaṇa genealogists. The rule *kastriyo raja ucyate* operated throughout the length and breadth of the country in early medieval times. The term *saṃskāravarjitah*, deprived of rituals, applied to the neo-kṣatriya called *vrātya* was a euphemism for his admission to the brāhmaṇical social order through inferior rites. The Bactrian Greeks, Śakas, Parthians, etc., because of the absence of any strong religion or culture of their own, were absorbed into the Hindu social system as second class kṣatriyas. Really the kṣatriya castes multiplied from the fifth and sixth centuries when the Central Asian peoples such as the Hunas and Gurjars joined their ranks as Rajputs. Probably the Solaṃkīs (Caulukyas), Paramāras, Cāhamānas, Tomaras, Gāhaḍvālas, etc., also had Central Asian origins. Although the Jats are not regarded as Rajputs, they had racial affiliations with Central Asian peoples. The composition of their present caste unions called *khaps* suggests that their was a composite caste of peasants and soldiers who were recruited from the Gurjara, Tomara and other Rajput clans.[51] We hear of Tomar Jats and Gujar Jats, and a document of the thirteenth century shows that Tomar and Gujar representatives sat on the Jat assembly.[52] We also find that the Jats, the Ahirs, and the Gujars smoke and drink together. It would be wrong to think that all foreigners were accepted as kṣatriyas and Rajputs, for in course of time the Gujar people broke up into brāhmaṇas, banias, potters, goldsmits, not to speak of herdsmen and cultivators (kunbis) who were looked upon as śūdras.[53]

The śūdras came to have the largest number of castes in early medieval times. The earliest law-books mention 10 to 15 mixed castes, but the law book of Manu, a work of the first century AD, enumerates 61 mixed castes.[54] This number exceeds 100 if we add to it the list of additional castes given in the *Brahmavaivarta Purāṇa.*[55] A huge increase in the number of śūdra castes can be inferred from the *Vaijayanti* of Yādavaprakāśa and also from the *Abhidhanacintamani* of Hemacandra. The *Viṣṇudharmottara Purāṇa*, a work of about the eighth century AD, states that thousands of mixed castes are produced as a result of the connection of vaiśya women with men of lower castes,[56] although these are not specified.

The conquest of the backward peoples living in the jungles, forests, etc., by brāhmaṇised princes from agriculturally advanced areas enormously added to the number and variety of śūdra castes. The suppression of Śabaras, Bhillas, Pulindas, etc., is referred to in a medieval inscription from central India.[57] For five hundred years from the ninth century almost all the Deccan powers fought against the Ābhīras,[58] who could not be easily assimilated into the brāhmaṇical order. An inscription of AD 861 shows that the Pratihara prince Kakkuka destroyed and conquered a village of Ābhīras near Jodhpur and settled it with brāhmaṇas and vaiśyas, who were promised safety and livelihood.[59] A Kalacuri inscription of the twelfth century speaks of the deliverance of the Ratanpur prince Jajjalladeva II from the clutches of a tribal people called Thirus or Tharus, which was celebrated by his donation of a village to two brāhmaṇas.[60] It is not clear whether this village lay in the Thiru area, but priests were granted land in many subjugated territories, where they inducted the indigenous aboriginal tribal peoples into their cultural fold. This process may have been also peaceful, but peaceful or otherwise it succeeded because of the superior material culture of the brāhmaṇas who not only taught new scripts, language and rituals to the preliterate people but also acquainted them with plough cultivation, new crops, seasons, calendar, preservation of cattle wealth, etc. The tribal peoples were not always given the same place in the brāhmaṇical order, and even the same tribe broke up into several varṇas and castes. We hear of Ābhīra brāhmaṇas, Ābhīra kṣatriyas, Ābhīra vaiśyas, Ābhīra mahaśūdras, and of Ābhīra carpenters and goldsmiths[61] although most Ābhīra seem to have been admitted into Hindu society as śūdras. However, in all such cases *jātidharma* was strictly respected, and each constituent caste was allowed to retain its customs and manners. The Ābhīras, Āgarīs, Ambaṣṭhas, Bhillas, Caṇḍālas, Kauñcas, etc., mentioned as mixed castes in the *Brahmavaivarta Purāṇa*[62] and other texts, were originally tribal people who were accommodated in the brāhmaṇical social framework either as pure or impure śūdras.

The middle ages saw a phenomenal growth in the number of impure śūdras or untouchables, who are first noted in the fourth century BC by Pāṇini. Medieval legal texts describe the untouchables as eaters of cow, and list them as antyajas, barāṭa, barūḍa, bheda, bhilla, caṇḍāla, carmakāra, dāśa, naṭa, rajaka,[63] etc. Some of these appear in about the beginning of the Christian era. Bhedas and tantuvāyas are mentioned by Albiruni, who also refers to bhadhatu, cāṇḍāla, ḍoma, hāḍi,[64] etc. Twelve categories of untouchables are mentioned in early medieval law books, but the actual number might be much more. Detailed rules in the law-book of Parasara suggest an increase in the number of cāṇḍālas and svapakas.

It is difficult to explain this large increase in the number of untouchables. Most untouchable castes were backward tribes whose induction into the Hindu system was accomplished through brāhmaṇisation and through the spread of Hinduized Buddhism. This can be inferred from brāhmaṇical texts as well as from Buddhist Caryāpadas. The latter refer to the ḍomas, niṣādas and their women-folk and to the kāpālikas, all of whom generally lived on mounds outside the villages and were untouchables for the brāhmaṇs.[65] Apparently certain tribal people could not be fully absorbed in Hindu society because of their being very backward and hence had to be pushed to the position of untouchables; or possibly those who offered stiff resistance to the process of conquest and Hinduisation were dispossessed of their lands in the villages and forced to settle outside. Perhaps this happened to the Kaivartas who were finally overpowered by the Pālas in the eleventh century. This may also be true of the Ḍomba tribe, who appear to be an important people in the Dombīpādacaryā.[66] Since brāhmaṇization took place on a very large scale in early medieval times, the number of untouchable castes increased substantially. In earlier times certain varieties of hunters and artisans were rendered untouchables, but now even some agriculturist castes were condemned to this position. This may have happened not so much on account of the hatred of princes and priests for agriculture as on account of their contempt for the backward agriculturists who opposed the new order. On the other hand the fact that a good number of śūdras were reduced to the position of untouchables must have given satisfaction to the reminder who now practically took the place of the vaiśyas in social hierarchy.

Another significant process which led to the multiplication of śūdra castes was the transformation of crafts into castes. As trade and commerce languished in post-Gupta times, craft guilds tended to become stagnant, immobile, more and more hereditary, and more and more localized. Trades and guilds gradually constituted themselves into closed, exclusive groups resembling castes for all practical purposes. Aparārka quotes Bṛhaspati to show that heads of guilds may reprimand and condemn wrong-doers and may also excommunicate them.[67] It seems that *nāpita, modaka, tāmbulika, svarṇakāra, mālākāra, śaṅkhakāra, sūtrakāra, citrakāra*, etc., who, like aborigines, are all called mixed castes in medieval texts,[68] obviously emerged as castes out of various crafts.

Craft villages are mentioned in ancient texts, but now they find place in medieval inscriptions. Thus we hear of two villages called Kumbhāra-padraka,[69] which evidently belonged to the potter caste. Modern specialization means skill and proficiency in the craft wherever and whenever it can be acquired but medieval specialization meant attachment to the master, to his place, and to the family which practiced the craft.

A factor which multiplied the number of castes among both the higher and lower orders of Hindu society, especially in the Deccan and South India, in medieval times, was their religious affiliation. The parallel between the multiplication of sects and that of castes in medieval times is very close, and the former helped the latter. Śaivism, Viṣṇavism, Buddhism, and Jainism—each one of these religions—proliferated into numerous sects not so much due to basic differences in doctrines as due to minor differences in rituals and even in food and dress, which all were sustained by regional practices. Some religious teachers kept moving from place to place, but many others were tied down to maṭhas, monasteries and temples by means of land grants.

Buddhism came to be divided into 18 sects, and Jainism came to be divided into seven sects in Karṇātaka. Each one of these sects came to be led by its teacher or guru who demanded unquestioned allegiance from his followers. Between the followers and the Supreme God the teacher acted as an intermediary just as a vassal acted as an intermediary between the actual tiller of the soil and the king. In course of time members of the sect began to behave as members of a caste. They remained confined to their sects and refused to interdine and sit together with members of another sect. By late medieval time these sects had become full-fledged castes. The Liṅgāyats and Viraśaivas in Karṇātaka and Rādhāsvāmīs in northern India formed separate castes. In Rajasthan and Western India the Jains came to constitute a large caste divided into so many subcastes. In the Gangetic valley the goalas, who worshipped Kṛṣṇa and thought themselves to be racially connected with the divine hero, called themselves Kisnots.

It is an irony of history that the religious sects which sprang up to remove caste disparities and privileges based on birth were themselves swallowed by the caste system. But without any fundamental change in social and economic structure, this was inevitable, for reforming zeal and idealism of the initial reformers had no solid foundations to sustain themselves.

The present survey shows that the pre-Muslim society in northern India underwent some important changes. Unequal distribution of land

and military power created feudal ranks which cut across varṇa considerations, especially at the higher and literate level. Frequent land grants and partitions led to the rise and growth of a new literate class, called the kāyasthas, whose place in the varṇa system could not be clearly defined. The varṇa system was also modified by the transformation of the śūdras into cultivators and the relegation of the vaiśyas to the position of the śūdras, with the result that the newly founded brāhmaṇical order in Bengal and South India provided mainly for brāhmaṇas and śūdras. The most spectacular development was the proliferation of castes, which affected the brāhmaṇas, the kāyasthas, the kastriyas or the Rajputs and above all the śūdras. The number of the mixed castes rose by leaps and bounds, and the untouchable castes increased enormously. These social changes can be understood in terms of a strong sense of feudal localism fostered by closed economic units based on intense preoccupation with land and in the context of the absorption of the tribal peoples into the brāhmaṇical fold through conquests and land grants to brāhmaṇas.

ABBREVIATIONS

CII *Corpus Inscriptionum Indicarum*, i–iii, London, 1888–1929; iv, Ootacamund, 1955

EI *Epigraphia Indica*, Calcutta and Delhi

NOTES

1. R.S. Sharma, *Indian Feudalism: c.* 300–1200 (Calcutta, 1965) Ch. V.
2. Richards Pankhurst, *An Introduction to the Economic Hisory of Ethiopia* (London, 1961), pp. 46–7.
3. VI.3. 105.
4. *CII*, iii, no. 60, II, pp. 12–13.
5. *EI*, xx, no. 14, B plates, 1, 19.
6. *EI*, iii, no. 40; *Epigraphia Carnatica*, vii, Shikarpur Talk 20a.
7. *EI*, xxx, no. 30, II, pp. 8, 28.
8. Ibid., I, 6.
9. *Indian Feudalism*, pp. 54–6.
10. *EI*, xxxv, no. 17. I owe this reference to Dr B.N.S. Yadav.
11. *EI*, xxx, no. 17.
12. *CII*, iii, no. 80, 1, 10.
13. *Indian Feudalism*, pp. 118–19.
14. Batuknath Bhattacharya, *The 'Kalivaijyas'* (Calcutta, 1943), p. 67; P.V. Kane, *History of Dharmaśāstra*, iii, 953, 955.
15. Kane, op. cit., iii, 934.

16. *Alberuni's India*, ed. Edward C. Sachau (Delhi, 1964), ii, pp. 134–5.
17. Quoted in B.N. Sharma, *Social Life in Northern India* AD 600–1000 (Delhi, 1966), p. 12.
18. Kane, op. cit., iii, 953.
19. *Devibhagavata* cited in R.C. Hazra, *Studies in Upapuranas*, ii, 325. I owe this reference to Dr B.N.S. Yadav.
20. III.201.
21. *Brhannaradiya Purana*, 22.11.
22. *Skanda Purana*, Brahma Khanda, II. 40.5.
23. XXIX, pp. 80–2.
24. 81, pp. 2–12.
25. 71.33–4, 39; V.S. Agrawala, *Harshacharita-Ek-Sanskritik Adhyayan* (Patna, 1953), p. 178. fn. 3.
26. Quoted by Agrawala, op. cit., p. 203.
27. P.K. Acharya, *Hindu Architecture in India and Abroad, Manasara Series* (Oxford, 1946), vi, 125; this is found in Chapters 45 and 46 of the text.
28. P.K. Acharya, op. cit., vi, 125.
29. Benoytosh Bhattacharya, *The Indian Buddhist Iconography* (Calcutta, 1958), Chapters I & II.
30. *Indian Feudalism*, pp. 22–3, 99.
31. *Aparajitaprccha*, 81, pp. 21–4.
32. *Inscriptions of Bengal*, iii, ed. N.G. Majumdar (Rajshahi, 1929), no. 5, verse 36.
33. *Indian Feudalism*, pp. 153–4.
34. Kane, op. cit., ii, 77.
35. *EI*, xv, no. 19.
36. I.322.
37. IV.620 ff; VIII, 560 ff.
38. Quoted in B.N. Sharma, op. cit., p. 311.
39. T. Watters, *On Yuan Chwang's Travels in India*, ed. T. Rhys Davids and S.W. Bushell, 2 volumes (London, 1904–5), i, 168.
40. Sachau, i, 101.
41. Nagara Khanda, VI, pp. 242, 31.
42. III.554.
43. Brahma Khanda, II., pp. 39, 291–2.
44. Sachau, ii, p. 136.
45. *Bangalir Itihasa* (Adi Parva) (Calcutta, 1948), p. 343.
46. R.C. Majumdar (ed.), *The History of Bengal*, i (Dacca, 1943), pp. 558–9.
47. Puspa Niyogi, *Brahmanic Settlements in Different Subdivisions of Bengal*, Calcutta, 1967, p. 55.
48. *Inscriptions of Bengal*, iii, no. 4, verse 3.
49. Niyogi, op. cit., p. 33.
50. Brahma Khanda, X. 14; cf. 168.
51. M.C. Pradhan, *The Political System of the Jats of Northern India,* Oxford, 1966, Appendix, 1, p. 249.

52. Ibid., pp. 254–5.
53. D.R. Bhandarkar, 'Foreign Elements in the Hindu Population', *Journal of Ancient Indian History*, i, pp. 301–3.
54. X, pp. 1–51.
55. Brahma Khanda, X, pp. 14–136.
56. II, pp. 81–2.
57. *EI*, i, no. 38, II, verse 22.
58. Bhagwansingh Suryavamsi, *The Abhiras: Their History and Culture*, Baroda, 1962, pp. 39–40.
59. Ibid., p. 40.
60. *CII*, iv, no. 99, pp. 1, 28.
61. D.R. Bhandarkar, op. cit., pp. 286–8.
62. Brahma Khanda, X, pp. 17–136.
63. Quoted in Vasudeva Upadhyay, *Socio-Religious Condition of North India* (AD 700–1200), Varanasi, 1964, p. 92, footnote nos. 3 & 4.
64. Sachau, i, pp. 101–2.
65. Atindra Mojumder, *The Carypadas*, Calcutta, 1967, p. 10.
66. Ibid., pp. 48–9.
67. Quoted in B.P. Mazumdar, *Socio-Economic History of Northern India* (AD 1030–1194), Calcutta, 1960, p. 211.
68. *Brahmavaivrta Purana*, Brahma Khanda, X, pp. 17–136.
69. Puspa Niyogi, op. cit., p. 53.

17

Need for an Integrated Approach*

The Congress [Indian History Congress] was set up in the intellectual climate of 1930s when reaction against colonialist views on India's past was at its peak. Naturally papers read at its sessions questioned the nature of the western contribution to India's progress in different periods of our history, and our scholars tried to show that Indian rulers were neither despotic nor incapable of setting up large political entities. The fact of the composite culture of India was also emphasized and so also its past achievement in governing the people. There is no doubt that the national approach enabled the historians to make notable progress in various fields of scholarship. But it would be wrong to gloss over the important contribution to Indian history made by western scholarship. Similarly it would not be right to gloss over the elements of chauvinism and obscurantism that has crept into the nationalist approach and diluted its content.

The relevance of India's past assumes special significance in the context of the problems we face in modern times. In the name of nationalism some people clamour for the restoration of ancient Indian culture and civilization, and a good many are sentimentally swayed by the propaganda about the past glories of India. This is different from the concern for the preservation of ancient heritage in art and architecture. What they really want to bring back is the old pattern of society and culture. Such a situation demands a far better understanding of the past. There is no doubt that ancient Indians attained distinction in different fields of life, but these advances cannot enable us to compete with the achievements of modern science and technology. We cannot ignore the fact that the ancient Indian society was marked by gross social injustice. The lower

*Inaugural lecture of Golden Jubilee Session of the Indian History Congress delivered at Gorakhpur, December 1989.

orders, particularly the śūdras and untouchables, were encumbered with disabilities which are shocking to the modern mind. The restoration of the old way of life will naturally revive and strengthen all these inequalities. Ancient India's march to civilization was accompanied by the growth of social discriminations. The success of the ancients in surmounting the difficulties presented by nature and human factors can build our hope and confidence in future, but the attempt to bring back the past will mean the perpetuation of social inequity which has plagued the country for long.

We have many survivals of ancient, medieval and later times persisting in the present. The old norms, values, social customs and ritualistic practices are so deeply ingrained in the minds of the people that they cannot easily get rid of them. Unfortunately these survivals inhibit the development of the individual and the nation. They were deliberately fostered in a colonialist situation. India cannot make rapid strides unless such vestiges of the past are removed from its society. Obsolete social traditions and institutions hinder the integration and development of the country on democratic lines. Caste barriers and prejudices do not allow even the educated people to appreciate the dignity of manual labour and prevent our unity for a common cause. Though women have been enfranchized, their age long social subordination prevents them from playing their due role. The study of the past helps us to go deeply into the roots of these prejudices. We may try to find out the causes that sustain the caste system, subordinate women, and promote narrow religious sectarianism.

We have to look into the causes of the origin of various religious sects, and also of social and political institutions with economic life as their focal point. We would also like to understand the nature of the changing interrelationship between the superstructural institutions on the one hand and the essentials of economic development on the other.

Interaction can be illustrated in several cases. It is true that the Buddhist emphasis on the non-killing of cattle and other animals arose out of the needs of animal husbandry which underwent a qualitative change with the introduction of iron in the middle Ganga plains. The doctrine of non-killing taught by the Buddhists was further strengthened by the stress laid on its sacredness by the brāhmaṇical writers. All kinds of dire consequences awaited those who committed the sin of killing cow and brāhmaṇas. Though this instruction was not followed completely, without doubt the doctrine of the non-killing of cows contributed to the progress of agriculture in ancient times and contributed to the agrarian economy and state system. But the same doctrine came to be considered an obstacle to further progress when it became difficult to feed all types of animals. At present the economics of sacred cow does not favour a developing country like India.

Similarly, social division of labour and unequal access of various social strata to the surplus produce created a kind of varṇa system which was of particular help to the brāhmaṇas and the kṣatriyas. Since both of them were divorced from the work of primary production they wanted to perpetuate the system by stressing the idea of heredity which spread the myth of the blue blood of the higher classes. Social divisions were considered natural and based on qualities inherent in human beings (*guṇakarmavibhāgśah*). Such ideas formed the bedrock of the varṇa system. This system facilitated division of labour and also promoted specialization in various professions at the earlier stage. But the same ideology prevented further progress because of the advance of technology. When technology advances and indusrialization begins, mobility becomes a common feature, and impersonal relations based on the use of machines are established in place of personal relations. In such a society the old ideology, based on ascriptive ideas, cannot work.

Another example of interaction between base and superstructure could be seen in the case of family. In a patriarchial set-up women are at the receiving end and have to live under male domination. Such a society is also marked by the exclusive domination of the consuming classes over the producing classes. It is significant that whereas in Rome women and slaves were placed in the lowest category, in India women and śūdras were generally placed in the same position. But the patriarchical values, which governed the behaviour pattern of people in prefeudal and feudal times and continue to do so even now, are being challenged in the changed material situation. Although male domination sanctified by the Dharmaśāstras was willingly accepted at one time, it is getting undermined by avenues available for the employment of women. Women are gradually becoming selfreliant. In the conditions created by industrialization women workers can earn their livelihood independently, can vote, can have access to education and other facilities. Although old prejudices die hard, new conditions of work make it possible for women to demand just and equal rights. Those who stand for social reform need not quote extensively from ancient texts but study the stages through which the matriarchal element was submerged under the patriarchal element on account of social, economic and other compulsions.

It seems clear that the practices and institutions which originate in the context of certain means, processes and relations of production become redundant when those economic factors change. Although there is no doubt that these institutions keep on influencing economic developments, they also continue to exercise the minds of the people even after the situation in which they had originated has disappeared.

The main focus of the Indian History Congress in the first 20 years or so of its existence was on political history. Consequently under its influence a large number of monographs were published on the political and administrative history of various periods. These histories are both pan-Indian and regional. They show streaks of nationalism which illumine our understanding at many points. Overemphasis on political history led to a shift in favour of social and economic history. Since 1960, during the last 30 years or so much work has been done on social and economic history although this has not been fully reflected in the history courses in different universities. But because of this political history has not suffered. On the contrary it has been immensely enriched by insights derived from the study of society and economy. For example we can give a much better explanation for the rise and the formation of the first large states in early India. What is needed now is to integrate the results obtained from the study of social and economic history with those acquired from political and other types of history and to create a new type of integrated history as far as possible. I am aware of many new ideas which are being discussed by younger researchers, and I see a bright future for the study of history in this country.

18

Main Trends in Indian History

Recently it has been argued by a foreign researcher William Dalrymple, in the *The Times of India*, Patna 5 November 2006, that since the British had ended the power of the Muslim ruler Tipu Sultan and also that of Awadh, mainly the Muslim leaders revolted in 1857 against the British. The Muslims were not only anti-British but also anti-Christian. But this is a wrong view. The Hindus including Kuwar Singh and some leaders of Meerut actively joined the 1857 revolt. The Hindus and the Muslims fought together as they did in Singapur in 1915 against the British and Japanese. Sabyasachi Bhattacharya quotes Kaye who explains the causes of Hindu reaction in 1857. Hindu sentiments were hurt by the beginning of female education, legislation on widow re-marriage, violation of caste rules in jails and the use of animal fat including that of pork in some rifle cartridges. ('Rethinking 1857, page 5') This Hindu reaction and Muslim revolt worried the British. They realized the urgent need of studying the life of Indians for ruling over them. Although they did not ignore the study of Islam, they translated Sanskrit and Pali texts into English and also prepared several dictionaries and English books covering India.

The Revolt of 1857 made Britain realise that it badly needed a deeper knowledge of the manners and social systems of an alien people over whom it had to rule. Further, the Christian missionaries wanted to find out the vulnerable points in the Hindu religion to win converts and strengthen the British empire. To meet these needs ancient scriptures were translated on a massive scale under the editorship of Max Mueller. Altogether fifty volumes, some in several parts, were published under the *Sacred Books of the East* series. Many of them appeared in the eighties and nineties. Although some Chinese and Iranian texts were included, the ancient Indian texts predominated in the series. The texts included not only the brāhmaṇical law books, but also covered the Jain and Buddhist books.

The Vedic Index by Macdonell and Keith was an important contribution. Further the *Pali-English Dictionary* by Rhys Davids and Stede and the *Dictionary of Pali Proper Names* by G.P. Malalasekara were two Pali works, both sponsored by the Pali Text Society in Britain. The study of linguistics also made great progress and even after the end of British rule Sir Ralph Turner brought out a *Comparative Dictionary of Indo-Aryan Language* in 1966. In Britain oriental studies were started in important universities, but now they are being dropped in several of them.

British academic work also inspired Indian scholars. They started the preparation of the Critical Edition of the *Mahābhārata* in 1927 and completed it in 1963. All this matter together with evidence from archaeology and inscriptions facilitated the study of different aspects of early life. In Great Britain all the efforts supported by the British finance helped the understanding of the various aspects of early Indian life. These included not only the study of political institutions but also covered the caste system, status of women together with the economic life of the people.

Max Mueller and other western scholars made certain generalizations about the nature of ancient Indian history and society. They stated that the ancient Indian lacked a sense of history, especially of the factor of time and chronology. They stressed that the Indians were accustomed to despotic rule. They added that since the Indians were engrossed in the problems of the next world they felt no concern about the problems of this world. The western scholars stressed that the Indian had experienced neither feelings of nationhood nor any kind of self-government.

Vincent Arthur Smith wrote *Ancient India* and devoted almost one-third of it to Alexander's invasion. India was presented as a land of despotism which did not experience political unity until the establishment of British rule. As he observes: 'Autocracy is substantially the only form of government with which the historian of India is concerned'.

Generalizations made by colonialist historians were by and large either false or grossly exaggerated, but these served as good propaganda material for the perpetuation of the despotic British rule. Their emphasis on the Indian tradition of one-man rule could justify the system which vested all powers in the hands of the viceroy. Similarly, if the Indians were obsessed with the problems of the other world, the British colonial masters had no option but to look after their life in this world. Without any experience of self-rule in the past, how could the natives manage their affairs in the present? At the heart of all such generalizations lay the need of demonstrating that the Indians were incapable of governing themselves.

NATIONALIST APPROACH AND CONTRIBUTION

All this naturally came as a great challenge to Indian writers, particularly to those who had received western education. They were upset by the colonialist distortions of their past history and at the same time distressed by the contrast between the decaying feudal society of India and the industrial capitalist society of Britain. A band of scholars took upon themselves not only the mission to reform Indian society, but also to reconstruct ancient Indian history in such a way as to plead for social reforms and, especially, for self-government. In doing so most historians were guided by the nationalist ideas of Hindu revivalism, but several scholars adopted a rationalist and objective approach. To the second category belongs Rajendra Lal Mitra (1822–91), who published some Vedic texts and wrote a book entitled *Indo-Aryans.* A great lover of ancient heritage, he took a rational view of ancient society and produced a forceful tract to show that in ancient times people took beef. Others tried to prove that despite its peculiarities the caste system was not basically different from the class system based on division of labour found in Europe's pre-modern and ancient societies.

In Maharashtra, Ramakrishna Gopal Bhandarkar (1837–1925) and Vishwanath Kashinath Rajwade (1869–1926) emerged as two great dedicated scholars. They pieced together varied sources to reconstruct the social and political history of the country. R.G. Bhandarkar reconstructed the political history of the Deccan of the Satavahanas and the history of Vaishnavism and other sects. A great social reformer, through his researches he advocated widow marriages and castigated the evils of the caste system and child marriage. With his unadulterated passion for research, V.K. Rajwade went from village to village in Maharashtra in search of Sanskrit manuscripts and sources of Maratha history; which were published in twenty-two volumes. He wrote the history of the institution of marriage in Marathi in 1926 based on Vedic and other texts. He marked the stages in the evolution of marriage in India. Pandurang Vaman Kane (1880–1972), a great Sanskritist wedded to social reform, wrote the *History of the Dharmaśāstra* in five volumes in the twentieth century. It is an encyclopaedia of ancient social law and customs, and even refers to beef eating. It indicates social processes in ancient India.

The Indian scholars diligently studied polity and political history to demonstrate that India did have its political history and that the Indians did possess expertise in administration. Thus Devdatta Ramakrishna

Bhandarkar (1875–1950), an epigraphist, published books on Asoka and on ancient Indian political institutions. More valuable work was done by Hemchandra Raychaudhuri (1892–1957), who reconstructed the history of ancient India from the time of the Bhārata (*Mahābhārata*) war, that is, the tenth century BC to the end of the Gupta empire. Being a teacher of European history, he adopted some modem methods and comparative insights. Though he recognized the contribution of V.A. Smith to the reconstruction of early Indian history, yet Raychaudhuri criticized the British scholar at many points. His writings show impeccable scholarship but reveals a streak of militant brāhmaṇism when he criticizes Aśoka's policy of peace. A stronger element of Hindu revivalism appears in the writings of R.C. Majumdar (1888–1980), who was a prolific writer and the general editor of the multi-volume publication *History and Culture of the Indian People.*

K.A. Nilakanta Sastri (1892–1975), the great historian from south India, was not such a revivalist. His *History of South India* is a very dependable book. Nilakanta Sastri emphasized the cultural supremacy of the brāhmaṇas and also highlighted the harmony that prevailed in early Indian society.

K.P. Jayaswal (1881–1937) and A.S. Altekar (1898–1959) overplayed the role of the indigenous ruling dynasties in liberating India from the rule of Shakas and Kushans, though these foreigners became an intrinsic part of India's life and did not exploit its resources for their original homeland.

But the greatest merit of K.P. Jayaswal lay in exploding the myth of Indian despotism. As early as 1910–12, he wrote several articles to show that republics existed in ancient times and enjoyed a measure of self-government. His findings finally appeared in *Hindu Polity* in 1924. Although Jayaswal is charged with projecting modern nationalist ideas into ancient institutions, and his republican government is attacked by many writers including U.N. Ghoshal (1886–1969), Jayaswal's basic thesis regarding the practice of the republican experiment is widely accepted, and his pioneer work *Hindu Polity*, now in its sixth edition, is considered a classic.

There is no doubt that the works of Indian orientalists and historians deeply influenced the mental make-up of the educated people and paved the way for the freedom struggle. It is significant that a good many freedom fighters were literate. But at the same time generally the writings of Indian historians ignored the problems of socio-economic and cultural inequality in ancient India.

MOVE TOWARDS SOCIAL CHANGE AND PROBLEMS OF INEQUALITY

British historian, A.L. Basham (1914–86), a Sanskritist by training, questioned the wisdom of looking at ancient India from the modern point of view. He first showed deep interest in the materialist philosophy of some heterodox sects. Later he thought that the past should be read out of curiosity and pleasure. His book, *The Wonder That Was India* (1951), is a sympathetic survey of the various facets of ancient Indian culture and civilization free from the prejudices found in V.A. Smith and many other British writers.

Basham's book gave more space to social, economic, and cultural aspects. The same shift is evident in D.D. Kosambi's (1907–66) book, *An Introduction to the Study of Indian History* (1957), later popularized in *The Civilisation of Ancient India in Historical Outline* (1965). Kosambi blazed a new trail in Indian history. His treatment follows a materialist interpretation of history, derived from the writings of Karl Marx. He presents the history of ancient Indian society, economy, and culture as an integral part of the development of the forces and relations of production. He made the first survey to show the stages of social and economic development in terms of tribal and class processes. Though criticized by many scholars, including Basham, his book continues to be widely read.

In Sanskrit literature the Aryans were considered highly cultured and civilized. They were supposed to act according to the Dharmaśāstra which stress caste distinction and sex discrimination. However the genetic evidence now shows that earliest Indo-Aryans did not originate in India.

Agriculture and white skin American researchers may have worked hard, but their finds about the presence of the white skin in India and Africa are not supported by the present realities. Both Africans and south Indians are mostly engaged in agriculture, but they are generally black. Most probably the skin colour is conditioned by the nature of the climate in which the people live. This can be well illustrated on the basis of the skin colour of people in different part of the Indian subcontinent. As we proceed eastward we encounter more and more black-skinned people. On the other hand when we travel north-westward we meet more and more white skinned people. Recently such people belonging to an Indo-Aryan tribe have been found in north Kashmir. Some researchers have reported this in the *Times of India*, 11 March 2006. We learn from this report that an Indo-Aryan tribe called Dards live in north Kashmir in the

Ladakh area. This tribe is different from other peoples who live in Ladakh. Members of this tribe practised polyandry till recent times, but they continue polygamy till today. A picture of a woman from this tribe has been given in the Times Report, but there is no doubt that she is white-skinned. On this basis one could say could climatic conditions helped the production of white-skinned people.

19

From Kin to Class*

The work starts with an excellent summary and critique of the current anthropological theories regarding the origin of the State. In the process Romila Thapar explains the lineage theory in which elders enjoy authority and better access to resources at the cost of the juniors because of their kin-based seniority. She also clarifies the concept of the householding economy, which means a large, self-sufficient household comprising several small houses, all belonging to the same kin group. The head of the household enjoys power and authority over its members, and also employs labourers not belonging to the kin. It is Thapar's thesis that the Vedic communities, which practiced reciprocity and redistribution, were organized on the basis of lineage and householding economy and the development of these institutions led to the formation of the State. The State, on the basis of Lawrence Krader, is understood as a political authority operating with its functionaries within a territory, deriving its income on an impersonal basis, and integrating social segments with different ritual roles and economic functions (p. 11).

The problem of transition from classless and stateless societies to class-based and state-based societies is very complex. Anthropologists have tried to tackle it in the context of Black Africa and Latin America. Some work relates to tribal India in modern times. A similar exercise in respect of ancient India is made doubly difficult by the intractable and fragmentary nature of the sources and the inadequacy of generalized anthropological findings. Vedicists and other scholars including K.P. Jayswal and U.N. Ghoshal have referred to the tribal, kin-based character of Vedic institutions. Some others have stressed the pre-class and pre-State nature of Vedic society and highlighted the tribal character of *jana,*

*This is a review of *From Lineage to State* by Romila Thapar. Previously published in *Economic and Political Weekly*, vol. 20, no 22 (June 1, 1985), pp. 960–1.

vis, grama and *vrata* together with that of the Vedic assemblies. But Romila Thapar's search for the operative kin group at a lower level has materially advanced this argument further. In the context of Vedic society she finds the term 'tribe' to be imprecise and inadequate. She considers *sabha, samiti, vidatha, parishad*, etc., to be clan gatherings. More importantly, she uses the concept of 'lineage' to explain the nature of society in Vedic times and its change-over to class and State society in the middle Ganga plains around 500 BC. In doing so the ecological and archaeological evidence is put to good use. Her study leaves no doubt that a major portion of the Vedic age had its archaeological counterpart in the western Ganga plains. However she bases her argument mainly on the Vedic and Pali texts. She shows an acute awareness of the current anthropological concerns with the problem of transition, particularly in the writings of French Marxists on the subject. In her view lineage, which is different from the egalitarian band, plays a dominant role in determining access to economic resources, power and status; this is true of the predominantly pastoral society of Rigvedic times and the agricultural society of the later Vedic age. No significant agrarian changes took place between the second millennium BC and *c.* 500 BC. Although iron was known, its use was limited to weapons. The lineage distinction appeared in the *Rigveda* in the form of that between the *rajanya* and the *vis* and it continued in later Vedic texts. But the relationship between the two became more distant in later Vedic times (p. 32). The *rajanya* represented the senior lineage and the *vis* the junior lineage. The place of the *rajanya* was taken by the kshatriya who represented power. The *vis* made prestations (payments of levies or a kind of forcible presentation) to the chief, who reallocated to the kinsmen the things that he received. However claims to sovereignty and increasing demands for prestations were justified through coronation rituals.

The development of the lineage system led to an 'arrested development of the State' in the west Ganga plains in later Vedic times. Though territory emerged as an important element and the raja enjoyed a high status and effective control, increase in resources through agriculture was 'not sufficient to finance a state system'. The destruction of wealth in the ritual placed severe limitations on chiefdoms and prevented easy transition to a State system (p. 66). [We could add that cattle sacrifice hindered the progress of agriculture.] There developed several impersonal institutions round the kshatriya king who emerged as the head of the State because of the authority conferred on him by the senior lineage. The twelve *ratnins* or functionaries who took part in the 'royal' coronation 'remained essentially within the orbit' of the clan (p. 60), though their existence shows 'the emergence of a group of non-kinsmen' (p. 61). Lineages were so important that *janapadas* or territorial states were named after them. Apparently because of its inherent exploitative tendencies lineage led to the institutionalization of the political leadership. Further, because of the principle of descent the kshatriyas and brāhmaṇas emerged as separate varṇas. The element of heredity in the varṇa system was derived from the lineage system. Those who view the varṇa as class or as a symbol of social status ignore the importance of lineage leading to its formation.

This bare outline may not do full justice to the various other ideas, insights and interpretations found in this study, which puts forward some original views on the nature of the *gana-samgha* of the Vrijis and distinguishes between the internal working of the monarchies and that of the *gana-samgha* in the middle Ganga plains. Romila Thapar rightly points out that in post-Vedic times the functioning of the sudra and not of slavery was the crucial variable. Her study is further enriched by a critical appraisal of historiography, both Buddhist and brāhmaṇical, and by a keen perception of the role of the geographical factors in economic and social changes.

NATURE OF PRE-CLASS SOCIETY

The nature of the pre-class and pre-State society is viewed in different ways. The French Marxist anthropologist Maurice Godelier talks of the nuclear family, the enlarged family, the clan and the tribe as kin-based units of consumption which could also coincide with production units. The Soviet ethnographers think of (i) the extended family (which is identical with the lineage system), (ii) patronymic community, (iii) late gens (or clan), (iv) primitive (heterogeneous) neighbouring community, (v) the fraternal family community, etc. These do not occur in any sequence and may exist simultaneously in pre-State societies. In their views the concept of 'military democracy', propounded by Engels in his pioneering work on the origin of the State, 'fails to cover the whole of the period of the transition to class society', for military hierarchical and oligarchical structures emerge in the process. Those who have not done field work are likely to pick up any of the models or think of some other on the basis of confrontation between their hypothesis and the empirical evidence.

In Romila Thapar's view the term 'lineage society' is 'perhaps more precise' than 'tribal society' (p. 18) in the context of the Vedic society. She therefore uses it as a tool of analysis, which taken together with the 'householding economy' contains 'a certain degree of hopefully creative speculation' (p. 18). A few comments may be offered. The notion of kin is central to the tribe, clan and lineage. Of the three, the tribe is the largest and lineage the smallest kin unit. In between comes the clan. Both clan and lineage are descent-based either on the male or the female side. Descent in the first may be stipulated, but in the second it is true and remembered. In our view kin groups are not purely biological phenomena, but they are formed to obtain subsistence and make the group reproduce itself. Certain Vedic terms such as *gotra, vra, vraja, vrata*, etc. which connote kinship at a later stage, originally indicate groups of those who come together either for cattle herding or for 'body production' through wars. *Vamsa* rightly considered in this study as the equivalent of lineage. But the term does not occur in early Vedic texts, and later texts use it for the family tree of the kshatriyas and brāhmaṇas. Nevertheless the basic idea that in a kin group chiefs, elders or seniors enjoy more access to resources and better claim to status and authority is true of many primitive societies. Privileges flow from age, skill and experience in procuring subsistence, ability to lead in wars and so on, but these are frozen and formalized on the basis of heredity. Eventually seniority based on genealogy is turned into that based on the ideology of patrilineal descent, and genealogical kinship converted into ideological kinship. Some Marxists equate the lineage system with relations of production in which seniors strengthen their position *via* booty, elite goods, redistribution, genealogical knowledge, and above all through control of exchange of women. Many of these have been discussed in this book, but the idea that the control of young men's marriage amounts to the control of labour force needs exploration. Claude Meillassoux and Emmanuel Terray hold that the seniors can perpetuate their supremacy only if they control the circulation of women and bride-prices. But the detailed description of Surya's marriage with the two Asvin brothers in the *Rigveda* does not support this generalization. Similarly the well known marriages of Rama and Arjuna do not indicate that the elders enjoyed such a control, although they occasionally arranged marriages in the epics. In post-Vedic texts, the *arsha* and *asura* forms of marriage indicate bride-price comprising a pair of cow and bull, probably provided by the seniors. But such bridal gifts cannot be called 'elite' goods. On the other hand bride-price attests the importance of women, and marriage in the matrilineal context may mean exchange of men rather than that of women.

The concept of the lineage mode of production is based on the study of very few primitive societies; to make it more viable many stateless communities, including those in India, will have to be studied by the anthropologists. Lineage does not exist among the Mbutis in the Congo region of Africa. In some primitive societies no chiefs are found, and in others they are elected not because of their lineage but because of their generosity. Hereditary chiefs appear in Vedic texts, which also indicate that a person was elected raja because of his physical and other personal qualities. Indra was chosen for the great coronation because he was 'the most vigorous, the most strong, the most perfect, the best in carrying out any work'. Even then many kin-based or 'lineage' societies show the distinction between its 'elder' and junior members. Kin groups or lineages generate genealogical inequality, but it is not the same as class inequality based on access to land (p. 41) and its products. Kin-based differences may give rise to classes only in a productive economy. The surplus, over and above the subsistence needs of the cultivators, may not alone explain the rise of the class and the State, but its centrality cannot be ignored. Only in the agricultural society of later Vedic times the tribal chief appears as the eater of the settlers/cultivators (*visamatta*), that is, of their products. Although the context alters the meaning of a term, Vedic scholars may find it difficult to render *vis* either into lineage or junior lineage. Generally the term indicates clan (occasionally tribe) in the *Rigveda* and settlement or tribal cultivators in later Vedic texts. Originally a kin group, when the *vis* took to agriculture, it came to mean a house or a settlement. The analogy of *grama* is well known. But the *rajanya*, literally the kinsmen of the raja, may have been divided into junior and senior lines. How hierarchies in various lineages or kin groups were combined in to the network of domination and exploitation called the State needs more research.

Polanyi's householding economy, equated by him with the patrilineal lineage (p. 39), is applied to the later Vedic period. It presupposes the employment of labour outside the extended family circle, for which we have little evidence in Vedic texts. Sudras do appear as the most inferior group, but they are rightly considered 'addenda' by Thapar; at best non-kin labour covered domestic servants and women slaves. A large household could be an intermediate economic unit between the clan control over land and its family possession. Its non-kin component could undermine the lineage system, but if the household meant the extended family (p. 33) 'the natureof its association with the lineage', which was a wider unit, may need some rethinking. Evidently a family needed extra labour only if it grabbed more land than it could manage. Such units of production became important in post-Vedic times, when the vaiśyas or the *gahapatis* became the principal tax-payers.

The 'lineage'-varṇa continuum cannot be denied. Hutton and others held that caste endogamy was derived from tribe endogamy and *gotra* exogamy from clan exogamy. Recently the idea of the tribe-caste continuum has been elaborated by Indian anthropologists. But the continuity of lineage was overshadowed by the social division of labour on which the varṇas were erected. Division of functions paved the way for the rise of new lineages. In post-Vedic times priests and warriors tried to congeal their surplus consuming privileges by reinforcing heredity and fabricating family trees. The author rightly holds that the brāhmaṇas comprised several non-Vedic elements. This is also true of the kshatriyas, who understood the ideological and validitary value of the lineage. In the past both the raja and the *vis* practiced agriculture. Gradually the vaiśyas were compelled to stick to it. How some families monopolized war and tax-collection, others adopted religion and the receipt of gifts, and the two together pushed the majority to producing and paying has to be solved satisfactorily.

Many other valuable points made in Romila Thapar's book deserve attention. She has undoubtedly produced a thoughtful and stimulating study, full of fresh ideas. Analytical and interpretative in the main, the book also supplies new pieces of information. It provides several leads for further inquiry. As a significant contribution to the study of ancient Indian polity and society, it is indispensable reading not only for ancient historians but also for those who are interested in the problem of transition from kin-based societies to class-based and state-based societies.

20

Rahula Sankrityayana and Social Changes

Rahul Sankrityayana was a multi-faceted personality. He received formal education only up to Class VII, through the medium of Urdu, but he managed to educate himself and outside schools and colleges. He learnt three dozen languages, and in an active life of about 50 years he wrote as many as 134 books in a period of less than 40 years. These included original works, translations and edited books. He mostly wrote in Hindi though he published a few pieces in English mainly in the form of lectures delivered at some research institutes abroad. He possessed remarkable memory because usually he neither had too many books nor notes around him when he started writing. He possessed phenomenal memory which made it easy for him to write or give dictation. It is really astounding that although Rahul kept on moving all the time from place to place in India and outside the country, he found time for writing so many books. Two and half years before his death in 1963 at the age of 70 years, he lost his memory and sometimes could not recognize even his wife Kamala. He could have certainly contributed several other books during this period of two and half years had he retained his memory power.

Sometimes he would work for almost 20 hours a day. Though his handwriting was not legible, he kept on constantly writing and also gave dictation. During the period of writing he would not read any newspaper continuously for a month until the book was finished. At the end of the month he finished reading the newspaper in 3–4 days. He translated *Majjhima Nikaya* into Hindi in 28 days, although it is a book of nearly 300 printed pages. Similarly he wrote the bulky book consisting of nearly 1000 pages on Soviet Russia in Hindi in a month. It was said about him that he would not take his breakfast unless he had written 20 pages. However, this great writer never cared to look at what he had written.

When complained to him about mistakes in his writing his pet reply was that the editors could take care of them. Rahul also emphasized the point that in order to enrich Hindi, it was necessary to write on new subjects as much as possible. He was a man in hurry, and had no time to waste on revising the manuscript and correcting it.

The worldwide travels of Rahula Sankrityayana are wellknown. But his most outstanding achievements were made in his four trips to Tibet from where he brought altogether more than 4500 zylographs and manuscripts now preserved in the Bihar Research Society, Patna. His collection contains the complete *Kanjur* and *Tanjur* corpus. The *Kanjur* comprises the canonical Buddhist texts and the *Tanjur* consists of commentaries on them. He also brought eighty valuable Buddhist manuscripts in Hybrid-Sanskrit language written in the script of tenth to twelfth centuries. Some of these Buddhist manuscripts have been deciphered and published by the K.P. Jayaswal Research Institute, Patna. Mention may also be made of 619 manuscripts in Tibetan languages; some of these are translations from Sanskrit texts and others are original works in Tibetan. Unfortunately in contrast to the large funds provided for post-independence scholars Rahul was not provided with any grant except for a sum of Rs 6000 in 1938 by the Bihar Research Society.

Rahul's thirst for knowledge was insatiable and his commitment to rationalism firm. Rationalism came to him through the process of constant questioning. This led to his conversion to Arya Samaj and was followed by that to Buddhism and finally to Marxism. The intellectual making of Rahul could well be a subject for an in-depth investigation. I can touch on it by stating that because of his birth in Brāhmin family in eastern UP, where the vestiges of the traditional varna systems were strong, he was steeped in orthodoxy. At the age of 19, he became the Mahant of a Vaishnava Math in Chapra district. From Kedarnath Pande he came to be known as Ramodardas. At the age of 27 he went to Sri Lanka where he became a Buddhist. The new religion made such a deep impact on him that even when he joined the Communist Party in 1940 he occasionally justified communism on the basis of the teachings of Gautama Buddha.

Rahul was not an ivory tower scholar. Throughout his active career he was involved in one movement or the other. He played an important part in the non-cooperation movement in Saran district and has even written a book on his contemporaries who had taken part in this movement. At the same time, he also took an active part in the Arya Samaj movement and exposed the evils of Brahmanical orthodoxy. When he found the Arya Samajist ideas inadequate for promoting social equality, he became a Buddhist in 1930. In the 30s he was very much influenced by Socialist and Marxist ideas and became extremely critical of the Gandhian aspects of the Nationalist movement. His book *Why Communism* in Hindi brought out in 1933 was one of his earliest publications. Eventually Rahul became one of the founders of the Communist Party in Bihar in 1940 and actively participated in the Amwari Satyagraha for restoring to the peasants the land that had been grabbed by the landlords. He was subjected to lathi-charge which resulted in serious injury to his head. Since 1930 he remained an active supporter of the leftist movement until his death, though he strongly criticized the language policy of the Community Party.

It is difficult to make a critical assessment of the contribution of Rahul to history, literature, religion, philosophy, travel literature, biographical accounts, lexicography, Buddhist scholarship, study of social problems and political thought. In fact I do not know of any other scholar who has enriched the different genres of Hindi so much. I would make some comments on his contribution to history. There is no doubt that the historical writings of Rahul were deeply influenced by the Marxist theory of historical materialism. He wrote a book on dialectical materialism, which popularized this philosophy among the Hindi readers because of its lucid exposition. Lucidity coloured almost all his writings whether they related to history, philosophy, literature and other disciplines. Because of his love for Indian history, Central Asia had a great fascination for him. He wrote the history of Central Asia in two volumes in which he gave only an outline of political history. His main subject was ethnic, social, economic and cultural history. Rahul wrote several Hindi novels and collection of stories to illustrate the course of history in ancient times. In his book called *Volga to Ganga* in Hindi, he dealt with the origins of the Aryans in the Volga basin, their migration to India and marked the main stages in the evolution of human society from matriarchy to capitalism. It is remarkable that archaeological excavations during the last 30 years or so have lent enormous weight to the hypothesis that the Indo-European lived in the steppes of south Russia in the Volga basin. Horse, wheeled chariots, sacrificial remains of horse, cattle and sheep all belonging to 4000–2000 BC have been discovered in south Russia. All these are associated with the Indo-European peoples, and especially the sacrificial rituals connected with the animals are typical of the Indo-Iranians. Some of the burials found in south Russia belonging to 4000–2000 BC show that male members were buried separately from the female ones and when they were buried together the male was placed on the right side and the female on the left side. That suggests the supremacy of the male element.

That matriarchy was important in the horticultural stage of society is now recognized by most anthropologist. Only when the plough driven by animals began to be used in agriculture and women were found physically unequal to the task of driving oxen, they were relegated to the background. Similarly in a phase of continuous cattle raids in a stock-breeding society women were not able to fight all the time. These developments materially undermined matriarchal elements in the early Indo-Aryan society, but there is doubt that such an element did precede the emergence of patriarchy. Although Rahul was not aware of these developments he refers to both stages of society in many of his writings.

The various stages in the evolution of the human society are clearly brought out in his book entitled the *Manav Samaj* published from Patna in 1942. In this book as well as in his other historical or history-oriented publications, Rahul follows a schematic evolution of society based on orthodox Marxism. Primitive communism appears as the first stage, slavery as the second, feudalism as the third and capitalistic as the fourth. The author considers socialism to be the final stage, and it is exemplified by Soviet Russia. During the last 50 years there have been many refinements in this historical scheme, and it has been found that they do not apply to several specific cases. But considering the state of Marxist historical thinking around 1940 *Manav Samaj* is a pioneering book, and so far as Hindi is concerned it is the first book of its kind.

The application of historical materialism to the study of the evolution of the Indian society by Rahul must be regarded as a significant development. His findings may not be acceptable today in the light of subsequent research, but the general direction and orientation can still prove to be rewarding. Rahul speaks of the existence of slavery in the earliest Indian society which is also the view of several eminent Russian Indologists. But the ancient texts do not provide adequate evidence to support the view that the slave mode of production obtained in ancient India.

Similarly the great scholar postulates that feudalism arose in India in the time of Gautama Buddha, grew up to Harshavardhana's time and then became stagnated. Although some western scholars are trying to bring down the date of the Buddha, there is no doubt that the earliest Pali texts belong to the fourth century BC and may reflect the state of affairs existing somewhat earlier. If we therefore accept the view of Rahul it will mean that feudalism started around 500 BC and continued until the seventh century AD. If feudalism is defined by the presence of a class of landlords supported by a class of servile peasantry, this social phenomenon did not exist in the age of the Buddha. We hear of a few rich landowners who employed slaves and wage-earners in agricultural production, but by and large the early Pali texts as well as the earliest law books written in Sanskrit speak of peasant proprietors enjoyment autonomy in their production unit. The process of the creation of a class of landlords started with the system of land grants for religious purposes which became considerable in the fourth seventh centuries AD. Therefore feudalism really appears as a full-fledged social, economic and political phenomena in the age of Harsha. It does not stagnate with his reign.

I have referred to slavery and feudalism to illustrate that the first does not apply to ancient India and that the second appears in early medieval times and not in ancient times. But all this does not take away from the basic validity of the Marxian approach adopted by Rahul. There is no doubt that irrespective of the Indian society being ancient or medieval the ruling class and its ideologues lived on the surplus produced by the peasants and artisans and collected from them in the form of taxes, tributes, tithes and various forms of religious gifts.

Rahul was a rare combination of an outstanding intellectual and a social and political activist who fought for the transformation of society not only on the ideological plans but also through active participation in various mass movements. Rahul was completely dedicated to the cause of rationalism and socialism on which he did not make any compromise. He had always before him the vision of a socialist India for which he argued in a book as early as 1933. It was in pursuance of this ideal that he wrote an utopia called *22nd Century* in Hindi. He also wrote another book called *Naye Bhārat ke Naye Netā*, which included biographies of many mass leaders and activists including Sahajanand Saraswati, Muzaffar Ahmed, P.C. Joshi, Ajoy Ghosh, Kalpana Dutta and several others. Rahul dreamt that these leaders would be able to build a new India in which society would be reorganized on the principles of social and economic justice.

Rahul felt deeply concerned not only about the need for just distribution but also about increase in production. His concern for increase in production is evident from his book on *22nd Century*. It is also shown by his great attention paid to the importance of science in his writing. In fact he brought out several publications on science in Hindi, and in his speeches he pleaded for a higher place for science in our educational system.

Finally I would like to emphasize the point that Rahul never lost touch with the common man. It is because of this that his writings provide us with more insights into the working of the life of the masses than the results of the field work of many sociologists. In order to educate the masses of the people, he pleaded for education and state formation on the basis of what are called dialects such as Magahi, Bhojpuri, Awadhi, etc. In the Bhojpuri area he made public speeches in Bhojpuri. He also wrote books in Bhojpuri; one contains three and the other five dramas. Thus Rahul strongly felt that no cultural progress could be made unless people were educated through the medium of their mother tongue. Certainly he could write in English and some other foreign languages, but he successfully resisted the temptations to be recognized internationally at the cost of being unknown to the common people in India.

Rahul Sankrityayana's writings have proved to be so powerful that even without the support of the ruling groups they continued to be reprinted and read particularly in the Hindi-speaking world. There is no doubt that they generated ideas of socialism, rationalism and gender equality between 1930 and 1950 and continue to do so even now.

21

Rethinking the Past

PROBLEM OF MEMBERS OF LOWER ORDERS

An important question relates to changes in the occupations of the people based on caste. Some early medieval texts emphasize the importance of resources. It is stated that all the good qualities emanate from wealth. A person who possesses wealth is noble. He possesses beauty, scholarship and other qualities. Whether this applies also to persons from lower orders is not clear. But if we look at the status of lower orders in modern times it appears that rich people are found even among the śūdras though in small numbers. It is curious that the central government of India recognizes the continuity of the caste system in this country. It reserves some offices, privileges, educational facilities according to the caste order. Those who belong to backward castes are given reservations for their upkeep and progress. Many backward castes are easily recognized, though others are not. The present government faces the problems of OBC or 'other backward castes', dalits (untouchables) and tribal groups. It also follows the policy of locating those who are below poverty line (BPL). But it ignores the distinction between various groups and orders on the basis of what they possess. Even the creamy layer among the śūdras and the dalits are allowed some special privileges on the caste basis. Thus the impact of early law books is so strong that it is formally felt by the central government.

Although I brought out a book on the śūdras in 1958, I did not discuss the problem of the rich and the poor in this community or within the higher communities. It needs to be done. The prevalence of some titles in various castes throw some light on this problem. I will begin with the Dusadhs. In my village the food and water touched by the Dusadhs is not accepted by members of the higher castes. The Dusadhs are agricultural labourers who are called untouchables or *dalits.* In the nineteenth century the British government also recorded them as criminals. Interestingly however, in my early days all the fourteen choukidars or guards of my village were Dusadhs.

It seems that in early medieval times the Dusadhs challenged the rulers in the rural areas. The term *dusadh* is derived from *duhsadhya*, which means difficult to control. For this purpose an officer was appointed in Pala times. He was called *dauhsadhasaohanikas*, that is, one who controlled the uncontrollable. The term also appears in post-Gupta inscriptions in early medieval times in north India. It may be suggested that the present Dusadhas are the descendents of those who occasionally rebelled against the ruling authorities and discarded the Dharmaśāstra or law book rules. Probably some Dusadhs were also employed in controlling their caste men; they may have possessed some resources. Some present titles suggest a creamy layer in the lower varṇas. This can be said on the basis of the present prevailing title *mahto*. This title is derived from *mahattara*, a term that occurs in Gupta inscriptions. *Mahattara*, or elder, was an officer, who probably controlled the lower orders. At present the title *mahto* is used by both members of the higher castes and the lower castes. In my village, members of the backward castes such as Dhanuks and Kahars are called *mahto*. In its neighbourhood the Kurmis who are better of are also called *mahtos*. Those who bear these titles may be regarded as descendents of the *mahattaras* or the elders who served as controlling officers.

The bearers of the title *choudhari*[1] are also found not only among the higher castes but also among the śūdras. This indicates the presence of some kind of resourceful order in the lowest castes in early times. The term *choudhari* is derived from the Sanskrit word *caourodharnika* or extirpator of theft. The Sanskrit word seems to have appeared around AD 1000 in inscriptions. Later this title was also adopted by the Muslim rulers and landlords. It seems that considerable theft prevailed in medieval times which made it necessary to appoint officers for tackling it. The present prevalence of *choudhari* suggests that theft authorities were appointed not only from higher castes but also from lower castes. Thus in this respect social inequality did not prevent some high offices for lower caste people.

The varṇa titles are prescribed by the law books called the Dharmaśāstra. They lay down that a brāhmaṇa should be called *sharma* which means auspiciousness, a kśatriya should be called *varma* which means defensive armour, a vaiśya should be called *gupta* which means preserver, and a śūdra should be called *dasa* which means a slave or servile person.

Many present names of the castes do not occur in literary sources, but few appear in Gupta and early medieval inscriptions. At present some castes are recognized by their skin colours. In my rural area this is specially true of the Dusadhs. Though varṇa means colour, the colours of the four varṇas are neither indicated in the law books and probably nor in literary texts.

Though I did a doctoral thesis on the history of śūdras I did not discuss the problem of racial or colour differences between different castes. In this context the rural relics of ancient culture are important. They speak of colour distinction as a factor connected with caste distinction between the highest caste and the lowest caste. In my village the Babhans, now called Bhumihars are commonly considered of white skin and the śūdras are considered black skinned. The saying *karbabhan gora suddar tekra dekh ke kampe ruddar* is widely prevalent in my area. It means that even the god Rudra trembles at the presence of black-coloured Babhans and white-coloured śūdras. Thus colour discrimination seems to have been an important factor in promoting and maintaining social inequality which continues till today.

Although DNA tests are available it is very difficult to co-relate colour distinction with the caste distinction. The study of genetic system is relevant to human history. There was not much change in material life so long as humans were engaged in hunting and food gathering. Changes occurred in 10,000–5000 BC period when they started agriculture and founded settlements in the Neolithic phase. Geographical and biological research shows that the advent of agriculture changed skin colour, hair texture and bone structure. These features determine the social identity which is absent in pre-agricultural times. Change in physical features are noticed by some American researchers in the humans of the regions of Europe and East Asia. We may add that in 2006 the Aryan tribes found in the Ladakh valley of Kashmir are tall and good looking. They are fair with big light-coloured eyes, full lips and pointed nose.[2] Toshi, an educated Aryan said, 'that is why we consider ourselves superior to others and don't marry in other communities'.[3] In any case the agricultural past of the humans differed from their pre-agricultural past. Ideas of colour distinction appeared in the agricultural age.

The human mind is moulded by these above-mentioned changes. Theorists of psychological evolution attribute changes in human choices to genetic developments. In Europe humans first lived on beef. Later they noticed sugar-like element lactose in milk which became more important than beef. In any case the agricultural past of the humans differed from their pre-agricultural past.[4]

In India changes in skin colour, hair texture and bone structure indicate racial identity. They may suggest many races. The Indo-Aryan identity is being discussed in India, the USA and elsewhere, and white skinned people are considered Aryans. Sanskrit texts represent the Aryans as highly cultured and civilized in post-Vedic times when they are supposed to act according to the Dharmaśāstra. But the rules of these law books stress only caste distinction and sex discrimination, they hardly refer to racial distinctions.

In the Indian subcontinent generally white skinners are found in Kashmir, Afghanistan, Baluchistan and Punjab. They also appear in western U.P., M.P. and Bihar in good numbers. The Bengalis are mostly black and so is the case with people from Jharkhand. From this generalization it seems that despite continuous co-mingling of various peoples in the country climatic changes affect skin colour and possibly hair texture and bone structure. Now it is well known that the speakers of the Aryan language lived earlier in the cold climate of Central Asia from its one end to the another. The DNA evidence suggests that they had certain special genetic characteristics. These characteristics are found in 30 per cent Hindi speaking people of Delhi and only in 10 per cent Dravidian speaking people of that area. Although genetic evidence may be decisive it is difficult to say that śūdras were primarily black coloured as distinct from other castes. Thus although some works had been done on continuous commingling of cultures and effect of climatic conditions on colour of people it is still necessary to work on this problem not only from the genetic point of view but also from the climatic point of view in different parts of the Indian subcontinent.

PROBLEM OF UNTOUCHABILITY

I wrote on untouchability in some detail in my *Sudras* in 1958. Suvira Jaiswal dealt with this problem in 1998.[5] Vivekanand Jha discussed, 'Stages in the History of Untouchability' in 1975 in his doctoral thesis in Patna University.[6]

Untouchables are not found in any other country. But in India they are as old as 400 BC. The grammarian Panini uses various names for the untouchables, their castes and functions. These terms are: *bahya, antya, antyaja, antavasayin, antayoni* and *nirvasita sudra*. The term *asat sudra* used in the law books means untouchable.

The untouchables increased in early medieval times. Some of them rebelled against the disabilities imposed on them. Thus in the sixth century the Kalabhras of south India occupied the land given to the brāhmaṇas.

Similarly Kaivartas revolted against the rulers in Bangladesh in the eleventh century. They are called *antyaja* (born at end) or *varnasamkara* (low caste of mixed orders). But generally the peasants and agricultural labourers reconciled themselves to the existing social order. Hierarchy in gradations made it difficult for the lowest order to come together and revolt. The idea of *karma* philosophy and the belief in *punarjanama* (rebirth) and also in the heredity of earlier birth checked dissensions. The bhakti movement and religious teachings also prevented revolts. Varṇa indoctrinations, *tirthas*, temples and the Gita teachings to Arjuna regarding varṇa duties also helped reconciliation. Feasts of redistribution covered most castes, and occasionally even the untouchables.

Despite all the causes mentioned above we have to find out why untouchability continued in medieval times and why does it exist today? Curiously the Indian government recognizes the caste system and reserves offices, privileges, according to this system.

PROBLEM OF TRANSITION TO CHIEFDOM AND STATE AMONG THE ARYANS

In discussing the origin of the class and state ancient anthropologists and historians usually refer to examples found in non-Indo-Aryan tribes. Relics of Indo-Aryan tribes in modern times have not been found. In my book *The State and Varṇa Formation in the Mid-Ganga Plains* I have pointed out several cases of transition from kin to class and also from tribal equality of tribe members to chiefdom. A case of the presence of an Aryan tribe in Ladakh valley in Kashmir has been reported in the *Times of India* in Patna on 11 March 2006. It refers to an Aryan tribe living in three villages in the valley and suggests that they practiced agriculture. They are presented as fair people with good eyes and noses. Though their colour is not mentioned they seem to be white-skinned. Till 1870 they practiced polyandry and polygamy and kissed one another openly. They are Buddhists by religion. Under modern protests they gave up polyandry and open kissing. However, no information is given about their social organization or tribal headship. Historians have to take up this problem and pursue it further. This will enable the historians and sociologists to explain the rise of class and state in the Sanskrit speaking Aryans in a better manner.

On 3 August 2006 at Patna, I discussed this problem from kin to class with an anthropologist who has worked on this subject. He is Professor Satish Kumar of Patna University. He notices three processes in the formation of the tribal chiefdom. Among the Mundas in

Jharkhand one who first occupies land and begins agriculture is entitled to chiefdom. Among the Oraons in the same area the best hunter is entitled to chiefdom. Also among these and other tribes such as the Gonds and others the one who appears as the best fighter in intertribal war becomes the chief. It seems that in all cases the need for acquiring resources for livelihood is vital to the transition from tribal equality to chiefdom. The ability to collect food through hunting, land location or intertribal war was essential to the rise of chiefdom.

But such examples have still to be found among the remnants of the Indo-Aryan tribes. The information supplied by Satish Kumar can be supplemented by the tribal practice found in Mizoram situated at the end of eastern India. Among the Lushais or Mizos, knowledgeable farmers were asked to locate suitable lands for jhum cultivation. Those who succeeded were allowed the first choice of cultivating the fields (ibid.). Probably these distinctions in land cultivation emerged in the Chalcolithic phase and contributed to the consolidation of chiefdom.

Finally the Sanskara section of the television, meant for illustrating ancient Indian achievements, also perpetuates and strengthens the idea of social inequality. It supports the varṇa system. However this propaganda is confined to the members of the middle class who can afford the use of the television. A study of India's past has also to consider such questions.

There is no dearth of problems in the study of ancient Indian history. We have referred to only a few questions for consideration. In order to promote research and historical knowledge various issues relating to religion, polity, society, production, tax-collection, economy, etc., have to be pursued in an organized manner.

NOTES

1. Though *C* is used for *ch*, in this case the widely prevalent ch for it has been used.
2. *The Times of India*, Patna edn, Thursday, March 2006.
3. Ibid., 11 March 2006.
4. *The Times of India*, Patna edn, Thursday, March 2006.
5. *Caste, Origin, Function and Discussion of Change*, Delhi, 1998.
6. *Indian Historical Review*, 1975, vol. II, pt. 2, July 1975, pp. 19–20.

Index

Digha Nikaya 158
Divyavadana 156, 158

Fa-hsien 162, 174
feudalism/feudal state 128, 171, 189, 20, 201, 206–28; beneficiaries 79, 82; conception of property 79; land grant 44, 128; beginnings of 166; regional culture 183; closed economy 184, 248; regional scripts 185; ornate prose style 185; role of temples 187; subinfeudation 187, 201, 248; economic factor 193; extra economic means 195; parcellization of land 197; from below 198; seigniorial rights 214–18

gahapati 4, 87, 100, 148, 213, 280
gana-samgha 278
Gautamiputra Satkarni, Satvahana king 29, 172
Gordon Childe 2
Grhyasutras 33
guilds/nigamas 149, 159; issuing currency 164
Gupta 59, 77, 81, 96, 115, 118, 157, 164, 161–7, 171, 174, 187; beginning of feudalization 161; inscriptions 198
Gurjara-Pratihara 26

Harappa 23–4, 140–2; granaries 23; Indus valley civilization 26
Harsavardhana 164, 174–5
hinterland/nuclear zones 10
hiranya 29
historical materialism 60, 285
Hsuan Tsang 174, 176; on several nationalities 184

Indo-Greek 26
Indo-Roman trade 42, 129–30, 159; decline in 244
inheritance laws 5, 14, 15, 31, 32, 33, 117, 119, 121, 181, 202, 207; laws primogeniture 14, stridhana 14; in law-books 32
inscriptions 27; land grant inscriptions 27, 29; Asokan pillars 27–8; Lumbini pillar 28; Nasik cave inscriptions 28; Hathigumpha inscription of Kharavela 29; Sohgaura inscription 124; Mahasthan inscription 124; Mehrauli iron pillar 165, 228; Allahabad inscription of Samudra Gupta 196; Deopara inscription 253
iron 13, 24, 25, 31, 49, 50, 51, 134, 135, 145, 216, 228, 240, 267, 277; technology 10, 13, 48, 180; tools 14, 24, 25, 145, 170
irrigation 29, 34, 75, 77, 82, 157, 179, 228; local initiative in 163; repair of tank by Kharavela 157; Rudradaman 157
I-tsing 176

jajmani 2, 80, 81, 182, 226
janapadas 164
Jatakas 106
jati 100

Kaivarta revolt 36, 54, 197, 203, 225
Kalabhra revolt 54
Kalhana 199, 255
Kali crisis 47, 54, 137, 172, 251
Kalidasa 165
Kalinga 137, 197
Kanjur and *Tanjur* corpus 288
Kautilya 20, 57, 80, 106, 123, 126, 129, 135–6, 173, 212, 242; (on sharecroppers 4; evidence of urban settlements 16, on marriages 34; on slaves 34; on taxes 124
Kaveripattinam 241
kayastha 253, 254